Kelvin Joseph Bwalya, Stephen Mutula
E-Government

Global Studies in Libraries and Information

Edited by Ian M. Johnson

Volume 1

Kelvin Joseph Bwalya, Stephen Mutula

E-Government

Implementation, Adoption and Synthesis in Developing Countries

DE GRUYTER
SAUR

ISBN 978-3-11-030475-6
e-ISBN (PDF) 978-3-11-030527-2
e-ISBN (EPUB) 978-3-11-039605-8
ISSN 2195-0199

Library of Congress Cataloging-in-Publication Data
A CIP catalog record for this book has been applied for at the Library of Congress.

Bibliographic information published by the Deutsche Nationalbibliothek
The Deutsche Nationalbibliothek lists this publication in the Deutsche Nationalbibliografie; detailed bibliographic data are available on the Internet at http://dnb.dnb.de.

Typesetting: Michael Peschke, Berlin
Printing: CPI books GmbH, Leck
♾ Printed on acid free paper
Printed in Germany

www.degruyter.com

Acknowledgements

This book is the result of collective effort by many colleagues and specialists in Computer Science, Information Management and Public Administration who indirectly and directly rendered their contributions.

We are greatly indebted to Prof. Ian Johnson who is the Chief Editor, IFLA/ De Gruyter series: 'Global Studies in Libraries and Information', Aberdeen, Great Britain and Dr. Christina Lembrecht who is the Project Editor of the 'Library & Information Science', Munich, Germany. Without their critical eyes and advice, this book would never have materialised.

We wish to acknowledge the pivot role played by the University of Kwa Zulu Natal and the University of Botswana in providing conducive academic environments, without which this publication would not have been possible.

We thank our families and beloved ones who endured our long absence from home during the preparation of this book. Last but not least, we acknowledge the favour of God in providing us with His guidance to overcome challenges during the different cycles of this production.

Dr Kelvin J. Bwalya
Prof Stephen Mutula

Table of Contents

List of Abbreviations —— xiii

List of Figures —— xvii

List of Tables —— xviii

Chapter 1: Prologue —— 1
1.1 Introduction —— 1
1.2 Focus and Locale —— 1
1.3 Background: E-Government and Society —— 3
1.4 Semantic Understanding of e-Government —— 3
1.5 Practical Uses of e-Government —— 4
1.6 E-Government Impact —— 5
1.7 E-Government Research and Practice —— 6
1.8 Book Rationale —— 8
1.9 Conclusion and Summary —— 12

Chapter 2: The e-Government phenomenon —— 14
2.1 Introduction —— 14
2.2 Background to e-Government Conceptualization —— 14
2.3 Motivation for e-Government Implementation —— 16
2.4 What is e-Government? —— 18
2.5 Factors Influencing e-Government Proliferation —— 22
2.6 Levels of e-Government —— 23
2.7 E-Government versus e-Governance —— 24
2.8 Types of e-Government Applications —— 28
2.8.1 Government-to-Citizens (G2C) —— 29
2.8.2 Government-to-Businesses (G2B) —— 29
2.8.3 Government-to-Government (G2G) —— 30
2.8.4 Government-to-Employees (G2E) —— 30
2.9 Success or Failure of e-Government Implementation —— 32
2.10 E-Government Implementation Worldwide —— 39
2.11 Conclusion and Summary —— 43

Chapter 3: E-Government and Society —— 44
3.1 Introduction —— 44
3.2 Benefits, Disadvantages and Implications of e-Government —— 44

3.2.1 Benefits of e-Government Applications — 45
3.2.2 Economy and e-Government — 48
3.2.3 Negative Implications of e-Government — 50
3.3 Multi-Dimensional Aspects of e-Government Applications — 51
3.4 Conclusion and Summary — 52

Chapter 4: E-Government Readiness — 53
4.1 Introduction — 53
4.2 Socio-technical Infrastructure for e-Government — 53
4.2.1 E-Readiness and the Digital Divide — 54
4.2.2 The Role of Policy and Leadership in e-Government — 58
4.2.3 Social Infrastructure — 60
4.2.4 Technical Infrastructure — 61
4.3 E-Government Maturity Models — 63
4.3.1 West Four-Stage Model — 63
4.3.2 Gartner Maturity Model — 64
4.3.3 Layne and Lee Four-Stage Maturity Model — 64
4.3.4 Deloitte's Six-Stage Maturity Model — 66
4.3.5 Howard's Three Stage Model — 67
4.3.6 Hiller and Bélanger's Five-Stage Model — 68
4.3.7 United Nations Five-Stage Model — 68
4.3.8 World Bank Three-Stage Maturity Model — 70
4.3.9 Asia Pacific Six-Stage Model — 70
4.3.10 Moon Five-Stage Model — 72
4.3.11 Chandler and Emanuel Four Stage Model — 72
4.3.12 Accenture Five-Stage Model — 73
4.3.13 Public Sector Process Rebuilding (PPR) Four Phased Model — 74
4.4 Importance of e-Readiness Assessment — 80
4.5 E-Readiness and e-Government — 82
4.6 Guidelines in e-Readiness Assessment — 82
4.6.1 The Computer System Policy Project's Readiness Guide for Living in the Networked World — 82
4.6.2 Guide for Developing Countries, Asian Pacific Economic Cooperation's E-Commerce Readiness Assessment — 83
4.6.3 Harvard University's Center for International Development Readiness for the Networked World — 84
4.6.4 Case Studies for e-Readiness Assessment — 84
4.6.5 International Telecommunications Union Internet Country Case Studies report, Mosaic Methodology — 85

4.6.6 United States Agency for International Development Tool and Report — 85
4.6.7 Sweden International Development Agency — 85
4.6.8 Association of South East Asian Nations e-Readiness Assessment — 86
4.6.9 Third Party Survey and Reports — 86
4.6.10 McConnell International Risk e-Business — 86
4.6.11 World Information Technology and Services Alliance's International Survey of e-Commerce — 87
4.6.12 The Economic Intelligence Unit: e-Business Readiness Rankings — 87
4.6.13 Statistical Indicators Benchmarking the Information Society — 88
4.6.14 World Bank's Knowledge Assessment Methodology Report — 88
4.6.15 Information Society Index Report by the International Data Corporation — 88
4.6.16 Networked Readiness Index in the Global Information Technology Report — 89
4.6.17 Kenny's Assistance to Overcome the Digital Divide (World Bank) — 89
4.6.18 World Telecommunication Indicators — 90
4.6.19 Digital Access Index by International Telecommunications Union — 90
4.6.20 Analysis of the e-Readiness studies — 90
4.7 Conclusion and Summary — 92

Chapter 5: E-Government Assessment Methods and Frameworks — 93
5.1 Introduction — 93
5.2 Background to e-Government Assessment — 94
5.3 Conceptualization of e-Government Assessment — 97
5.4 E-Government Assessment Methods — 102
5.4.1 Considering the Digital Divide — 103
5.4.2 E-Government Assessment Frameworks — 105
5.4.2.1 India's e-Government Assessment Framework — 106
5.4.2.2 United Nations Department of Economic and Social Affairs Global e-Government Readiness Series — 106
5.4.2.3 The MAREVA Framework — 106
5.4.2.4 The UK Criminal Justice IT Benefits Management Framework — 108
5.4.2.5 Accenture e-Government Leadership Survey Framework — 110
5.4.2.6 CPP-BU Global e-Government Rankings Series — 110
5.4.2.7 Balanced Scorecard (BSC) Theory — 110
5.4.2.8 The European Union e-Government Economic Project Framework — 111
5.4.2.9 Standard Cost Model — 113
5.5 Other e-Government Measurement Frameworks — 114

5.6 Shortcomings of Some of the e-Government Assessment Frameworks — 116
5.7 E-Government Assessment Metrics and Tools — 117
5.7.1 Web Measure Index — 117
5.7.2 Telecommunications Infrastructure Index — 117
5.7.3 Human Capital Index — 118
5.7.4 E-Participation Index — 118
5.7.5 E-Government Index — 118
5.7.6 E-Government Readiness Index — 119
5.7.7 E-Government Measurement Systems — 119
5.7.8 Organisational Readiness Assessment — 119
5.7.9 Business Processes Assessment — 120
5.7.10 Organisation Hierarchal Structure — 120
5.7.11 Leadership and Governance Readiness Assessment — 121
5.7.12 Customer Readiness — 121
5.8 Heuristic e-Government Assessment Framework — 122
5.9 Conclusion and Summary — 125

Chapter 6: E-Government Adoption and Synthesis — 127
6.1 Introduction — 127
6.2 Factors Affecting e-Government Adoption — 127
6.3 E-Government Adoption Models — 133
6.3.1 Innovation Diffusion Theory (IDT) — 134
6.3.2 Theory of Reasoned Action (TRA) — 134
6.3.3 Theory of Planned Behaviour (TPB) — 136
6.3.4 Technology Acceptance Model (TAM) — 136
6.3.5 Unified Theory of Adoption and Use of Technology (UTAUT) model — 139
6.4 Critique of Some of the Adoption Frameworks/Models — 143
6.5 Conclusion and Summary — 145

Chapter 7: E-Government Technology Design Frameworks — 146
7.1 Introduction — 146
7.2 Technology Nuances for e-Government — 146
7.3 Advances in Technology Designs — 153
7.4 Future Prospects — 155
7.5 Summary and Conclusion — 156

Chapter 8: Selected Cases of e-Government Implementation — 157
8.1 Introduction — 157

8.2 Current Status of e-Government Adoption Worldwide — 157
8.2.1 America (North and South) — 157
8.2.2 Europe — 161
8.2.3 Asia — 164
8.2.4 Africa — 169
8.3 Distinct Cases of Failure of e-Government Applications — 174
8.3.1 Gambia — 174
8.3.2 India — 179
8.3.3 Lessons learnt from failed e-Government projects — 181
8.4 Detailed Case Study for e-Government Implementation: Zambia — 183
8.4.1 Supply Side of e-Government Implementation in Zambia — 184
8.4.2 Demand Side of e-Government Implementation in Zambia — 187
8.4.3 Questions and Responses Counter — 189
8.5 Testing Hypotheses — 192
8.6 Regression of CU on All Other Variables — 210
8.6.1 Anticipated Interventions for e-Government Proliferation — 213
8.7 Contextual Challenges of e-Government implementation in Zambia — 215
8.8 General Barriers to e-Government Implementation — 218
8.9 Summary and Conclusion — 219

Chapter 9: E-Government Development Paradigms — 221
9.1 Introduction — 221
9.2 E-Government Design Frameworks — 222
9.3 Interoperability and Process/Application Integration — 223
9.4 E-Government Interoperability Frameworks Worldwide — 226
9.5 e-Government Implementation Frameworks — 231
9.6 Conceptual and Theoretical Frameworks/Models — 231
9.7 Closer look at Zambia's Case — 233
9.8 Proposed e-Government Strategy Design Framework — 236
9.9 Conclusion and Summary — 239

Chapter 10: Methodology and Practical Perspectives for e-Government Research and Practice — 241
10.1 Introduction — 241
10.2 Research and Practice Focus — 242
10.3 Methodology of Research — 244
10.4 E-Government and Multi-dimensional Methodological Inclination — 246
10.5 Further Look at the Zambia Case Study — 252

10.6 Statistical Analysis — 263
10.7 Summary — 265

Chapter 11: E-Government Funding Models and Sustainability Frameworks — 267
11.1 Introduction — 267
11.2 Background to e-Government Funding — 268
11.3 E-Government Funding Frameworks and Models — 268
11.4 Implications and Future Work — 272
11.5 Summary and Conclusion — 273

Chapter 12: Contemporary and Future Research and Practical Directions — 274
12.1 Introduction and Background — 274
12.2 The Future Outlook of Public Service — 274
12.3 Convergence of e-Government Applications — 275
12.4 Future Technologies and Impact on Governance Practices — 277
12.5 Future Transformation in Government — 279
12.6 M-Government Initiatives — 280
12.7 Future Issues in m-Government — 281
12.8 Issues in e-Government Practice and Implementation — 284
12.9 Conclusion and Summary — 285

Chapter 13: Conclusion — 286

Appendix 1 — 288

Appendix 2: Research Questionnaire — 292

Bibliography — 303

About the Authors — 337

Index — 338

List of Abbreviations

ADF	African Development Forum
ABM	Active Benefits Management
APEC	Asian Pacific Economic Co-operation
APEC	Asian Pacific Economic Corporation
ASPA	American Society for Public Administration
BcN	Broadband convergence Network
BPR	Business Process Reengineering
BSC	Balanced Score Card
CAM	Citizen Advantage model
CAZ	Communications Authority of Zambia
CEGE	Executive Committee on e-Government
CID	Center for International Development
CITC	Central IT Committee
CIO	Chief Information Officer
CNP	Contribution Network Project
CPI	Corruption Perception Index
CPRDs	Provincial Digital Resource Centers
CRM	Customer Relationship Management
CSPP	Computer System Policy Project
CTGCIE	Brazilian Technical Committee on Knowledge and Strategic Information Management
DAI	ITU Digital Access Index
DBM	Department of Budget and Management
DPSA	Department of Public Service and Administration
EAF	E-Government Assessment Framework
ECT	Electronic Communications and Transactions
EGDMs	E-Government Development Models
eGEP	Union e-Government Economic Project
EGR	Electronic Government Readiness
EIU	Economist Intelligence Unit
EVA	Economic Value Added
EGDMs	Government Development Models
eGAP	E-Government action plan
FOI	Freedom of Information
FNB	First National Bank
GDP	Gross Domestic Product
GePS	South Korea's Government e-Procurement System
GIB	Government Interoperability Board
GOC	Government Online Centre
GOL	Government Online
GSM	Global System for Mobile Communications
G2B	Government-to-Business
G2C	Government-to-Citizens
G2E	Government-to-Employees

G2G	Government-to-Government
G2B	Government-to-Business
HANIS	Home Affairs National Information System
HMIS	Health Management Information System
ICTs	Information and Communication Technologies
IDs	Identification Documents
IDA	Infocomm Development Authority of Singapore
IDT	Innovation Diffusion Theory
IEEE	Institute of Electrical and Electronics Engineers
IFMS	Integrated Financial Management Information System
IRR	Internal Rate of Return
IS	Information Systems
ITU	International Telecommunications Union's
KAM	World Bank's Knowledge Assessment Methodology
KBE	Knowledge-Based-Economy
KE	Knowledge Based Economies
KEI	Knowledge Economy Index
KII	Korea Information Infrastructure
LAN	Local Area Network
LDC	Least Developed Countries
LDC	Least Developed Country
MDGs	Millennium Development Goals
MIOS	Minimum Interoperability Standards
MISS	Minimum Information Security Standards
MMS	Multimedia Messaging Service
MMR	Mixed (or Multiple) Research Methodology
MPCTs	Multi-Purpose Community Telecenters
NCP	National Computerisation Plan
NGOs	Non Governmental Organisation
NHS	National Health System
NIIB	National Information Infrastructure Backbone
NPV	Net Present Value (),
OPEN	Online Procedures Enhancement for civil applications initiative of Korea
PB	Payback Period
PDA	Personal Digital Assistant
PEOU	Perceived Ease of Use
PHPNP	Participatory Health Population and Nutrition Project
PMIS	PMO Management Information System
PMO	Personnel Management Organisation
PoPs	Internet Points of Presence
PPR	Public sector process rebuilding
PTC	Posts and Telecommunications Corporation
PU	Perceived Usefulness
PoPs	Internet Points of Presence
PSRP	Public Service Reform Programme
PSCAP	Public Service Capacity Building Project
PTC	Posts and Telecommunications Corporation

PPP	Public Private Partnerships
PVIT	Public Value of IT
PU	Perceived Usefulness
RFID	Radio-Frequency IDentification
ROA	Return on Assets (ROA),
ROI	Return on Investments
ROS	Return on Sales (ROS),
SADC	Southern African Development Corporation
SARS	South African Revenue Service
SCM	Standard Cost Model
SGEA	Singapore Government Enterprise Architecture
SIAFI	Integrated Financial, Budgetary and Asset Management System
SIDA	Sweden International Development Agency
SISP	Integrated Public Health System
SITA	State Information Technology Agency
SLA	Service Level Agreement
SMS	Short Message Service
SPs	Internet Service Providers
SSA	Sub-Saharan Africa
SVA	Shareholder Value Analysis
SWTA	Service-Wide Technical Architecture
TAM	Technology Acceptance Model
TESTA	Trans-European Services for Telematics between Administrations
TOI	Trust of the Internet
TOG	Trust of Government
TRA	Theory of Reasoned Action
TQM	Total Quality Management
UAP	Universal Access Programme
UN	United Nations
UNCAC	United Nations Convention against Corruption
UNDESA	United Nations Department of Economic and Social Affairs
UNDP	United Nations Development Programme
UNDPEPA	United Nations Division for Public Economics and Public Administration
UNDP	United Nations Development Programme
UNESCO	United Nations Education, Scientific and Childrens' Fund
UNICEF	United Nations International Children's Emergency Fund
UNPAN	United Nations Public Administration Network
UTAUT	Unified Theory of Adoption and Use of Technology
VSATs	Very Small Aperture Terminals
WEF	World Economic Forum
WHO	World Health Organisation
WIS	Web Interface Standards
WITSA	World Information Technology and Services Alliance
WMRC	World Markets Research Centre
WTI	World Telecommunication Indicators
ZANACO	Zambia National Commercial Bank
ZAMTEL	Zambia Telecommunication Company

ZICTA	Zambia Information and Communication Technology Authority
ZNFU	Zambia National Farmers' Union
ZRA	Zambia Revenue Authority

List of Figures

Figure 4.1 High-level e-Government Infrastructure —— 62
Figure 4.2 The Layne and Lee e-Government Maturity Model (Layne & Lee, 2001:124) —— 66
Figure 4.3 Public sector process rebuilding (PPR) maturity model (Andersen & Henriksen, 006:237) —— 75
Figure 4.4 A six stage e-Government roadmap (Adapted from: Forrester Research, Inc.) —— 80
Figure 5.1 The CJIT Benefits Management framework (Adapted from Jenner, 2005:11) —— 109
Figure 5.2 The eGEP measurement framework model (adapted from: EU Report (2007:11) —— 112
Figure 5.3 Activities that inform the Cost of Administrative Burden (adapted from: SCM, 2005:8) —— 113
Figure 5.4 Blueprint for Designing e-Government Assessment Frameworks —— 124
Figure 6.1 The TRA Model (Adapted from: Fishbein & Ajzen, 1975) —— 135
Figure 6.2 TPB Model (Adapted from: Ajzen, 1991) —— 136
Figure 6.3 Technology Acceptance Model (Adapted from: Ajzen, 1991) —— 137
Figure 6.4 Extended TAM2 model (Adapted from: Venkatesh and Davis, 2000:188) —— 139
Figure 6.5 UTAUT Model (Adapted from: Venkatesh, et al., 2003:447) —— 141
Figure 8.1 Gaussian normal data fit of PU on PEOU —— 195
Figure 8.2 P-P plot for standardised residue of PU on PEOU —— 196
Figure 8.3 Scatterplot of the Mahalanobis distance of PU on PEOU —— 197
Figure 8.4 P-P plot for standardised residue of actual usage on PU —— 198
Figure 8.5 Gaussian normal data fit of actual usage on PEOU —— 199
Figure 8.6 P-P plot for standardised residue of actual usage on PEOU —— 200
Figure 8.7 Gaussian normal data fit of PEOU on ICT infrastructure —— 201
Figure 8.8 P-P plot for standardised residue of PEOU on ICT infrastructure —— 202
Figure 8.9 Gaussian normal data fit of trust on actual usage —— 203
Figure 8.10 P-P plot for standardised residue of trust on actual usage —— 204
Figure 8.11 Gaussian normal data fit of actual usage on computer self-efficacy —— 205
Figure 8.12 P-P plot for standardised residue of actual usage on computer self-efficacy —— 206
Figure 8.13 Gaussian normal data fit of continuance usage on all other variables —— 207
Figure 8.14 P-P plot for standardised residue —— 208
Figure 8.15 Gaussian normal data fit of PU on PEOU and ICT infrastructure —— 209
Figure 8.16 P-P plot for standardised residue of PU on PEOU and ICT infrastructure —— 210
Figure 8.17 Gaussian normal data fit of CU on all other variables —— 211
Figure 8.18 P-P plot for standardised residue of CU on all other variables —— 212
Figure 9.1 e-GIF Architecture —— 226
Figure 9.2 Proposed conceptual e-Government adoption model (e-Government consumers) —— 235
Figure 9.3 Proposed framework for e-Government strategy development —— 239
Figure 10.1 Areas under the ambit of e-Government research and practice —— 245
Figure 10.2 Research classification quadrants (Stokes, 1997:73; Barnard, 2007:125) —— 247
Figure 10.3 Study design and research process —— 256
Figure 10.4 Snapshot of research motivation and process —— 257
Figure 10.5 Fundamental research models and anticipated conceptual model —— 259
Figure 10.6 Expanded view of the research model utilised in this study —— 260
Figure 10.7 Interdependence among different factors in the research model —— 261
Figure 11.1 Pool for e-Government funding —— 270

List of Tables

Table 2.1 Areas under the ambit of e-Government (Source: partly adapted from Godse & Garg, 2007:14) —— **21**
Table 2.2 Distinction between e-Government and e-Governance —— **27**
Table 2.3 Characteristics of e-Government applications —— **31**
Table 2.4 Overcoming e-Government implementation challenges (Source: Almarabeh & AbuAli, 2010: 32-34) —— **36**
Table 3.1 Benefits of e-Government implementation (Source: Capgemini analysis, November 2007) —— **46**
Table 4.1 Summary of models' characteristics —— **77**
Table 5.1 The French MAREVA measurement methodology —— **107**
Table 5.2 Task Group on e-Government of the Partnership on Measuring ICT for Development – draft list of core e-Government indicators (Adapted from source: UN e-Government Survey, 2010:94) —— **115**
Table 6.1 Models and frameworks of technology adoption —— **142**
Table 8.1 Mitigation of failure of HMIS implementation (Partially sourced from DoSH&SW, 2002) —— **178**
Table 8.2 Information Management Interventions in Zambia —— **185**
Table 8.3 Characteristics of participants —— **189**
Table 8.4 Awareness of e-Government initiatives in Zambia —— **189**
Table 8.5 Descriptive statistics of the PEOU and the PU data set —— **193**
Table 8.6 Correlations between PU and PEOU —— **193**
Table 8.7 Model Summary predictive value of PEOU on PU —— **194**
Table 8.8 Analysis of Variance —— **194**
Table 8.9 Predicting capacity of the model (Dependent Variable: Log_PU) —— **194**
Table 8.10 Residuals Statistics —— **195**
Table 9.1 E-Government Interoperability Frameworks —— **227**
Table 10.1 Comparisons between quantitative and qualitative research approaches —— **251**
Table 12.1 Emerging Technologies and Governance impact —— **278**
Table 12.2 E-Government and the emerging technology landscape —— **280**

Chapter 1
Prologue

1.1 Introduction

The use of Information and Communications Technologies (ICTs) in public delivery frameworks (e-Government) is gaining ground both in the developed and developing world countries. E-Government implementation may entail that other socio-economic developmental programmes are not given priority so that financial resources are devoted to putting in place requisite e-Government infrastructure and systems. Therefore, many countries and e-Government stakeholders now emphasize the need to ensure that carefully thought e-Government interventions, programmes and designs are pursued to avoid paying the huge opportunity costs in case of failure. Because e-Government is still in its nascent stage, there are many issues that centre on conceptual frameworks/models that in turn inform practice. Given this understanding, there is need to ensure that the general and context-specific principles that inform e-Government designs are referenced when designing e-Government applications or programmes.

The main objective of this chapter is to outline the major focus of this book, outline the topics discussed, articulate the intended audience and anticipated impact on e-Government research, practice and development. This chapter provides an overview of this book and accentuates its contribution to the e-Government body of knowledge. It is understood that the use of ICTs is slowly getting centre-stage based on the drive by governments around the world to provide efficient, effective, and responsive public service delivery.

1.2 Focus and Locale

This book intends to delve deeper into the understanding of e-Government given different contextual settings. It is not a secret that many e-Government interventions and/or programmes in the world fail completely and partially or do not completely meet their intended targets (Heeks, 2004). Huge opportunity costs paid as a result of failure of these e-Government programmes are unbearable in both developing and developed world contexts. With this in mind, many research endeavours have been devoted to understanding the inherent characteristics of e-Government as a multi-dimensional phenomenon, how its implementation strategies can be optimized in heterogeneous environments, and how to best draw e-Government implementation strategies given a context. This book, therefore, intends to highlight the multi-dimensionality of e-Government, highlight emerging trends in e-Government conceptualisation, and discuss requisite conceptual frameworks and e-Government Interoperability frameworks (e-GIFs) commensurate for the developing world contexts. The book further brings out the core attributes of e-Government given the revolving technology circles, and discusses both the supply (available e-Government applications, interventions, etc.) and the demand (citizens' and businesses' willingness to engage in e-Government) aspects of e-Government. The discussion of the aforementioned aspects of e-Government is important as the ultimate stumbling block of any effervescent and successful e-Government implementation is how to achieve equilibrium between the demand and supply sides.

To achieve the aforementioned, this book intends to discuss the following themes and/or topics:

1. Evolution of e-Government (accentuating on its multi-dimensionality and outlining the emerging trends of e-Government in the changing technology platforms);
2. E-Government readiness, the digital divide and the different e-Government readiness measurement frameworks;
3. E-Government assessment models and frameworks;
4. The attainment of equilibrium between supply and demand sides of e-Government outlining desirable e-Government interventions and adoption at both individual and organisational levels;
5. E-Government technology design frameworks highlighting technology principles that should guide e-Government development in any environment given emerging technology convergence;
6. E-Government development paradigms and frameworks; and
7. Discussion of the contemporary and future best-practice and research opportunities.

The book can be used by both e-Government researchers and practitioners, including policy makers, and students interested in e-Government. It is anticipated that this book will be used as a cardinal reference resource on issues concerning e-Government especially for the developing world context.

This study posited that e-Government is a multi-dimensional phenomenon which calls for a multi-dimensional approach. The book focuses on discussing both the technical and managerial issues around e-Government. The main case study presented in this book is drawn from empirical research that was done in 2011 as part of a doctoral study by the author. This study aimed at understanding the inherent factors that impact on e-Government adoption in Zambia at various levels of the socio-economic hierarchy. Three towns in Zambia, Livingstone, Kitwe and Lusaka were included as study sites. The discussions utilise the case study of Zambia as a focal point in order to understand the ramifications involved in e-Government development in a diverse, multi-cultural context. The conceptual framework discussed in the book and the e-Government Interoperability Framework (e-GIF) proposed may be adapted to suit a given contextual environment and therefore be utilised as a mirror for prioritization of interventions or inform policy frameworks and/or direction.

1.3 Background: E-Government and Society

The emergence of knowledge economies and extensive use and adoption of ICTs in business entities have placed more pressure on governments to implement e-Government in their public service delivery platforms. Because of efficiencies brought about by the adoption and appropriate use of ICTs in businesses and other private sector entities, e-Government is slowly becoming a *sine qua non* for responsive and transparent governance and is seen as one of the most important ingredients to national competitiveness (Klievink & Janssen, 2009:276). This has culminated into a greater call for governments both in the developed and developing world to promote the utilisation of ICTs in their public service delivery frameworks.

1.4 Semantic Understanding of e-Government

E-Government has been defined differently by many scholars as listed below (cf: Appendix). The simplest definition is that e-Government refers to the use of ICTs in the governing process of a country. Thus, it facilitates the utilisation of ICTs in the interaction amongst the government, citizens and businesses. Some common definitions of e-Government are given below:

- E-Government is an enabler for public service innovation and productive health (UN e-Government Report, 2008:69).
- E-Government refers to the use of ICTs by public administration to create a networked structure for; interconnectivity, service delivery, efficiency, effectiveness, transparency, and accountability (Yildiz, 2007:649–650).
- E-Government runs wide across all aspects of government, deep within the core of every governmental entity, and will inevitably be a transforming agent for government and governance (Boyle & Nicholson, 2003:92).

- E-Government is a strong tool for responsive and transparent governance and facilitates access to information, freedom of expression, greater equity, efficiency, productivity and social inclusion (ADF IV, 2004:64).

It is worth noting that the use of ICTs in public service delivery platforms (e-Government) is relatively a new wave that is sweeping through countries all over the world (Mutula, 2010). Global usage of ICTs in the public service delivery value chains not only brings about many tangible benefits but also helps a country participate in the contemporary knowledge value chains (Ndou, 2004:2; Misra, 2007:2). As mentioned above, ICT facilities mainstreaming of e-Government into the service delivery platforms of different government agencies and organs thereby culminating into efficient and quality service delivery (Lenk & Traunmüller, 2001:69; Pascual, 2003:6; Bwalya & Healy, 2010:23).

1.5 Practical Uses of e-Government

With many studies evaluating the positive returns on e-Government implementation, pronouncements of positive impacts of e-Government on public service delivery and its ability, the political and socio-economic landscape, have been grandiose (Wong & Welch, 2004:275,289; Kumar & Best, 2006:6,9). Many studies have documented the benefits associated with successful implementation of e-Government initiatives as follows: it facilitates interactive, vertical, collaborative and participatory engagement of citizens, businesses and other governments, reducing the cost of service delivery; encourages global participation of citizens in the decision-making processes; provides an opportunity for governments to rethink and reformulate their administrative praxis and provides a framework where governments continuously re-engineer their business processes to retain currency and relevance to best practice (Wu, 2007:89–90; Sarantis, Charalabidis & Askounis, 2011:117). E-Government may further be utilised to mitigate corruption levels in the public sector. For example, the introduction of e-Procurement and e-Tendering can greatly reduce corruption in tendering processes. E-Government has direct positive impacts on the individuals, businesses and the government itself. For example, it is thought that huge chunks of information generated on a day-to-day basis from government business processes can now be appropriately archived for future references. E-Government further facilitates affective information management practices within public service delivery platforms (Navarra & Cornford, 2007:2). E-Government also provides an appropriate platform for governments to engage the private institutions through the Public Private Partnerships (PPP) arrangements in development programmes.

In its entirety, e-Government aims to benefit the community by drawing together the civil society, public sector, international partners, and other stakeholders with a view of encouraging a participatory and inclusive process of governance and decision-making (Navarra & Cornford, 2007:3). Further, e-Government reduces or eliminates institutional fragmentation of public administration because the citizens and/or businesses are given a chance to access public services from a single point source (Shareef, Kumar, Kumar & Dwivedi, 2011:18). In so doing, e-Government presents itself as an intuitive decision support tool for informed public service decision-making (Fang, 2002:9).

Accruable benefits of successful e-Government implementation culminate in enabling citizens to participate in decision-making processes regarding issues of national importance regardless of their socio-economic status, promoting participatory democracy and social inclusion, reducing the cost of public service delivery, reducing corruption, and encouraging an efficient public service delivery system (Cho & Choi, 2004:721; Wong & Welch, 2004:275; Kumar & Best, 2006:4; Navarra & Cornford, 2007:3; Iqbal & Seo, 2008:68; Bwalya & Healy, 2010:23; Papadopoulou, Nikolaidou & Martakos, 2010:5; Syamsuddin & Hwang, 2010:1). E-Government benefits business entities in that it creates business sense and value so that good relationships between the government and the different businesses are maintained.

1.6 E-Government Impact

Although the utilisation of ICTs in public service delivery frameworks comes with many positives; at no time should it be seen as a universal remedy for the challenges faced by public administration especially in the developing world. Although e-Government has shown a lot of promise for positive impact on the overall public service delivery frameworks, revitalising the way government, citizens and businesses interact, it is not a panacea to problems associated with public service delivery. To successfully implement e-Government, there are certain prerequisites that need to be in place.

Another obvious impact of e-Government implementation is that other socio-economic programmes are neglected as huge financial resources are devoted towards putting in place requisite infrastructure for e-Government. For example, requisite e-Government implementation requires the putting in place of appropriate information architecture which is responsible for integrating all the other business processes in the e-Government domain (Navarra & Cornford, 2007:4). The putting in place of a requisite and responsive information infrastructure costs a fortune. In a real e-Government environment, government departments have heterogeneous information systems and platforms which need to be integrated if effervescent e-Government implementation were to be achieved. Information system integration makes it possible for inter-organisational information sharing in the public domain (Schooley & Horan, 2007:756). The importance of system integration in the e-Government realm cannot be overemphasized as the establishment of a shared information infrastructure is a major milestone in the e-Government implementation (Bekkers and Moody (2010:9). A lack of shared standards and a compatible infrastructure between government departments and agencies can impede inter-agency collaboration.

1.7 E-Government Research and Practice

Research of e-Government mushroomed at the time when computers were just being adopted worldwide (Stamoulis, Theotokis, Martakos & Gyftodimos, 2003:83; Tassabehji, 2005:1). The genesis of e-Government was rooted in the motivation to promote citizens' access to government information through online platforms in a ubiquitous manner and to generally promote efficiency in public service delivery. Despite this being the case, e-Government is still a novel concept in many developing countries (Ochara-Muganda & Van Belle, 2010:1). It is evident that a number of developing countries are still building the basic ICT infrastructures and some are only in the preliminary phases of articulating the vision of e-Government such as drawing ICT policies to act as e-Government enablers (Ochara-Muganda & Van Belle, 2010:3).

In support of the perception that e-Government is still at the conceptual stage in most developing countries, literature on the experiences of implementing e-Government in developing countries is scarce. Further, despite the burgeoning number of studies on public sector information systems especially in the developed world, very few scholars have focused on understanding the relationship between e-Government policies and information systems choice and design. This largely depends on the local context such as the characteristics of the anticipated users (Lee, 2010; Lee, Li, Yen & Huang, 2010:225; Bwalya, Du Plessis & Rensleigh, 2011:231). For these reasons, this study aims to understand the factors that impact on the development of e-Government taking full cognisance of the local context.

Knowledge-Based Economies (KBEs), which recognize knowledge as the major resource for competitiveness, are mushrooming everywhere in the world. Countries are recognizing the concept of KBE because aim to utilise few resources for maximum benefit and efficient/effectively use their knowledge resources to place themselves at a competitive edge in the global socio-economic value chains. With the emergence of KBEs, most countries have jumped on board the digital governance bandwagon and have started putting in place appropriate institutional, legal and regulatory frameworks to facilitate efficient information and knowledge management in the public sector using ICTs. As aforementioned, appropriate streamlining of ICTs in the socio-economic value chains translate into effective knowledge sharing and therefore competitiveness (Gerster Consulting, 2008:2; Každemikaitienė & Bilevičienė, 2008:186). For a country to be competitive in the contemporary economic order and information society, it is important that it has the high levels of productivity that can be brought forth by efficient and transparent management of information and national resources, coupled with a global participation of its citizenry in the various socio-economic value chains. Establishing efficient knowledge management value chains begins from the ability of the government to appropriately manage its information resources and how this replicates (ripple effect) to other socio-economic entities. The use of ICTs at a massive scale has proved to be an appropriate tool towards this agenda. For example, in a bid to amass the different benefits that e-Government has to offer, Botswana, Mozambique and Malawi have started putting in place strategic initiatives to aid e-Government development. Some of the interventions include the following: Botswana has drawn the National ICT Policy – Maitlamo (Sethibe & Bwalya, 2014), Zambia's ICT policy of 2006 (Bwalya & Healy, 2010), and South Africa has put in place de-regularised and liberalised telecommunication and other relevant policies (Mutula, 2010). Additionally, although Africa shows a regional average of 0.278 in regional e-Government development scale, it is evident that there are signs that e-Government will thrive in the near future (UNDESA, 2012).

Development agendas in many countries have been foiled because there is no outright accountability of priorities, no effective management of national resources, lack of participatory and transparent decision-making by ordinary citizens, and higher corruption levels (Ngulube, 2007:158; HIPSSA Project, 2008:10). Other studies have shown that effective use of ICTs in government processes may be used to remove these roadblocks to development (Kažemikaitienė & Bilevičienė, 2008:190). Global use of ICTs in the public delivery chains ushers in a paradigm where national resource management and decision-making are done with the full congruency and monitoring of all stakeholders including ordinary and marginal individuals with the full utilisation of ICTs.

In 2010, at least 184 countries attempted implementing e-Government with a view of reducing the cost of their public service delivery (Smith, 2011:90). According to Smith (2011:91), these countries have to some extent incorporated ICTs in their business value chains and processes and targeted the subsequent increase of effectiveness. However, it is important to note that the implementation of e-Government may be very difficult if the different modalities that aid successful e-Government implementation are not in place (Dada, 2006:6; Hossan, Habib & Kushchu, 2006:1). Successful e-Government implementation is dependent on an array of factors (multi-dimensional factors) which may be unique given the local context where it is implemented (Sharifi & Manian, 2010:63; Al-Khouri, 2011:23; Rokhman, 2011:3).

In the Southern African Development Community (SADC) region, there has recently been an escalation of e-Government initiatives with South Africa, Mauritius, Seychelles and Botswana leading the way towards this cause (Bwalya & Healy, 2010:23–24). These countries have established dedicated initiatives for the advancement of the e-Government agenda. An example of such dedicated initiatives is the case of Botswana where the government and various co-operating partners have invested heavily in ICT infrastructure development and a dedicated e-Government office has been put in place (Bwalya & Healy, 2010:23).

1.8 Book Rationale

There is limited text especially targeting e-Government development in less developed world countries. As posited above, this book intends to position itself as a key reference source for e-Government research and practice as it goes out to present the fundamental concepts that guide effervescent e-Government implementation regardless of context. This is because, although this book uses examples focusing on less developed countries, the fundamental principles for e-Government implementation and steps used to create e-Government strategies are global concepts.

Given the slow penetration of e-Government in the developing world countries compared to emerging and less developed world countries, it is important to investigate the factors that affect e-Government development in less developed world contexts. The understanding is that success of e-Government is largely influenced by context. Therefore, appropriate e-Government design should be informed by careful reference to local context and other successful implementation endeavours especially from the developing world context. The presentation of contextual scenarios in this book will help understand what it takes during the design of e-Government implementation modules and roadmaps for the less developed world. Generally, e-Government is underdeveloped in most less developed world countries. Widely held assertions have attributed the cost of establishing e-Government infrastructure as the major deterrent factor. However, recent understanding of e-Government has shown that context is much at play in drawing the development projectile for e-Government development in less developed countries. The underdevelopment of e-Government in the developing world is largely evident in countries' low score in international e-Government assessment metrics (See Chapter 6). For example, individual African countries have generally scored low in the different indexes that are used for measuring e-Government development status (such as 'Web Measure Index', 'Telecommunications Infrastructure Index', and 'Human Capital Index') as outlined in the global e-Government research by UNDESA (UN e-Government Survey, 2010:17).

As mentioned above, e-Government ushers in a paradigm of higher quality public and cost-effective service delivery, and facilitates better relationships and interactions between government entities and citizens or businesses (Ndou, 2004:5). Despite these pronounced benefits, many countries in the developing world have not taken advantage of the vast advantages that e-Government has to offer. For example, Rorissa and Demissie (2010:1) posit that the use of ICTs such as those necessary to provide e-Government services is minimal in Africa as compared to other parts of the world. In fact, at one time, Africa was considered a 'technological desert'. Further, as observed by Wescott (1999:4), Africa has inefficient and low-performance public administrations with under-resourced public institutions, unmotivated and unqualified workers, rigid centralism with neo-patrimonial leadership styles, and higher corruption levels. There is a chance that these inefficiencies can be minimised if ICTs are extensively utilised in the major government business processes, and that the e-Government designs are informed by an authoritative reference. Therefore, this book will fill in the gaps in e-Government literature to be used as a key reference source.

In order to amass the different benefits that come with effective e-Government implementation, there is need to develop context-aware (i.e. design informed by the local context) e-Government initiatives (Bwalya et al., 2011:295). Schuppan (2009:121) posits that e-Government initiatives should be designed with reference to the prevailing local conditions. Most e-Government implementation projects in the developing world have adopted ready-made e-Government solutions and 'blueprints' from the developed world and have tried to implement them without due reference to local administrative contexts and rationalities (Maumbe, Owei & Alexander, 2008:768; Nour, Abdel Rahman & Fadlalla, 2008:449). This has resulted into many e-Government projects failing. A context-oriented design methodology is the most appropriate approach for implementing e-Government in the developing world. The developed world has shown that it is easier to implement e-Government in their environments than it is in the developing world because of differences in the level of development of the institutional, legal, cultural, administrative contexts, and the socio-economic environment (Schuppan, 2009:118). Valdés et al., (2011:1 3) posit that e-Government designers should be wary of e-Government's multi-dimensional nature and take a holistic implementation approach. This book, therefore, is timely as it tries to understand the contextual setting in selected developing world countries and unearths the different factors that impact on individuals' or businesses' decisions to either participate or not participate in e-Government. By so doing, the book proposes frameworks that can be adopted or adapted for use in other developing world contexts. The most important feature of this book is the outline of the steps and approaches that should be followed when designing e-Government programmes in less developed world contexts.

A look at e-Government development initiatives in other developing countries reveals that they have mostly been designed with due reference to the International e-Government Development Models (EGDMs). Zarei, Ghapanchi and Sattary (2008:200) have criticised the authenticity and appropriateness of the EGDMs as to their applicability to e-Government development in developing countries. This is because the EGDMs may not take into consideration the local context, especially at the grassroots levels such as the community and individual level, which may be critical to the success of e-Government implementation. Global studies provide little information about the state of e-Government implementation in developing countries in general, and in Sub-Saharan Africa in particular (Shareef et al., 2011:17). There is generally a shortage of studies on e-Governments' implementation endeavours and this presents a knowledge gap that needs to be filled (Kim, Pan & Ling-Pan, 2007:338). Further, very few studies have attempted to understand the cardinal factors that affect e-Government adoption especially at the community or individual level. In this regard, the importance of a book focusing on discussing e-Government from the lowest abstraction (fine-details) cannot be overemphasized.

The major case study in this book is a closer look at e-Government implementation endeavours in Zambia. The case study intends to provide insights into what is involved with regards to e-Government implementation in a specific context, and to assess the level of development of e-Government at the business and individual level. Whilst various other research projects (such as by Weerakkody, Dwivedi, Brooks, Williams and Mwange, (2007:484–505); Coates and Nikolaus, (2010:137–161)) have been done to ascertain the level of e-Government systems encapsulation in Zambia, no grassroots research has been done to ascertain the actual issues and challenges that impend the adoption of e-Government systems by the general public and businesses there. Although several challenges have been highlighted as affecting the growth of e-Government systems, these are mostly generic in nature and may not be applicable for Zambia because of its unique contextual environment. The UN e-Government Report (2008) compares different countries using common indexes. Comparing countries with these indexes across-the-board may not be the most appropriate way to assess countries' standing with their peers in as far as e-Government adoption and encapsulation is concerned. This is because 'context' is not at play in these comparisons. Countries have different contextual characteristics and this may impact greatly on their adoption rate of e-Government systems. Apart from context, there is also an issue of 'culture' which separates countries. Some countries may have higher propensity to change as compared to others and this may have either a positive or negative impact in as far as adoption of new technologies is concerned. These issues may possibly have an effect on the level of e-Government encapsulation and development in any developing world context. It is therefore imperative that these issues need be discussed and highlighted as key attributes informing e-Government development in the developing world. This book aims to bring out the context-specific issues with regards to e-Government development.

A set of general challenges have been identified in the paucity of efficient e-Government systems implementation in the developing world. Some of the key challenges for e-Government applications have been identified as the following: a) the inadequacy in the development of telecommunication infrastructure; and b) the limited or lack of commitment of governments and other co-operating partners to usher in a genuine transformation paradigm towards more transparent and citizen-centered government processes (Ngulube, 2007:158). The other profound challenge for e-Government development in developing countries largely highlighted is the low literacy levels. For example, Sub-Saharan Africa has one of the world's lowest adult literacy rates, with only 60% of the population of 15 years and over able to read and to write, well below the world average of 80%. Literacy levels are as low as below 40% in Benin, Burkina Faso, Ethiopia, Gambia, Guinea-Bissau, Mali, Niger and Senegal (Simenda, 2009:5). Highlighting the impact of such factors is one of the objectives of this book.

The major objective of this book is to contribute to the understanding of the design of appropriate, responsive, and scalable e-Government applications regardless of the environment in which e-Government is implemented. Responsive e-Government applications are desired given the rapidly changing technologies. The book specifically looks at the issues of context, the up-take status of e-Government, and the challenges and factors impacting on e-Government development in less developed world contexts. Some of the contributions of this book are as follows:

8. After identifying the challenges and factors impacting on e-Government implementation and development in a developing world context, the study recommends ways of how different e-Government enablers can be streamlined into the design of an e-Government development strategy. Some of the major outcomes will be the appropriate technical standards and other operational support to facilitate progress in e-Government utilisation such as promotion of a smooth interoperability between various e-Government systems

and appropriate security arrangements, between different e-Government applications (such as in the use of e-Signatures and for other aspects of electronic identification management). The book provides cases of how the different technical and managerial aspects of e-Government implication should be linked to the e-Government Interoperability Framework (e-GIF) which is seen as the cornerstone of any robust e-Government strategy.

9. Identifies critical success factors for domestication and ownership of e-Government applications by the individual citizens and businesses in heterogeneous environments.
10. Provides a comparative assessment of the willingness and ability of ordinary citizens to get involved in e-Government; and provides a benchmarking tool for monitoring the progress of e-Government implementation as it moves towards higher levels of digital public service delivery in the near future.
11. Assesses efficiency and effectiveness of a selected set of traditional public service delivery systems and carries out feasibility analysis of how e-Government systems can fit in to create value for public service.
12. Probes the importance of e-Inclusion of all citizens into the governance hierarchy. This entails making sure that all citizens, including socially disadvantaged groups and people in remotest parts of the country, have equal chances of accessing e-Government applications.
13. Proposes start-point appropriate institutional, legal and regulatory frameworks which can allow for the protection of users in the e-Government environment.

It can thus be said that this book will likely positively contribute to both theory and practice owing to the fact that there is currently very limited literature on e-Government in developing world contexts. Therefore, it is anticipated that this book will be a major reference source especially for researchers, policy makers and practitioners with regards to designing their e-Government solutions and interventions.

1.9 Conclusion and Summary

This chapter has introduced the focus of this book by clearly outlining its boundaries and locale. The chapter outlines the motivation for this book out of the scarcity of literature or research outputs emanating from e-Government implementation in the less developed countries. Also, the chapter posits that, by providing the text in this book, e-Government practitioners will be better placed on how to design e-Government strategies. The chapter further articulates the anticipated impact of this book.

The next chapter will further articulate detailed specifics of e-Government and outline the major characteristics of e-Government especially highlighting its multi-dimensionality.

Chapter 2
The e-Government phenomenon

2.1 Introduction

The global usage of Information and Communication Technologies (ICTs) in the public delivery frameworks (e-Government) is relatively a new wave that is sweeping through countries all over the world (Mutula, 2010). Its effective implementation not only brings about many tangible and intangible benefits but also helps a country participate in the contemporary knowledge value chains (Ndou, 2004:1; Choi, 2007:6; Misra, 2007:2). Therefore, the benefits for successful e-Government implementation span through individual, organisational, national, and societal levels. In order to appreciate and amass these benefits definable at various levels of the socio-economic hierarchy, there is need to completely understand the whole gamut of e-Government conceptualization. Therefore, this chapter intends to understand what e-Government entails in different contextual settings. The chapter also discusses the different forms and characteristics of e-Government given its multi-dimensionality and heterogeneity. The drive towards thorough understanding of e-Government is important because it enables both researchers and practitioners design e-Government applications, interventions, or programmes based on globally agreed-upon principles and best practice.

2.2 Background to e-Government Conceptualization

E-Government aims at ensuring that the diverse information resources from the government are put in the public domain for everyone's consumption so that it may be utilized to inform socio-economic activities. On another hand, e-Government provides a platform for decisions affecting the general citizenry and attempts to ensure that businesses are made transparently in the public domain. By so doing, the level of corruption in the public sector may be reduced and efficiency and/or accountability are increased. At an individual level, the e-Government platform ensures that citizens are abreast with decisions made on their behalf in parliament and that they are able to participate in the governance hierarchy with the help of ICTs. With regards to businesses, e-Government platforms ensure that business entities are aware of business opportunities that they may pursue with government departments, e.g. open tenders through e-Tendering. Further, e-Government ensures that both citizens and businesses abide to the behavioural code and business ethical code of conduct, respectively. The benefits of e-Government at different levels of the socio-economic hierarchy may be too numerous to mention at this stage.

The use of ICTs in government business processes brings about service integration which culminates into effective, efficient and quality public service delivery (Lenk & Traunmüller, 2001:68; Pascual, 2003:6; Bwalya & Healy, 2010:23). Further, there is evidence that robust usage of ICTs in government business processes translates into higher innovation and productivity levels of the public service employees (Wonglimpiyarat & Yuberk, 2005:414; Zhu, Kraemer & Xu, 2006:1558). Additionally, successful implementation of e-Government would allow marginal individuals to freely participate into discourse regarding issues of national development regardless of their socio-economic status. Given the aforementioned, one can easily note that e-Government is slowly becoming a *sine qua non* for good governance and is seen as one of the most important pillars for effective and sustainable development of a nation.

The enormous benefits that come with e-Government implementation only become rhetoric if a strategic and robust implementation strategy is not put in place as the overall e-Government programme is bound to fail in such circumstances. Any e-Government strategy should be context-aware – informed by the local contextual characteristics and setup (Bwalya et al., 2011:231). A well informed e-Government strategy is a beacon to successful e-Government implementation. Further to the outlined focus of this book, the book intends to unearth the different factors that influence engagement or non-engagement of individuals and businesses in developing world contexts and subsequently design a conceptual reference for e-Government strategy design.

Taking cognizance of the different characteristics of e-Government, many governments in the world as well as different stakeholders have started considering the implementation of e-Government as a priority to public service reforms. Most of the governments have also realized that e-Government provides a platform for inclusiveness and open governance. As of April 2010, a total of 184 countries have attempted implementing e-Government with a view of reducing the cost of their public service delivery and have attempted to incorporate ICTs in their business value chains and processes (Smith, 2011:90). This means a lot of millions of US dollars are being devoted to e-Government implementation worldwide. The huge financial resources devoted to e-Government entail that careful thought and consideration need to be given as e-Government is designed to reduce incidences of failure and therefore losing out on expected return on investment. Careful design of e-Government is necessary because it is a well known fact that the implementation of e-Government may be a very difficult dream to realize when the different modalities that aid its successful implementation are not in place. This is because it is an established fact that most e-Government implementation fail (Heeks, 2003a; Dada, 2006:39; Hossan et al., 2006:2; Kumar, Mukerji, Irfan & Ajax, 2007:70). The success of e-Government implementation partly depends on the environment in which it is implemented, the ICT skills levels of the general citizenry, the type of applications being promoted, and the type of e-Government strategies in place (Heeks, 2003a:5).

The starting point in understanding what it takes to successfully implement e-Government includes the need to completely understand what e-Government entails. The totality of e-Government has to be clearly decoded to determine what kind of strategies have to be put in place to encourage its proliferation and sustainable development. This chapter, therefore, intends to succinctly define what e-Government is and discuss the different forms of e-Government. Further, it discusses the different e-Government maturity models and outlines the different pre-requisites necessary for successful implementation. Before the main discussion outlining the conceptual and technical understanding of what e-Government entails, it is important to discuss the different factors that have motivated countries the world over to implement e-Government.

2.3 Motivation for e-Government Implementation

Research of e-Government mushroomed at a time (*ca* the mid-1990s) when computers were just being generally adopted worldwide as global platforms for information management (Stamoulis et al., 2003:83; Tassabehji, 2005:1). The genesis of e-Government was rooted in the motivation to promote citizens' access to government information through online platforms anytime and anywhere (ubiquitous or pervasive access). The pivotal understanding by governments is that when information is in the public domains, citizens will be engaged at various levels of the governance hierarchy and that there will be enhanced trust in the entire governance establishment. In addition, the idea of e-Government also stems from the business world. Governments around the world have also been motivated to implement e-Government looking at businesses who have globally utilized ICTs in their business processes thereby achieving higher levels of effectiveness and efficiency culminating into overall business competitiveness.

The business world has matured from Fredrick Winslow Taylor's principles of scientific management to Total Quality Management (TQM) and 6 Sigma, and now utilising ICTs in processes such as Business Process Management (BPM), electronic procurement (e-Procurement and tendering processes) and Business Process Re-engineering (BPR) culminating into operational effectiveness and increased productivity and agility. With this in mind, businesses, citizens, developmental stakeholders and cooperating partners started mounting pressure on governments to also employ ICTs in a view to improve public service delivery, accountability and inculcate social inclusiveness in their governance paradigms (Weerakkody et al., 2007:486).

It can be posited that the specific motivations for e-Government implementation throughout the world are not homogeneous. The unique contextual setting and other political factors may largely impact on whether to implement e-Government or not, and dictates the format in which it is implemented. For example, in the USA, the main objective for implementing e-Government is to automate and provide an integrated platform between different islands of government information so as to simplify and harness the full benefit of what technology has to offer (Iyer, Baqir & Vollmer, 2006;Baqir & Iyer, 2010). In Europe, the major motivation stems from the desire to modernise public services and offer better public services to the citizens (Cuddy, 2003). It is clear that in corruption-prone areas, a major motivation of e-Government is to promote accountability and thereby reduce corruption levels in the public sector (such as implementing e-Procurement to reduce corruption in the tendering and procurement processes), and promote socio-inclusiveness where citizens regardless of their socio-economic status have the right to access government information and participate in issues of national interest (Iqbal & Seo, 2008:52). Other countries are motivated to implement e-Government in their public service delivery frameworks so as to jump onto the bandwagon of countries implementing e-Government and *'keep up with the Joneses'*.

A majority of countries have opted to implement e-Government in expectance that its major benefits are going to be amassed if successful implementation is achieved (Heeks, 2003b:15; Ndou, 2004:10; Misra, 2007:4). The major benefits of successful e-Government implementation are well documented in literature (Heeks, 2004; Weerakkody et al., 2007:489; Anttiroiko & Malkia, 2006; Kumar & Best, 2006:2; Tassabehji & Elliman, 2006:3; Ngulube, 2007:161; Iqbal &Seo, 2008:59;Palvia & Sharma, 2007:1,4; Papadopoulou et al., 2010:5; Syamsuddin & Hwang, 2010:2). Despite the many benefits that come with e-Government implementation, it should not be seen as a panacea towards solving all the complex and well-entrenched problems of corruption and poor public service delivery that are evident in many emerging economies of the world. However, e-Government is recognised as one of the potential tools which should be recognised to mitigate some of these problems.

E-Government not only provides a platform through which the citizens and different businesses can get in touch with the government, but also enables them to participate in decision making processes on issues of national importance (Bwalya & Healy, 2010:25). In addition, it reduces the cost of public service delivery, encourages and enables participatory democracy and social inclusion (citizens, regardless of their socio-economic status may participate in decision-making and will be abreast with government information and policies), reduces corruption, and facilitates an efficient public service delivery system (Heeks, 2004; Kumar & Best 2006:3; Navarra & Cornford, 2007:5; Iqbal & Seo, 2008:52; Bwalya & Healy, 2010:23). Public service delivery improvement through e-Government is brought about by its provision of a platform where different departments can network and integrate their services by mainstreaming ICTs in their business value chains (Ngulube, 2007:164).

Despite the many motivational factors and anticipated benefits of successful e-Government implementation as outlined above, e-Government implementation is still a complex phenomenon dependent on a multi-dimensional set of factors. Further, understanding of e-Government's conceptual or intellectual outlay is still in its nascent stage. Good e-Government implementation practice should be informed by a robust e-Government strategy designed with proper reference to the contextual environment in which e-Government is to be implemented. Not only that, the different intrinsic factors such as individual factors (for example, perceived usefulness (PU), perceived ease of use (PEOU), and ICT skill levels – (discussed in chapter 6 of this book)), and organisational factors (for example, resistance to change, mainstreaming ICTs into various organisations' business value chains, and technological buy-ins) need to be addressed.

2.4 What is e-Government?

Simply put, e-Government entails the use of ICTs in the government processes and in public service delivery systems. E-Government may be used as an umbrella term that may envelop local usage of ICTs in public services such as e-Health (use of ICTs in providing health services, e.g. remote diagnosis), e-Voting (technology-enabled voting), e-Passports (electronic readable passports), e-Debate (facilitating of citizens' participation of parliamentary debates using ICTs), etc. The implementation of e-Government involves the interaction between the government, citizens and businesses through online platforms. . There are many differences between traditional government systems and e-Government. Therefore, the major distinction between traditional government and e-Government is the later employs different forms of ICTs to enable citizens and businesses access government information and services pervasively. In the former, government services are accessed by visiting a physical office Apart from the need to visit a physical office to access a service, traditional government systems have most of their business processes done manually on paper and have limited operating hours (Godse & Garg, 2007:15). E-Government presents itself as a platform where government services and information can be accessed online by citizens anywhere and anytime to the convenience of the e-Government consumers (Iqbal & Seo, 2008:65). Most of the government services may be provided online depending on the maturity of e-Government where it is operated.

The root of e-Government is 'government'. It is important to understand what government is so as to appreciate the complete meaning of e-Government. The origins of the word 'government' can be traced from a Greek word *κυβερνᾶν* (kybernan), which means 'to steer' (Godse & Garg, 2007:13). Broadly, it refers to a body that has the authority to make laws and the power to enforce them within civil, corporate, religious, academic and other organisations (Dimitrova & Chen, 2006:176).Contemporary understanding of government takes a participatory approach where citizens and other development stakeholders are cordially involved in the decision-making processes and steering of the socio-economic undertakings. With this paradigm shift, the concept of connected government comes in. Connected or networked government entails that the different facets or entities of the governance infrastructure are linked together. This means that the emergence of ICTs in governance platforms further advance this concept. Connected government has been derived from the 'government' approach and considers technology as a strategic tool and enabler for public service innovation and productivity improvements (UN e-Government Report, 2008:132). The emergence of connected government is the genesis of e-Government conceptualization.

E-Government is growing at a faster rate owing to the fact that the usage of ICTs on the world stage has grown to unprecedented heights. This correspondingly means that adoption and usage of ICTs by ordinary or marginal citizens and businesses has the potential to transform the generation and delivery of public services by public institutions (Siftung, 2002; Haris, 2006:12). With ICT taking center stage in many socio-economic processes and productivity value chains, it becomes increasing apparent to delve towards using ICTs in government business processes for streamlined and efficient service delivery. The paradigm of using ICTs in delivering public services has been experienced by both the developed and the developing world. The importance of e-Government even in developing world contexts cannot be overemphasized as it enables countries to effectively participate in the emerging information and knowledge society.

The Internet, coupled with massive adoption of ICTs, positions e-Government as a public good. This is because the growth of the Internet has a transformational effect on the global society, making information and services accessible in ways that were not conceived not long ago (Napoli, Ewing & Pitt, 2008:78). Further, the use of the Internet and Web tools for supporting participatory actions in legislative processes, political or societal decision-making in governmental or communities' context in the context of e-Government services is becoming a common practice.

With the anticipated benefits of effective e-Government implementation, governments and other independent policy/law makers have realised the importance of e-Government as a strong tool for responsive and transparent governance (UN e-Government Survey, 2010:10). It has been known traditionally that many governments have been using paper-and-file approaches in managing their businesses and this has proved disadvantageous in as far as accountability is concerned (Hiller & Bélanger, 2001:165; Mehrtens, Cragg & Mills, 2001:166). Recently, the world has seen a paradigm shift where the majority of governments' transactions and interactions with citizens, business entities and private partners now take place at the local level (decentralisation). This calls for efforts to be devoted towards putting in place mechanisms which allow maximum collaboration and participatory governing involving ordinary citizens and the government through appropriate means as far as possible (Anttiroiko & Malkia, 2006; Coleman, 2006). One of these means is the use of ICTs in providing efficient public service delivery. It is to be noted that the use of ICTs in governance value chains further decentralises governance from the local to the household or individual level (Grönlund, Andersson & Hedström, 2005:5). This entails that even marginal individuals have a chance to participate in decision-making through ICTs.

The e-Government paradigm has ushered in an environment where ICTs are being utilised in public delivery systems by governments throughout the world (Kumar & Best, 2006:2; Alsaghier, Ford, Nguyen & Hexel, 2009:296). This has brought about a shift from traditional paper-based governance system to paperless governance systems where all interactions between the government and citizens or businesses are executed online. The implementation of e-Government entails that a country can positively participate in the emerging information, knowledge and technology age (Srivastava & Teo, 2007:20).

Many researchers have defined e-Government in different ways. The following paragraphs aim to present the different definitions of e-Government as found in different contexts.

A synthesis of definitions provided by Cho and Choi (2004), Crump (2005), Iqbal and Seo (2008) and Verdegem (2011) suggests that the simplest definition of e-Government would be:

> The use of ICTs to promote interaction amongst different players (government, citizens, and businesses) in the socio-economic value chains towards the promotion of participatory decision-making, reduction of corruption, facilitation of easier and efficient public service delivery, electronic voting (e-Voting) and social inclusiveness.

Coleman (2006) defines e-Government as the combination of electronic information-based services (e-Administration) with the reinforcement of participatory elements (e-Democracy) to achieve the objective of 'balanced e-Government'. Muir and Oppenheim (2002:175) define e-Government as the delivery of government information and services through the Internet or other digital means. In other settings, e-Government has been defined as the delivery of improved services to citizens, businesses, and other members of the society in pursuit of enforcing change in the way governments manage information using ICTs (Wong & Welch, 2004:278; Kumar et al., 2007:65). E-Government is one of the ingredients for strengthening the democratic process and institution, enhancing productivity in the public services, encouraging citizen participation through the ICT platform on different national development issues, and facilitation of social inclusion. In essence, e-Government impacts on three different areas of the governance hierarchy: governance, economic and social (cf: Table 2.1).

Table 2.1: Areas under the ambit of e-Government.

Governance	Core business	Management of workflow, finances, personnel, documentation, records, information, knowledge, internal communication, executive information and decision-making
	Transparency	E-Procurement, government portal, online availability of laws, regulations
	Participation	Online petitions, notices, comments, citizen's network, publication of election results, e-mails to parliamentarians
Economic	Revenue general	Taxation, custom, fee information and management
	Financial management	Budget planning, accounting, expenditure, investment, payroll and other information
	Resources management	Geographic and natural resources information and management, land/property/dwelling management, urban planning, development planning
	Business management	Enterprise registration, investment, technology and technology transfer information, patent information, market information, statistical analysis, economic forecasting, laws or regulations

Social	Social services	Civil applications, civil registrations, land and property registrations, personal identification documents, social security, vehicle registration
	Education and culture	Digital libraries, community information centers, education institutions – information and management
	Health	Distant medicine and prescription services, hospital information and appointment, blood availability reports, health insurance reimbursements, direct settlement
	Public safety	Crime information, drug monitoring and control, prison information and management, transportation information and management, natural disaster forecasting and management
	Natural environment	Natural environment information and management, weather forecasting

(Source: partly adapted from Godse & Garg, 2007:14)

A popular definition of e-Government was provided by McClure (2000) who stated that e-Government incorporates the use of Web-based Internet technology applications by the government to enhance citizens', businesses', partners', employees', and other agencies' access to government information and services. This is a more basic definition of e-Government in comparison with other definitions in literature. Other definitions of e-Government are evident in the literature, e.g.: Hiller and Bélanger, (2001); Fang, (2002:1); Dobnikar andNemec, (2007:357); Aichholzer, (2010:1); and Arora, (2011:167), etc. It is worth noting that all the definitions of e-Government lie in the use of ICTs in providing public services to the general citizenry and businesses within a certain band of areas as outlined in Table 2.1 above. Within each of these areas, Godse and Garg, (2007:14), Suinat, (2007), and Prybutok, Zhang and Ryana, (2008:143), stress the role of leadership in e-Government.

2.5 Factors Influencing e-Government Proliferation

In e-Government, there are two scales that need to be balanced in order for favourable e-Government development to occur. The first scale is the supply side – there is need for requisite interventions, strategies and programmes to be put in place based on the local contextual characteristics. The second scale is the demand side – individual citizens and businesses need to be aware of the e-Government solutions and/or applications available and be able to adopt and use them. Generally, the different factors that affect e-Government adoption are divided into individual and organizational (businesses) categories (Kitaw, 2006:14). An individual capacity to engage in e-Government may be determined by age, sex, culture and level of education, among other factors. An organisation (e.g. government department) may utilize ICTs in its business processes depending on its flexibility in its structural arrangement. The attainment of organisational readiness (that is, the ability of any government department or business establishment, together with its workers and the different business processes in that institution to adopt and utilise ICTs in its everyday business value chains) ensures that e-Government may permeate through organisational structures and business processes. In chapter 4, e-Government readiness is further discussed, outlining what should be in place if e-Government were to thrive.

In addition to the above, some of the most basic requirements for successful e-Government implementation include the following (Lenk & Traunmüller, 2001:72):
- There should be robust ICT infrastructure in place.
- There is need to put in place informed and appropriate legal, institutional, and regulatory frameworks.
- ICT-literate citizenry in order for them to engage in e-Applications (e-Participation – usage of ICTs to engage in various e-Applications).
- Good political will evidenced by the putting in place of relevant ICT policies.
- The willingness of the different government departments to seamlessly integrate their public service delivery networks.

These basic requirements outlined above are topped by leadership as a fundamental requirement and cardinal component of e-Government development. Leadership is very important in any e-Government implementation environment because it provides strategic roadmaps to be followed by e-Government development. Further, it is know that technology keeps changing, so in order for e-Government to observe its scalable nature and be able timely adapt, there is need for foresighted leadership.

2.6 Levels of e-Government

There are different levels of e-Government with different players and stakeholders. Michel (2005:213–218) identifies three different levels of e-Government services, namely:

14. In the first level, 'customers' are considered at the centre of all the e-Government initiatives. The primary motive of governments in this stage is to increase citizen satisfaction by increasing efficiency in the public service delivery systems.
15. The second level enables governments to deploy such techniques as electronic voting which enables citizens to rate their acceptance levels of government's policies and overall management of a nation's socio-economic resources.
16. In the third level, citizens are not only looked at as spectators, customers for public services or inert actors who should be submitting to the political will, but also as active agents who are taking part in the decision and policy-making processes (Markellou, Panayiotaki & Tsakalidis, 2003:59; Baumgarten, 2009). The third level is considered as the integrated stage where government's engagement with the citizens is thought to have reached advanced levels.

These three levels are the conceptual stages of contemporary e-Government implementation and are the cardinal and desired characteristics of all e-Government applications. Further, the three levels outline the different characteristics of e-Government development. This may aid the focus when designing e-Government strategies. The different e-Government maturity levels based on the common levels of e-Government development shown are discussed in Chapter 4.

The activities of e-Government implementation demand appropriately designed front-end and back-end processes and computerisation. This entails that e-Government development strategies should be properly planned with clearly-defined objectives and desired functionality considered right from the start of the strategy design endeavours. In order to do that, it is appropriate that we understand the whole concept of e-Government applications and distinguish between e-Government and e-Governance.

2.7 E-Government versus e-Governance

As evidenced in the proceeding sections, there are many varying definitions of e-Government. The existence of the many definitions of e-Government entails that there are no generally-accepted fit-all definitions of electronic governance (e-Governance) and e-Government. As such, these words are used synonymously and interchangeably. However, in this book, these terms are strictly distinguished. In order to obtain a succinct understanding of what e-Government and e-Governance entail, a discussion follows of the fundamental views of these two terms as evidenced from the literature review, emanating from different e-Government researchers.

Despite the growing number of studies of public sector information systems, very few scholars have focused on understanding the relationship between e-Government policies and information systems choice and design (Leeet al., 2010:220). The discussion of e-Government versus e-Governance stems from an attempt to understand the meanings of government and governance in their raw forms. As has been hinted in the previous sections, e-Government, together with e-Administration and e-Governance, is the final result of the digitisation process of public service delivery systems (Okot-Uma, 2000; Bedi, Singh & Srivastava, 2001; Holmes, 2001; Michel, 2005:213). Backus (2001) defined e-Government as the transformation of the business of the government; including processes, operations, and transactions; which are driven primarily by effective use of ICTs. Finger and Pecaud (2003) posit that e-Government brings about socio-economic development opportunities by opening up new channels and platforms for accessing government information and services, and contemporary systems for organising and managing information and public services.

Keohane and Nye (2000) offers a definition that spreads the net wide: e-Governance is not confined to the government only. They posit that governance, in its entirety, includes the different processes and institutions (both from the formal and informal sector) that guide and restrain the collective activities of a group. The civil society, non-governmental organisations (NGOs), and private firms all engage in governance in one form or another.

Further, Palvia and Sharma (2007:1) have offered an excellent account of what e-Government and e-Governance mean. They posit that e-Government involves the delivering of government (national or local) information utilising the Internet and other digital means to the general citizenry, businesses or other government agencies. E-Government allows pervasive access to government's information resources replacing the traditional operations of physical government offices with their characteristic red tape; facilitates participation of citizens in public-policy making processes; facilitates improved productivity; and enhances cost savings (Palvia & Sharma, 2007:6). E-Government presents itself as a platform that enables interaction of different individuals with a bid to obtain information, tax filings, making payments and a host of other activities (Sharma & Gupta, 2003; Sharma 2006). The eminent characteristic of e-Government is that it focuses on stakeholders and constituencies that are outside its organisational perimeters whereas e-Governance focuses on administration and management of resources within the organisational boundaries. Examples of e-Government activities include e-Procurement of government tenders, electronic voting (e-Voting), tax filing (e-Filing), and payments of bills. On the other hand, e-Governance includes applications that manipulate information to calculate retirement benefits, access to important public service delivery applications, and collaboration amongst government employees.

E-Governance is basically the use of ICTs and the Internet by managers and supervisors to execute their functions effectively. This involves internal business processes that are generally executed on the back-end of e-Government applications. E-Governance entails the use of ICTs at various levels of the government hierarchy for the purpose of enhancing the overall quality of governance (Bedi et al.,2001). The entirety of e-Governance includes the actual process of governing using ICTs. Sheridan and Riley (2006) posit that e-Governance envelops the whole concept detailing the different networks and relationships within government departments regarding the application of ICTs.

E-Government entails ICT usage to promote responsive government and encompasses such characteristics as electronic workflow, e-Voting, electronic service delivery which correspondingly culminates into increased electronic productivity. In addition, e-Governance entails the procedural aspects of e-Government and brings forth the societal synthesis of government policies and developmental programmes thereof. E-Governance is the process that brings about participation in the government processes using ICTs. Some of the characteristics of the e-Governance phenomenon are the following: electronic consultation (e-Consultation), electronic controllership (e-Controllership), electronic engagement (e-Engagement), and networked societal guidance (Sheridan & Riley, 2006; Palvia & Sharma, 2007:7).

E-Government and e-Governance have been defined by the World Bank (2003), UNDP (2003), and the United States of America (US) e-Government Act of 2002 according to their contextual understanding. These three definitions generally relate to e-Governance as a procedural approach to encompassing basic and standard procedures within the confines of public administration whereas e-Government is an institutional approach to jurisdictional political operations.

The World Bank (2003) has defined e-Government as:

> [T]he use by government agencies of information technologies (such as Wide Area Networks, the Internet, and mobile computing) that have the ability to transform relations with citizens, businesses, and other arms of government. These technologies can serve a variety of different ends: better delivery of government services to citizens, improved interactions with business and industry, citizen empowerment through access to information, or more efficient government management. The resulting benefits can be less corruption, increased transparency, greater convenience, revenue growth, and/or cost reductions.

Further, the US e-Government Act of 2002 (Section 3601:3) defines e-Government to mean:

> [T]he use by the Government of Web-based Internet applications and other information technologies, combined with processes that implement these technologies, to–
>
> (A) enhance the access to and delivery of Government information and services to the public, other agencies, and other Government entities; or
>
> (B) bring about improvements in Government operations that may include effectiveness, efficiency, service quality, or transformation (Public law, 2002).

UNDP (2003) has defined e-Governance as:

> [T]he exercise of political, economic and administrative authority in the management of a country's affairs, including citizens' articulation of their interests and exercise of their legal rights and obligations. E-Governance may be understood as the performance of this governance via the electronic medium in order to facilitate an efficient, speedy and transparent process of disseminating information to the public, and other agencies, and for performing government administration activities.

The common differences between the characteristics of e-Government and e-Governance are listed in Table 2.2 below.

Table 2.2: Distinction between e-Government and e-Governance.

e-Government	e-Governance
ICT superstructure and institutional approach to public service delivery systems using ICTs	System functionality and performance
Rules and roles in public service delivery frameworks	Business processes for public service delivery
Implementation of e-Government	e-Consultation
Electronic productivity (e-Productivity)	e-Participation
Electronic voting (e-Voting)	Coordination of public service delivery systems
Electronic workflow	Goals and outcomes

Despite the variations in the actual definitions of e-Government, the common denominator of all e-Government applications lies in the fact that ICTs and the Internet are utilised to improve the delivery of government services to the general citizenry and businesses. E-Governance involves ICTs' utilisation in a bid to transform and support business processes and the different structures of a governance system (Godse & Garg, 2007).

One of the critical success factors of e-Government is the ability of the government to re-structure and transform their long entrenched business processes thereby potentially re-defining the entire array of relationships between the public bodies with citizens and businesses in an ICT-enabled, online environments (Fraga, 2002; Leitner, 2003).Although e-Government is often defined as 'online government' or 'Internet-based government', many non-Internet technologies such as telephone, fax, short message service (SMS), multimedia messaging service (MMS), wireless networks, Bluetooth, television and radio-based delivery of government services can be used in the context of e-Government (Heeks, 2004; Anttiroiko & Malkia, 2006; Ngulube, 2007:158). With the rampant innovation in ICTs, and the appearance of emerging technologies (such as wireless and social networking media or Web2.0), e-Government can now be accessed through a multitude of platforms. These platforms can both be static and mobile (pervasive computing paradigm), the latter leading to a new form of e-Government, namely mobile government (m-Government). M-Government services centre on the wider use of wireless technologies like mobile phones and Personal Digital Assistants (PDAs) for providing public offices.

2.8 Types of e-Government Applications

In pursuit of reaching the different stakeholders of e-Government applications, e-Government is implemented in basically four different types, each with different specifications and targeted at reaching specified users. These different e-Government applications are meant to provide automation and streamlining of government business processes so that efficiency and accountability are maximised and ordinary transaction costs are reduced.

There are many forms of e-Government: Government to Government (G2G), Government to Business (G2B), and Government to Citizen (G2C) (Kokkinaki, Mylonas & Mina, 2005:2) and these different forms present the different stakeholders that participate in the different interactions brought about by e-Government. With these different forms of e-Government, different users (such as citizens and businesses) are accorded the chance to experience the benefits of e-Government. The different forms of e-Government also make it possible for different governments to implement e-Government with varying motivations.

2.8.1 Government-to-Citizens (G2C)

This mode of e-Government enables constructive interaction between the government and its citizens. Citizens are accorded the chance to effectively participate in the governance protocols and influence the direction of policy using ICTs. Alsaghier et al., (2009:296) defines G2C applications as all the dealings that occur between the government and its citizens over the online platform. G2C facilitates appropriate citizen-government interaction and is generally perceived as the primary goal of e-Government (Seifert, 2008:194). G2C is based on information symmetry between the government and its citizens. From the government's side, citizens can be able to access basic services such as application for passports, license renewals, agriculture services, acquiring of marriage/birth/death certificates, applying for government schemes, income taxes, and information on basic public services such as health care, libraries, hospital information, and education. G2C applications enable e-Participation of citizens and correspondingly make it possible for e-Government to develop (Palvia & Sharma, 2007:8; Kumar & Umashankar, 2010).

2.8.2 Government-to-Businesses (G2B)

G2B allows interaction between the government and different business establishments. This enables the business community to participate in policy formation and to be abreast with government information such as memos, policies, rules and regulations. Businesses can also benefit from this arrangement because they can download business registration forms, obtain permits, renew business licenses and pay taxes. G2B also involves e-Procurement, which is a government dispensation for the exchange and purchase of goods and services (Backus, 2001; Palvia & Sharma, 2007:5). E-Procurement makes the bidding process for government projects transparent and does not leave room for corruption practices (Banerjee & Chau, 2004). This is one of the many ways through which e-Government contributes to reducing corrupting in the public service delivery networks. Correspondingly, e-Procurement enables cost savings on the part of the government as there are no middlemen or agents in the procuring process (Mimicopoulos, 2004:3).

2.8.3 Government-to-Government (G2G)

G2G enables different government line ministries and agencies to seamlessly integrate, thereby facilitating faster and efficient public service delivery and transparency. G2G also provides an ICT platform for governments in different countries to collaborate and exchange ideas on developmental issues (Ebrahim & Irani, 2005:600). When used in this way, G2G is seen as an application for international relations and diplomacy. In the G2G frameworks, messages can easily be passed between departments to add to efficiency of service delivery and collaboration amongst the departments. Seifert (2008:195) attributes the main driving force to G2G applications as the quest to reduce government business transactions costs and the desire to increase efficiency and speed of these transactions, reduce the number of personnel needed to comprehend a task, and improve business process outcomes. Some of the examples of G2G applications include electronic document management, e-Security, e-Identity and process management services. G2G applications present the major backbone of e-Government applications.

Effective e-Government implementation demands that the internal systems and procedures which allow collaboration amongst different government departments be strengthened before electronic transactions with citizens and businesses can be successful. It is worth noting that G2G is a good example of e-Governance as it delves to improve efficiency of public service delivery from within the internal business processes.

2.8.4 Government-to-Employees (G2E)

This mode of e-Government aims to place the public service human resource base at a competitive advantage so that appropriate and competitive service delivery is achievable (Markellouet al., 2003:59). With this platform, government provides human resource training so that they are abreast with their professions. This mode also allows interaction between the government and the employees and would-be employees as it advises for any available employment opportunities, scope of work, employee welfare schemes, rules and regulations and articulation of the desired public service work culture (Palvia & Sharma, 2007:4). G2E platforms also promote collaboration amongst the different employees and can be used as an e-Learning platform.

A summary of the characteristics of the four different types of e-Government interaction modes presented above is shown in Table 2.3 below.

Table 2.3: Characteristics of e-Government applications.

e-Government type	Major consumers of e-Government content	Major service characteristics
G2C	Ordinary citizens	An interaction platform for citizens to access public services and government information
G2B	Business enterprises	Reduction of administrative costs and burden by offering appropriate ICT platforms to enable businesses access public services (such as e-Procuring/tendering, paying taxes, and renewing of business licenses)
G2G	Government departments and agencies	Effective inter-departmental interaction and collaboration space Seamless integration of government business processes at different tiers of the government (such as local and regional governments)
G2E	Civil servants and volunteers	Automation of government administrative processes Internal efficiency and appropriate productivity of the government agencies Optimisation of government business processes

The different types of e-Government applications present an opportunity where all the stakeholders active in online government are taken into consideration. Backus (2001) outlines tangible examples of the different types of e-Government applications; these are used in this book to list the following e-Government initiatives and e-Democracy initiatives:

a) E-Democracy Initiatives in Less Developed Countries

- **South Africa:** e-Government portal – http://www.gov.za/ (G2C). Used for informing, representing, encouraging, consulting and involving the citizen with information such as names of Ministers and Members of Parliament, the democratic structure and online constitution. Allows citizens to interact with, and provide feedback to the government organs. Various forms (such as ID applications, birth certificates, and voter registration) can be downloaded.
- **Uganda:** Parliament Portal – http://www.parliament.go.ug/ (G2C). Used for informing the citizen with such information as the constitution, country facts, and any information pertaining election results.

- **Burkina Faso:** National Portal – http://www.primature.gov.bf/ (G2C). Used for providing the citizen with such information as online constitution, laws and the current government structure.

b) E-Government Initiatives

- **South Africa:** government online services – http://www.gov.za/. (G2B) provides citizens with the necessary information such as tender documents online.
- **India:** new Internet established to enable digital signatures (G2G, G2B, G2C).
- **Peru:** an information system for rural development has been set up. (G2G, G2B).
- **Gabon:** Gabonese Ministry for Water, Forests, Fisheries, Environment and Protection of Nature – http://www.gabon-forests.org/ (G2C, G2G) aims to reach out to the people using ICTs.
- **Brazil:** Standardisation of public web pages in the state of Bahia so that uniform information display techniques are utilised.

The examples outlined above show that even less developed countries are rigorously implementing e-Government in order to modernize their government operations towards efficiency and effectiveness.

2.9 Success or Failure of e-Government Implementation

Governments are increasingly noticing the benefit of implementing e-Government systems and a paradigm shift has occurred where even governments are equally interested in using the Internet in carrying out its day-to-day activities (Nurdinet al., 2011:1). Despite this interest, determination and support from the government, failure and success of implementing and adopting e-Government into various socio-economic realms have been reported (Heeks, 2004). As posited above, implementation of e-Government comes with a higher opportunity cost. Therefore, e-Government stakeholders and co-operating partners would not be amused to witness failure of e-Government implementation where huge financial resources have been committed.

Depending on a government's motivation to implementing e-Government, when e-Government is implemented in a hurry, its anticipated benefits are more likely not to be realized (Seifert & Petersen, 2002:194; Anttiroiko & Malkia, 2006). This is because when e-Government is implemented in a hurry, certain cornerstone principles in e-Government implementation may be masked and therefore ignored. Such circumstances lead to many e-Government projects to fail. The motivation to implement e-Government may culminate from the governments' desire to retrieve the maximum benefit out of their huge financial expenditures towards setting up appropriate ICT infrastructures, and other interventions necessary for global ICT uptake (Almarabeh & AbuAli, 2010:40).

Heeks (2003b:4) partitions e-Government implementation in three different categories as detailed below:

- **Largely successful**: most stakeholder groups attained their major goals and did not experience significant undesirable outcomes.
- **Total success**: all stakeholder groups attained their major goals and did not experience significant undesirable outcomes.
- **Too early to evaluate**: it is too soon after implementation and/or there is too little evidence yet to evaluate the outcome.

Other forms of success have been identified as detailed below (Heeks, 2003a; Andersen & Henriksen, 2006:237; Wimmer, Scholl, Grönlund & Andersen, 2006:272):

- Total failure is a situation when the initiative was never implemented, was implemented but immediately abandoned, or was implemented but achieved none of its intended purposes. A largely unsuccessful case is one where some goals were attained but most stakeholder groups did not attain their major goals and/or experienced significant undesirable outcomes.
- Partial success/partial failure is a case where some major goals for the initiative were attained but some were not and/or there were some significant undesirable outcomes.

A question worth asking is what makes main e-Government implementations to fail? Case studies (Heeks, 2003a; Ali et al., 2009:3) from different countries on the implementation of e-Government suggest that there are many challenges to the implementation of e-Government systems. These studies show that the adoption factors are distinct for any particular country, and correspondingly depend on the local context and culture (Ali et al., 2009:1; Baumgarten & Chui, 2009). Of the many countries that have been surveyed, e-Government has shown a lot of maturity in Canada partly owing to the Canadian government's commitment to its implementation (Kumar et al., 2007:65). One of the commitments that the Canadian government has done is the allocation of CAD$880 million to support the development of e-Government initiatives and frontiers in Canada (Kumar et al., 2007:64). However, despite this huge investment, Canada still faces the challenge of low citizen's usage of the available e-Government platforms such as e-Government portals and websites. One of the major causes of this has been issues of trust and usability which have continued acting as barriers to wider uptake and adoption of e-Government services (Wimmer et al., 2006:273; Napoli et al., 2008:79). The low levels of citizens' engagement in e-Government applications for the case of Canada may be attributed to ignorance of appropriate website navigability and aesthetics (Coleman, 2006), personalisation and customisation (Horst et al., 2007:1841; Thorbjornsen et al., 2002:19) and loyalty programs (Kumar et al., 2007:73) which are seen as key strategies to attracting individuals to visit a website or e-Government portal.

In the developing world context and specifically the Sub-Saharan Africa's (SSA) case, lack of adequate ICT infrastructure seriously prevents the growth of the Internet and correspondingly e-Government. In addition, Internet connection and service charges are far much beyond the reach of ordinary citizens in many countries in SSA. According to Avila (2009:137), Africa's share of the worldwide mobile subscribers is 7.2% with a huge potential of growth. The number of mobile subscribers has now continued to grow because of the commitment of various stakeholders to ensure appropriate ICT infrastructures are in place so that information permeates in all the socio-economic frameworks (Avila, 2009:136). It is surprising to note that most of the existing telecommunications infrastructure does not reach even a half of the population. In most cases in the SSA, the rural environments are not provided with enough connectivity and telecommunications infrastructure despite having more than 50% of the population. Fifty percent (50%) of the available lines are concentrated in the cities, where only about 10% of the population lives. Another factor that adds to Africa's infrastructure impairments is the irregular or non-existent reliable electricity supplies which are a major barrier to use of the ICTs and correspondingly e-Government systems. This lack of robust and adequate ICT infrastructure has made many e-Government endeavors in SSA fail.

The success of e-Government very much relies on the e-Readiness of the area where e-Government is implemented and the available e-Government strategies. For example, New Zealand's success of e-Government implementation can be attributed to the following initiatives which have been put in place by the E-Government Unit (Boyle & Nicholson, 2003:91):

- Developed an e-Government strategy.
- Formulated standards and guidelines.
- Provided leadership to facilitate the achievement of the e-Government vision and strategy.
- Identified and coordinated opportunities for collaboration across government departments.
- Monitored progress towards achieving successful e-Government implementation.

The above examples show that in environments where e-Government thrives, there are sound ICT infrastructures, strong government commitment, clearly defined e-Government strategy and vision, information literacy and e-Literacy, and connectivity. In SSA, the exact opposite of this is the case. Ngulube (2007:158) has ascertained that this is mainly because citizens in SSA are IT-illiterate and the quality of government information is poor, and that standards to ensure interoperability and portability of government information systems are inadequate and sometimes not existing at all. Also, human capacity is compromised in most of the cases because human resources are scarce because of the brain drain and lack of capacity building programs (Coleman, 2006; Ngulube, 2007:162). It is also true that many governments have not put in place laws, policies and standards for privacy protection and information access and thus an enabling environment for e-Government implementation is basically lacking. Many governments in SSA have a lot of red tape and corruption in their public service delivery systems and this limits the development of e-Government. For example, in applying for passports in Botswana, one can download the forms from the Internet (http://www.gov.bw) but still has to visit a public office to complete the application process.

For successful e-Government implementations, Almarabeh and AbuAli (2010:32–34) provide a list of recommendations which should be utilised to overcome certain challenges of e-Government implementation. These recommendations, shown in Table 2.4 are generic in nature and may be applicable to any environment where e-Government is to be implemented. Further, these recommendations may act as guidelines when developing an e-Government strategy for any given area in both the developed and developing world contexts.

As mentioned above, the recommendations shown in Table 2.4 may be used to assess the maturity levels of e-Government implementation. These recommendations are guiding principles of how the assessment of e-Government maturity should be done. The next section presents some maturity models which target certain aspects of the recommendations shown in Table 2.4. The choice of which model to use largely depends on what specific attributes of e-Government development you want to assess and in which environment e-Government is being implemented.

Table 2.4: Overcoming e-Government implementation challenges.

Challenges	Recommendations
Infrastructure development	– Develop projects compatible with nation's telecom infrastructure – Use public access kiosks and mobile centers if telecommunication density is low – Introduce telecom competition and lift regulation on wireless and other digital technologies to accelerate their deployment – Build on microenterprise model to bring connectivity to underserved areas and ensure sustainability – Consider government's current use of technology and learn from the past successes and failures – Establish an action framework at the beginning of the process to allow for a rational and coordinated investment effort down the road
Law and public policy	– Consult with stakeholders to assess how existing laws may impede desired results – Give legal status to online publication of government information – Clarify laws and regulations to allow electronic filings with government agencies – Reform processes by simplifying regulations and procedures
Digital divide	– Provide communal access through village computer centers or kiosks – Combine access and training – Provide incentives to the private sector to donate equipment and training – Emphasise local language and content tailored to different communities – Use for-profit entrepreneurs to build and sustain access points in small communities

E-literacy	– Ensure the content is in local languages and that interfaces are easy to use – Develop applications that use speech or pictures in addition to, or instead of, written text – Include an educational component of e-Government projects – Provide aides at access points who can train citizens in basic computer skills – Create programs that include traditional media, like radio programs or newspaper columns, where citizens can learn about e-Government – Special attention should be given to groups difficult to integrate (such as women, immigrants, and the elderly)
Accessibility	– From the onset, design applications that accommodate the disabled, such as an audio option for the blind – Establish as a legal requirement that the government must adopt technology to assist the disabled – Set performance criteria and measure progress
Trust	– Map key internal and external partners and build a strategy to open lines of communications – Start with short-term projects that yield early results. This helps build trust and could point to areas for larger scale ventures – Strong leadership can help build confidence in programs – *(Continues)*
Privacy	– Educate and train government officials on the importance of privacy – Design applications that integrate privacy protections – Follow 'fair information practices'. Minimise the collection and retention of personal information
Security	– Designate a senior official responsible for computer security – Continually assess systems to make sure that security precautions are being implemented – Backup information regularly and store backups in a secure location – Provide ongoing training to employees on computer security – Evaluate performance of system managers in adhering to sound security principles

Transparency	– Highly-placed public officials can expedite transparency and accountability efforts by making their offices positive examples of openness – Post online rules, regulations and requirements for government services (such as requirements for obtaining a license) to minimise subjective actions by officials – Train civil servants and provide incentives to reform – When outing services online, give citizens the ability to track status of their application – Integrate transparency and process reform to simplify regulations and procedures
Interoperability	– Map and assess existing record systems – Identify and reform regulatory schemes that make interaction with the government onerous – Use common standards throughout the government to shorten development time and ensure compatibility – Adopt a common IT infrastructure for the government
Records management	– Encourage data sharing and co-operation between government departments – Streamline online record keeping processes to make the transformation to online publication easier – Creation and standardisation of meta-data is critical for conducting successful data searches across institutions and networks
Permanent availability and preservation	– Design applications according to need – Consider relevance, usability, language compatibility and affordability – Encourage co-operation between departments and with the private sector in collecting, storing and utilising data, but proceed continuously with personally identifiable information
Education and marketing	– Develop publicity and training campaigns that will engage the public about e-Government initiatives – Conduct research to ensure that online services respond to actual needs and that the implementation suits the target audience
Public/private competition/ collaboration	– Forge multi-sector partnerships – Review and reassess laws and policies that impede public/ private co-operation – Ensure the agreements with contractors and partners are equitable and can be reviewed and revised over time – Seek assistance and involvement from organisations that already have experience in providing services and information using the same or similar technologies

Workforce issues	– Articulate a timeline for implementation in a step-by-step manner so the reforms will not seem overwhelming to the bureaucracy – Hold regular meetings between e-Government policy leaders and the affected workforce so employees are active participants in the process – Create incentives by rewarding individuals and agencies that apply the reforms rapidly
Cost structures	– Avoid advertising-based or fee-based services. – Articulate functionalities clearly and try not to add details that will push budgets into deficit. – Develop projects that are achievable with resources available – Consider the government's current use of technology and study past successes and failures – Designate an officer or organising body that will oversee cost
Benchmarking	– Create measurable goals during early planning phases – Designate an office to oversee e-Government implementation – Make sure the office is sufficiently funded and is recognised by all relevant agencies and departments – Conduct regular audits to ensure progress is being made to achieve the stated goals – Review benchmarks regularly to ensure that accurate measures are appropriate for rapidly changing technology – Create collection system to support program operation – A common IT infrastructure and architecture standard is key to ensuring that ongoing development takes place in coherent and integrated way – Advanced planning of common IT infrastructure standards result in shortened development time and system compatibility – Quantitative measure can be beneficial as qualitative ones

(Adapted from Almarabeh & AbuAli, 2010:32–34)

2.10 E-Government Implementation Worldwide

In order to understand the attention being attributed to e-Government in the developing world, there is need to consider the current status of e-Government development in Africa, Asia and South America. It is evident that e-Government is a very important undertaking as evidenced by the number of countries who are seriously implementing it in their governance value chains. Generally, as posited above, e-Government is being implemented in the developed and developing world contexts. In the developed world context, the e-Government institution is well advanced in Canada, the United States, and the United Kingdom. The Americas have relatively advanced e-Government development as compared to other countries. For example, the status of e-Government in other countries such as Chile, Mexico, and Argentina is comparatively developed (Gil-Garcia et al., 2007:267; Lau, Aboulhoson, Lin & Atkin, 2008:88–100). Another region with relatively developed e-Government is Asia. The Asian economic boom, especially with the tiger nations – South Korea, Singapore, Hong Kong-China, Malaysia – has brought about faster adoption of ICTs in almost all the socio-economic establishments. These countries are the world leaders in the Digital Opportunity Index (DOI) (Ok, 2011:326).

In order to appreciate the status of e-Government development in the developing world, the following paragraph highlights e-Government penetration amongst African countries.

Realising that e-Government brings about many benefits such as improving power relations between the politicians (and the government at large) and the general citizenry, most African countries have started pursuing e-Government implementation with high degree of commitment (Coleman, 2006; Schuppan, 2009:118; Bwalya & Healy, 2010:27). Although almost everywhere in Africa it can be shown that the level of adoption of ICTs, and correspondingly e-Participation, is still very low, most countries do not want to pay the opportunity cost that comes from shunning away from implementing e-Government. Mauritius, South Africa, Seychelles, are some of the countries that have dedicated e-Government projects (Kitaw, 2006:10) whereas Mali and Niger have the least developed e-Government institutions (Kitaw, 2006:10). Other countries such as Botswana, Uganda, Tanzania, Namibia, Nigeria, and Kenya have also started drawing e-Government development plans and have one or two e-Government applications running online (UN e-Government Survey, 2010:18). All these countries have at least a government portal with static information display as an entry point to accessing government information and guidelines on accessing public services. Two-way communication interactivity brought about by dynamic Web content as detailed in most of the maturity models discussed above is missing even amongst the leaders of e-Government implementation in Africa. The rest of the countries are mostly at the ICT policy development levels (Gerster Consulting, 2008:13; Coleman & Kaposi, 2009:71–78).

Mauritius is the leader of e-Government readiness and implementation on the African continent (UN e-Government Survey, 2010:75). Its strength lies in its implementation of an integrated Web portal, http://www.gov.mu, allowing access of a wide array of sophisticated transaction-based services to static information to different e-Government stakeholders and users; and a relatively high Human Development Index (0.800) and an adult literacy rate of 87.4% (Pudaruth, Moloo, Mantaye & Bibi, 2010:415). Mauritius's e-Government has steadily developed because of government's desire to transform it into a cyber island and transcend towards putting in place an information-based society where interactive platforms are readily available for citizens and businesses to allow appropriate interaction with the government (E-Government Initiatives, 2005:10)

Some of the e-Government projects implemented in Mauritius include the Contribution Network Project (CNP) which is a Government-to-Business (G2B) initiative of the Ministry of Finance. The CNP allows large employers to pay tax electronically. In 2001, the e-Government Task Force was set up to spearhead the e-Government mandate in Mauritius. E-Government Initiatives (2005:10) details the following specific initiatives that were implemented in a bid to promote e-Government: set up of the Government Online Centre (GOC) infrastructure at the Ebene Cybercity; unveiling of e-Government Master Plan for the civil service and set up of the Government Web Portal; appointment of Chief Information Officers (CIO) within individual ministries; set up of a Central IT Committee (CITC) at the Prime Minister's Office; and the set up of a CIO Council. These different initiatives have contributed to the rapid growth of e-Government in Mauritius. To account for appropriate change management initiatives, a training programme targeting 5000 civil servants was set up in 2002 to provide the necessary IT-related training. In the same year, the e-Government Interoperability Framework (e-GIF) which sets out the technical policies and specifications to achieve interoperability and information coherence across the public service was introduced.

Another country that has made significant inroads in as far as e-Government implementation is concerned is South Africa (SA) because of its relatively advanced mainstreaming of ICTs in the public service delivery platforms. With the successful hosting of the World Cup 2010, it is anticipated and thought that more robust and appropriate ICT infrastructures have further been put in place (Fisher, 2008:4; Abrahams & Goldstuck, 2010:18). These are correspondingly going to contribute towards encouraging faster adoption of ICTs. Some of the notable e-Government initiatives are the e-Filing that is used by the Southern African Revenue Service (cf: http://www.sars.gov.za/home.asp?pid=340); and the Cape Gateway portal presented in three languages – English, Afrikaans and iXhosa (cf: http://www.capegateway.gov.za/eng/). These websites practice transparency in public service delivery by offering government information online. There is also the Judicial Inspectorate of Prisons, the South African Department of Correctional Services, and the Home Affairs National Information System (HANIS) where citizens can access birth and death registration forms online (E-Business Handbook, 2005). Commitments have been shown by co-operating partners such as the government and the private sector to transform SA into an information society. Some of the notable initiatives have been the Electronic Communications and Transactions Act of 2002 which came up with an e-Strategy especially hinged on developing a world class telecommunications infrastructure; and the putting together of a presidential National Council on ICTs directly answerable to the president. All the e-Government interventions and vision are entrenched onto SA's Vision 2014 (Farelo & Morris, 2006:3).

A closer look at the e-Government initiatives of South Africa and Mauritius reveals that there is commitment from different stakeholders both at the technical and policy level; ICT infrastructure is relatively developed to allow the possibility of successful implementation of e-Government applications; and institutional framework and foundation is laid for successful e-Government implementations. The only tenet of e-Government which comes out silent is on the interventions that have been put in place with regards to encouraging wider participation of citizens in e-Government. As mentioned above, the cases of South Africa and Mauritius are ones where the implementation of e-Government are on course with cross-sector expectations.

Despite the success stories outlined above in as far as e-Government implementation is concerned, there are some countries that have failed to attain the desired goals in the realm of public service. One such example is depicted by The Gambia which implemented an e-Government project which had shown a lot of potential on the onset but eventually failed because of lack of strategic sustainability plans for its implementation (Sander, Bell & Rice, 2005). With the help of the United Kingdom Department for International Development (DfID), The Gambia implemented the Personnel Management Information System (PMIS) which was designed and installed around 1998–1999 and was aimed at managing the entire human resource base. This system did not serve its intended purpose because of several contextual challenges which were met during implementation. The technical advisors from DfID, together with the local consultants did not take the local contextual characteristics much into consideration and implementation was approached as if it was done in a developed world. An additional e-Government system which failed to live to its mandate was the Health Information Management System. Another developing world country where many e-Government projects have been seen to fail is India (Kumar & Best, 2006). This shows that without a careful design philosophy, e-Government may likely fail resulting into huge opportunity costs.

2.11 Conclusion and Summary

The discussion in this chapter has outlined the multi-faceted understanding of e-Government. The chapter has highlighted the fact that e-Government cannot be understood from one dimension as it depends on many factors to thrive. E-Government has been misconceived as a technology-centric undertaking without considering the managerial and socio-economic, individual and organisational factors that have a big say on whether e-Government interventions succeed or not.

In summary, this chapter provided in-depth definitions of e-Government and discussed the scope of e-Government applications. It gives an overview of different characteristics and forms of e-Government together with its different maturity models. The chapter outlines the multi-dimensionality of e-Government given different contextual settings. A distinction between 'e-Government' and 'e-Governance' is explained so that the when these two terms are utilised throughout this study their exact meanings can be decoded. The basic characteristics of e-Government, together with the different types of e-Government applications have been discussed. Amongst the characteristics, this chapter has clearly presented e-Government as a multi-dimensional phenomenon which requires both social and technical infrastructure for it to succeed.

The next chapter builds on the discussion of e-Government development initiated in this chapter by highlighting the different benefits that can be amassed if successful e-Government implementation is achieved. The next chapter further looks at the negative implications on the socio-culture setup of implementation. In addition, the next chapter accentuates the multi-dimensional nature of e-Government and articulates the e-Government evolution trajectory.

Chapter 3
E-Government and Society

3.1 Introduction

If implemented successfully, the cumulative benefits from e-Government in as far as ushering in an efficient, effective and responsive public service cannot be over-emphasized. On the other hand, when e-Government implementation fails, the opportunity cost incurred is insurmountable. E-Government implementation is not a small undertaking as it involves huge financial commitments which could otherwise be utilised towards other socio-economic developmental programmes. This chapter intends to discuss the impact of e-Government on different hierarchies of the society especially considering the government, community, individual and businesses. The understanding of the overall impact of e-Government on the society is important because it allows e-Government stakeholders appreciate the value of e-Government and therefore justifies the worthiness of investing in e-Government social and technical infrastructure.

As posited in the previous chapters in this book, e-Government is a multi-dimensional phenomenon which involves a lot of strategic planning, careful design and effervescent implementation for it to succeed. In the last section of this chapter, a discussion on the multi-dimensional nature of e-Government is presented in order to allow e-Government stakeholders, practitioners and designers appreciate and understand the different intricacies that need to be considered when conceptualizing or designing e-Government interventions or programmes.

3.2 Benefits, Disadvantages and Implications of e-Government

Understanding the anticipated benefits of e-Government is cardinal to the motivation of its implementation. Organisations and individuals are interested in any innovation if it is guaranteed their participation will be met with reciprocal benefits to their wellbeing. Understanding the actual benefits is very important, e.g. on an individual, how will e-Government improve a person's work or life's experience? Understanding the impact and value of e-Government also involves considering the different disadvantages and implications that come with e-Government implementation on the individual and the socio-economic setup of a given area. This section aims to present different aspects of e-Government in a detailed manner with some evidence emanating from empirical studies.

3.2.1 Benefits of e-Government Applications

It cannot be over-emphasised that appropriate usage of e-Government applications offers a wealth of socio-economic development opportunities (Pascual, 2003:13; Hawamdeh, 2005; Ma, Chung & Thorson, 2005:21). Extensive utilisation of e-Government services may potentially create value on the part of the citizen and the business community in terms of cost and convenience. Examples of e-Government may include the application of Information and Communication Technologies (ICTs) to access government services such as application for passports, renewing drivers' licenses, accessing policy and law documents, taking advantage of interactive platforms and forums to communicate with political leaders, and accessing government services anywhere, anytime. This entails that citizens can collaboratively participate in decision and policy-making through the use of ICTs (e-Participation). Further, implementation of e-Government enables citizens and businesses to efficiently and timely access information and services (such as accessing business opportunities in the public sector, utilisation of e-Procurement channels, and e-Commerce). Accessing such e-Government opportunities may change people's general perception on government which has always been that governments are complex, mammoth bureaucratic establishments with disjointed information infrastructures making it very cumbersome and frustrating to access public information and services (Coleman, 2006).

Accruable benefits of successful e-Government implementation translate into a situation where citizens are empowered to participate in decision-making processes regarding issues of national importance, enabling participatory democracy and social inclusion, reducing the cost of public service delivery, reducing corruption, and encouraging an efficient public service delivery system (Cho & Choi, 2004:721; Wong & Welch, 2004:277; Kumar & Best, 2006:2; Navarra & Cornford, 2007:5; Bwalya & Healy, 2010:24). Other than on the positive impacts on individual citizens, e-Government also brings about a myriad of benefits on the part of businesses. When e-Government is successfully implemented to act as an information management between the government and the different business entities, it creates business sense and value so that cordial relationships between the government and the different businesses are maintained. Table 3.1 shows the different benefits of successful e-Government on the part of businesses and the government itself (Capgemini analysis, 2007).

Table 3.1: Benefits of e-Government implementation.

Benefits to businesses	Benefits to government
– Reduction of compliance burden – More efficient interaction with government – Cost reduction – Greater flexibility, for example, in the ability to submit returns 24/7 – Online access to detailed information – Improve the transparency of interaction with government	– Improves competitiveness – More efficient processes and functioning of government – Higher productivity – Economies of scale when targeting higher volume services – Cost reduction – More innovative and competitive economy – Ability to offer 24/7 services incurring additional costs from longer opening hours – Higher data quality – Reduces man-days required for data collection – More trust in government

(Adapted from Capgemini analysis, November 2007)

Not only promoting civic and business engagement, ICTs in the framework of e-Government can also facilitate the engagement of government and business/ civil society entities by augmenting their capacity to work as organised networks (Hamel, 2010:9; Sutinen & Tedre, 2010:222). Organized networks are premised on the realization that there should be free interchange of information between/ among participating networks nodes so that the entirety of the network maintains a certain level of competence. For example, Infonet, which has been created by the Social Development Network of East Africa, and FarmSubsidy.org, a non-profit project in Sweden, have been built on the principle of Freedom of Information (FOI). E-Government is a promising vehicle for enforcing the Freedom of Information and therefore improving the level of democracy in a society.

For the above mentioned benefits of e-Government to be amassed, it is imperative that there should be put in place appropriate organisational and institutional reforms, dysfunctional centralised governance systems and traditional patterns of social interaction should be removed, and robust e-Government awareness campaigns promoted (Ma, Chung & Thorson, 2005:23; Srivastava & Teo, 2007:33; Hafkin, 2009:7). The above interventions should be coupled with active ICT streamlining initiatives within the public sector business value chains (Misra, 2007:4).

Other than the above mentioned benefits, successful e-Government implementation may translate into the reduction of the penetration of corruption in public service business value chains. With the increased corruption levels in most of the developing world, e-Government implementation may provide a platform where decisions are made in the open space and therefore corruption largely reduced. (Banerjee & Chau, 2004:32; Cho & Choi, 2004:720; Wong & Welch, 2004:290). The following list of empirical studies highlights the impact of e-Government implementation on fighting corruption and access to information by ordinary citizens (Palvia & Sharma, 2007:1):

- South Korea's Seoul Metropolitan's online procedures enhancement for civil applications (OPEN) project, and South Korea's Government e-Procurement System (GePS) have been extensively utilised as anti-corruption platforms (Iqbal & Seo, 2008:53).
- In India, the impact assessment of five e-Government projects was conducted and resulted in reduction in the percentage of transactions involving bribes (Bhatnagar, Rao, Singh, Vaidya & Mandal, 2007:14).
- In Pakistan, the entire tax department was restructured in 2002 in a bid to combat corruption. ICT systems were introduced so that contact between tax collectors and taxpayers can be reduced, and correspondingly chances of corruption done away with (CTDI, 2002).
- Pathak and Prasad (2006:436–439) analysed nine e-Government initiatives in India and arrived at a conclusion that e-Government is effective in reducing corruption or eliminating it altogether. Also, from a study by Csaki and Gelleri (2005:254), effective use of decision support systems which can be embedded into e-Government applications, in public procurement systems (G2B e-Government) can limit the damaging effects of corruption.
- In the Philippines, the Department of Budget and Management (DBM) was established to oversee the implementation of an online e-Procurement system (can be found online at http://www.procurementservice.org). This system allows the public to bid for government needs. This system has led to increased transparency in tendering procedures (Gonzalez, 2007:3).

The points articulated above point to the fact that effervescent implementation of e-Government go a long way in mitigating corruption levels in the public service delivery business processes. Despite this being the case, as posited in Chapters 1 and 2, e-Government is not a panacea to the inherent problems in the public sector delivery hierarchies. For example, e-Government implementation in one government department in India showed that the number of bribes recorded actually increased. Specifically, the e-Government strategy impact assessment conducted in India showed that there were increases in bribes in the departments dealing with passport computerization whereas the Ministry of Corporate Affairs' computerisations showed signs of a reduction in bribes (NeGP Report, 2007). This shows a case where e-Government culminates into different results in different contextual settings.

To amass the aforementioned benefits, it is important that there are appropriate trust levels in e-Government and the government itself. In addition to mitigating corruption in the public sector delivery value chains, the Online Procedures Enhancement for Civil Applications (OPEN) initiative in South Korea (Bhatnagar, 2003:25), and the Bhoomi project in India (Bhatnagar & Singh, 2008:115) aimed to show the impact of trust in encouraging engagement of citizens in e-Government applications.

The different benefits outlined in the previous sections do not make any sense if citizens do not actively participate in e-Government application. As mentioned previously, trust in the government at large and the ICTs platforms dictate the engagement or non-engagement of citizens in e-Government applications. Erosion of citizens' trust in government because of corruption at various levels in the government ought to be an area of serious concern which should be addressed if far-reaching e-Government projects were to be developed (Tassabehji & Elliman, 2006:9; Horst, Kuttschreuter & Gutteling, 2007:1842). A well-designed e-Government strategy can lead to a more efficient, accountable and transparent government. If planned in consultation with representation from key stakeholders, e-Government applications can rebuild citizen trust in government by improving service delivery, reducing corruption and empowering citizens to participate in advancing good governance. It is a well-known fact that two major factors that contribute to the growth of corruption are the low probability of discovery, and perceived immunity against prosecution. Secrecy in government, restrictions on access to information by citizens and the media, ill-defined/complex and excessive rules, procedures and regulations can all lead to a low chance of discovery (Cho & Choi, 2004:722; Wong & Welch, 2004:288). The weak character of institutions which are supposed to investigate charges of corruption and prosecute the guilty, as well as an inefficient or corrupt judiciary further exacerbate the problem of corruption and facilitate immunity of perpetrators against prosecution. Appropriate implementation of e-Government gives hope regarding all the different facets of corruption.

As well as positively impacting on individual citizens and businesses, e-Government has both indirect and direct impact on e-Government.

3.2.2 Economy and e-Government

In countries where e-Government has been successfully implemented, there is enough evidence to suggest that there are a couple of economic advantages that come with successful e-Government implementation (Pascual, 2003:14; Hawamdeh, 2005; Ma et al., 2005:34; Kitaw, 2006:14; Hafkin, 2009:4). These benefits impact on all the stakeholders of e-Government and contribute to the overall socio-economic development of a country in the context of ICT for development (ICT4D).

The idea of e-Government culminates from the conceptual understanding of ICT4D as an arrangement where ICTs are recognised as the main enabler for socio-economic development (Gurstein 2003; Visser & Twinomurinzi, 2008:1). This entails that it does not only have a socio-technical, but also an economic development dimension. This economic dimension is mostly achieved from financial and time savings on both the businesses/citizens and the government side out of successfully implementing government business processes using ICTs. The Economist (June 28, 2000) has identified e-Government as the next revolution after e-Commerce and e-Business. With this revolution evidently onsite in many parts of the world, it is logically coherent to state that the implementation of e-Government will culminate into harnessing many economic advantages. The following list presents the different economic advantages of successful e-Government implementation:

- On the government side, implementation of e-Government ensures that the annual financial cost of providing efficient public service delivery is significantly reduced (Ebrahim & Irani, 2005:595).
- There are massive cost-savings resulting from not employing a large workforce in the public sector service delivery frameworks (such as handing out application forms for government services, e.g. passports, and national registration cards (Mimicopoulos, 2004:3).
- Time saved by accessing e-Government services by ordinary individuals can be devoted to other economic development activities (Fang, 2002:4).
- There is a potential to fundamentally change the way people relate to government as they can interact with government agencies and line ministries at anytime and anywhere when need arises (Dada, 2006:6; Misra, 2007:3). The more information people can access ubiquitously, the more competitive the citizenry becomes and therefore this competence translates into socio-economic development.
- Electronic service delivery joins up service provision across departmental boundaries, breaks down silo-based delivery networks and allows citizens to interact with government whenever they deem fit (Misra, 2007:3).
- Better government, better policy making, better responsiveness to what people want and better public services by reforming the machinery of government (Ndou, 2004:9).

With many countries seeking to establish themselves as knowledge-based economies (KBEs), e-Government is one of the major ICT applications that should not be overlooked (Bwalya et al., 2011:231). This is because the cornerstone of a KBE is having the capacity to efficiently and appropriately manage information with citizens having equal rights to access this information using ICTs. The establishment of a KBE relies on efficient knowledge management channels and a majority of the actors of the economy are given chance to freely participate in the knowledge value chains (Bwalya, 2009:2). In such an establishment, e-Government is rightly recognized as one of the most appropriate tools to establish and strengthen national competiveness and therefore can create an environment for its effective development.

So far, the discussion in the previous sections has been centred on the positive sides of e-Government. Surely, there should be some negative implications of implementing e-Government. Understanding these negative implications will further solidify design endeavours of any e-Government strategy.

3.2.3 Negative Implications of e-Government

The true value of e-Government cannot be realised if its negative implications are not objectively considered when designing any interventions targeted at e-Government proliferation. This book posits that negative implications of e-Government very much depend on the local contextual characteristics and setting. For example, in the Southern African region where most of the socio-economic processes are driven by the local culture, the following may be some of the negative implications of e-Government implementation (Zhan-qi, Xue & Zhang, 2009:289–290):

- If not properly monitored, access to networked computers intended as e-Government platforms may further permit minors to access unsuitable content in cyber space, such as pornography or social networking sites where some members take advantage of minors psychologically or emotionally.
- E-Government applications may be disadvantageous to most developing countries because setting up appropriate institutional, legal and regulatory frameworks may be quite expensive – financially and resource-wise. The implementation of e-Government comes with a huge opportunity cost. The resources and finances dedicated to advancing e-Government development might alternatively be allocated to other sectors of the economy such as building or renovating social infrastructure such as roads, hospitals, and schools (Ndou, 2004:21). In cases where these e-Government interventions fail, the opportunity cost incurred is huge.
- E-Government facilities may have an adverse effect on the culture setup in a developing world context. As well as trying to access e-Government network

with heterogeneous applications and information content, citizens may also access other online content that may impact negatively on the local culture. Most African cultures are almost extinct because many of the citizens have adopted western cultures in the name of modernisation.

- Full-scale e-Government implementation may mean that more and more people who do not have access to the Internet and other ICTs will further be excluded from government processes. This may happen when there are higher levels of the digital divide (differences in the access to ICTs and correspondingly to information). In essence, it can be said that instead of promoting e-Participation and e-Inclusion of rank-and-file citizens into the governance hierarchy, e-Government implementation may further encourage e-Exclusion and foster a digital divide.
- E-Government enforces a paradigm where the face-to-face aspect of public service delivery is eliminated. This may culminate in massive retrenchments of government employees if e-Government were successfully implemented.

As can be observed from the foregoing, the different implications of e-Government may be evident depending on what kind of e-Government model is being implemented.

3.3 Multi-Dimensional Aspects of e-Government Applications

Various studies mentioned in the previous chapters have identified several factors that influence e-Government usage by the general citizenry, and the organizational characteristics that influence e-Government development as a whole. The identified different factors point to the fact that successful e-Government development depends on both the supply (government) and the demand (consumers) sides of e-Government. E-Government's success is mainly hinged on technical and managerial attributes in a given environment and may be influenced by culture, community setup, individual or collective beliefs, individual characteristics (literacy levels, ICT skills, etc). The list of factors that influence e-Government proliferation cannot be finalized as factors that may influence e-Government's success also depend on the context. Given the aforesaid, the multi-dimensionality nature of e-Government cannot be over-emphasised. Therefore, e-Government should be seen as a multi-dimensional entity whose design and implementation should employ a multi-dimensional approach.

In its entirety, e-Government presents itself as a multi-dimensional phenomenon because of its complex nature with many entities and because of its characteristic dependence on many variables for its implementation regardless of the environment in which it is implemented (Al-Khouri, 2011:24; Rokhman, 2011:2). Despite e-Government's complex phenomenon characteristic and being one of the most expensive IT applications to implement owing to its need for appropriate ICT infrastructures, it also brings about multi-valued benefits when implemented correctly (Dutta & Mia, 2010a:4; Smith, 2011:91). Among other benefits, as posited earlier, e-Government brings about transparency to public service delivery and administration; helps mitigate social ills such as corruption and misappropriation of national resources; and allows ordinary citizens to participate in decision-making. Further, citizens are further accorded timely information on government decisions; and serves as an enabler to enforce quality public service delivery at a comparatively low cost. Given these benefits that the implementation of e-Government has to offer, it is necessary that all citizens be given an opportunity to access ICTs for social demands and development in an equal manner (Kažemikaitienė & Bilevičienė, 2008:190).

3.4 Conclusion and Summary

This chapter has highlighted the major benefits and disadvantages of e-Government implementation. The chapter highlights the need to look at e-Government as a multi-dimensional phenomenon in order to come up with requisite design modules. Despite the widely-held misconception that e-Government is technology centric, this chapter has articulated the fact that e-Government depends on main factors for it to thrive. In addition to the technology capabilities required of all e-Government applications, appropriate e-Government design should consider the managerial and socio-economic, individual and organisational factors.

Having clearly defined the concept of e-Government and its anticipated impact in Chapter 2 and 3, the next chapter discusses the concept of e-Government readiness. Although e-Government is closely related to the common e-Readiness concept, it is unique with defined focus on measuring the multi-dimensional nature of e-Government.

Chapter 4
E-Government Readiness

4.1 Introduction

In any given context, e-Government cannot thrive if the overall e-Government readiness is not achieved. E-Government readiness is defined by multiple factors defining the overall characteristics of an environment which support sustainable e-Government implementation. The multiplicity nature of e-Government entails that the assessment of its readiness calls for observing organisational, individual and business entity characteristics, together with enablers such as culture, technology and societal beliefs.

There have been many different ways that have been used the world over on how to measure e-Government readiness and development. These heterogeneous measurement approaches are informed by diverse theoretical or conceptual understanding of e-Government. This chapter intends to review the different methodologies used to measure e-Government readiness, articulate the link between e-Government readiness and e-Readiness, and explore the emerging e-Government development projectile as proposed by Forester research. By the end of this chapter, it will be clear that there is no global (one fits all) e-Government readiness assessment methodology and that all the available assessment methodologies are informed by local contextual characteristics or the practitioners'/researchers' understanding of e-Government. This accentuates the fact that the understanding of what e-Government is a cardinal component to realizing any appropriate and sustainable e-Government design and implementation.

4.2 Socio-technical Infrastructure for e-Government

E-Government requires appropriate ICT and socio-technical infrastructure as one of the first pre-requisites for its effective implementation. Recently, different researchers and practitioners have identified the digital divide and e-Readiness phenomenon as two more independent factors that impact on the probability of success of e-Government implementation. E-Readiness enables the depth of e-Government implementation to be assessed using multi-dimensional attributes such as ICT skills, policy framework, e-Participation, and ICT adoption indexes (Sipior & Ward, 2005:137). The digital divide shows the likelihood of access to information resources by people from different social strata. T

4.2.1 E-Readiness and the Digital Divide

For e-Government implementations to thrive, it is important that the area/context where it is implemented is e-Ready and the gap between the *information-haves and information-have nots* (digital divide) is as low as possible. One of the first steps before implementing e-Government on a bigger scale entails assessing whether a country is e-Ready or not (Codagnone, 2008:16). When an environment is e-Ready, it is easy for the citizens to accept and adopt the new technological applications such as e-Government. The Computer Systems Policy Project (CSPP) posits that it is important for an 'e-Ready' community to have high speed access to, and robust applications of ICTs in various socio-economic sectors such as hospitals, schools, government offices. These ICT applications should have acceptable levels of user privacy and online security; and government policies favouring such endeavours should be in place (Mangena, 2004:3). E-Readiness can be determined by assessing the strength of the human resource base, policy regimes, ICT infrastructure, degree of independence of the institutional, legal and regulatory frameworks, ICT usage in various socio-economic endeavours such as in e-Commerce, e-Learning, e-Banking, and e-Forums, budgetary resources, investment climate, the industry, the social sector, etc.

As articulated above, there are many factors that affect e-Government penetration and these should be adequately addressed if meaningful e-Government development were to be achieved. These factors depend on which environment (local context) e-Government is implemented. Empirical evidence from studies done elsewhere show that context determines peoples' attitudes towards information sharing and privacy (Lips, Eppel, Cunningham & Hopkins-Burns, 2010:4). For example, in a study addressing the adoption of e-Government, public Internet access was found to be the most important factor affecting the use of online government services (Prattipati, 2003; Sipior & Ward, 2005:137). This may point to the fact that e-Government cannot take place if there is no defined ICT infrastructure, affordable costs, and easy access to the Internet. Access is one of the most important facets of e-Government development as it translates into e-Participation. The recent growth of ICT usage, Internet in particular, has exacerbated the digital divide as a socio-economic problem which needs to be given attention (Gonzalez, Adenso-Diaz & Gemoets, 2010:4).

The digital divide has been a very contentious issue with regards to its characteristic of negatively impacting on e-Government uptake (in its various forms). It is common knowledge that differences in information content, representation, lack of interoperable e-Government applications, limited content in local languages, limited ICT skills and literacy amongst the general citizenry, limited ICT infrastructure, and limited usability of e-Government platforms exacerbate the extent of the digital divide in emerging countries (Scott & Marshall, 2005:639–640; Wynne, Perry & Cooper, 2007:6–13). The digital divide limits access to different e-Government applications and therefore translates into electronic exclusion (e-Exclusion). This entails that any appropriate e-Government strategy should aim towards finding ways on how the digital divide should be practically reduced for the proliferation (positive adoption and continuance use) of e-Government applications (Salman, 2010:7). The recognition of the multi-dimensional and multiplicity nature of e-Government and its scope beyond technology is cardinal to effective implementation and development of germane e-Government strategies. E-Government does not only evolve around technology but requires re-organisation, appropriate change management strategies, new skills and training, and strategic insights into user needs (Codagnone, 2008:18).

Further, it can arguably be stated that the digital divide has acute impact on the major sectors of the socio-economic hierarchy. For example, it has an underlying impact on contemporary education systems where ICTs are extensively used. Researchers or students who do not have requisite access to the Internet find it very difficult to remain at the competitive edge. In another context, Pilling and Boeltzig (2007:38) have done a study investigating how the digital divide can be reduced so that marginalised individuals acquire the chance to use the Internet as the first step to accessing public services. The study came up with strategies that could be employed in the United States and United Kingdom with much emphasis to the local contextual setup.

It cannot be denied that e-Government and the digital divide are intertwined (Helbig, Gil-Garcia & Ferro, 2005:89), which emphasises the need to understand how the two impact on one another (as complementary social phenomena). As aforementioned, e-Government is a tool for government administrative reform (Kraemer & King, 2003:4) and has potential not only to improve quality of service in the public delivery value chains, but also enhance cost savings, effectiveness and efficiency (Grönlund, 2001:26). With this in mind, it is important to understand how the digital divide impacts on e-Government so that relevant e-Government strategies are put in place.

There are several measurement criteria utilised for e-Readiness assessment. The measurement of e-Readiness is important as it provides an indication on e-Government readiness (discussed in Chapter 4). These criteria indirectly measure the extent of the digital divide (Bui, Sankaran & Sebastian, 2003:6; Budhiraja & Sameer, 2004:2; Hanafizadeh, Hanafizadeh & Khodabakhshi, 2009:189). The following are some of the approaches that have been used to measure e-Readiness:

- The **1998 Computer Systems Policy Project (CSPP)** measures e-Readiness for living in the networked world. This is a self-assessment tool used by individuals and communities to determine how prepared they are to participate in the networked world (CSSP, 1998). The CSPP identifies five categories for measurement of e-Readiness as ICT infrastructure, applications and services, access, economy, and enablers such as policy, privacy, security and ubiquity. The CSPP measurement framework can be used to determine how ready a country is to participate effectively in the networked world. When the attributes measured by CSPP are satisfactory, it means the likelihood for the adoption and usage of e-Applications such as e-Government, electronic commerce (e-Commerce), and electronic democracy (e-Democracy) is high. .

- **Harvard's Center for International Development (CID)** e-Readiness guide for developing countries organises assessment of a variety of factors for determining networked readiness of a community in the developing world (CID, 2000). The CID defines an e-Ready society as one that has the requisite infrastructure (adequate bandwidth, reliability, and affordable prices), a good degree of ICTs integrated into various business establishments (e-Commerce), communities (content depicting the local flavour, ICTs integrated into everyday socio-economic networks (e-Learning, e-Health, e-Government), strong ICT regulatory bodies promoting acceptable competition amongst different market players, and an ICT-mature environment where direct foreign investment is encouraged. Such an e-Ready environment promotes rapid mainstreaming and adoption of e-Government in various socio-economic establishments.
- The **Asian Pacific Economic Co-operation's (APEC)** measures the e-Readiness for e-Commerce applications using the following metrics (Bridges, 2005):
  1. Internet usage in government business processes (e-Governance), interaction of different stakeholders with the government through application of ICTs (e-Government)
  2. Facilitation and promotion of industry led standards
  3. Availability of relevant ICT skills and human resource base
  4. Positioning for the digital economy
  5. Access to networked services
  6. Basic ICT infrastructure and technology. An area that is able to score positively when assessed using this e-Readiness tool means that it is ready to adopt and use e-Applications such as e-Government. If Internet usage is high amongst the general citizenry and businesses, there are high chances that government information and public services may be readily accessed by citizens and businesses through online platforms.
- **McConnell International and World information Technology Services Alliance (WITSA)** global e-Readiness metrics. This measures e-Readiness with the following five metrics (McConnell, 2000:5):

1. Information security, with motivation from intellectual property, privacy and electronic signatures.
2. Connectivity, which includes ICT infrastructure, access and pricing.
3. E-Leadership, whose success is embedded in government policies and regulations.
4. E-Business climate, which is defined by competition, political and financial stability, foreign direct investment (FDI), and the financial infrastructure.
5. Human capital, with appropriate ICT education and available skilled workforce.

These different factors are used to assess the readiness of an area to adopt ICTs and utilise them in their different socio-economic frameworks. A closer look at the targeted factors in e-Readiness measurement by WITSA reveals that it focuses on both the social and technical aspects of readiness. This is good as these factors are the bedrocks for e-Government implementation.

- **Network Readiness Index (NRI)** is computed using three main attributes (Dutta & Mia, 2010b):
  1. ICT environment in a specific environment – political, market, regulatory and ICT infrastructure readiness.
  2. Community stakeholders' readiness to adopt and use ICTs – individual psychological and technical readiness, business, government readiness.
  3. The extent to which ICT is used among these stakeholders – individuals, businesses and the government. As in the previous cases above, network readiness also demonstrates that an area is ready to implement different e-Applications such as e-Government, e-Commerce and e-Learning.
- The **e-Government Index** by the United Nations Division for Public Economics and Public Administration (UNDPEPA) and the American Society for Public Administration (ASPA) aims to assess the capacity of UN member countries to implement online government (e-Government). Today, measuring e-Readiness for e-Government implementation includes a multitude of measurement indexes (because of its multi-dimensional nature). The UN e-Readiness and e-Government development assessment methodology is limited because it does not consider the actual adoption levels of e-Government at the grassroots (community) where actual adoption takes place at the individual level. This measurement framework basically focuses on the institutional readiness when measuring e-Government development (Almarabeh & AbuAli, 2010:39).

The factors affecting actual adoption, and therefore, development of e-Government are discussed in Chapter 6 of this book. Apart from e-Readiness, another attribute of e-Government readiness is the policy framework. Appropriate policy and institution framework is desired for e-Government to thrive.

4.2.2 The Role of Policy and Leadership in e-Government

Appropriate leadership is required to maintain and coordinate the body of rules guiding e-Government initiatives, standards and agreements that define intra-relationships amongst different e-Government stakeholders (Anttiroiko & Malkia, 2006). It is evident from different endeavours of e-Government implementations that it (e-Government) cannot succeed without appropriate commitment and support from the leadership hierarchies and ICT champions who should take a leading role in the implementation endeavours. E-Government success demands that the different stakeholders involved in its implementation (such as public officers, political leaders, and individuals) collectively work together so that their coordinated efforts applied from multiple fronts can yield amalgamated positive results.

Appropriate leadership ensures both the managerial and technical attributes of e-Government are taken care of. For example, there is need to have Line Managers who should ensure that ICTs are actually employed in the day-to-day activities in the civil service, and also monitor and evaluate the status of implementation and impact. Further, Applications Designers may be needed to ensure that context-aware (made with clear focus and reference of the local contextual characteristics) applications that respond with local needs and demands are designed.

In realising the benefits of e-Government implementation, many countries in Africa are in the process of enacting their national ICT policies that will act as reference points for mainstreaming ICTs into different socio-economic platforms (Heeks, 2002:1; Kitaw, 2006:6; Hafkin, 2009:3; Bwalya & Healy, 2010:24). Only a handful of countries such as Mauritius, Seychelles, Namibia, Tanzania, South Africa, Egypt, Morocco, and Botswana have drafted dedicated e-Government strategies to aid e-Government development in their countries (UN e-Government Survey, 2010:64). At the regional level, the Southern African Development Community (SADC) has put in place several policy instruments that would create an environment conducive for its member countries to transcend towards knowledge economies, and correspondingly implement e-Government (SADC, 2002; Mamelodi-Onyadile, 2008; Bwalya & Healy, 2010:28). For example, Zambia launched an ICT policy in 2007 but not much was done on the e-Government front (Chikanta& Mweetwa, 2007; Konde, 2007:37). It is only now that some efforts are being pronounced by the political elite that it is imperative to engage consultants for direction on how to implement e-Government.

The above paragraph clearly shows that among the developing world countries, those in Africa have seriously put in place interventions to ensure that ICTs permeate through the different public service delivery channels. The genesis of e-Government implementation endeavours in Africa have been encouraged by the communiqué which was released by the 4th African Development Forum (ADF IV, 2004:64) and reads in part:

> The implementation of e-Government involves following many contextual factors that influence success or failure of e-Government projects (Heeks, 2003:12). This being the case, it is appropriate to study the contextual setup of any environment before any e-Government implementation can be commissioned. The different contextual environments come with different challenges that may be unique to any environment.

For most of the developing and emerging countries, especially those in Sub-Saharan Africa (SSA), there are many leadership challenges that prevent e-Government proliferation. This is because, on a general point of view, preliminary requirements that aid effective e-Government implementation are not evident in most of the cases (Ngulube, 2007:162). Some of these key challenges are the lack of basic ICT skills on the part of government employees and citizens who may want to engage (adopt and use) e-Government applications, lack of appropriate ICT backbone infrastructure especially in the rural areas, lack of political will, and incapacitated legal and regulatory frameworks (Konde, 2007:39; Ngulube, 2007:159).

Codagnone (2008:58) has identified the leadership pillars of connected government as the following: standardised common infrastructure, new organisational model, back-office re-organisation, governance, and social inclusion. Sorrentino and Niehaves (2010) opine that all e-Government initiatives should incorporate social-awareness by ensuring that it is delivered through multiple delivery channels so that the heterogeneous demand side is accorded the choice of which service alternatives (physical and electronic) to explore. Abrahams and Newton-Reid (2008) suggest that the key components of e-Government include an enabling contextual environment where ICTs can easily be streamlined into the different socio-economic business value chains, public sector reform, and good governance value chains.

One of the starting leadership points to consider when designing effective e-Government development strategies is to ensure that there is a strong institutional, legal and regulatory policy base. Properly designed e-Government strategy has a positive impact on the success of any e-Government implementation. As e-Government is a multi-dimensional entity, its success depends on many factors. One of these important factors is trust (Thorbjornsen, Supphellen, Nysveen & Pedersen, 2002:13; Tassabehji & Elliman, 2006:9). Trust is spread over citizens' and businesses' perception of the privacy and security regarding their personal information. Trust in e-Government also depends on the overall trust in leadership – the government at large.

4.2.3 Social Infrastructure

Since e-Government is a multi-dimensional phenomenon, it does not only depend on technology prowess of a given area but also the social ramifications including the general people's perceptions with regards to newly introduced social phenomenon, beliefs and general community characteristics. The social infrastructure for e-Government applications presents the totality of all the social frameworks and entities that can be encapsulated into electronic applications to access public service delivery (Wynne et al., 2007:6–13; Petrauskas, Bilevičienė & Kiškienė, 2008:50). It can further be posited that the social infrastructure does not only include ICTs but also the favourable conditions (such as culture perceptions on e-Government, ICT literacy levels of individual citizens, security and trust of e-Government applications) that exist in society and allow proliferation of e-Government applications.

The far-reaching factor that impacts on e-Government of all the social infrastructure attributes is the ICT skills of a given individual or what is collectively called information literacy (Materska, 2004:144). The common understanding is that if someone does not have the requisite (and appropriate) information literacy skills, he or she cannot effectively engage in e-Government applications. Correspondingly, this entails that the level of information literacy is directly proportional to e-Government engagements. Many researchers and practitioners have largely emphasised that information literacy is fundamental to the use of information resources in the knowledge age (Dowling, 2001:4; Braaksma, 2004:154; Materska, 2004:144; Shanbhag, 2006:2). In a developing world context, where collaborative and participatory governance systems are still in their nascent stage despite colonial rule ending several decades ago in most countries, information literacy is very important in order to ensure that individuals can decode the digital content and effectively participate in governance value chains.

Information literacy refers to the person's ability to possess the power of cognition of heterogeneous information resources presented before him/her and be able to locate, evaluate and use it according to his/her information needs (American Library Association, 1989). Today, literacy has been extended to include ICT literacy and skills (DESA, 2003:15). Adequate ICT literacy skills among citizens are a big determinant to ensuring that e-Government is adopted and synthesised as part of the local culture. Developing world countries have low literacy rates which make it very difficult for citizens to effectively participate in global socio-economic value chains (Cho & Choi, 2004; Wong & Welch, 2004). For example, in the case of Zambia, despite the general literacy rate being above 78%, information literacy policies are deficient and skills levels are extremely low (Hoffman & Gibson, 2005:2).

It is logical to expect that the more people a country has who have adequate ICT skills and are ICT literate, the higher the chance of them engaging in e-Government. If more people engage in e-Government applications, it means there will be a higher e-Participation rate. E-Participation is the number of individuals that are involved in any electronic applications (are able to access digital content using ICTs). The metrics that impact on e-Participation may include, among others, the ability to operate common computer applications such as e-mail, downloading and uploading content from and to the website or knowledge portals, reading and accessing File Transfer Protocol (FTP) operations, using fax, telephone, and operating a mobile phone.

Local culture may also have an implication on the adoption of, and correspondingly the success of e-Government applications (Ebrahim & Irani, 2005:603; Kovacic, 2005:152; Ali, Weerakkody & El-Haddadeh, 2009:2; Wescott, 2010; Nurdin, Stockdale & Scheepers, 2011:1). The more deceptive a culture is to new practices, the easier it will be for people to accept e-Government applications.

Since most of digital content is presented in international languages and English being the most dominant, this may have a negative implication on individuals who only understand local dialect. This implies that even if citizens have access to ICTs, it is important that the digital content on e-Government platforms be also presented in the local languages for universal comprehension. It is not only the local language that is important but also the existence of the local e-Government content that dedicates whether citizens will engage in e-Government applications or not (Ali et al., 2009:3). Local generation of digital content on e-Government platforms will entail that the content is relevant to the local context as well.

4.2.4 Technical Infrastructure

Technical infrastructure for e-Government applications entails the availability of the technical capability (such as ICT accessibility, usability of ICT platforms, ICT skills of individual citizens, and soundness of the national ICT infrastructure backbones) that may support basic e-Government applications (Backus, 2001; Chandler & Emanuel, 2002). Anticipated e-Government technical infrastructure should accommodate broadband Internet communication to allow users to download and upload content on government websites. Typical e-Government technical infrastructure basically comprises three tiers: the client tier, application tire, and the data storage tier as shown in Figure 2.1 (Abramsom & Morin, 2003:42; Al-Omari, 2006:846). These tiers are used to realise the different forms of e-Government as outlined above. Figure 4.1 shows high level of abstraction in as far as details in the e-Government architectural arrangement are concerned.

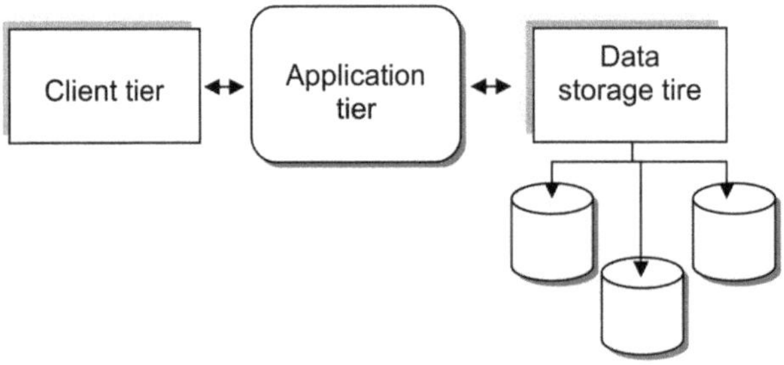

Figure 4.1: High-level e-Government Infrastructure.

The client tier presents the graphical user interface (GUI) for the e-Government consumers (citizens and businesses) to access the different government information on heterogeneous conventional ICT platforms. The application tier presents the business logic i.e. determines the rules of interaction in the e-Government environment and enforces the rules on how e-Government users can access e-Government content. In a relatively developed e-Government environment, the application tier also precedes the rules of application integration which are outlined using the e-Government interoperability framework (discussed in chapter 8 and 9). The data tier is the storage component of the e-Government infrastructure which hosts all the data components and the e-Government content.

As discussed above, it is a known fact that a majority of e-Government implementations fail (Heeks, 2003a:13). The degree of failure of any e-Government implementation is proportional to the level of maturity of e-Government implementation. The maturity models show the degree of readiness of e-Government implementation to amass the general benefits attributed to successful e-Government implementation.

4.3 E-Government Maturity Models

Implementation of e-Government follows some distinct phases as outlined in different maturity models of e-Government. The maturity models detail the steps and processes that need to be followed when e-Government initiatives are being implemented. The following are some of the common maturity models for e-Government implementation.

4.3.1 West Four-Stage Model

West four-stage e-Government maturity model was proposed by West (2000). The four stages in this model are described as follows:

1. **Billboard:** Is the first stage that e-Government development has to pass through. In this stage, static websites are used for information display. Various types of information can be posted on the website including reports and publication. Citizens (visitor) could easily access and consume the displayed information. The flow of information is uni-directional and the customer of e-Government content accesses it for information purposes only. There is no direct interaction between the customers and the government.
2. **Partial service delivery:** Allows governments to set services online for citizens to access. At this stage the static website in the first stage is developed to include more capabilities and functionalities and also allow sorting and searching of information.
3. **Full integrated service delivery:** Is a stage where a one-stop government portal is created with fully-integrated online services. In this stage, citizens can easily access government and agencies' information from one service centre.
4. **Interactive democracy:** With public outreach and accountability is the final stage of e-Government development which encompasses political transformation with executable and integrated online services. In this stage, the e-Governance institution is quite developed so as to provide back-end streamlining of government business processes.

This model's focus is on functionality and citizen-centric. Some fair consideration is given to both technical and non-technical security attributes. The model also considers the benefit of e-Government implementation to political changes at its highest level. The next section presents the Gartner model.

4.3.2 Gartner Maturity Model

The Gartner Group proposed a four-stage e-Government maturity model involving Web presence, interaction, transaction, and transformation (Baum & Di Maio, 2000). The descriptions of the four stages are given below:

1. **Web presence:** Is a stage where government agencies provide a static website to post information for people to read.
2. **Interaction stage:** Allows a bi-directional communication opportunity. Users are able to contact the different government agencies using e-mail or download forms or any documents from the website.
3. **Transaction stage:** Makes it possible for users (citizens, customers and businesses) to complete transactions (such as filling in forms, application for licenses and e-Procurement) online.
4. **Transformation stage:** Makes it possible for the government to transform the existing operational processes in a bid to provide a more efficient, integrated, unified, and personalised service.

The model basically concentrates on e-Governance (back-end business process integration) maturity and assesses the degree of efficiency of e-Government applications. The next section presents the Layne and Lee model which has four distinct stages for measuring e-Government maturity.

4.3.3 Layne and Lee Four-Stage Maturity Model

Based on Layne and Lee's (2001:124–128) understanding of the evolutionary nature of e-Government, a four-staged model is proposed which details the different levels of e-Government development. The following are the detailed specifics of the four stages:

1. **Catalogue:** The first stage details the capability of e-Government to be delivered through static webpages. Here, government information is basically displayed for information purposes only and is basically uni-directional (information is from the government side only with businesses and citizens acting as passive consumers). Government information in this stage may be such information as 'announcements for vacancies in government agencies', 'regulations for accessing government services', and 'policy documents for the public consumption'.

   At this stage of e-Government development, the government does not expect feedback from the consumers of the information posted on web pages (Ebrahim & Irani, 2005:594). Citizens can download forms from government websites, print them, and fill them in before they are return to a physical government office.

2. **Transaction:** The second stage entails that e-Government has developed more than the description given above for the catalogue stage. A limited bi-directional interaction between the government and citizens is evident. Citizens can now fill in government forms online.
3. **Vertical integration:** The third stage involves the transformation of government services rather than activities that automate its existing business processes. The major focus at this stage is the integration of government functions such as those at the local governments with those at the central government level in the realm of G2G applications (Pathak & Prasad, 2006:445). This means that the focus of this stage is basically making sure that the e-Governance institution is solidified so that ICT is streamlined into the different government business processes translating into service integration and government functions across different government departments.
4. **Horizontal integration:** The fourth and final stage of the Layne and Lee's adaption model is the horizontal integration. This stage aims to integrate different functions from standalone systems to provide a unified and a seamless public service model. In this stage, a citizen can make payments in one department and access the service at a different department as long as the two departments are connected with an appropriate telecommunications channel (Stiftung, 2002).

Figure 4.2 below, originally developed by Layne and Lee, (2001:124), shows the summarised characteristics of each of the different stages.

The model focuses on e-Government efficiency and service integration. The following section discusses the Deloite's six-stage e-Government maturity model which has more detailed stages as compared to the Layne and Les's model.

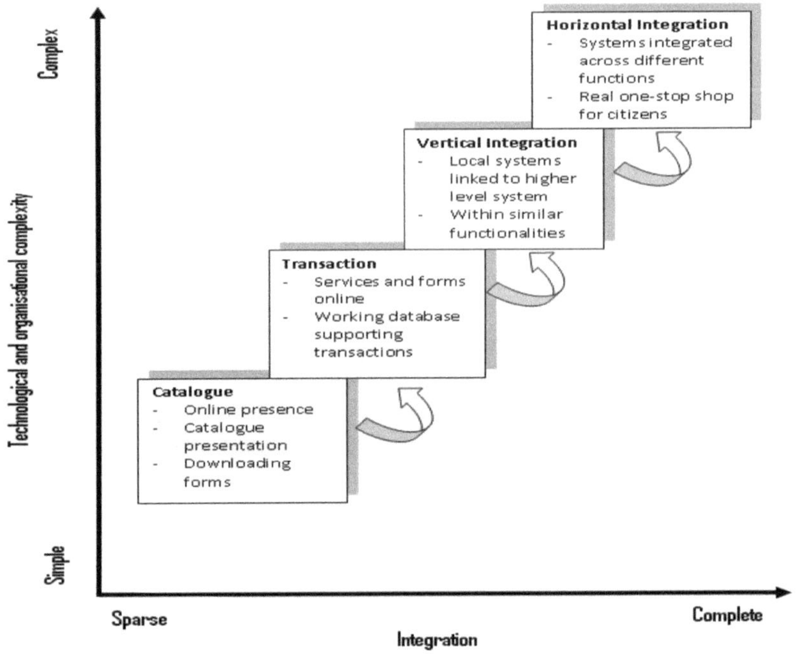

Figure 4.2: The Layne and Lee e-Government Maturity Model (Layne & Lee, 2001:124).

4.3.4 Deloitte's Six-Stage Maturity Model

Deloitte's e-Government maturity model emphasises that e-Government applications should be aimed at serving citizens and customers effectively and should build long-term relationships with them. Deloitte and Touche (2001) propose the following six-stage maturity model for e-Government applications:

1. **Information publishing/dissemination:** Enables governments to provide users with increased access to information using ICT platforms. This is basically a uni-directional service as citizens and businesses are only able to access information from the government websites without being expected to provide feedback.
2. **'Official' two-way transaction:** Provides a platform for agencies to provide interaction between governments and users by using ICTs such as digital signatures and encryption keys. As the name implies, there is bi-directional flow of information between the government and the citizens/businesses.
3. **Multi-purpose portals:** Allow governments utilise a single portal to provide universal service across multiple departments and line ministries.

4. **Portal personalisation:** Is a platform which allows governments to enable users to customise portals according to their own desires. At this stage, interaction is quite developed and citizens can modify the way content is shown on the government portal to their own specification. In other words, the display of information on the web pages has matured from being static to fully dynamic.
5. **Clustering of common services:** Is a stage where governments are able to enhance collaboration and reduce intermediaries (between operational processes) in order to provide a unified and seamless service. The e-Governance institution is quiet advanced at this stage and almost all the back-end government business processes are done using ICTs.
6. **Full integration and enterprise transaction:** Represents an ideal e-Government vision where governments provide sophisticated, unified, and personalised services to every customer according to their own needs and preferences.

This model assesses evidence of integrated e-Government service. The next section presents Howard's model which has only three stages.

4.3.5 Howard's Three Stage Model

Howard (2001:6–7) presents a three stage model with the following attributes:
1. **Publishing:** Is the initial stage of e-Government development with information about government activities available online and citizens can access it.
2. **Interacting:** Is the advanced stage of the former where citizens have the ability to do simple interactions with governments. The available services at this level may include sending e-mail, chat rooms, and/or filling and sending forms.
3. **Transacting:** Is based on the model is the highest stage of e-Government development with possibilities for citizens to conduct transactions over the Internet, including purchasing/payment of licenses and permits.

Howard's model puts more emphasis on maintaining acceptable functionality of e-Government applications, not ignoring the issue of citizen-centric applications. It does not, however, consider the adverse effects or potential benefits of political changes and ignores non-technical issues of e-Government applications (Howard, 2001:6). The next section presents the Hiller and Bélanger's model.

4.3.6 Hiller and Bélanger's Five-Stage Model

Hiller and Bélanger (2001:162) proposed a model with five stages, namely:

1. **Information dissemination:** Is the initial stage of the government to disseminate information to the general citizenry by posting it on a static website in a one-way communication platform. This is the most basic form of e-Government, which involves dissemination of information by simply posting it on the websites.
2. **Two-way communication:** Is a stage where the government uses enhanced or dynamic websites with e-mails and downloadable forms to interact with its citizens.
3. **Service and financial transaction:** Is an advanced stage, with more sophisticated technology, where the government offers online services including financial transactions to citizens. Bi-directional communication occurs between the government and individuals (such as in VISA application processes or businesses (e-Tendering, applying for trading licenses, ordering office facilities, and paying taxes).
4. **Vertical and horizontal integration:** E enables the government to integrate various systems in its business value chains both vertically (systems from different levels) and horizontally (systems from different departments). A look at the Layne and Lee (2001:123–127) four-stage maturity model discussed above reveals that this stage is similar to the last two stages of that model.
5. **Political participation stage:** is the most advanced stage of the Hiller and Bélanger's five-stage model which enables ordinary citizens to participate in politics through online voting (e-Voting) and e-Forums.

This model focuses on e-Participation. The next section presents the UN e-Government maturity model. The UN five-stage model has been used in a series of e-Government surveys by the United Nations Division for Public Economics and Public Administration (UNDPEPA) in its assessment of e-Government development throughout the world.

4.3.7 United Nations Five-Stage Model

The UN Global e-Government survey of 2003 outlines the five-stage e-Government maturity model as follows (UN e-Government Report, 2003:13):

1. **Emerging presence:** Is the first stage of e-Government which presents limited and basic information such as a webpage and/or an official website; links to ministries/departments of education, health, social welfare, labor and

finance may/may not exist; links to regional/local government may/may not exist; some archived information such as the head of states' message or a document such as the constitution may be available on line; usability options are not that developed and there is no interactivity in these options. The website or webpage presents a static online platform that is specifically for display of information resources.

2. **Enhanced presence:** Is the second stage of e-Government implementation and involves government's provision of greater public policy and governance sources of current and archived information, such as policies, laws and regulation, reports, newsletters, and downloadable databases. The website enables a user to search for a document and access the help feature and a site map. There is also a larger selection of public policy documents such as an e-Government strategy, policy briefs on specific education or health issues. Though more sophisticated than in the first stage, the interaction is still primarily unidirectional with information flowing essentially from the government to the citizen.
3. **Interactive presence:** Is the third stage, online public service delivery enters the interactive mode with services to enhance convenience of the consumer such as downloadable forms for tax payment, application for license renewal and so forth. Audio and video capability is provided for relevant public information. In this stage, communication is enhanced as most government officials can be contacted via e-mail, fax, telephone and post. There is also spontaneity update regularity of the site's content so that it is as current as much as possible.
4. **Transactional presence:** Is the fourth stage, e-Government applications allow bi-directional interactions between citizens or businesses and government. It includes options for paying taxes; applying for ID cards, birth certificates/ passports, license renewals so that these services are accessed online at any time of the day. Citizens and businesses are able to pay for relevant public services, such as motor vehicle violation, taxes, fees for postal services through their credit, bank or debit card. In addition, providers of goods and services are able to bid online for public contacts via secure links.
5. **Networked presence:** The fifth stage is the most sophisticated level in the online e-Government endeavours. It can be characterised by an integration of G2G, G2C and C2G (and reverse) interactions. This stage can be reached when the government encourages participatory deliberative decision-making and is willing and able to involve the society in a two-way open dialogue. Through interactive features such as Web comment forms and innovative online consultation mechanisms, the government actively solicits citizen views on public policy, law making, and democratic participatory decision-making.

Implicit in this stage of the model is the seamless integration of the public sector agencies (such as the different line ministries) with full co-operation and understanding of the concept of collective decision-making, participatory democracy and citizen empowerment as a democratic right.

The World Bank three-stage model has been used extensively in e-government studies and has been extensively utilised as a reference model for e-Government applications (World Bank, 2003; Bui et al., 2003:6; Wescott, 2010). There are no much differences, for example with the Layne and Lee, and Deloitte's models, only that the World Bank model presents snap-shot stages of what has been presented in the models discussed above.

4.3.8 World Bank Three-Stage Maturity Model

The World Bank (2003) came up with a three-stage e-Government maturity model which comprised the following:

1. **Publishing:** Is the first stage of this model which makes it possible for the government to disseminate information to its citizens through the website. All the important information that the government wants to disseminate is posted on the website.
2. **Interactivity:** Is the second stage of the World Bank model which enables the installation of a paradigm where the government interacts with its citizens. In this stage, websites are enhanced with interactive capabilities such as feedback forms and e-mail.
3. **Completing transaction:** Is the last stage this model and enables citizens/users to take advantage of the available ICTs to the full and conduct secure and complete transactions online.

Apart from the World Bank maturity model, the UN model discussed above has also been extensively used in assessing e-Government maturity throughout the world.

4.3.9 Asia Pacific Six-Stage Model

The Asia Pacific region has made significant strides in the implementation of e-Government projects. With the experience gained from the implementation of these projects, the Asian Pacific six-stage e-Government maturity model was proposed in 2004. The different stages are:

1. **Setting up an e-mail system and internal network:** This is the initial stage of this model. In this stage, ICTs are used actively mostly at the government administrative level (such as e-mails for internal collaboration and payroll) to make sure internal government business processes are efficient as much as possible.
2. **Enabling inter-organisational and public access to information:** Involves activities that will make it possible for the government to develop systems that will allow it to manage its workflow from paper-based to electronic format. At this stage, ordinary citizens are able to access information and other public services through effective use of the Internet.
3. **Allowing two-way communication:** Is a stage which involves the active usage of ICTs in the bi-directional communication between the government and the citizens. On the government websites, fax numbers or e-mail addresses are posted so that citizens can use these media to interact with the government.
4. **Allowing exchange of value:** Is the fourth stage of the Asian Pacific maturity model which makes it possible for ICT to be used to support development of more flexible and convenient ways for citizens to conduct business with the government in accessing public services such as tax assessment, visa application and applications for license renewals.
5. **Digital democracy:** Enables ICT to be used as an enabler to support participatory and democratic processes. Citizens and the civil are encouraged and empowered to use ICTs in the voting processes (e-Voting).
6. **Joined-up government:** Is the final stage which makes it possible for both vertical and horizontal service delivery to be integrated. A robust Web portal is used to integrate information and services from various government agencies and line ministries. This allows integrated and seamless public service delivery.

Asia Pacific maturity model mainly focuses on citizen-centric and functionality together the potential impact on e-Government applications which can be brought about by sudden political changes. Also it considers the potential benefit of political changes. The model, however, does not succinctly consider security issues (Wescott, 2009:8, 27). This model posits that it is acceptable for e-Government to develop without minimal security levels. This might be a problem because there is no guarantee that privacy of e-Government customers will be observed as they engage in e-Government applications.

4.3.10 Moon Five-Stage Model

Moon's model identified five stages of e-Government maturity (Moon, 2002:425) as presented below:

1. **Simple information dissemination (one-way communication):** Is the first point reached in e-Government implementation where information is disseminated simply by placing it on static websites.
2. **Two-way communication (request and response):** Is the second stage of Moon's model which entails that dynamic websites are in place and there is bi-directional communication between the government and users.
3. **Service and financial transactional:** Is the second stage of Moon's model which involves transactions between governments and individuals.
4. **Vertical and horizontal integration:** Is the fourth stage of Moon's model and is similar to the last two stages in Layne and Lee's (2001:124) four-stage model.
5. **Political participation:** Involves promotion of political participation through online voting and surveys (Moon, 2002:425).

Note that Moon's maturity model is the exact replica of Hiller and Bélanger's five-stage model. The Hiller and Bélanger's and Moon's models focus on system functionality and gives some consideration to the potential benefit of political changes. The limitation of these models is that they do not give consideration to any security-related issues including those which are non-technical. Note that security is only given at the financial transaction stage (Moon, 2002:429).

4.3.11 Chandler and Emanuel Four Stage Model

Chandler and Emanuel (2002) present a four stage e-Government maturity model which is being described below:

1. **Information stage**: Is the preliminary stage of Chandler and Emanuel's four stage model. In this stage, citizens are able to access government information through a static website. A unidirectional communication exists between the government and the citizens in this stage.
2. **Interaction stage**: Presents an advanced stage of the 'information stage'. Simple interaction between citizens and governments is enhanced and various website features and functionalities such as search and e-mails are added to the static website developed during the first stage. This enables bi-directional communication to exist.

3. **Transaction stage:** facilitates value-based transactions between citizens and the government with citizens able to pay taxes, submit forms online. Citizens and other e-Government stakeholders can engage the government through heterogeneous Web platforms creating scenarios where public service delivery is brought to the citizens ubiquitously.
4. **Integration stage:** This stages presents an advanced stage in as far as mainstreaming of e-Government applications into government business processes is concerned. It facilitates business intelligence applications allowing both vertical and horizontal integration of services across government and agencies. When e-Government is developed to this stage, state-of-the-art ICT infrastructure is erected in government departments to promote responsive service delivery which evolves with changing trends.

The Chandler and Emanuel model mainly devotes its focus to ascertaining the functionality and whether e-Government applications are citizen-centric. A fair deal of consideration is given to the security aspects of the applications. The model, however, ignores the non-technical security issues and does not give due consideration to sudden political changes on the e-Government environment (Chandler & Emanuel, 2002).

4.3.12 Accenture Five-Stage Model

Accenture in its report on 2003 (Irani, Al-Sebie & Elliman, 2006:5) identifies five stages for effective e-Government development as detailed below:
1. **Online presence:** Is the first stage of this model and involves the publication of essential government information online for citizens' use. This includes simple public services like downloading forms and does not need advanced technical capabilities.
2. **Basic capability:** Involves building on what has been developed in the first stage and includes creating a central plan, developing a legislative framework, addressing the security and certification problem, broadening the online presence, and implementing some easy transaction capabilities. Digital signatures are introduced to securing personal and agency information. Correspondingly, this stage requires a higher level of technical abilities.
3. **Service availability:** Means that a basic portal website is available and acts as a gateway to the e-Government system. In this stage, services from different agencies are integrated and cross-agencies or horizontal co-operation is introduced.

4. **Mature delivery**: Entails that e-Government implementation has reached an advanced stage where even customer service has fully emerged into the system. At this stage, there is clear ownership, responsibility and authority, intra-agency relationships and collaboration across different levels of government.
5. **Service transformation:** Is the final stage of e-Government maturity and the different e-Government platforms are able to deliver all the public services which could otherwise be provided in a paper world.

This model is customer-centric and focuses on whether the e-Government service is being utilised by basic customers.

4.3.13 Public Sector Process Rebuilding (PPR) Four Phased Model

The Public sector process rebuilding (PPR) model was proposed by Andersen and Henriksen (2006:237) as an extension of the Layne and Lee (2001:125) model. PPR takes the customer-centric approach whereas the Layne and Lee model puts more emphasis on technological capability. The paragraphs to follow succinctly describe the different phases of the PPR model shown in Figure 2.2 (next page).

1. **Cultivation:** This is the onset of e-Government applications where horizontal and vertical integration of public service delivery is sheltered with limited usage of front-end systems and adoption of intranet with government departments and line ministries. Forms can be downloaded from static websites, completed and returned as e-mail attachments or mailed back using ordinary postal services. At this stage, there are limited digital services accessible through the Internet and it is unclear whether considerable effort is devoted to promoting the use of the Internet to increase user frequency and increase quality of public service delivery. The general experience in this phase is that the public institution will be experienced as inaccessible, have long case processing time, and no accessibility for accessing the processing of requests (Andersen & Henriksen, 2006:239).

For the purpose of this book, it is worth noting that most governments in developing world countries are busy implementing e-Government initiatives. Having characteristics of this first phase may be counter-productive to different government business processes and customer focus. Figure 4.3 below, originally developed by Andersen and Henriksen, (2006:237), provides a diagrammatical representation of the PPR model and details the contrast between the customer-centric and activity-centric applications.

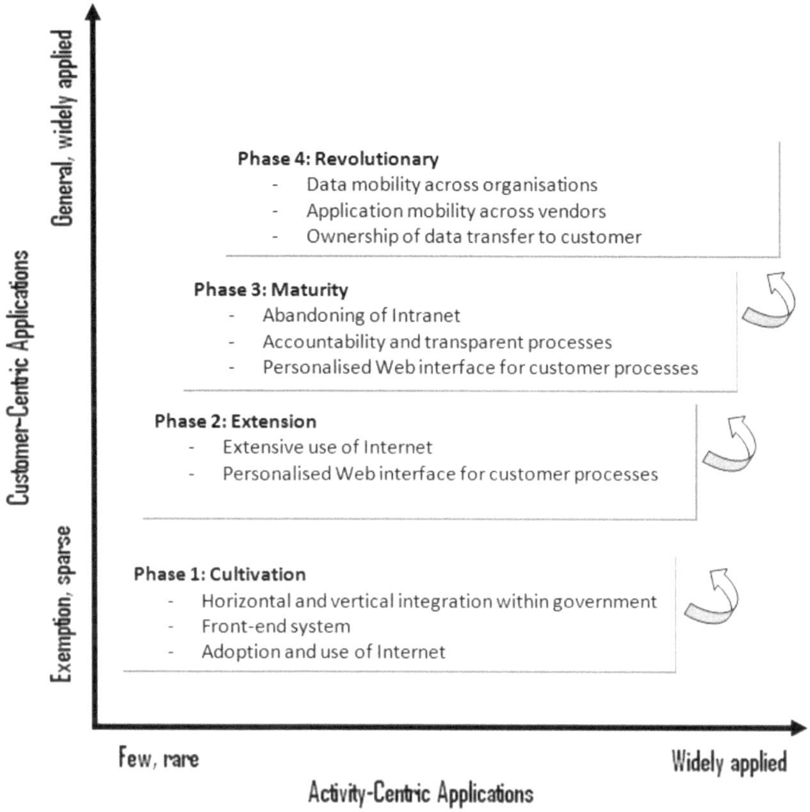

Figure 4.3: Public sector process rebuilding (PPR) maturity model (Andersen & Henriksen, 2006:237).

2. **Extension:** As expected, this stage builds on the cultivation phase to the possibilities of user experience in this e-Government platform. In this phase, there is extensive use of the Intranet, adoption of personalised Web user interface brought about by improved interactivity of the Web platform, and better Web platform usability for customer processes. To enhance usability, the Web interface is targeted towards end-users rather than public agencies or any government authorities as the emphasis is on the 'user-centric' paradigm. Many manual routines still exist at this stage, and in most of the cases users are re-directed to other agencies for specific information that they may be interested in. This stage is considered intermediary as a desired one stop e-Government platform is not yet achieved.

3. **Maturity:** At this stage, the government has matured enough and has put in place transparent processes coupled with other personalised Web interfaces for processing customer (citizen) requests. This stage provides a chance for the Internet and the Intranet to merge (converge) so that marginal costs in the processing of customer information are kept minimal. Unlike with the 'extension stage' where there are links to other institutions, the homepage in this stage feeds information from other institutions to users online. The website is highly interactive and can handle requests from users convincingly. Self-service is the key priority in this phase.
4. **Revolutionary:** At this stage, public service delivery has completely matured and provides service integration and data mobility across organisations. It also provides application mobility and interoperability across vendors. Rather than seeing the Internet as exclusively a means to create increased mobility with the government, it is seen as a platform for transfer of data ownership and orientation of the database infrastructure to the end-users (Andersen & Henriksen, 2006:238).

Comparison of the different models discussed here reveals that these models can work with serious consideration to the local context in the area where e-Government is implemented. This is to say that there is no global or optimal e-Government maturity model amongst the existing e-Government maturity models. These models provide a guideline as to what issues any e-Government strategy should consider at any stage of the e-Government maturity level.

A summary of the different e-Government maturity models according to each model's characteristics identified from the literature review is presented in Table 4.1.

Table 4.1: Summary of models' characteristics.

Name of model	Discoverer	Maturity levels	Model focus
West four-stage model	West, 2000	4	– Online presence – Transaction processes – Full integration (e-Governance) – Digital democracy – e-Government functionality and citizen-centric – technical and non-technical security attributes
Gartner	Baum and Di Maio, 2000	4	– Online presence – Integration of business processes (e-Governance) – Full integration (e-Governance) – Efficiency of e-Government applications
Layne and Lee	Layne and Lee, 2001	4	– Online presence – Transaction process – Vertical and horizontal integration – Streamlined public service delivery – Full service integration
Deloitte	Deloitte and Touche, 2001	6	– Online presence – Transaction processes – Integrated e-Government service
Howard	Howard, 2001	3	– Maintaining acceptable functionality of e-Government application – Considers issues of citizen-centric applications
Hiller and Bélanger	Hiller and Bélanger, 2001	5	– Online presence – Integration – Transaction processes – Vertical and horizontal integration – Digital democracy – E-Participation

United Nations	UN, 2003	5	– Online presence – Interaction (e-Participation) – Transaction processes – Full integration and e-Government functionality
World Bank	World Bank, 2003	3	– Efficient e-Government services – E-Government overall development
Asia Pacific	Wescott, 2009	6	– Integration – Transaction processes – Full integration (e-Governance) – Digital democracy – Citizen-centric and functionality – Potential impact on e-Government applications
Moon	Moon, 2002	5	– System functionality
Chandler and Emanuel	Chandler and Emanuel, 2002	4	– E-Government functionality
Accenture	Irani, Al-Sebie and Elliman, 2006	5	– Online presence – Interaction (e-Governance) – Transaction processes – E-Government service availability – Assesses availability of user-centric applications – Full integration

It can be shown from Table 4.1 that most e-Government maturity models assess the development of e-Government with reference to the functionality of e-Government applications, the privacy mechanisms employed by those applications, and the general e-Participation levels of the general customers. This entails that e-Government maturity is partly evidenced by the number of citizens and businesses that are able to do business with government using online platforms. These different e-Government maturity models can be used to gauge the penetration of e-Government in any area.

Apart from the maturity models presented in Table 4.1, Forrester Research has proposed a 6 level e-Government development trajectory. The model has been drawn with careful reference to the changing trends in the way world entities interact with each other given the current and emerging technology trends and the emerging Knowledge-Based-Economies (KBEs). The wider recognition of information as a strategic resource to organisations has led to KBEs where the unit of competitiveness is information and knowledge. KBEs are basically economical setups which have bought-into the idea that the different knowledge types (tacit and explicit) need to be amassed appropriately and integrated into the different organisational business processes. The emergence of knowledge economies entails that knowledge is the major source of competitive advantage, an acute departure from the generally held conception according to the old economic models which recognized land, labour and capital as vital factors of production and therefore competitiveness (Drucker , 1995; 1999; Stiglitz, 2003; Butler et al., 2004). The wider recognition of the role information plays in business contexts and the need for it flow across organisation silos entails that process integration and dynamic technology applications are needed. As has been mentioned earlier, one of the main enablers of e-Government is information. Therefore, there is need to check what advancements have been achieved by both e-Government practitioners and researchers on the technology front. In order to appreciate the role of technology in the e-Government landscape, Figure 4.4 below shows a six-stage e-Government development roadmap.

The roadmap in Figure 4.4 shows that e-Government development starts from back-office process automation where the organisation has procured one or two types of databases, the enterprise architecture has been established and the workflow automation has been put in place. The advanced stage comprises the existence of interoperable government systems which lead to ubiquitous governance systems. The future development stage of e-Government will vie towards international interoperability where government systems from across borders of different countries will be integrated. At each of these stages, it is important to note that technology is extensively utilised. Therefore, as much as other non-technology strategies are cardinal to the success of e-Government, ignoring requisite technology design frameworks for e-Government applications is a huge opportunity cost.

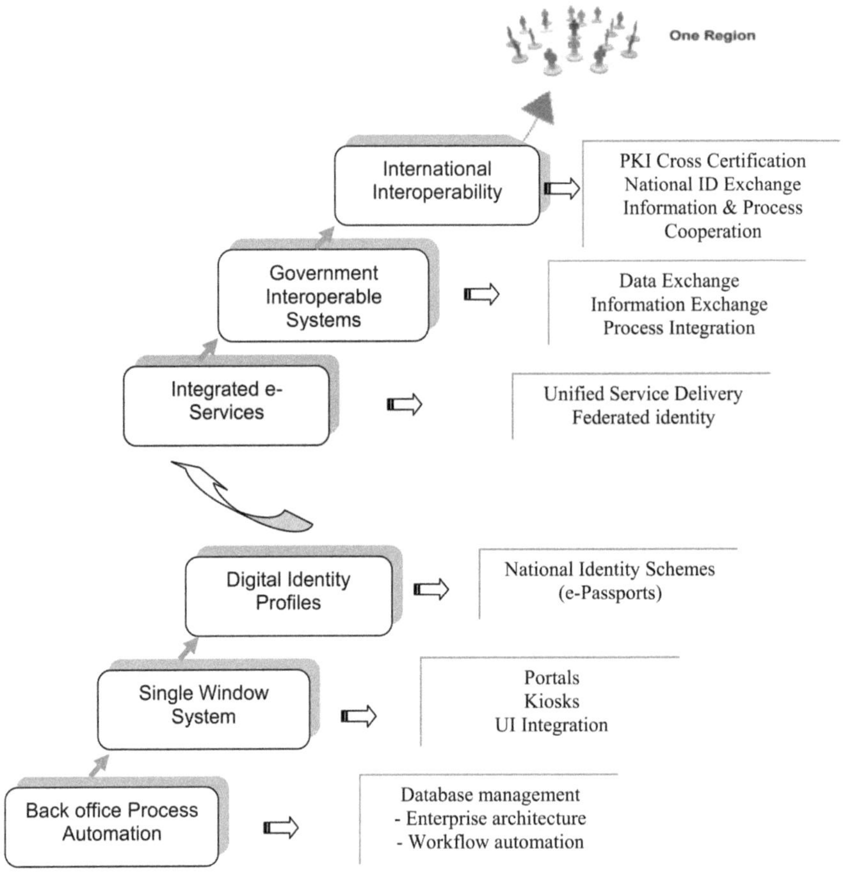

Figure 4.4: A six stage e-Government roadmap (Adapted from: Forrester Research, Inc.).

4.4 Importance of e-Readiness Assessment

E-Readiness assessment is an important undertaking to determine the readiness of an environment to participate in the information or digital economy. In any socio-economic frameworks, setting a solid and enabling environment for nurturing an information society is prerequisite to any endeavours for the uptake, adoption and penetration of ICT applications (such as e-Government, e-Democracy, e-Learning, and e-Health). Ojo, Janowski and Estevez (2007:2) have identified three factors that motivate countries to advance and promote e-Readiness. In the first place, ICT contributes towards alleviating some of the most basic economic problems by facilitating job creation through the ICT industry or productivity enhancements through ICT-intensive sectors. Secondly, countries want to avoid the notion of being digitally isolated and non-competitive. Thirdly, ICT development sits at the center of any multi-national organisation's and many foreign donors' agendas (such as the UN's Millennium Development Goals (MDGs) or the World Bank's InfoDev programme (CDTI, 2002)).

For a country to participate in the information society, it is important that it is e-Ready; an assessment that can be provided by utilising e-Readiness assessments or frameworks outlined below. According to Mutula and Van Brakel (2006:214–217), some of the various reasons for e-Readiness assessments are discussed in the following paragraphs.

Appropriate levels of e-Readiness will enable countries to inclusively participate in global economies where individuals regardless of status are able to create, receive, share and utilise information for their social, cultural, economic and political development (Consulting and Audit Canada, 2004:1). The level of e-Readiness directly determines a country's competitiveness as it is able to effectively use the Internet to create new opportunities and maintain a competitive edge over countries that are not e-Ready (Mutula & Van Brakel, 2006:214). E-Readiness assessments help understand the potential of enterprises to take advantage of ubiquitous and mobile marketplaces which are made possible by adequate levels of Internet penetration (e-Commerce). These assessments further help to understand whether a country has capacity to have all its citizens participate in national social, economic, political and cultural endeavours; development information flows and ICT-based development opportunities; and the digital divide among different economic strata.

E-Readiness assessments enable individuals to probe the likelihood of success of any anticipated ICT-based applications such as e-Government, e-Health, and e-Learning and correspondingly how ready a country is to transcend towards a KBE. E-Readiness assessments further provide guidelines on what interventions to take and policies to enact so as to realistically achieve goals that allow participation in the information society.

E-Readiness assessments can help to understand a country's e-Readiness strengths and weakness and guide policy prioritisation and facilitate appropriate usage of scarce resources to encourage ICT adoption. The SADC e-Readiness task force report (2002) noted that e-Readiness assessments are based on a theory that countries having pervasive information infrastructures and use ICT applications effectively possess advantages, against those that do not, in as far as economic growth and social development is concerned.

4.5 E-Readiness and e-Government

From the discussion above, an environment that is not e-Ready cannot effectively implement e-Government. The point of departure is that for an environment to be able to stand any chance of successfully implementing e-Government, it must be e-Ready. Azab, Kamel and Dafoula (2009:12) have ascertained that assessing e-Government Readiness also transcends into the investigation of the overall e-Readiness and vice-versa. E-Readiness entails socio-economic and culture-technical maturation which outlines the willingness to adopt and use technology in daily routines.

4.6 Guidelines in e-Readiness Assessment

On the technical side, just like in huge software engineering projects where established methodologies apply a logical series of steps to analyse and redesign or rearrange the features of the subsystem; for example Boehm's description of waterfall (and later the spiral) approaches (Eddowes, 2004:118), e-Government assessment also follows the similar paths. Kamal-Vaezi and Bimar (2009:502–507) have identified a number of e-Readiness assessment tools that have generally been utilised to assess the uptake of ICTs in any given environment. Since e-Government is accessed on ICT platforms, it follows that without the use of ICTs, success of e-Government cannot be achieved.

The following sections present some of the most common tools that have been widely used to assess e-Readiness. As aforementioned, the discussion of e-Readiness is pre-requisite to understanding the likelihood of success for e-Government implementation.

4.6.1 The Computer System Policy Project's Readiness Guide for Living in the Networked World

Published in 1998 the Computer System Policy Project's (CSPP) Readiness Guide (cf: www.cspp.org; CSPP, 1998; CSPP, 2000) helps individuals and communities to assess how prepared they are to participate in the Networked World; measures the integration of ICTs in homes, schools, businesses, healthcare facilities and government departments. Measurements are divided into five categories: infrastructure, access, applications and services, economy, and enablers (policy, privacy, security, and ubiquity). Averaging the score on these categories obtains an estimation of the community's readiness to participate in the digital world (CSPP, 1998; Bridges, 2005).

The definition of e-Readiness according to this guide is extensive, namely:

> An e-Ready society is one that has the necessary physical infrastructure (high bandwidth, reliability, and affordable prices); integrated current ICTs throughout businesses (e-commerce, local ICT sector), communities (local content, many organisations which are online, ICTs used in everyday life, ICTs taught in schools), and the government (e-Government); strong telecommunications competition; independent regulation with a commitment to universal access; and no limits on trade or foreign investment (Bridges, 2005).

This definition of e-Readiness, although missing out on contemporary understanding of e-Readiness captures most of the attributes for assessing e-Readiness.

4.6.2 Guide for Developing Countries, Asian Pacific Economic Cooperation's E-Commerce Readiness Assessment

A guide for Developing Countries, Asian Pacific Economic Cooperation's (APEC) e-Commerce Readiness Assessment helps governments to develop their own focused policies which are adapted to their specific environment for the health of e-Commerce (business transactions over online media). Six categories are used to measure readiness for e-Commerce which may as well apply in an e-Government context, namely:

1. Basic infrastructure and technology (speed, pricing, access, market competition, industry standards, and foreign investment).
2. Promotion and facilitation (industry led standards).
3. Use of the Internet (use in business, government, homes).
4. Access to network services (bandwidth, industry diversity, export controls, credit card regulation).
5. Skills and human resources (ICT education, workforce).
6. Positioning for the digital economy (taxes and tariffs, Industry self-regulation, government regulations, consumer trust).

In assessing participants' e-Commerce readiness, participants are asked 100 multiple-choice questions grouped into the six categories listed above. The APEC guide recognises a country as being e-Ready when it is 'ready' for e-Commerce transactions, has free trade, industry self-regulation, ease of exports, and has compliance with international standards and trade agreements (Bridges, 2005).

Since e-Government is the next technological wave after e-Commerce, it is logical to ascertain that for an environment to be e-Ready, it must have achieved e-Commerce readiness in the first place.

4.6.3 Harvard University's Center for International Development Readiness for the Networked World

Published in 2000, the Center for International Development (CID) Readiness for the Networked World guide systematically organises the assessment of numerous factors that determine the networked readiness of a community in the developing world. It measures 19 different categories, covering the availability, speed, and quality of network access, use of ICTs in schools, workplace, economy, government, and everyday life, ICT policy (telecommunications and trade), ICT training programs, and diversity of organisations and relevant content online, and provides a grid with descriptions of four stages of advancement in each of 19 categories (placed into five groups).

This guide defines e-Readiness as follows:

> An e-Ready society is one that has the necessary physical infrastructure (high bandwidth, reliability, and affordable prices); integrated current ICTs throughout businesses (e-Commerce, local ICT sector), communities (local content, many organisations online, ICTs used in everyday life, ICTs taught in schools), and the government (e-Government); strong telecommunications competition; independent regulation with a commitment to universal access; and no limits on trade or foreign investment (CID, 2000:6).

These different guidelines for e-Readiness assessments are utilised in case studies carried in different regions of the world aimed at assessing e-Readiness for an area to participate in various aspects of the digital economy. The following section presents some of the common studies that have been done on a regular basis.

4.6.4 Case Studies for e-Readiness Assessment

Case studies from the International Telecommunications Union's (ITU) Internet Country Case Studies, the ASEAN e-Readiness assessments, and case studies conducted or funded by USAID (United States Agency for International Development), infoDev and Swedish International Development Agency (Bridges, 2005) are presented in this section.

4.6.5 International Telecommunications Union Internet Country Case Studies report, Mosaic Methodology

The ITU Internet Country Case Studies or Mosaic Methodology measures availability of ICT infrastructure, use of ICT, legal and regulatory frameworks and macroeconomic and local business environments. These studies seek to understand Internet penetration in different economies around the world and are based on the methodology developed by the Mosaic group (Bridges, 2005; Kamal-Vaezi & Bimar, 2008: 503).

These studies analyse the factors that impact on the use of the Internet and provides some recommendations, thereof. The case studies provide an opportunity for country Internet penetration to be assessed in relation with other countries using a unique methodology developed by the Mosaic group (Bridges, 2005).

4.6.6 United States Agency for International Development Tool and Report

The USAID case studies are produced using a framework of 'Pipes (Access), public sector (Government Policies, e-Government), private sector (Usage), people (Training), and existing development Programs' (Kamal-Vaezi & Bimar, 2008: 503). The analysis is done with the help of data from the ITU's World Telecommunications Indicators. The report details the progress that has been made and what plans or interventions are earmarked for future implementation.

4.6.7 Sweden International Development Agency

Sweden International Development Agency (SIDA) conducts some country case studies to examine the available ICT infrastructure, its usage, availability of competent human resource base, and the existence of acceptable legal and regulatory frameworks. These case studies are done using survey methodology, interviews and CID's guide for readiness for the networked world (Bridges, 2005; Vaezi & Bimar, 2008: 503).

The study further seeks to describe the given country's ICT landscape, as well as 'a basic analysis of factors of major interest for the promotion of ICT usage for development purposes' (Bridges, 2005).

4.6.8 Association of South East Asian Nations e-Readiness Assessment

The Association of South East Asian Nations (ASEAN) e-Readiness Assessment aims to investigate the readiness of countries in the ASEAN region to participate in the digital economy. Six different sets of indicators are used to measure the digital economy and the extent to which the ASEAN information infrastructure (such as e-Society, e-Commerce, e-Government, liberalisation of trade in ICT goods and services and the available ICT infrastructure) is developed (Bhatia, 2001:7; Bridges, 2005).

This assessment tool allowed 10 different countries from the ASEAN region to be assessed and clustered according to their level of e-Readiness development: emerging, evolving, embedding, and extending. The tool also allows the unearthing of common issues and challenges towards achieving a developed e-Ready economy in the ASEAN region (Bhatia, 2001:6).

4.6.9 Third Party Survey and Reports

Third party reports rank countries with regard to their e-Readiness and e-Competitiveness (use of ICTs in various socio-economic value chains). Many of these reports, with others using questionnaires, depend mostly on statistical analysis of data gathered from other sources. Some of these reports do not directly measure e-Readiness *per se* but their measurements help in the understanding of e-Readiness. Some of the third party surveys are: WITSA's International Survey of e-Commerce; the World Bank's Knowledge Assessment Methodology (KAM); Crenshaw and Robinson's Cyber-Space and post-industrial transformations; McConnell International's Risk e-Business; Benchmarking the Information Society (SIBIS); World Economic Forum's (WEF) Networked Readiness Index (NRI); Mosaic's global diffusion of the Internet project; CIDCM's negotiating the net model; and the Economist Intelligence Unit's (EIU) e-Readiness rankings (Bridges, 2005).

4.6.10 McConnell International Risk e-Business

Released in August 2000, prepared in conjunction with WITSA (2000), this report was aimed at assessing national economy's e-Readiness, or capacity to participate in the global digital economy. The major measurement areas for the report are:

1. Information security (intellectual property, privacy, electronic signatures).
2. Political and financial stability and human capital (ICT education, available skilled workforce).
3. E-Business climate (competition, foreign investment, and financial infrastructure) and connectivity (infrastructure, access and pricing).
4. E-leadership (government policies and regulations).

The report assesses 42 countries by performing a 'dynamic evaluation of the relevance and accuracy of available quantitative data with an understanding of myriad cultural, institutional, and historical factors' (Vaezi & Bimar, 2008:504) and describes a complex e-Readiness picture. McConnell International contends that the report provides a basis for which planning towards a digital economy should be based (Bridges, 2005).

From the report, it is inferred that an e-Ready country should have extensive utilisation of computers in various socio-economic setups such as businesses (e-Commerce), schools (e-Learning), government (e-Government), and homes; affordable and reliable ICT access in the competitive market; free trade; skilled workforces, government-business partnerships, transparency and stability in public service delivery systems; and secure networks and personal privacy with regulations allowing digital signatures and encryption (Bridges, 2005).

4.6.11 World Information Technology and Services Alliance's International Survey of e-Commerce

The WITSA's survey was aimed at understanding the different companies' experience with conducting their businesses using e-Commerce, and to further obtain views on what should be done to promote e-Commerce penetration. Varying set of questions are used in this survey ranging from barriers to technology industry; problems with e-Commerce technology in terms of users' trust, usability and availability; internal business practices that support e-Commerce, workforce problems; ICT and public policy issues; and to understanding resistance to e-Commerce technology adoption by the consumers.

4.6.12 The Economic Intelligence Unit: e-Business Readiness Rankings

The Economic Intelligence Unit (EIU) aims to measure the extent to which an environment is able to adopt Internet-based opportunities, taking into account a vast array of factors such as quality of IT infrastructure, ambition of government interventions to promote Internet penetration, and real value of commercial efficiencies brought about by the Internet. About 100 qualitative and quantitative criteria are organised into six categories: supporting e-Services (10%); regulatory framework (15%); business environment (20%); connectivity (30%); e-Commerce consumer and business adoption (20%); and social and cultural infrastructure (5%).

The rankings target 60 of the world's largest economies and provide pointers as to where government policy should be directed. The rankings are important because they are also referred to by multinational business entities who would like to invest in technologically innovative or isolated countries and tailor their ICT strategies to the local context. The countries that participate in this survey are ranked using an e-Readiness score (out of 10) and ranked from 1 to 60 (Bridges, 2005).

4.6.13 Statistical Indicators Benchmarking the Information Society

Statistical Indicators Benchmarking the Information Society (SIBIS) assesses the e-Readiness of an environment to envelop the information society. It mostly concentrates on measuring the benchmarking indicators in ten areas: Telecommunication and access; education; security and trust; work, employment and skills; social inclusion; e-Commerce; e-Government; Internet for research; health and transport (Bridges, 2005; Kamal-Vaezi & Bimar, 2008:506).

4.6.14 World Bank's Knowledge Assessment Methodology Report

The Knowledge Assessment Methodology (KAM) Report is an interactive benchmarking tool used by countries to assess the challenges and opportunities they face in their bid to transform to KBEs. The KAM identifies four pillars of a KBE as follows: economic incentive and institutional regime, education, innovation, and ICTs. These four pillars are used to assess 146 countries with regards to their KBE status using a normalised scale of 0 to 10. The KAM further derives a country's overall Knowledge Economy Index (KEI) and the Knowledge Index (KI).

4.6.15 Information Society Index Report by the International Data Corporation

The International Data Corporation's (IDC) Information Society Index (ISI) Report was produced in 2003 to assess readiness of countries to envelop the information society using four 'infrastructure pillars' or sub-indexes: telecommunications and social factors, use, computer Internet, and e-Commerce.

This report assesses 53 countries and ranks them according to the likelihood that they would adopt IT in the near future. Mainly, the report is used by governments, telecommunications and asset management companies to assess the market potential of a given region (Bridges, 2005).

4.6.16 Networked Readiness Index in the Global Information Technology Report

Comprising three components (the readiness of the community's key stakeholders including individuals, businesses, government to use ICT; the ICT environment offered by a given country or community; and the actual use of ICTs amongst different stakeholders), the Networked Readiness Index (NRI) measures the willingness of the community to reap the benefits that ICTs have to offer. The NRI is officially defined as 'the degree of preparation of a nation or community to participate in and benefit from ICT developments' (Hu, Xiao, Pang & Xie, 2005:4; Dutta & Mia, 2010b).

The report defines 'ICT environment' as comprising three components: ICT market, political or regulatory factors, and the actual ICT infrastructure. Readiness is defined as comprising a tripartite of individual, business and government readiness. Use of ICT is looked at as comprising the totality of individual, business and government usage (Bridges, 2005).

The report also captures core factors that determine the performance of a nation on ICT development using the three major stakeholders in ICT usage (individual, businesses, and government).

4.6.17 Kenny's Assistance to Overcome the Digital Divide (World Bank)

According to Bridges (2005:6), the Kenny report serves as a tool to assess the ease with which access to quality information infrastructure is achieved. It outlines the gap regarding access to information resources. Kenny assesses the per capital income of a country with strong reference on econometric studies looking at determinants of how developed the information infrastructure is. The per capital income is used to assess the potential of a country to utilise ICTs in its various socio-economic value chains.

Using four different indicators (competition, small economies, rural needs, and institutional investor), the report identifies countries that have 'both a lower than expected level of ICT provision given their GDP level and a quality and cost of service that is less than satisfactory' (Bridges, 2005:6). The outcomes of these reports are correspondingly used for prioritisation for donor funding.

4.6.18 World Telecommunication Indicators

Questionnaires are sent worldwide to telecommunication authorities and operating companies on an annual basis. The indicators are also based on data obtained from annual reports, statistical year books, and data from national broadcasting authorities, together with other demographic and macro-economic data (Bridges, 2005).

These indicators are produced by the ITU in the form a comprehensive set of tables for 196 economies, with basic indicators (population, GDP, total telephone subscribers), data on local telephone networks, ISDN, telephone tariffs, International telephone traffic, equipment trade, telecommunications revenue, IT, cellular subscribers, and network growth, among others.

4.6.19 Digital Access Index by International Telecommunications Union

The ITU aims to investigate the level of access of digital content by citizens and businesses throughout the world using the Digital Access Index (DAI). This information is important as it helps shape the direction of ICT policy towards proliferation of ICT usage in various socio-economic sectors in individual countries.

The DAI utilises eight variables to cover five areas (quality of ICT services, availability of infrastructure, educational level, affordability of access, and Internet usage) to provide overall country scores on digital access opportunities. This index is based purely on quantitative indicators.

Using the four categories (high, upper, medium, and low) countries are classified with reference to the actual ICT adoption trends. These categories can be used to understand the country's weaknesses and strengths to ICT access and adoption.

4.6.20 Analysis of the e-Readiness studies

These different case studies provide a basis for which the e-Readiness of any given area can be deduced. Although some of these case studies measure e-Readiness indirectly, they help a great deal in understanding what initiatives have been put in place for an area to be e-Ready and be better placed to participate in the digital economy.

The above e-Readiness assessment models demonstrate that the major parameters used for e-Readiness assessments can categorically be put in five distinct groups as shown below:

- Assessment of human resource base – availability of ICT champions to lead ways of advancing global usage of ICTs, and the percentage of people in a given country who have been trained in IT.
- Availability of ICT infrastructure – probability of ease of access to robust infrastructure that may be utilised for basic and advanced ICT applications.
- Availability of appropriate policies and regulatory frameworks – to guide interaction in the digital environment, how ICTs should be regulated so that no one is disadvantaged.
- The social, cultural, economical and political environment – detailing leadership and the political will for ICT mainstreaming in different socio-economic sectors.
- Maturity levels of e-Government – the usage levels of ICTs in public service delivery frameworks.

However after a critical look at the measurement capabilities of these tools, and being in agreement with Dada (2006:4), these e-Readiness assessment tools do not take in-depth assessment and analysis of factors that may directly affect e-Government proliferation such as culture and technology acceptance. Since these case studies mainly measure global aspects of e-Readiness and mainly concentrate on macro aspects of e-Readiness, they do not bring out the individual and grassroots (community) aspects of e-Readiness. This means these surveys may not be effective to any appreciable extent in as far as understanding the level of e-Readiness at an individual and micro level such as a community is concerned. With this understanding, it is logical to ascertain that further studies still need to be pursued on how e-Readiness assessment frameworks should be designed especially the ones that target the community levels.

As can be deduced from the discussions of the different e-Readiness assessment tools above, e-Readiness tools and models can potentially be divided into two major categories: those focusing on the availability of basic ICT infrastructure and an environment's capacity and readiness to support meaningful businesses and economic growth; and those focusing on the general citizenry (the society) to benefit from ICTs. These two categories are correspondingly referred to as e-Economy and e-Society, respectively. It is worth noting, however, that the concept of e-Economy and e-Society are not mutually exclusive.

The researcher's conception of e-Economy and e-Society (as a result of the preceding literature review) is roughly categorised based on the different tools used in e-Readiness assessments as follows:

- **E-Economy:** APEC's e-Commerce Assessment; Crenshaw and Robinson's Cross-National Analysis of Internet Development; McConnell International's e-Readiness Report; Mosaic's Global Diffusion of the Internet Framework; and the WITSA e-Commerce Survey.
- **E-Society:** CIDCM's negotiating the Net Model; The various models for evaluating e-readiness from 'digital divide' reports; CID's E-Readiness Assessment Guide; and the CSPP's E-Readiness Assessment Guide.

This section has presented tools and concepts used in e-Readiness assessments which may indirectly indicate how probable it may be for an area to adopt novel applications such as e-Government. The following section presents the different frameworks that directly measure e-Government penetration in a given area.

4.7 Conclusion and Summary

This chapter has highlighted the different measurement approaches and tools that may be used to ascertain the readiness of any area to implement e-Government. Despite no direct e-Government readiness assessment methodologies or tools, e-Readiness shows the likelihood of any e-Government to thrive in any given environment. It does this by analyzing the readiness of an area to envelop the idea of 'information society' where information and knowledge resources are managed and streamlined into the socio-economic processes using ICTs. The different e-Government assessment methodologies are unique given their understanding of e-Readiness is, and the area being assessed. This shows that proper assessment of e-Government readiness should start from first understanding what it entails.

The next chapter discusses e-Government assessment methods and frameworks. Although the previous chapters have precursory outlined the benefits and impact on e-Government on the society, there is need to now discuss concrete methods used the world over. This is important as this book delves towards proposing a robust e-Government framework that will positively impact on e-Government research and practice.

Chapter 5
E-Government Assessment Methods and Frameworks

5.1 Introduction

Just like other projects implemented on a large scale, e-Government also needs monitoring and evaluation (appraisal) along the implementation cycle. The monitoring is important because it accords chance to the implementing team and other stakeholders to assess whether the original goals are being realized and whether e-Government is being implemented sustainably with ability to follow the changing societal trends. Further, e-Government appraisal is very important because it helps in the understanding of the different factors that dictate success or failure of e-Government projects (Gupta & Vasishta, 2008). The understanding of the likelihood of failure or success of e-Government project is important because, from the onset, it enables governments avoid the diversion of scarce resources (e.g. finances) to unfruitful socio-economic projects. This chapter intends to discuss the appraisal of e-Government endeavours done using various e-Government assessment methods, tools and frameworks. The chapter intends to highlight the different e-Government tools and available frameworks and how these can be adapted to be used in any environment in the less developed countries.

From the onset, it is important to acknowledge the fact that e-Government assessment (ascertaining its development trajectory and value on the different strata of the socio-economic setup) is a much complicated undertaking. The level of e-Government adoption or penetration of e-Government in different government business processes cannot be established if appropriate and tested techniques and tools are not employed to investigate the status of e-Government development. For this reason, this chapter discusses methodologies and approaches of carrying out an e-Government development audit (i.e. checking the availability of desired attributes for successful e-Government implementation) and presents some discussions on the different tools and methods that are commonly used in e-Government assessment frameworks. The chapter provides an overview of the reasons why continuous assessment and process re-engineering of e-Government initiatives is important to maintain currency and relevancy of different ICT applications in the public service business processes. Process re-engineering procedures aim to continuously assess stakeholder value prepositions and ensure that the different e-Government applications are designed within the confines of expected public value. Finally, to ameliorate common flawed positions in e-Government research and practice, some thoughts on e-Government assessment tools and methods' capabilities are presented at the end of the chapter.

5.2 Background to e-Government Assessment

It cannot be over-emphasised that the Internet has transformed the way citizens and businesses interact with their government and with one another. It has famously been asserted that the opportunity cost, in as far as overall efficiency and effectiveness is concerned, incurred in ignoring the usage of Information and Communication Technologies (ICTs) is huge (Gupta & Jana, 2003; Dada, 2006; Hargreaves, 2011). As articulated in Chapter 2 and 3, the huge benefits of e-Government eventually culminate into individual, regional and international advancements with regard to harnessing socio-economic opportunities. Despite this being the case, as already articulated in this chapter, it is also true that e-Government implementation comes with many disadvantages, costs and risks.

On the positive side, e-Government is viewed as a lever to transform outmoded bureaucracies and red tapes, thereby promoting efficiency and effectiveness of public service delivery and facilitating e-Participation and e-Democracy (Rowley, 2011:54). To amass the maximum benefits of e-Government, there is need to closely monitor and evaluate the e-Government initiatives and interventions at each stage of the implementation lifecycle (Evans & Yen, 2005:355–357). This can only be possible if there are well-defined e-Government assessment tools, approaches and methodologies. Further, continuous assessment of e-Government is important so that the designers and implementers put in place scalable e-Government solutions which evolve with the evolving and emerging technologies. For example, the developing world has now seen many mobile technologies and platforms which have enabled many citizens' overdependence on accessing ubiquitous e-Applications.

In the pursuit of transforming e-Government penetration, investments directed towards the same have been techno-centric. It is only recently that governments and other e-Government core stakeholders have realised that initiatives aimed at encouraging e-Government proliferation should incorporate a great deal of managerial specifications of technology and the different business processes in the e-Government environment. The contemporary understanding of e-Government implementation is that interventions should be devoted towards both the managerial and technical aspects of ICT usage in public delivery value chains. Further, germane e-Government initiatives should firmly be targeted at citizens and businesses as they are the major stakeholders (Rowley, 2011:54). In this regard, it is right to suffice that e-Government assessment models should also aim to measure the value that e-Government brings forth to all stakeholders. Thus, it can be posited that appropriate e-Government assessment models should consider the value created by e-Government from both the public and private domains (Raus, Liu & Kipps, 2010:124).

Knowing the status of penetration of e-Government both on an individual and businesses' level is very important so as to understand whether the original purpose/intention of engaging in e-Government is being achieved. Not only that; the financiers of e-Government initiatives may need to be convinced that their investments have created the necessary social and economic value originally anticipated. In this regard, assessment of e-Government includes ascertaining the conception of value in the public and private sector domains (Raus et al., 2010:124). E-Government assessment at any implementation level is important because it presents an opportunity to assess the currency and relevancy of e-Government applications and the approach utilised to implement them.

Assessment of e-Government initiatives can be done in the framework of monitoring and evaluation of e-Government development. This presents a continuous cycle which can further inform the strategies that should be employed to re-engineer and improve certain e-Government business processes. It is not a secret that the current approaches employed in the design, management and monitoring of e-Government interventions reveal gaps that need to be filled (Sarantis et al., 2011:117,120). Therefore, there is need to understand the strengths and weaknesses of each of the tools as used in e-Government assessment and find ways of how robust and most responsive assessment tools can be designed.

It is a well-known fact that e-Government is a multi-dimensional phenomenon (cf: Chapter 2 and 3) and its success depends on multi-dimensional factors. Therefore, desired tools for measuring e-Government development should also incorporate a multi-dimensional or disciplinary approach. This being the case, different sets of e-Government tools and methodologies are reviewed in this chapter and aspects of how these can be integrated are discussed. As mentioned in chapter three, the factors that influence e-Government depend on the local context where e-Government is implemented. Since the assessment tools will have to measure these local factors, it is logically coherent to presume that appropriate e-Government assessment tools should also be designed with reference to the local context. This aspect of e-Government assessment tools and frameworks has been lacking in literature.

It can further be ascertained that most assessment metrics use global metrics regardless of which area is being assessed. The objective of this chapter is not only to propose new assessment models but to highlight these pertinent issues as gaps for future research and find ways on how these different models can be integrated to achieve a more balanced assessment. It is visible from a search from common databases (such as *ScienceDirect*, *Emerald*, *GoogleScholar*, and *Portal)* that e-Government assessment research is still in its infancy and therefore a lot needs to be done (Jones, Irani, & Sharif, 2007:1; Esteves & Joseph, 2008:119).

E-Government initiatives mostly succeed when certain conditions are fulfilled. One of the most critical conditions is that of availability of management (implementation process management) and technical leadership and experts who have the adequate managerial and technical expertise to develop context-specific e-Government applications (Prybutok, Zhang & Ryana, 2008:143). It is also important to have project management heuristics incorporated into the e-Government implementation roadmaps. In the e-Government environment, the project management principles are enforced by project managers who are mandated to plan, monitor and re-engineer (reschedule) the necessary tasks, responsibilities and milestones (Sarantis et al., 2011:121). A robust e-Government assessment tool should not ignore the need to assess the depth of project management/ continuous assessment of e-Government interventions and take inventory of what leadership capital is in place.

Many studies have been conducted in a bid to design robust and accurate e-Government assessment tools. In an effort to provide a robust e-Government assessment methodology, Billon, Marco and Lera-Lopez (2009:596–605) identified the use of multivariate techniques in a view to capture the relative and multi-dimensional character of the digital divide as one of the major determinants that positively impacts on ICT diffusion. In another study, Jones et al., (2007:2) proposed an e-Government evaluation framework utilising four major constructs: decision-making, evaluation methods, performance assessment, and practitioner concerns. These different factors impact on e-Government penetration regardless of where it is implemented. In another study, Esteves and Joseph (2008:121) designed a three-dimensional ex-post framework for evaluating e-Government penetration and development. This framework considers technological, strategic, and organisational perspectives of e-Government. These different e-Government frameworks have also concentrated on finding out whether such e-Government initiatives culminate into financial or social value and trust in e-Government applications. Citizens' trust and therefore adoption (as outlined in Chapter 3) comes about when citizens are assured that their information which has been submitted on e-Government websites will not be compromised. Zhao and Zhao (2010:49–56) carried a study that investigates the level of security on e-Government websites as an indirect measure of e-Government maturity. In general, there are few studies which have concentrated on e-Government assessment methodologies and tools *per se*.

Only a few researchers have attempted to document the motivation for e-Government assessment. It is important, therefore, to understand the conceptualization of e-Government assessment and its contextual background, thereof.

5.3 Conceptualization of e-Government Assessment

Since e-Government is a multi-dimensional phenomenon, its measurement should also take the multi-dimensional measurement approach and utilise diverse indices and measurement tools as much as possible to come up with a correct and well-rounded measurement e-Government assessment. The use of the different measurement tools and indices delve to ensure that the hidden factors that influence e-Government development are unearthed. As has been highlighted in Chapter 4, e-Government evaluation encompasses evaluating the e-Readiness of an environment where e-Government is implemented as the first point in accessing feasibility of engaging in e-Government implementation. E-Readiness depends on many factors such as ICT access and availability, ICT affordability, ICT quality and reliability, electrical power supply and government public service delivery system. E-Readiness provides an indication of whether a country is ready to participate in the networked and information society or not (Mutula & Van Brakel, 2006:216). In essence, it is right to posit that a country that is not e-Ready may find it very difficult to effectively implement e-Government.

The first point of call in assessing e-Government development and value is to first measure e-Readiness. For example, Gauld, Goldfinch and Horsburgh (2010:178–179) measure the penetration of ICTs and e-Government using the following indicators: e-mail usage or website visits frequency, usage of e-mail to contact government, visit to e-Government website, and frequency of financial transaction on a government website. Further, Gauld et al., (2010:179) aimed to investigate whether the 'digital divide' existed in Internet-based ICT and e-Government measures by using multiple regression models. This is an example of combining the concepts of e-Readiness and digital divide in as far as measuring e-Government penetration is concerned owing to its multi-dimensional characteristic.

Using the information system theory, Koh, Prybutok and Zhang (2008:540) proposed three levels at which governmental offices' e-Government readiness should be based: strategies, system and data. The strategies entail the different strategic initiatives in place which directly contribute to the proliferation of e-Government. Examples of strategic initiatives may include investment into robust ICT infrastructure, awareness campaigns, establishment of appropriate institutional, legal and regulatory frameworks, recruitment of competent human resource cadre, etc. System entails the different technology systems and ICT platforms in place. Data means the information that the e-Government systems hold which are availed to citizens and businesses through the different ICT platforms. The research by Koh, Prybutok and Zhang (2008) culminated into an e-Government readiness model which was empirically tested in a US municipal government. This model proposed an integration strategy for strategic goals, system and data and brought together different desperate functions (informational, transactional, and operational) into an integrated e-Government portal. The assessment of the potential of e-Government success using the model suggested by Koh, Prybutok and Zhang (2008) entails checking the different strategies in place, systems and data available in different governance value chains.

Successful implementation of e-Government encompasses a vast array of factors and therefore it is important to emphasise the need to utilise many e-Government assessment methodologies so as to be certain that all the factors impacting on e-Government are considered. Many studies, such as Fang, (2002), West, (2003), Mutula and Van Brakel, (2006), Koh et al., (2008), and Gauld et al., (2010) have emphasised the importance of considering the multi-dimensional aspects and factors when assessing e-Government penetrations. For example, Koh and Prybutok (2003:34) recognise that strategic e-Government implementation should encompass and consider in its design a myriad of factors that impact on success of any e-Government business processes. Fang (2002:12) outlines the characteristics of successful e-Government interventions such as being comprehensive and interoperable, integrated, ubiquitous, easy to use, accessible, secure and private, and re-engineered business processes. Further, West (2003) identifies six factors that should be considered if e-Government initiatives were to succeed. These are: disability access, readability, non-English language accessibility, interactivity, equity of access across agencies, and user fees. Robust assessment on the potential for e-Government success therefore includes understanding aforementioned desired interventions and the six factors outlined by West (2003).

Prior to the studies by Fang (2002) and West (2003), Caldow (2001) had already identified seven factors as milestones for successful e-Government implementation. These factors are still largely valid in many environments where e-Government is to be implemented even today, and can be summarised as follows (Caldow, 2001):

- **Process integration and technology integration** – ensuring that all the business processes are compatible with the technology on disposal.
- **Economic development** – which is a determinant to such economic aspects as what kind of an ICT infrastructure a given country can afford, how much financial resources can be dedicated towards the design of robust and effec-

tive e-Government strategies, and the ability of a country to put in place a relevant institutional, legal and regulatory frameworks.
- **E-Democracy** – the capacity of the e-Government platforms to allow free participation of citizens on national issues through arrangements such as electronic voting (e-Voting) and public debates.
- **E-Communities** – ascertains the degree to which ICTs are being utilised at the community and individual levels in various socio-economic platforms.
- **Inter-governmental relation** – the transparency levels between different governments, especially regional ones, and the probability that these can utilise ICTs to forge their interactions ahead.
- **Policy environment (legal framework)** – the availability of appropriate policy and legal environment which could protect users in the online environment.
- **Internet connections** (that are fast, always on, everywhere, natural, intelligent, easy, and trusted).

With these different factors on which e-Government depends, coherence prescribes that its assessment should incorporate a multi-dimensional approach. As has been identified by Caldow (2001:36), Fang (2002:12), Koh and Prybutok (2003:34–35), and West (2003), e-Government generally encompasses social (impact of the e-Government initiative on the social outlay of an area), economical (costs of implementing and Return on Investment (ROI)) and technical constructs (such as usability and interactivity of the available systems, the systems on which it is implemented, and software specifications).

Apart from assessing the e-Readiness of a given area, it is important to measure the ROI in erecting ICT infrastructures and putting in place appropriate regulatory frameworks. As outlined by Ferro, Carratta and Dadayan (2006:1–2), assessing the return of public investments in ICT is not easy. The difficulty is mainly brought about by intangible benefits that can be amassed from ICT investments, shorter timeframes, and cross-sectional nature of ICTs. In most cases, IT investments are looked at as having negative or zero returns because of their lack of readily visible results (Dehning, Richardson & Zmud, 2003:638) and in this regard may not attract private business entities because they are specifically interested in positive returns. To a greater or lesser extent, the probability of obtaining a positive return on IT investments depends on the type of IT investment and for which purpose it was meant (Raus et al., 2010:122–123). It is worth noting that even in situations where organisations have invested huge sums of money to acquire latest technologies to increase efficiencies and profits, failure to re-engineer their organisational processes transcends into delays in realising the return on that investment (Dos Santos & Sussman, 2000:430–431).

Most of the tools employed to measure ROI in IT have been traditional in nature and are typically based on financial models such as Net Present Value (NPV), Return on Sales (ROS), and Return on Assets (ROA), (Arlotto & Oakes, 2003). Such tools may be deficient with regards to appropriately measuring ROI on e-Government interventions since e-Government is a multi-dimensional phenomenon. Because of the differences in the contexts of private and public sectors, a positive ROI in the public sector may not be perceived as positive in the private sector. This is because public sector organisations face more competing goals and are more bound to legal and staffing restrictions than private sector organisations (Guy 2003). An example could be a situation where a private organisation wants to invest in IT to automate tasks and reduce headcounts. Reducing headcounts would be a potential risk to public agencies with limited discretion to dismiss and/reassign employees in a view to improve productivity or improve the general public service delivery.

As outlined by Raus et al., (2010:123), the true value of e-Government assessment can be obtained by assessing the different innovations for both public and private stakeholders. This is because what may appear to be genuine value to one may not be value to another. Value in the private sector is more related to business value – the returns obtained on a business undertaking. Business entities measure value using a myriad set of ratios such as Economic Value Added (EVA), Net Present Value (NPV), ROI and the Social Return on Investment (SROI) (Brewer, Chandra & Hock, 1999:7; Raus et al., 2010:125). Around the 1980s, the concept of public value was conceived the New Public Management (NPM) approach where greater emphasis was placed on private styles of resource management which culminated into greater parsimony for resource utilisation and accountability (Raus et al., 2010:124). The Public Service Value (PSV) model was developed in 2003 by a group of Accenture executives working in collaboration with the Harvard Kennedy School of Management. The concept of public value involves more than the provision of an efficient and cost effective public service. It also involves a quest to develop a balanced understanding of the trade-offs along the process of public service delivery (Jupp & Younger, 2004:20).

To conceptualise the idea of private management into the public service, Creswell (2006:379) presented the Public Return on Investment (PROI) as a framework for evaluating ICT investments by governments. While analysing the financial and economic aspects of these investments, PROI concentrates on an umbrella view of how these ICT investments result into value creation for the citizens and the society as a whole. This value is split into two: value resulting from government's improvements from a citizen's perspective, and the value obtained from specific service benefits directly to persons, groups or the public at large (Creswell, 2006:380).

Apart from the metrics outlined above, there are other metrics that have been utilised to measure public value either directly or indirectly. Gartner Inc. coined the phrase 'Public Value of IT (PVIT)' which measured and demonstrated how IT investments can, over time, contribute towards political return and operational efficiency (World Bank, 2007). The PVIT phenomenon posits that value for money (measured with such metrics as the payback period, NPV, Internal Rate of Return (IRR), and EVA may not be the ultimate goal for investing in ICTs. Public value encompasses such attributes of governance as the political return and operational efficiency. Political return shows the impact of ICT investments on political goals and consensus, with some emphasis on wider reach of information to the general citizenry and the bridging of the intra-national digital divide. Operational efficiency is the internal impact of an initiative, cutting across individual government departments and across government agencies and organs (Kao, Lu & Chiu, 2011).

Other approaches in e-Government value assessment have been utilised. For example, Kertesz (2003) highlighted the need to utilise a Cost-Benefit-Analysis (CBA) methodology to assess the impact of e-Government projects. Using the CBA, the three major categories of costs are the following:

1. In order to transcend towards e-Government, there are quantifiable investments towards acquiring requisite ICT infrastructure (hardware peripherals, software, etc), computerized database platforms and digital information management practices;
2. Costs (in terms of finances and human resource) required to build the e-Government portal and cost incurred during the implementation cycle (operation costs).

In addition to the general costs outlined above, e-Government implementation involves cost incurred in establishing e-Government institutional, regulatory and legal frameworks, digital migration, personnel training, recruiting and laying off employees, awareness campaigns, and organisational work process re-engineering.

The different forms of costs incurred during e-Government implementation outlined above are compared against the gains obtained as a result of e-Government implementation. E-Government impacts on different socio-economic frameworks as follows:

- citizens/businesses (service satisfaction (win-win), time gains, access of desired public services ubiquitously regardless of socio economic status, etc.);

- government departments and its employees (increased efficiency and effectiveness, business process automation, reduction in the quantity of the human resource base); and
- society (transparency in public service delivery value chains).

The CBA aims to check whether there is equilibrium between the supply (cost) and the demand (benefits, effects or positive impact) sides of e-Government, or whether e-Government implementation is negatively or positively inclined.

In conclusion, e-Government assessment comes in two types: assessing the value of e-Government applications to the stakeholders, and assessing the penetration or adoption of e-Government by the citizens and businesses. Most of the metrics for measuring the value of e-Government have been incorporated into a set of methodologies and tools for e-Government assessment.

5.4 E-Government Assessment Methods

Another important factor that contributes to the slow development of e-Government is the digital divide. The discussion of the digital divide lays background to e-Readiness assessment which indicates the readiness of any given area to participate in the digital economy and globally uses contemporary ICT applications such as e-Government.

Assessment of e-Government at each stage of the maturity level is very important to ascertain the original purpose with which these applications were made is achieved. There are many e-Government assessment methodologies that are in existence and utilised to carry out surveys on overall e-Government development. These methodologies use the financial, non-financial, and economical metrics to assess value brought above by e-Government applications, and assesses the adoption levels i.e., the number of people who are willing to engage in e-Government. Further, some of these methodologies also assess the e-Readiness of an area to accept e-Government and the impact of the digital divide on the development of e-Government as a whole. Quantification of the digital divide and its other attributes such as e-Inclusion and social inclusion may also give a clue on the potential or status of e-Government diffusion in a given area.

This section assesses some of these methodologies and presents scenarios where these methodological underpinnings can be applied.

5.4.1 Considering the Digital Divide

As already discussed in the previous chapters, the digital divide is a concept detailing the differences between opportunities to access ICTs and information amongst different entities such as individuals and countries. Low digital divide entails that there is universal access to ICTs and thereby increasing the likelihood of success of e-Government implementation. Almarabeh and AbuAli (2010:29) ascertain that with the unprecedented growth in the adoption of ICTs in various socio-economic setups, the world has moved from the industrial age (resource-based) to the information age. It is clear that encapsulation of the information age presents challenges of the digital divide where discrepancies in the levels of access to information is a major concern. The digital divide is not a new phenomenon. James (2002) acknowledges the fact that the digital divide was evident in the world as early as 1970 where it was referred to as 'international technological dualism' which meant unequal developments in science and technology between richer and poor countries. The emergence of ICT utilisation on the political landscape may result into exclusion of individuals from online voting; and other interactive opportunities such as e-Government, will weaken the voice of those who are techno-disadvantaged (Althoff, 2004:26; Sipior & Ward, 2005:138).

The root concept of the digital divide has been social stratification which is usually applied to studies of systematic inequalities between groups of people (Scott & Marshall, 2005:639–40). People are classified into social strata in a superior or inferior position, which has given way to the understanding of the differences in access and utilisation of ICTs, culminating into the notion of inclusion/exclusion which is a spatial concept pointing to the idea of being inside or outside. The digital divide has always been looked at as a problem of ICT access which is generally approached with political *naïveté*, since interpretation of ICT adoption has always been looked at from the economic viewpoint. The digital divide (gaps on digital literacy and broadband access) presents itself as a deterrent to appropriate civic engagement, community network, educational methods and outcomes, and overall economic development of the community (Wynne et al., 2007).

The concept of the digital divide involves not only access to physical ICT platforms, but goes further to include the concept of e-Inclusion. E-Inclusion details engagement and participation in different socio-economic frameworks using ICTs. This reasoning has been supported by several researchers (Fortunati, 2008; Salman, 2010:7). Cultural homogeneity in most emerging countries (where behaviours towards ICTs consumption and adoption is influenced by a few experiences from a few individuals) may cause unison behaviour pattern towards ICTs adoption and use, let alone access to public services.

Petrauskas et al., (2008:1) define e-Inclusion as an activity or an instrument which is prerequisite for the creation of an information society and the different ICT applications in the information society. They further assert that e-Inclusion has many benefits when pursued correctly; such as decreasing the risk of digital disjuncture, to secure that marginalised individuals such as the disabled or elderly persons can be involved in the development of e-Government. This is done by avoiding new forms of disjuncture caused by information illiteracy, limited ICT skills and lack of access to the Internet. Petrauskas et al., (2008:1–2) has defined e-Inclusion with emphasis on its characteristic of outlining the extent to which ICTs have been employed to equalise and promote participation in society at all levels of the socio-economic hierarchy by enhancing social relationships, facilitating economic opportunities for work and entrepreneurship, developing cultural aspects of society, and encouraging civic participation. Thus, from the above definition, it is clear that e-Inclusion centers on using ICTs to remove obstacles which limit (or in other instances prevent) people from meaningful participation in the KBE. E-Inclusion aims to overcome the known barriers to access to ICT products and services that would otherwise translate into another form of exclusion – the digital exclusion.

Mancinelli (2008:5) posit that social exclusion principles need to be redrafted so that they can take into consideration the fact that the digital divide is essentially about social access to digital technologies as distinct to the idea of mere 'access to the technical kit'. It is important to be clear about the role of e-Inclusion in the e-Government development. Sahraoui (2007:44–45) posit that e-Inclusion should be advocated as a socially inclusive strategy for e-Government planning and not erroneously be considered as a further stage of e-Government development.

With proper understanding of the different tenets of e-Inclusion, new digital opportunities for marginal individuals and other traditionally excluded social groupings to participate in the information and knowledge-based economy are found. Wynne et al., (2007:2) posit that those who have online access coupled with digital literacy (including adequate and appropriate ICT skills) may be more likely to be economically secure and at less risk than those who do not have these attributes. This, although not empirically tested, may hold sense since lack of the aforementioned attributes may result into less participation, and realisation of the benefits and/or opportunities that come with the information and knowledge-based economy. Salman (2010:7) has outlined three key themes that should be pursued when designing and delivering projects that aim to tackle social exclusion. These are appropriate awareness campaigns, and universal access to ICTs and correspondingly information. Further, it is imperative that relevant ICT skills and appropriate literacy levels are attained by the general citizenry and businesses.

Fortunati (2008) has studied the most appropriate ways of approaching e-Inclusion and/or e-Exclusion and unearthed four different factors that should be considered in the design of any e-Government strategy. The following are the factors that should be considered:

- Recognition of the fact that the discussion of e-Inclusion/Exclusion takes cognisance of digital divide as a priori phenomenon that needs to be understood.
- E-Inclusion is not a universal aspiration; debate on e-Inclusion/exclusion seems to lack not only a robust sociological and political vision, but additionally, an anthropological awareness which leaves wide gaps in our reading of cultural differences.
- E-Inclusion must be related to the notion of 'administrative burden', which measures time and costs required from citizens in order to use online information and services provided by public administration.

As aforementioned, mitigation the disparity in access to information is the first step in successful e-Government implementation. High levels of the digital divide may have a negative impact on the access and adoption to e-Government applications.

5.4.2 E-Government Assessment Frameworks

There are many e-Government measurement frameworks that are used to guide the assessment of e-Government penetration. These different frameworks measure the degree to which a given organisation or individual is ready to utilise Information and Communication Technologies (ICTs) in public service delivery processes. If already implemented, the frameworks may be utilised to measure the degree to which ICTs have been streamlined into the government business processes. For the purposes of this book, e-Government Readiness is defined as follows:

The availability of requisite, context-aware interventions on the supply side and the degree of willingness of the citizens and businesses to engage in e-Government on the demand side.

The following are some of the different e-Government frameworks. Note that the number of frameworks presented below is not exhaustive.

5.4.2.1 India's e-Government Assessment Framework

In 2004, India came up with the e-Government Assessment Framework (EAF Version 2.0) to assess e-Government projects on attributes such as service orientation, sustainability, cost effectiveness, technology, and feasibility of replication. These attributes are further sub-divided to arrive at individual and overall e-Government scores on any service. The EAF was meant to assess the efficiency of G2G, G2B, and G2C e-Government services (cf: http://www.egovindia.org/eaf.pdf).

This model has a good intention because it can be used as an e-Government monitoring tool. The only negative aspects about this assessment framework is that it has not been subjected to empirical testing in other environments where e-Government has been implemented other than India (Bhatnagar & Singh, 2008). This, therefore, means that its validity can be contested.

5.4.2.2 United Nations Department of Economic and Social Affairs Global e-Government Readiness Series

The UN Department of Economic and Social Affairs (UN-DESA) has conducted e-Government surveys in 2001, 2003 and 2004 and documented these in UNDPEPA (2002), and UNDESA (2004) respectively. These surveys were meant to assess the development of the e-Government institutions worldwide, how these institutions impact on different societies, and to draw lessons from successful e-Government implementations.

Countries are benchmarked according to their online presence, human capacity development and telecommunication infrastructure. Online presence is determined by the use of the UN Web Measure Index (Bouaziz, 2008:13). Human capacity development is measured by the literacy level and gross enrolment ratios for primary, secondary and tertiary education. The telecommunication infrastructure considers the number of available PCs, the number of fixed telephone lines, mobile phone subscription, Internet users, the number of citizens with access to TV and the online population (Bouaziz, 2008:16).

5.4.2.3 The MAREVA Framework

The French MAREVA framework is the e-Government measurement methodology developed by Adele (*Agence pour le Développement de l'Administration Electronique*) which translates into 'Electronic Administration Development Agency'. This framework is mostly utilised in huge e-Government projects to ensure quality project management styles are employed. Table 5.1 shows the major constructs of the MAREVA framework.

Table 5.1: The French MAREVA measurement methodology.

Profitability for the state	Internal benefits for public administrations	Externalities for users	Necessity of the project	Risk of the project
Productivity gains – More Full Time Employees – Tasks elimination – Ergonomics improvement – Faster search: database	**Better work place for public sector employees** – Job content improvement – Working conditions improvement	**Quality Improvements** – Simpler services – Personalisation – New integrated services – Multi-channel delivery	**Necessity for Adele** – Cross infrastructure for Adele – Cross project referral system	**Project risk**
Efficiency Gains – Reduction of errors – Optimised receipt of documents – Improved decision-making	**Improvement of Efficiency of Public Service** – Support reorganisation – Improved planning – Improved and faster decision-making – Elimination of paper archives.	**Info Society Promotion** – Benefits for work and civic life – Benefits ICT skills – Benefits of groups at risk – Benefits for social cohesion – Benefits to democratic participation	**External Necessity** – Respond to regulatory requirement – respond to political obligation	**Technical Risk**
Accruing Economies – Avoid costs – Economies of scale	**Support to decentralisation** – Empowerment of local communities – Mutualised infrastructure for communities	**Number of users affected**	**Public Service Efficiency Necessity** – Avoid other expenses – simplify complex area	**Legal Risk**
Increased Revenue Collection	-	**Time/Money saved**	-	**Deployment Risk**
Increased Revenue	-	-	-	-

The MAREVA framework is an example of a tailored framework which has been applied in France utilising generic measurements elements (such as effectiveness, efficiency, and democracy) as outlined by the European Commission. These generic measurement elements are tailor-made to qualitatively and quantitatively conform to aspirations to measure impacts against measurable targets. These measurements can generally refer to standard calculations of ROI using indicators such as 'Breakeven point', 'IRR', and 'Recurring Gain from the project'. The MAREVA framework also enables the assessment of value using strategic indicators and alignment to overall organisational goals (as shown in Table 4.2), economic justification and consideration of internal benefits to users, the general measurements of the necessity of the project, and project monitoring and evaluation.

From its launch in 2005, MAREVA has been rolled out in over 100 e-Government initiatives and 10 French Ministries and other public entities. The general benefits for utilising the MAREVA framework are as follows:

1. Provides an innovative approach for value definition of a project by integrating the ROI analysis, public sector concerns around productivity, and impacts on the general citizenry.
2. Provides itself as a unique method to enable evaluable of different project (infrastructure projects, internal transformation projects, e-Services) in the public sector frameworks.
3. Helps facilitate discussion between project team members, decision-makers and the contractors.
4. Helps identify project risks and therefore enables project teams to concentrate on concrete objectives and deliverables.

The MAREVA framework utilises a pragmatic approach to measuring the e-Readiness of a given area and the potential to successfully adopt e-Government.

5.4.2.4 The UK Criminal Justice IT Benefits Management Framework

Any e-Government implementation can be justified by the anticipated benefits that such an application is going to offer. With the motivation of the fact that 60%-70% of IT projects under-deliver on projects (Hossan et al., 2006:3; Kumar et al., 2007:64), the UK Criminal Justice IT (CJIT) came up with a Benefits Management framework which aligns how different anticipated benefits of IT projects should be managed to retrieve maximum value of such IT projects. The CJIT posits that prior to the commencement of any IT project or in prioritising the portfolio of initiatives each program is evaluated against its 'attractiveness' and 'achievability'. A program that scores above the pre-defined minimum on these scores is taken forward for implementation. Some of the key benefits management issues are presented in Figure 5.1 below.

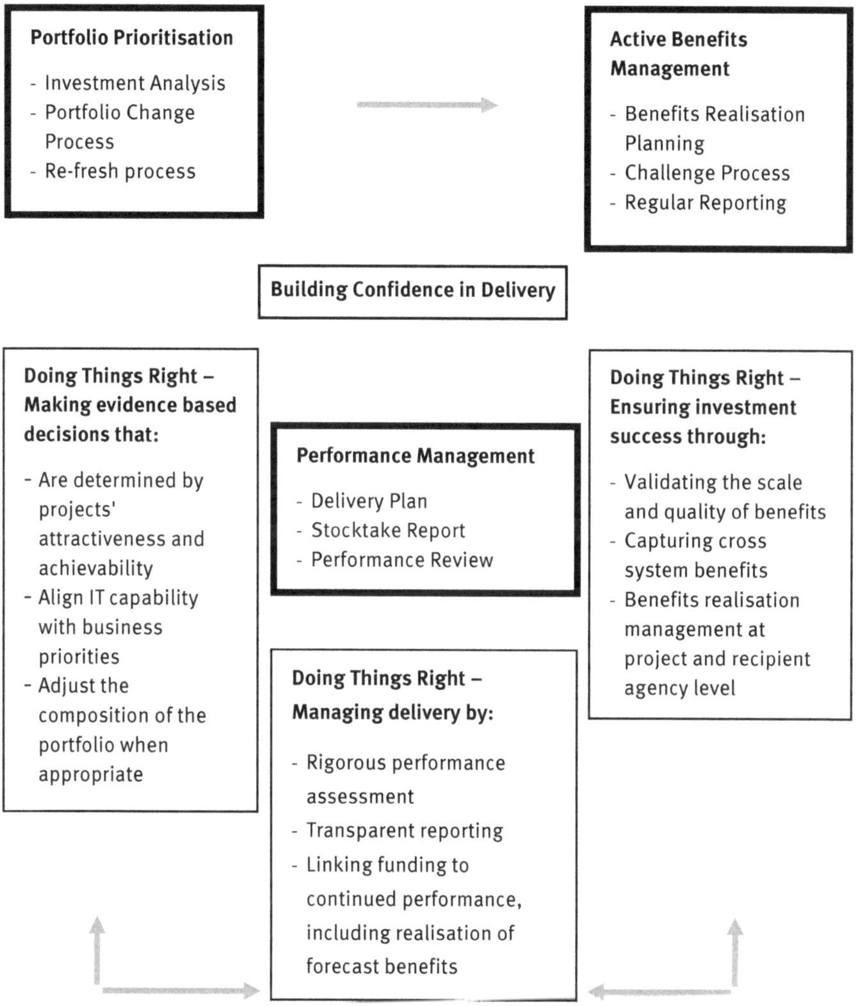

Figure 5.1: The CJIT Benefits Management framework (Adapted from Jenner, 2005:11).

For those projects that finally go into implementation, they go through an Active Benefits Management (ABM) phase which classifies each individual benefit either as efficient (cost or time saving) or effective.

5.4.2.5 Accenture e-Government Leadership Survey Framework

With a limited focus of just over 20 countries, Accenture has carried out e-Government leadership surveys since 2000 until 2004. Accenture considers service maturity (breadth and depth of e-Service delivery) and delivery maturity (Customer Relationship Management (CRM) support to end users). Service maturity is a function of the number of public services offered online whereas delivery maturity is the level of sophistication of such services (Accenture, 2004).

5.4.2.6 CPP-BU Global e-Government Rankings Series

In 2001, the Centre for Public Policy of the Brown University (CPP-BU) commenced surveys of national government websites, with over 1200 websites surveyed each year (West 2003; West 2004). The survey mainly focuses on online security, online services, disability access, foreign language access, advertisement and user fees, and public outreach.

CPP-BU provides a fairly simple methodology for ranking countries. It awards a certain number of points (for instance 4 points in the 2004 survey) for the presence of 18 specific features: publications, databases, audio clips, video clips, foreign language support, absence of adverts, absence of premium fees, absence of user fees, disability access, privacy policy statements, security policies statements, digital signature on transactions, options to pay through credit cards, e-mail contact information, areas to post comments, options for e-mail updates, options for website personalisation and Personal Digital Assistance (PDA) accessibility. Countries are further awarded a point for each executable service provided online (up to the maximum of 28 points). The maximum obtainable score is 100.

5.4.2.7 Balanced Scorecard (BSC) Theory

Kaplan and Norton (Kaplan & Norton, 1992:71–79; Wright, Smith, Jesse & Stupeck, 1999:4–41) developed the BSC to link a firm's strategic objectives to performance measurements. The BSC presents a theory that suggests measurements that guide a firm towards its strategic objectives; integrates measures of the causal determinants of financial outcomes; and concentrates on operation of business processes to permit a more accurate capture of the benefits that result from investments in IT.

The BSC concentrates on four performance perspectives: customer, financial, internal business process, and the learning and growth perspective. In the information systems perspective, the BSC can be used as a balanced scorecard that includes business-value measurement dimension, user orientation, internal-process, and a future e-Readiness dimension. The BSC was meant for many measurement perspectives. Specifically, the BSC was meant for the following: identify the performance drivers affecting electronic service delivery; establish a set of cause-and-effect relationships amongst the identified drivers; and set up explicit linkage to financials ultimate success indicators.

Other researchers such as Martinsons, Davison and Tse (1999:73) have also suggested an adaptation of the Kaplan and Norton BSC approach for the measurement of organisational performance related to information system. Lawson-Body and Miller (2006:76) extended the balanced score card (basing on previous efforts by Huang and Hu, 2004:59) to seek to address how the usability and interactivity aspects of government portals impacts on electronic service delivery performance. They also sought to find out what the benefits of usability and interactivity of Web portals are to the government agencies and citizens. In their study, they found out that usability and interactivity of Web portals can lead to more efficient and effective internal business processes through improved e-Service delivery capability, and re-inventing and re-engineering processes. Lawson-Body and Miller (2006:76) further probed the aligning strategies of usability and interactivity of Web portals with overall public service delivery platforms. Their study was made possible with the use of the BSC which proved useful in identifying the strategic impacts of usability and interactivity of Web portals on e-Government service delivery performance.

Basing on G2G and G2C applications, Lawson-Body and Miller (2006) further proposed a framework to match potential benefits of usability and interactivity of Web portals with government service delivery strategy using four dimensions: innovation and learning, internal business process, customer, and financial. Still, some other authors such as Wright et al., (1999:14–19) and Huang and Hu (2004:64–65) have examined the integration of IT or Web services with the BSC. The BSC can also be used to assess the public value of IT, unlike concentrating much on the business value of IT (Maio, 2003). The public value of IT can be articulated in terms of measures of how IT related investments, over time, contribute towards improved constituent service level, operational efficiency and political returns.

5.4.2.8 The European Union e-Government Economic Project Framework

Seeking to establish the rationale and feasibility of e-Government implementation in Europe, the European Union Commission launched the e-Government Economic (eGEP) project in 2005. The major aim of eGEP was to formulate an e-Government assessment framework that would analyse expenditure trends and funding of online government initiatives. This was done to assist agencies in individual European countries in developing transparent and auditable assessment of e-Government interventions.

The eGEP framework assesses the demand and value side of e-Government interventions. The demand side focuses on the end user whereas the value side concentrates on measuring the benefits and costs, social and governance implications, and other intangible benefits and risks. The goal of the eGEP measurement framework was to act as a general measurement framework rooted in pre-existing measurement methods, mandated to assess the impact of e-Government services in different countries. It is based on the following frameworks: The Danish e-Government Signposts methodology; the French MAREVA methodology; the German WiBe 4.0 methodology; the Dutch Monitor: Multiple Use of Information; and the UK business case methodology. Figure 5.2 below shows the eGEP measurement framework model.

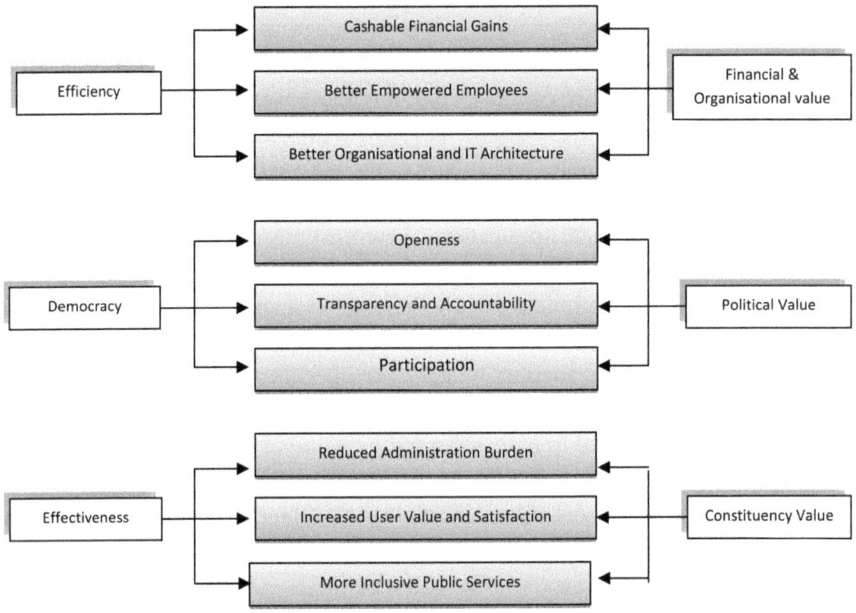

Figure 5.2: The eGEP measurement framework model (adapted from: EU Report (2007:11).

The eGEP framework measures both the quantitative and the qualitative impacts of e-Government interventions and services. Further, it produces a multi-dimensional assessment of potential and perceived public value of e-Government implementation.

5.4.2.9 Standard Cost Model

The Standard Cost Model (SCM) employs systematic analysis to simplify registration and lower registration burden for any intervention such as the introduction of the regulatory frameworks for e-Government. As shown in Figure 5.3, this method breaks down regulation into a range of manageable and measurable components including information obligation, data requirements and administrative activities. Cost parameters such as time, quantity, and price are also defined and measured.

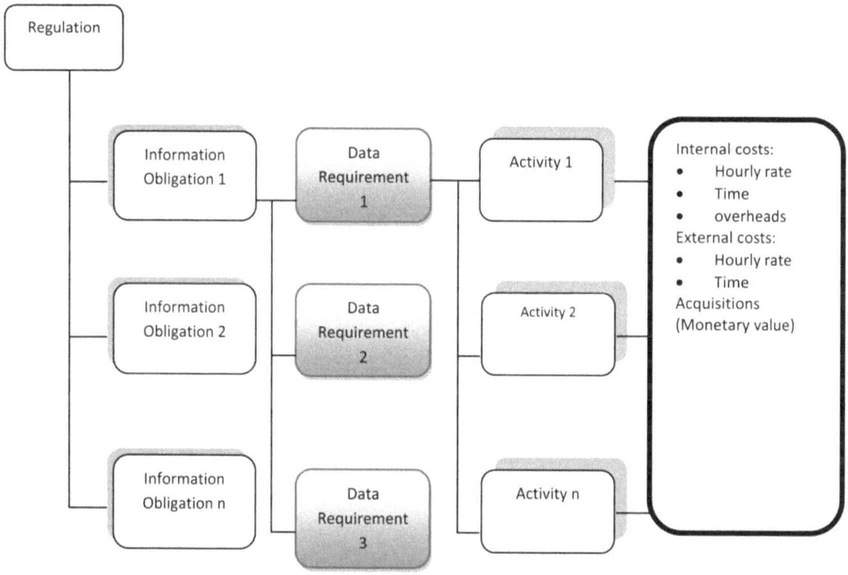

Figure 5.3: Activities that inform the Cost of Administrative Burden (adapted from: SCM, 2005:8).

The overall costs of the activities that form the SCM are represented in the formula below:

$$Activity\ Costs = Price \times Quantity = (tariff \times time) \times (population \times frequency)$$

Generally, the lower the activity cost, the more economic any administrative activity is. This tool can be used in the monitoring of e-Government activities from an economics point of view.

The models and assessment frameworks presented in this section detail how the different metrics and concepts discussed in the sections above can be used in practical assessment of e-Government interventions. These different frameworks have been used in different countries but initially designed using specified local conditions. This is disadvantageous and not conceptually correct because the local conditions of different areas may be different. This approach is not used in this study because the major objective here is to understand the factors that influence adoption of e-Government and then incorporate these factors in a conceptual model.

Despite the e-Government assessment frameworks discussed above, there are other frameworks that have been used in some places with specific targets. Reviewing these frameworks is important to inform the direction that e-Government research should take and to understand what factors to consider when designing an e-Government assessment model.

5.5 Other e-Government Measurement Frameworks

Other frameworks for evaluating the benefits of overall ICT investments have been suggested. Accenture adapted the principles of Shareholder Value Analysis (SVA) to justify IT investments in the public sector. SVA probes the hard-to-measure benefits such as transparency and competitiveness and translates them in capturing the value for anticipated ICT investments.

The 2004 Deloitte's Citizen Advantage model (CAM) utilises the bottom-up approach to evaluate the overall benefits of e-Government applications to socio-economic competitiveness (Deloitte, 2004). For example, if it is assumed that e-Government promotes an efficient public service delivery system in terms of reduction in time in citizen/business-government transactions, then the Citizen Advantage measures this time in financial terms and does some aggregation analysis across the economy.

In 2009, the Partnership on Measuring ICT for Development (2009) came up with a list of core e-Government indicators. These indicators have correspondingly been used to measure the e-Government readiness of any particular area. Table 5.2 shows the sets of these e-Government indicators. Most of these core e-Government development indicators have been utilised as input in the design of the questionnaire that is used in this study.

Table 5.2: Task Group on e-Government of the Partnership on Measuring ICT for Development – draft list of core e-Government indicators.

	General Indicators
EG1	Percent of staff in government institutions with a computer, disaggregated by gender
EG2	Percent of staff in government institutions with Internet access at the office, disaggregated by gender
EG3	Percent of government institutions with websites and/or databases
EG4	Percent of government institutions with corporate networks (LAN, Intranet, extranet))
EG5	Percentage of government institutions offering mobile phone technology accessible platforms
EG6	Percent of ICT personnel in government institutions, disaggregated by gender
EG7	Number of intrusions and hacking of networks and websites of government institutions
EG8	Percentage of spam messages per total e-mail messages received
EG9	Percentage of expenditure on ICT per total expenditure of government institutions
EG10	Percentage of ICT budget spent on institutional capacity-building and human resources development
EG11	Percentage of government institutions with access to the Internet by type of access (narrowband, fixed broadband, mobile broadband)
	Usage Indicators
EG12	Percent of open source software vis-à-vis proprietary
EG13	Percent and type of applications used, for example, word processing, accounting, data base, website
EG14	Percent of staff in government institutions who are trained on the use of ICTs, disaggregated by gender
	Transformation Indicators
EG15	Percent of government institutions providing services online and type of services; e.g. retrieval and printing of online forms, use of interactive online forms, online bids, payment of bills, tax filling applications, company registration, car registration, voting, public grievance systems, online feedback
EG16	Percent of requests processed using ICTs in respect of overall number of requests
EG17	Percent of requests processed online in relation to overall number of requests processed using ICTs
EG18	Degree of satisfaction of e-Government service users, disaggregated by gender

(Adapted from: UN e-Government Survey, 2010:94)

This list of indicators can be used to measure e-Government in diverse environments especially in the developing world. It is up to the people involved to either utilise all the indicators outlined in Table 5.2 or only utilize some of them.

5.6 Shortcomings of Some of the e-Government Assessment Frameworks

Azab et al., (2009:11–28) outline some of the shortcomings of e-Government development frameworks generally. The major outcome of their discussion corresponds with Peters, Janssen and Engers, (2004:481–482), and Hu et al., (2005:532–533), who provide inventory of shortcomings with regard to e-Government frameworks. It is anticipated that to overcome the different shortcomings visible in different e-Government frameworks, the design of e-Government frameworks should try as much as possible to avoid the following design errors:

- Focusing only on measuring the quantifiable factors of e-Government results into the masking of other inherent factors that may be at the center of determining the pace at which e-Government develops.
- Restricting assessment to factors that only affect e-Government; and taking a generic approach of investigating external factors such as availability of appropriate ICT infrastructures and competent human resource base.
- Focusing only on back office or e-Administration (such as Bertelsmann Foundation (2002)) and limiting assessments only on developed countries and excluding developing countries limits the ability of a given assessment framework to identify context-specific e-Government development factors.
- Approaching e-Government assessment at a national level rather than considering the micro level (such as a public organisation, community or individual level) of e-Government adoption may give inaccurate adoption assessment results.
- Measuring only the public websites in a bid to evaluate e-Service delivery. This completely leaves out the private businesses' website therefore limiting the correctness of e-Government perception.

Most of the e-Government frameworks rely on one of the following methodologies of obtaining information: citizen's feedback, secondary or baseline data, or feedback from policymakers of e-Government. Further, most of these models do not evaluate e-Government from the framework of employees to find their perceptions on e-Government benefits and usability, and most do not investigate the degree of awareness and employees' belief in e-Government viability.

In conclusion, the developed e-Readiness and e-Government Readiness assessment frameworks can only be used as the start point for developing local-context sensitive (context-aware) assessment models.

5.7 E-Government Assessment Metrics and Tools

In measuring the actual e-Government penetration, there are many indices that are collectively put together to determine the e-Government readiness basing on the fact that there are many factors that impact on e-Government given its multi-dimensional nature. The combinations of these tools and metrics very much depends on the framework that is currently in use. The noticeable limitation is that these metrics and tools use global concepts as the ones discussed above.

5.7.1 Web Measure Index

The Web Measure Index is based upon a five-stage model, and builds upon the previous level of sophistication, of a state's online presence. For the countries which have established an online presence, the model defines stages of e-Readiness according to a scale of progressively sophisticated citizen e-Services. The Web measure assessment model does not assess the quality of services by design. As such, any discretionary ratings are eliminated from the quantitative Web measure and the e-Government readiness indices minimising the bias inherent in combining qualitative assessments with quantitative measures (UN e-Government Report, 2003:13).

5.7.2 Telecommunications Infrastructure Index

The Telecommunications Infrastructure Index is based on basic infrastructural indicators which define a country's ICT infrastructure capacity. Some of the measurements that are used to determine this index are: PC's/1000 persons; Internet users/1000 persons; telephone lines/1000 persons; online population; mobile phones/1000 persons; and TV's/1000 persons (Potnis & Pardo, 2008).

5.7.3 Human Capital Index

The Human Capital Index mostly relies on the UNDP 'Education Index' which is a composite of the adult literacy rate and the combined primary, secondary and tertiary gross enrolment ratio (Mabila et al., 2010:6). Weighting of this index has a two third weight allocated to adult literacy and one third to gross enrolment ratio. The measurement of available human capital is cardinal to e-Government's success because a requisite human resource base is vital to developing context-aware e-Government applications and developing context-aware ICT management strategies.

5.7.4 E-Participation Index

The United Nations Public Administration Network (UNPAN) proposed the 'e-Participation' index which generally intended to measure the level of e-Access. Specifically, the e-Participation Index assesses the quality, usefulness and relevancy of the information and services provided by government and the willingness of countries to engage citizens in public policy making through the use of e-Government programs. The major goal of the e-Participation index is to assess the willingness of the general public in participating in the policy and related national decision-making establishments (Potnis & Pardo, 2008). The index is divided into three sections, namely, E-Information, e-Consultation and e-Decision-making across six general economic and social sectors. These three sections are the qualitative equivalent of the quantitative Web measure Index discussed in Section 5.7.1 above. Using the e-Participation Index, each country is assessed using a scale of 0 to 4 which are then later standardized.

5.7.5 E-Government Index

The World Markets Research Centre (WMRC) and Brown University proposed the e-Government Index in a survey of composite indices measuring country performance on ICT uptake in 2006. The index measures how appropriate governments deliver information over online platforms and media to its citizens and businesses (West, 2006).

A scale of 0 (having none of prescribed features, no portal or online services) to 100 (having all the prescribed e-Government website features and a majority of basic online services) is assigned to a country's website depending on what information is available on it and its interactivity (Potnis & Pardo, 2008). Points of assessment are: availability of contact information, databases, portals, government publications, links to other sites, audio and video clips, foreign language and disability access, allowing digital signatures on electronic transactions, areas where users can post comments, search capabilities, and option for e-mail updates.

5.7.6 E-Government Readiness Index

UNPAN proposed the e-Government Readiness Index as a composite measure of the capacity and willingness of countries to use e-Government for ICT-driven development (ICT4D). According to Potnis and Pardo, (2008), this index ranks the governments' interventions in developing e-Government with reference to their size, ICT infrastructure availability and ICT penetration, and the level of education of the general citizenry and ICT skill development. The index is used to asses over 50,000 features of e-Government websites in over 190 countries. The e-Government Readiness Index averages the abovementioned Web Measure Index, the Telecommunications Infrastructure Index and the Human Capital Index using a scale of 0 (lowest) to 1.0 (highest).

5.7.7 E-Government Measurement Systems

E-Government is directly measured by assessing the e-Government readiness of a particular area. Al-Omari and Al-Omari (2006:841–845) have outlined the general aspects of e-Government readiness metrics, which reflect the multi-dimensionality of e-Government applications. This includes leadership, strategic position, cross-coordination of initiatives and know-how, and the technology strategy which aims to take vision to reality.

5.7.8 Organisational Readiness Assessment

For e-Government to thrive, it is important that the overall organisational arrangement should be ready to adopt the utilisation of technology in its business value chains (Kitaw, 2006:14). Government organisations in most of the cases are structured in a bureaucratic style demanding users to study these structures before any services can be accessed from them. Most of these bureaucratic arrangements introduce delays in processing any transactions of the business setup of the government; have complex procedures in place resulting in duplication of work and efforts and also have data and process redundancy. It is anticipated that these unwarranted characteristics of the government institutional arrangement creates barriers between the government and its constituents (individuals and businesses) and can only be brokered with appropriate usage of ICTs. This calls for automation of government business processes incorporating a defined business re-engineering process and organisational hierarchy change management process. The overall organisational readiness is assessed by considering the 'mean' obtained from the overall business process assessment and the organisational hierarchical structure assessment (Kitaw, 2006:14).

5.7.9 Business Processes Assessment

According to Kitaw, (2006:14) the business process assessment mechanism is a set of guidelines to assess the different business processes in an environment. The following are the different metrics that are used in business process assessment: process electronic delivery; process automation; average number of journeys to receive the service; average time to complete the service delivery; and the average number of stations visited by the citizen to complete the service. The bottleneck for this assessment is the process flow which is set by high level management and domain experts to facilitate business process applications. The assessment centres on the availability of the different laws that govern and guide process flow execution and any management aspects such as process improvement. An environment ready for e-Government implementation is one that can accommodate easier process flow improvement paradigms.

5.7.10 Organisation Hierarchal Structure

An organisation that has enveloped process improvement will certainly need to also align its organisational structure to the new anticipated hierarchical structure, including the redefining of the new roles of employees and that of the organisation itself (Kitaw, 2006:14). The organisational structure also encompasses the laws that govern the organisation. Assessment of the organisational hierarchical structure also involves investing the possibility of implementing process-technical integration and the availability of the technical infrastructure that should support that integration.

5.7.11 Leadership and Governance Readiness Assessment

In part, the success of e-Government implementation partly depends on the political will and the leadership of all the e-Government initiatives. Leadership is a vital component of the body responsible to maintain and coordinate the rules guiding e-Government initiatives, standards and agreements that define intra-relationships amongst different e-Government stakeholders. It is evident from different endeavours of e-Government implementations (as detailed in Chapter 3) that it cannot succeed without due commitment from the leadership hierarchies, and does not merely involve drafting of laws and policies for e-Government implementation. E-Government success demands coordinated efforts from multiple fronts from different stakeholders (such as public officers, political leaders, and individuals) involved in its implementation.

Leadership and governance readiness assessments do not merely look for the availability of leadership in environments where e-Government is implemented but also look to determine the following metrics:

- Availability of re-engineered government business processes in individual agencies and across government departments.
- Existence of a Service Manager with end-to-end responsibility for service delivery.
- Existence of a Service Level Agreement (SLA) which evaluates the time, quality and cost, and evaluates customer service satisfactory.
- Existence of new policies which define the functional and non-functional requirements of e-Government applications.
- Existence of business continuity planning and content management processes.

5.7.12 Customer Readiness

E-Government services are directed towards all the consumers of the public service delivery systems such as businesses and the general citizenry. As discussed earlier in this book, e-Government is also directed towards other government departments in the G2G platform. It is worth noting that these different consumers of e-Government may be handicapped due to physical, geographical, cultural or socio-economic factors and therefore may not be able to fully amass the opportunities brought about by e-Government.

According to Al-Omari (2006:846), customer readiness revolves around accessibility, culture, and socio-economic status of the diverse groups. The major motivational factors to either participate or hold back from e-Government participation are accessibility and trust concerns. Accessibility of e-Government content depends on the way the content is displayed. Considerations include aspects such as the following:

- Are the visually impaired person taken into consideration;
- Is the customer colour blind; how well will people with low ICT skills be able to participate; and what language(s) is used for content presentation?
- Trust depends on how reliable e-Government information channels are;
- Are the necessary encryption standards in place that envelop e-Government applications, and what different legal frameworks are in place to protect the user in the e-Government environment?

By considering the above listed aspects of different e-Government consumers and other factors not outlined above, it becomes possible that appropriate and responsive e-government solutions can be put in place.

5.8 Heuristic e-Government Assessment Framework

Diverse approaches have been utilised to assess e-Government in different contexts the world over. Despite this, one thing is clear – there is no global assessment model that can be utilised to assess e-Government in the heterogeneous environments. This, therefore, calls for e-Government designers, researchers and practitioners to work towards developing frameworks that outline the globally agreed upon principles and entities. The general principles can be gotten from both developing and developed countries that have achieved a lot in as far as e-Government implementation is concerned. For example, reference can be made to countries such as Estonia in the middle income range which have accomplished better results in evaluation and implementation of e-Government policies than some countries with higher incomes (Stanimirovic & Vintar, 2013). It is also worth noting that most of the existing e-Government assessment models use website analysis (front office) which may not be enough to ensure comprehensive evaluation of e-Government interventions (Stanimirovic & Vintar, 2013).

Generally, the first point of call is that e-Government design should be informed by clearly defined principles, guidelines, and an overall understanding of the assessment process. In this regard, one needs to understand that, given its multi-dimensional nature, e-Government assessment involves, among other things, a tedious process that correlates the projects' achievements against the different goals on which it was designed and the need to check whether the project can be replicated or is sustainable (Gupta & Vasishta, 2008). As aforementioned, since e-Government has multiple stakeholders, its assessment should be done using multi-dimensional perspectives recognising the core entities of the e-Government implementation hierarchy and contextual setting. These different dimensions are as follows:

- Government (ROI, impact on the public service hierarchy, internal business process efficiency (effect on back-end business processes), overall impact with regards to morale or work approach on internal employees, sustainability, development goals, impact on the cost of public service delivery, etc.)
- E-Government consumers – citizens and businesses (impact on the cost of accessing government service, reduce on the time one has to wait before a public service is provided, convenience on the part of the consumer, impact on transparency (accountability, corruption, participation of citizens in the governance value chains and therefore being part-and-parcel of the decision-making infrastructure), convenience in as far as obtaining the service is concerned)
- Funding agency (direct and indirect economic benefits, ROI, business model being utilised, and the immediate or long term impact on the e-Government consumers, business process improvements, impact on the non-economic objectives of governance)
- Public Private Partnerships – (compliance to service levels, ROI, and the business model employed)

Therefore, effervescent e-Government assessment should ensure that most of the interests of the different stakeholders are addressed. In order for the different approaches utilised in designing e-Government implementation frameworks and/or models, it is essential that we review the different e-Government assessment frameworks and models that have been utilised worldwide.

Tavana, Zandi and Katehakis (2013), in a bid to evaluate the level of e-Government readiness at the community level, proposed a hybrid fuzzy model based on the group Analytic Network Process (ANP) and the Technique for Order Preference by Similarity to Ideal Solution (TOPSIS). The TOPSIS model accentuates the inherent complexities in e-Government assessment. Esteves and Joseph (2008) propose the KEeLAN framework which was meant to assess e-Government implementation readiness at both front-office and back-offices. In another contextual setting, Shareef, Ojo and Janowski (2008) proposed a component-based e-readiness assessment framework aimed at developing strategic e-Government planning. This framework comprises the following components: stakeholders (profile and interests of stakeholders), technology (available ICT infrastructure), demand, supply, international context (information such as Millennium Development Goals), national context and local context, enabling environment, perceptions (current understanding of e-Government by the practitioners and key stakeholders to inform design of e-Government interventions). Considering the multi-dimensional nature of e-Government, Iribarren, Concha, Valdes, Solar, Villarroel, Gutiérrez and Vásquez (2008) discussed the capabilities maturity model, developed by the Chilean government with the support of the Universidad Técnica Federico Santa María (UTFSM). This model largely considered the varying organisational contexts in Chile and described ways on how e-Government can thrive. Al-Khouri, Al-Mazrouie and Bommireddy (2010) proposed a model named **T**hrust, **R**esistance **A**nd **N**avigation **S**trategy Form (TRANSFORM). TRANSFORM aims to highlight the following: resistance, coordination issues, budgetary constraints, digital divide, security and privacy concerns, technical issues and inadequate standards, resistance to change, conflicting initiatives. TRANSFORM further highlights the major success areas for e-Government implementation as follows: vision, authority and leadership, demand, Public Private Partnership, human development, marketing and promotion, compliance, and navigation.

Figure 5.4 shows a diagrammatical representation that summarises the different principles that should be considered when designing e-Government assessment frameworks.

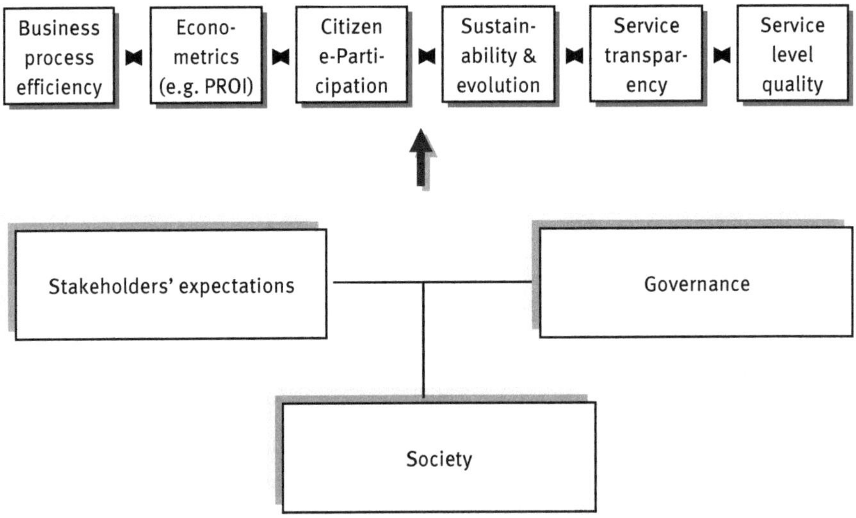

Figure 5.4: Blueprint for Designing e-Government Assessment Frameworks.

Figure 5.4 shows that a robust e-Government assessment framework should consider the needs of the anticipated e-Government stakeholders, the governance establishment and the impact on the anticipated consumers. The inherent characteristics of each of the entities shown in Figure 5.4 pretty much depends on the local contextual characteristics.

5.9 Conclusion and Summary

With e-Government being a multi-dimensional phenomenon depending on multiple entities (as outlined in Chapter 2 and 3), it follows that for e-Government to be successfully measured, there is need to utilise a multi-dimensional approach. This requires using a combination of more than one e-Government assessment framework, tool or indices to ascertain the actual development of e-Government. The measurement of e-Government interventions (and its penetration, adoption, and usage) is useful in many scenarios such as the following:

- Using measurement metrics such as NPV, EVA and IRR, it is possible to measure e-Government development. The financers of e-Government would like to establish whether expected returns on their investments are positive, and whether e-Government implementations culminate into value-added propositions or profits.
- The e-Government development partners would want to establish whether they are using the right approaches in their implementation of e-Government which may lead to either success or failure.
- The government may want to know how effective ICTs are being used to ensure that they appropriately involve citizens in decision-making (e-Participation), how ICTs on government platforms are being used for social-inclusion, how business entities conduct their businesses with the government (such as in e-Procurement), and how these should best be implemented.

Such measurements are very important as they inform the government and other e-Government stakeholders how useful e-Government applications are, help in monitoring and evaluating e-Government intervention, and further help in cost-benefit analysis of e-Government investments. Further, as proliferation of e-Government implementation depends on e-Readiness of an environment, measuring e-Government penetration may also give an indication as to whether a country is ready to participate in the global socio-economic value chains where the medium of interaction is basically ICTs.

This chapter has presented the different e-Government assessment frameworks, tools and indices. These e-Government frameworks incorporate a mix of e-Government tools and metrics discussed immediately after the e-Government frameworks. The chapter discusses the major motivation for e-Government assessments and attempts to answer the following question: 'Why is it necessary to assess e-Government interventions and development status?' Thereafter, the chapter presents some e-Readiness assessment tools. This is because e-Readiness is the starting point of e-Government. Any implementation of e-Government can only be successful if the environment where it is implemented is e-Ready. E-Readiness needs to be assessed, not forgetting that there are certain limitations with regard to assessment tools.

The limitations in the capabilities of the different e-Government assessment frameworks are noted in this chapter. It has been established that most of the e-Government assessment frameworks are generic in nature. In addition, almost all the frameworks have the following limitations:

- Most e-Government assessment frameworks focus on quantifiable factors of e-Government and are mostly result-oriented.
- Measurement tools do not restrict their research boundaries to factors that only affect e-Government, they take a generic approach of investigating external factors such as availability of appropriate ICT infrastructures and human resources which may not have a direct impact on e-Government.
- Assessments such as Bertelsmann Foundation (2002) focus on back office or e-Administration. Assessments are limited to developed countries and exclude developing countries in their assessments altogether.
- Frameworks approach e-Government assessment at a national level rather than also considering the micro level (such as a public organisation, community or individual level) of e-Government adoption. Therefore, there is lack of frameworks targeting the local or individual levels.
- Measurements concentrate on appraising only the public websites in a bid to evaluate e-Service delivery.

The chapter has also discussed the major metrics used in assessment of e-Readiness such as the assessment of human resource base, ICT infrastructure, policies and frameworks, and social, cultural and political environment. However, after a critical look at the measurement capabilities of these tools, it can be inferred that these e-Readiness assessment tools do not take in-depth assessment and analysis of factors that may directly affect e-Government proliferation such as culture and technology acceptance. Further, as can be deduced from the discussions of the different e-Readiness tools, e-Readiness tools and models can potentially be divided into two major categories: those focusing on the availability of basic ICT infrastructure and an environment's capacity and readiness to support meaningful businesses and economic growth; and those focusing on the general citizenry (the society) to benefit from ICTs.

The chapter concludes by discussing the blueprint for designing e-Government assessment frameworks that can be used in any context to measure both the value and development status of e-Government. The said framework can be used to guide e-Government assessments even in multi-cultural and complex e-Government environments.

Chapter 6
E-Government Adoption and Synthesis

6.1 Introduction

In any given context, e-Government cannot thrive if acceptable levels of e-Government readiness are not achieved. E-Government readiness determines the degree of adoption at both the individual and institutional levels. The general conceptualisation of this chapter is that if the anticipated e-Government consumers do not readily accept e-Government, then its value is much likely to be limited and the intended original purpose not met. In order to understand the general factors that influence the adoption and synthesis of ICTs in the public sector delivery value chains and business processes, there is need to employ the theories for explaining technology adoption. In this regard, this chapter devotes a significant portion to highlighting the different technology adoption models/frameworks that exist and subjecting them to a limited meta-physical assessment of their fit in explaining e-Government.

This chapter emphasises the softer side of e-Government design where non-technical issues are going to be thoroughly discussed. Further, the chapter intends to highlight the e-Government adoption models at both the individual and the institutional level.

6.2 Factors Affecting e-Government Adoption

As outlined in the previous chapters of this book, from the many e-Government projects that have been implemented world-over, it is evident that most e-Government projects fail. The high failure rate of the many e-Government projects culminates into substantial loss on the part of the government and other co-operating partners. Therefore, there is need to ensure that very careful thought is given during the design phase where all the multi-dimensional ramifications of e-Government are taken into consideration. The success of e-Government implementation comes about in cases where most of the multi-dimensional factors that aid successful e-Government implementation have been addressed or incorporated into the strategies to aid its implementation and development. Countries (such as South Korea, Canada, USA, Brazil, Singapore, Malaysia, and Mauritius) which have successfully implemented e-Government have well-authored e-Government strategies and implementation plans in place (Davis, 1989; Davis, Bagozzi & Warshaw, 1989; Warkentin et al., 2002:157; Choudrie & Dwivedi, 2004:323; Bwalya

& Healy, 2010:27). With this understanding, other countries such as Singapore, Tanzania and Mauritius have put in place their strategic initiatives in a bid to develop e-Government (Thong-Tee, 2003; Menda, 2005). The current status of e-Government adoption in these countries is slowly gaining a positive ground. With the knowledge that most e-Government implementation strategies fail, this chapter probes what has made e-Government in these countries to succeed and generally, what the different factors that may influence e-Government usage and adoption by ordinary citizens are.

As mentioned earlier, the different factors that influence e-Government adoption regardless of where it is implemented can be divided into individual and organisational factors. Warkentin et al., (2002:161) posit that data security, accessibility and perceived confidentiality greatly influence individual adoption of e-Government. Apart from organisational factors, individual beliefs of citizens have a significant influence on the adoption of e-Government services (Titah & Barki, 2006:31). It is worth noting that different personal factors may directly have an impact on the decision by an individual to either engage or not engage in e-Government applications. The following are some of the different personal factors identified in different studies:

- **Age:** Sciadas (2002:23) suggests that age and adoption are proportionate. In other words, the older a consumer is, the more likely he or she is to engage in e-Government services. This is not always the case as in the context of Saudi Arabia older users were found less likely to engage in e-Government services due to cultural trends or sometimes resistance to change (Baker, Al-Gahtani & Hubona, 2007:353).
- **Gender:** Al-Otaibi and Al-Zahrani (2009:5) suggested that females in Saudi Arabia are expected to adopt e-Oriented services, including e-Government services, more than males due to religious and/or socio-cultural pressures that limit their ability to physically visit government offices (Al-Otaibi & Al-Zahrani, 2009:4). Nevertheless, it is noted that females are almost out of the equation due to cultural barriers and lack of awareness about the existing e-Services (Baker et al., 2007:353).
- **Previous experience:** It was found that experience, where those who already use e-Government services are more likely to do so again. In this case, the mostly cited reason seems to be a higher degree of trust resulting from an increased familiarity with such systems (OECD, 2007).
- **Motivation:** Motivation plays a major role in tailoring adoption of e-Government services. Gefen and Straub (2000:5) argued that there are different levels of motivation between search for information and the firm's intention to engage. A firm whose competence depends on availability of requisite and current information on different aspects of its operation will be more moti-

vated to employ networked ICT platforms so that information is obtained as it is produced. When an organisation is motivated enough to have current information with higher integrity, then it invests into platforms and ensures that it has a well adaptive information infrastructure to achieve universal access to different employees in its business processes. Anandarajan, Igbaria and Anakwe (2002:49) on the other hand, suggested that motivation is determined by other factors such as system usefulness, enjoyment and social pressure.
- **Socio-cultural pressure:** Socio-culture pressure is commonly argued to be a major factor in the adoption of e-government within environments carrying very strong cultural values and social pressures (Al-Gahtani, Hubona & Wang, 2007:681–682; Dwivedi & Weerakkody, 2007:45). For example, Al-Otaibi and Al-Zahrani (2009:7) noted that religious and social issues in the Saudi community motivate the tendency towards electronic work, especially for females.

The influence of the individual factors on e-Government development has also been emphasised in Davis' technology acceptance model of 1989 (discussed in the next section), that individual beliefs such as perceived usefulness (PU) and perceived ease of use (PEOU) have been considered as the dominant factors that affect the intention to adopt or use technology in a business-to-consumer (B2C) model (Warkentin et al., 2002:161). Heeks and Santos (2009:3) posit that adoption of a technology is based on the behaviour of individual actors set within a contextual framework.

In a study aimed at understanding factors that affect e-Government uptake, Al-adawi, Yousafzai and Pallister (2005:2) identified four 'critical' questions in relation to the adoption and encapsulation of e-Government into different socio-economic setups. Their study identified the following questions which guide what should be incorporated into a model for e-Government adoption:
1. How are intentions towards the use of e-Government conceived and to what extent are they related to the actual use of e-Government?
2. To what extent are the intentions to get information and to conduct transactions different from each other?
3. What are the beliefs that influence citizens' propensity to use e-Government and do these beliefs affect their intentions towards the use of e-Government?
4. Are there any perception and adoption differences between segments of citizens on the basis of their technology readiness and demographic characteristics?

In yet a different study, Bélanger and Carter (2008:165–176) analyse the impact of trust and risk perceptions on one's willingness to use e-Government services and develop a model that includes constructs supporting Trust of the Internet (TOI) and the Trust of government (TOG). Their study utilised data from a citizen survey that indicated that the disposition to trust positively affects TOI and TOG.

These different organisational and individual factors affecting e-Government have been taken care by drawing e-Government strategies responsive to the specific needs (Feller, Finnegan & Nilsson, 2010:5). Hu, Chau, Liu Sheng and Tam, (1999:91) advance this argument and posits that the level of any technology acceptance must be measured using three different contexts: the individual, technological, and implementation context. This further translates into the behaviour of an individual's acceptance and usage of technology being influenced by the individual context (characteristics of individual end-users), the technological context (functionality and user-friendliness of the technology), and the implementation context which is the user's professional environment (Chau & Hu, 2002:297–298).

Many studies are in agreement with Warkentin et al.,'s (2002:158) identification of trust as one of the major factors that influence e-Government uptake (Papadopoulou et al., 2010:5; Subbiah & Ibrahim, 2011:445). If trust in e-Government services were to be attained, these two parties (uptake of e-Government and trust) should 'talk' to each other which would later culminate into an easier adoption process of e-Government applications. The importance of trust in e-Government on the part of citizens is a vital component that shapes the intention to participate, adopt or not adopt the different e-Government applications on offer. Many studies have attempted to understand the effect of trust on e-Government adoption (Bélanger & Carter, 2008:165–166; Papadopoulou et al., 2010:5; Hermana & Silfianti, 2011:156; Lee et al., 2011:223; Mohd-Suki & Ramayah, 2011) and have found that it is the cardinal '*enzyme*' to influence e-Government adoption. With regards to e-Government, trust generally depends on the e-Government service, the e-Government system, the government organisation, and the institution-based trust (Papadopoulou et al., 2010:7; Mohd-Suki & Ramayah, 2011). These different factors of trust in e-Government can further be extrapolated to include the following (Papadopoulou et al., 2010:8–9):

- Trust in stored data (data stored in legacy information systems should only be accessed with proper role authentication and authorisation procedures).
- Trust in channel transaction (use of SSL, HTTPS, and PKI encryption).
- Trust in service (ease-of-use); trust in information (publicly available, validated and accurate information); trust in system (update and relevant technology).

- Trust in government organisation (perception of general citizenry on government transparency); and institution-based trust which is based on existence of a strict legal and regulatory framework.

Karunasena and Deng (2010:1) investigated the penetration of e-Government in Sri Lanka, and found that, just as in other emerging countries, the public value of e-Government initiatives is not clear (Kelly, Mulgan & Muers, 2002:3–5; Talbot, 2008:4). Studying the possibility of e-Government penetration by investigating its public value is a new concept which is being widely followed by e-Government practitioners. Several methodologies have been proposed for measuring public value of e-Government implementation. One of these methodologies is the Golubeva (2007) methodology which concentrates on usability, transparency, interactivity, citizens' centricity of e-Services, and level of e-Services development. Another is a multi-dimensional framework proposed by Liu, Derzsi, Raus and Kipp (2008:85) which emphasises the importance of evaluating the e-Government value and the stakeholder satisfaction.

Current research practice suggests that there is an inextricable link between ICTs and socio-economic development and that 'development informatics' can be used to help bridge the digital divide in developing countries (Mutula, 2010). Development Informatics centers on the provision of ICT systems which are relevant to the social setups of the communities. The conceptualisation of 'development informatics' entails that e-Government be looked at as a social development phenomenon which should be hinged into available community infrastructures. It is anticipated that most e-Government strategies will be community-centric so that individual citizens can have sense of ownership of the different e-Government applications.

Apart from the importance of raising awareness and providing knowledge of security measures to citizens, Tassabehji and Elliman (2006:1) carried out a project that focused on finding ways on how information about the security of technology infrastructure can be collated accurately and precisely from citizens in a way to enable them make informed decisions on whether to participate in e-Government transactions or not. From this study, it was ascertained that citizens and businesses taking part in e-Government should be made aware of what security measures are in place to guarantee the safety of their personal or organisational information as they engage in e-Government. This includes explaining to the stakeholders what the hard technological (hardware and software is needed to protect systems and information) and soft management (management and organisational policies, controls, regulations, legislature, human resource management and training) factors have been put in place. In another study conducted earlier, Osterweil, Schweik, Sondheimer and Thomas (2004:64) outlined additional factors that impact on e-Government applications such as service automation. Service automation often involves intricate collaborations between computer systems, government staff, and the citizenry or businesses who are the users and recipients of these services. In addition to service automation, the Government managers and e-Government application developers are faced with the challenge of demonstrating that these applications are error-free so as to increase public confidence and trust (Hermana & Silfianti, 2011:157).

In line with findings of the earlier studies, Zhou and Hu (2008:208) outlined some of the factors that prevent citizens and businesses to completely trust e-Government applications. Some of the identified factors are information interception by unknown users, information tampering, denial of service, system resources stealing, and information faking. In addition, Papadopoulou et al., (2010:7) investigate the different constructs and factors that impact on citizens' trust and adoption of e-Government applications; and identify seven different types of trust in e-Government. As shown by earlier studies discussed in this and previous paragraphs, citizens' trust in e-Government as a whole has always been characterised as critical in legitimising huge investments in e-Government services and as a necessity for its wide adoption and usage.

Because of the complexity of trust in e-Government applications, it is worth noting that in any trust arrangement, there is a dyadic relationship involving two parties, a *trustor*, i.e. the party that trusts (citizens or businesses), and a *trustee* (government), i.e. the party to be trusted (Papadopoulou et al., 2010:2). Ensuring security of e-Government applications and infrastructures is crucial to maintaining trust among stakeholders so as to store, process and exchange information over the e-Government systems (Syamsuddin & Hwang, 2010; Rowley, 2011:57). If the e-Government establishment proves that there are secure channels between the trustor and the trustee so that information and public services are easily accessed, chances of effervescent e-Government development are huge.

In developing any e-Government agenda, there is need to put in place strategies that encourage trust of citizens in the e-Government applications. This is because trust has been identified as one of the most important factors for successful e-Government implementation because once it is present, it is expected that there should be wider engagement and participation of citizens and businesses (Tassabehji, 2005:7). It is worth noting that e-Government strategy is not entirely a national IT plan or policy but should be a separate strategy for social inclusion through e-Government (Sahraoui, 2007:45). As mentioned above, effective e-Government should find a balance between technological and community-centric e-Government approaches. Salman (2010:6) has articulated the importance of responsive and favourable ICT policy in encouraging the proliferation of e-Government initiatives. The ICT policy should delineate 'the role of private sector, Civil Society Organisations (CSOs) and Government and provide a road map for harnessing the ICT for addressing the development problems being faced by the country' (Joseph, 2002:12).

Having outlined different factors that affect e-Government adoption and development, different researchers and practitioners have come up with models to mimic the adoption trajectory of different technologies introduced for the first time to different people in different areas. It is understood that since the major platform of e-Government is ICTs, these different models mimic technology adoption are relevant to show the likelihood trajectory of adoption trends in e-Government.

6.3 E-Government Adoption Models

There are many factors that may affect adoption of a technology by individuals as outlined in the previous section. The different technology adoption models presented in literature define or mimic the behaviour of individuals when a new technology is first introduced to them to the extent that they may accept, reject or remain neutral about it (Lin et al., 2011:271; Shareef et al., 2011:18; Lee et al., 2011:226). Appropriate reference to and use of e-Government adoption models may aid policy makers and development partners in authoring interventions or drafting strategies that may transcend into successful implementation of e-Government applications (Bwalya & Healy, 2010:24).

The discussion of technology adoption models is very important as it helps in identifying the different factors that affect adoption and use of a new technology. These discussions may help in the understanding of the current adoption status of the limited e-Government applications in the developing world and decipher why this is so. Further, the discussions are important because they help shed some light on the design of e-Government adoption strategies and provide pointers on how these strategies can be modified to sustainable and meaningful encourage e-Government development. Drawing of well-informed e-Government strategies is a first step in the right direction for successful e-Government implementation.

The following sub-sections discuss the different technology adoption models that have been identified or utilised in different studies worldwide. These different models may shed some light on the common factors that influence adoption of e-Government regardless of location where it is implemented.

6.3.1 Innovation Diffusion Theory (IDT)

The Innovation Diffusion Theory (IDT), originates from Rogers (1962), and aims to explain how innovations diffuse or get adopted by the wider society and how the individual and organisational context of any environment accepts new innovations especially in the realm of new technology (Wonglimpiyarat & Yuberk, 2005:414; Zhang, Wen, Li, Fu & Cui, 2010:1428). Rogers (1962) puts a demarcation on the different meanings of 'diffusion' and 'adoption'. He views a diffusion process as one that occurs within a society or in a group; and adoption processes as those related to individuals. The IDT also notes that technological innovation is communicated over time amongst different members of a social system or grouping. The IDT further identifies the following five characteristics as being determinants to the success of a technology: compatibility, complexity, trialability, observability, and relative advantage.

There are many studies that have been conducted to test the pattern and rate of technological adoption in different areas (Mahajan, Muller & Bass, 1990:2; Rodger, Pendharkar & Bhatt, 1996:1; Zhang et al., 2010:1428). Not only has IDT been used to aid explanation of adoption and diffusion of technology-centric innovations but it has also been used to explain the assimilation and encapsulation of technology in multiple fields of study including health care (Sanson-Fisher, 2004:1–2), education (Wilson & Stacey, 2003:2), and e-Business (Zhu et al., 2006:1558).

Further, some researchers have opted to investigate the role of single factors such as social network structure (Liu, Madhavan & Sudharshan, 2005:242), gender (Ilie, Slyke, Green & Lou, 2005:13), and culture (Zhu et al., 2006:1562) in the adoption process of various technologies. Despite the IDT being one of the first major adoption models and having enjoyed wider usage as a reference point in many studies, it has still attracted critical views on its effectiveness (Lytinen & Damsgaard, 2001:2). Despite this being the case, it has continued inspiring many studies focusing on adoption of technology (Centrone, Goia & Salinelli, 2007:249; Panuwatwanich, Stewart & Mohamed, 2009:790; Hung, Chou & Dong, 2011:317; Verdolini & Galeotti, 2011:119–122).

6.3.2 Theory of Reasoned Action (TRA)

Developed by Martin Fishbein and Icek Ajzen in 1975, the Theory of Reasoned Action (TRA) is aimed at organising and integrating research concentrating on attitude of individuals into a systematic theoretical orientation. The emphasis of TRA is to probe the attitudes, beliefs, intention, behaviour, and subjective norms thereby unearthing the different distinctions and relations amongst these variables. Combined together, these concepts culminate into a model that predicts the overall behavioural intention and the actual behaviour towards an innovation or technology that has been just introduced.

Figure 6.1 shows that the actual individual's behaviour (such as the acceptance or rejection of a technology) is dependent on one's intention to perform the behaviour. Further, this intention is concurrently influenced both by the individual's attitude and subjective norm. The subjective norm points to the fact that the way a person behaves is to a lesser or greater extent influenced or susceptible to what other people expect of one's behavioural pattern (Fishbein & Ajzen, 1975).

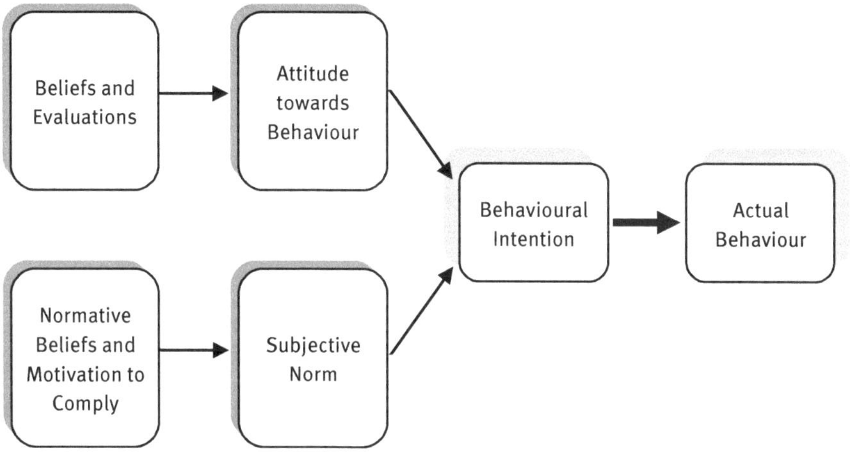

Figure 6.1: The TRA Model (Adapted from: Fishbein & Ajzen, 1975).

The TRA model is employed in the following situations: prediction of human choices in situations as diverse as acceptance of expert systems (Liker & Sindi, 1997:148), fast food restaurant consumption (Bagozzi, Wong, Abe, & Bergami, 2000:98), and teen sexual behaviour (Gillmore, Archibald, Morrison, Wilsdon, Wells, Hoppe, Nahom & Murowchick, 2002:885). Hansen, Jensen and Solgaard (2004) and Wu (2003:539–550) have also utilised the TRA in their respective studies for predicting online grocery buying intention. The late 1980s saw TRA being succeeded by the Theory of Planned Behaviour (TPB) of Ajzen (1988; 1991). In this model, it is ascertained that the behaviour of an individual when a new technology has been introduced to him/her is not 100% voluntary. This results into perceived behavioural control to be added to the original TRA model

6.3.3 Theory of Planned Behaviour (TPB)

Introduced by Ajzen (1988), TPB was a direct outcome of the modification of the TRA. The schematic representation of the TPB is shown in Figure 6.2.

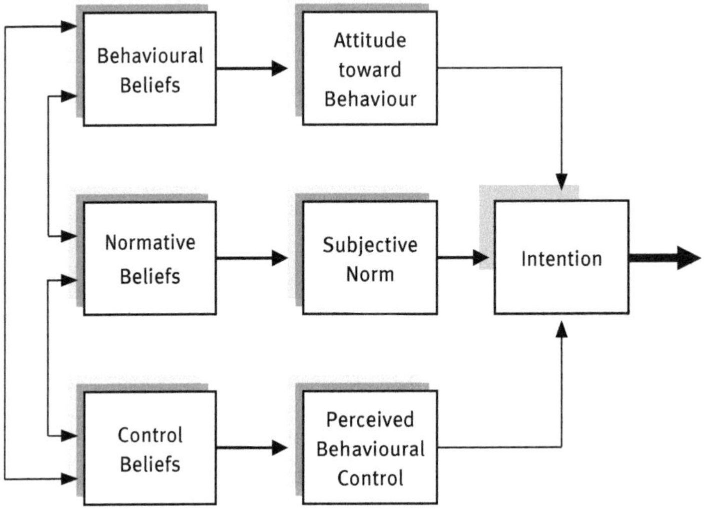

Figure 6.2: TPB Model (Adapted from: Ajzen, 1991).

TPB's usage extends the original usage of TRA to include such disciplines as environmental engineering (Flannery & May, 2000:644), computers (Workman, 2005:211–231), business (De Cannière, De Pelsmacker & Geuens, 2009:7) medical science (Andrykowski, Beacham, Schmidt & Harper, 2006:759), and traffic planning (Bamberg, 2006:820–821).

In essence, the TRA and IDT are basically foundational technology adoption models which influence the emergence of other models. One of the prominent models based on the understanding of the TRA and IDT is the technology acceptance model (TAM) developed by Davis in 1989.

6.3.4 Technology Acceptance Model (TAM)

The TAM adapts the social psychology theory or reasoned action which aims to model user acceptance of information technologies. The major constructs considered by the TAM are the 'Perceived ease of Use' (PEOU) and the 'Perceived Usefulness' (PU). PU is the extent to which a person considers and believes that the use of an information system will enhance task performance, whereas PEOU is the degree to which a person believes a system will be free of effort to a large or lesser extent (Venkatesh, Moris & Davis, 2003:438; Saadé & Kira, 2007:1190; Shen & Chiou, 2010:43). Across studies, PU is referred to as the most important determinant for a person's engagement in the utilisation of a technology (Venkatesh & Davis, 1996; Venkatesh et al., 2003:427; Horst et al., 2007:1843).

Figure 6.3 below presents the diagrammatical view of the TAM showing all the attributes responsible for determining a person's behavioural intention to use a system.

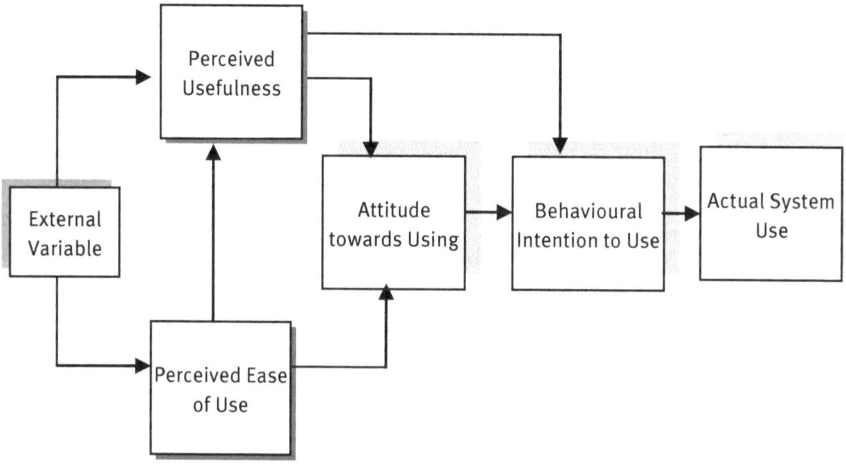

Figure 6.3: Technology Acceptance Model (Adapted from: Ajzen, 1991).

The TAM has found its use range from diverse applications from cellular telephone adoption (Kwon, 2000:1), online consumer behaviour (Koufaris, 2002:205), Personal Digital Assistant (PDA) usage (Liang, Xue & Byrd, 2003:373), electronic commerce (Pavlou, 2003:103), and World Wide Web (Dishaw & Strong, 1999:9–10; Lederer, Maupin, Sena & Zhuang, 2000:269; Venkatesh & Davis, 2000:187; Saade & Bahli, 2005:317). Because of its wide usage, many information technology/systems researchers use the TAM to measure the numerous aspects of Information Systems (IS) uptake (Gefen & Straub 1997:391; Straub, Keil & Brenner, 1997:1) as evidenced in leading Information Systems (IS) journals for the period from 1980 to 2001 (Legris, Ingham & Collerette, 2003:193). TAM's usage of PU and PEOU varies depending on the local and cultural context. It has been found that its prediction prowess is higher in the West with 45%-70% accuracy levels than in the East where it is 10%-35% accurate in most of the cases (Straub, 1994:1–11; Rose & Straub, 1998:42). Rose and Straub (1998:39), and Straub (1994:7) also note that

PU emerges as the most important attribute in all cultures studied. In the African and Asian context, the subjective norm rightly comes out with cultural factors being highlighted as the central determinants of the behavioural intention to use computers (Dinev, Hu & Goo, 2004:2).

In contrast to the IDT and TRA, the TAM is also utilised in situations comprising more than one individuals' (group or organisational) adoption of technology as distinct to the individual level. One such example is the adoption of new technologies in areas such as police investigations, e-Commerce, telemedicine, and sales force coordination (Chau & Hu, 2002:297; Olson & Boyer, 2003:225; Colvin & Goh 2005:89; Marshall & Stamps, 2005:1623; Yu, Ha, Choi & Rho, 2005:965). Grandon and Pearson (2004:197) explored the factors that influence small businesses to involve and accept technology in their different business endeavours. Their study concludes that the determining factors for accepting technology use in these businesses have been the perceived value of e-Commerce applications, external and internal factors, and perceived cost of technology, staff interests, and agency priorities.

Further, the TAM is used to measure the success of e-Government implementation. The PU and PEOU of the TAM measures the overall perceived value of engaging in e-Government. This perceived value can be split amongst three different entities: transactions (such as doing business with the government), seeking public service, and obtaining general information. Examples of transactions are applications such as e-Commerce, Internet banking, business-to-consumer (B2C) model and e-Learning. Seeking public services may involve downloading application forms for a passport from a government website and participating in decision-making may involve such things as engaging in e-Voting. Obtaining information involves such activities as checking recommended prices for farm products, and checking weather forecasts. If the considerable value is obtained from these three different e-Government entities and applications, this can further culminate into effective e-Government adoption (Legris et al., 2003:192; Ooh, Lean, Zailani, Ramayah & Fernando, 2009:462).

From its inception, the TAM has seen many modifications and enhancements to improve its effectiveness as a more relevant modelling tool for IS uptake. Pedersen (2005:209) suggests some extensions on the set of determinants for PU and PEOU. Of the main researchers (*viz* Venkatesh & Davis, 2000:186–204; Ramayah, 2005:71–82) that have endeavoured to extend the original Davis' version of the TAM, Venkatesh and Davis (2000:186–187) suggests a model which is arguably the most influential one because it attempts to take into consideration the local context and has been widely referenced. This model is referred to as TAM2 and is shown in Figure 6.4 below.

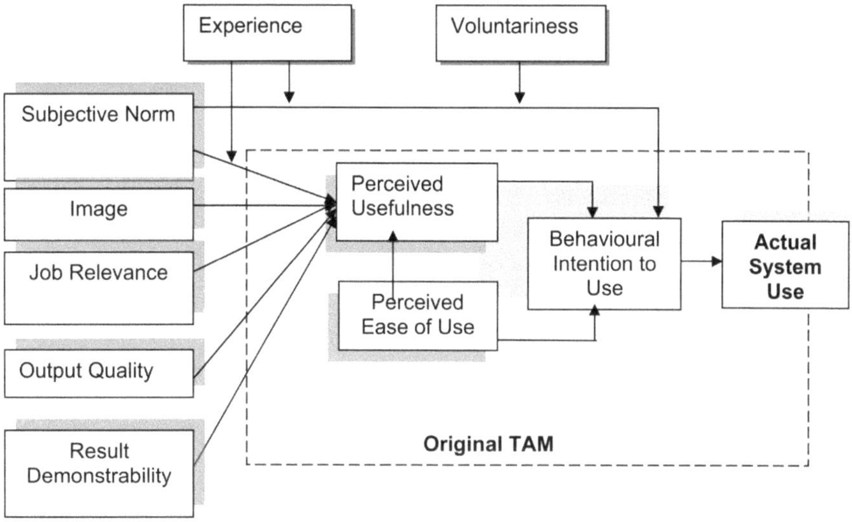

Figure 6.4: Extended TAM2 model (Adapted from: Venkatesh and Davis, 2000:188).

The TAM2 considers the impact of three inter-related social forces (subjective norm, voluntariness and image) which may influence an individual's choice of either to adopt or reject a new system. TAM2 adds the concepts of subjective norm, result demonstrability, job relevance, image, output quality, experience, and voluntariness into the original model as presented in Figure 6.4 above. Just like the original TAM, TAM2 is employed by a number of studies, *viz* Venkatesh and Davis, (2000:186); Singletary, Akbulut and Houston, (2002:1135); Chismar and Wiley-Patton, (2003:2–3); Marchewka, Liu and Kostiwa, (2007); and Lee et al., (2010), to model the factors that influence IS adoption. The TAM2 has opened up possibilities for tailor-made models to be designed with a focus to fit in to the local context where technology is to be introduced. With this possibility, Venkatesh, et al., (2003:428) developed the unified theory of adoption and use of technology (UTAUT) which aims to incorporate certain specifics of adoption as outlined in the next section.

6.3.5 Unified Theory of Adoption and Use of Technology (UTAUT) model

The UTAUT model is one of the main extensions of the TAM originally introduced by Venkatesh, et al., (2003:427). Also explaining user intentions to engage in IS, the UTAUT model further aims to capture the usage behaviour. The theory hinges on four key constructs of 'performance expectancy', 'effort expectancy', 'social influence', and 'facilitating conditions' as the major determinants that dictate usage behaviour (Venkatesh et al., 2003:425–426). These four constructs are mediated by age, gender, experience and voluntariness of use. The theory is based upon the conceptual and empirical similarities across a variety of technology acceptance models explained using the following factors:

1. Performance expectancy (individual's belief of the ability of the system to help him or her improve the job performance).
2. Effort expectancy (degree of ease of use of the system).
3. Social influence (individual perception that he or she is expected by other citizens to use the new system).
4. Facilitating conditions (individual's belief that organisational and technical infrastructure is in place to support the use of a system).
5. Behavioural intention (individual's decision regarding future system use).

The UTAUT model has been adopted in various studies to investigate the adoption technology being introduced for the first time (Kijsanayotin, Pannarunothai & Speedie, 2009:405; Wang & Shir, 2010:158; Zhou, Lu & Wang, 2010:760–761; Im, Hong & Kang, 2011:1). The study by Al-Shafi and Weerakkody (2009:2) applies the UTAUT to ascertain the diffusion and adoption of e-Government services in Qatar by determining citizens' behavioural intention. The results of this survey show that there is an established positive relationship between performance expectancy, effort expectancy, social influence and behavioural intention to use e-Government applications and services. In another study in Indonesia, Hermana and Silfianti (2011:156) examine the factors that influence utilisation, usage and adoption of technology to boost small manufacturing enterprise companies' performance using the TAM. Their study revealed that technology and Internet adoption is largely influenced by PU, PEOU, Internet self-efficacy, and Internet anxiety, thereby further supporting the validity of the UTAUT model.

These factors, with reference to the earlier models such as the IDT, TRA and TAM2 are incorporated into the UTAUT model. The UTAUT model is shown in Figure 6.5 below.

Different adaptations of the UTAUT have been utilised in different studies (Masrom, 2007:9; Nanayakkara, 2007:5; Keller, Hrastinski & Carlsson, 2008:395,400; Yuen & Ma, 2008:231; Wang & Shir, 2010:159; Zhou, Lu & Wang, 2010:760) to test the acceptance of e-Learning technology by both teachers and students. These studies have shown that the PU is the most important determinant for teachers to engage in e-Learning whereas PEOU is seen as the most important factor that influence students to engage in e-Learning.

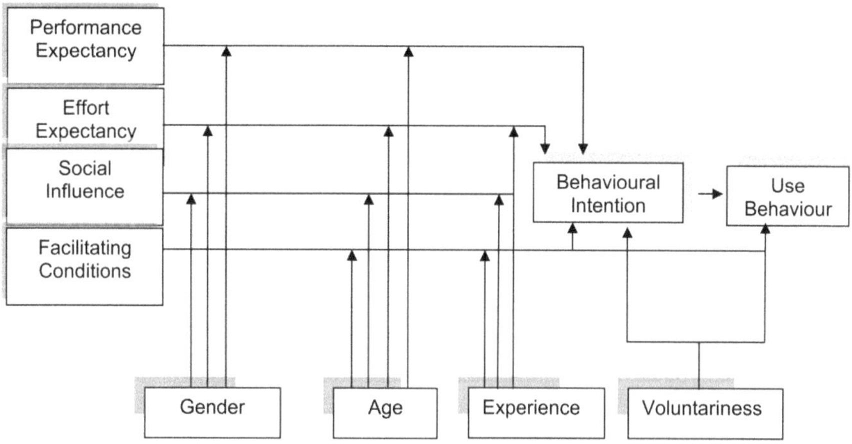

Figure 6.5: UTAUT Model (Adapted from: Venkatesh, et al., 2003:447).

From the discussion of the models above, it is evident that these models emphasise different sets of technology acceptance and adoption determinants, and underline the basic concepts underlining these models. The earlier models (such as IDT and TRA) concentrate on finding out factors that prompt an individual to adopt a technology that has just been introduced. The later models such as the UTAUT extend the understanding of adoption to include the future intention (continuance use) and actual frequency of use of the system. Further, the models do not in any instance focus on system characteristics of technologies and only provide limited guidance on how to influence the use of a technology through its design and implementation (Wixom & Todd, 2005:89). This emphasizes the need for models to be designed with strong reference to the local context (such as the local legal and market environment, government) and thereafter be subjected to properly-designed empirical testing procedures to confirm validity.

The different studies outlined above show that there are different factors that influence adoption of new technologies. In most of the cases, these factors depend on the local contextual characteristics. There is a general consensus, however, that PEOU (usability), PU (anticipated benefits), computer self efficacy, local culture and usage expectance are some of the major factors that determine adoption of a technology. The desire to understand the factors that impact on the adoption of technologies is important as technology is the main enabler of e-Government research.

It is not easy to discuss all the technology adoption models and/or frameworks in one write up. As shown in Sundaravej (2010), a summary of the different theoretical frameworks and models used to explain technology adoption are shown in Table 6.1 below. The entries in this Table are a snapshot of the key characteristics of each of the major theoretical frameworks, especially as utilised at the individual level.

Understanding the limitations of the technology adoption models is vital because it helps researchers to understand the intricate factors that are critical in measuring overall technology adoption and designing context-aware e-Government adoption models.

Table 6.1: Models and frameworks of technology adoption.

S/N	Models and Theories	Constructs
1	Fishbein and Ajzen (1975): The Theory of Reasoned Action (TRA) – it has its roots embedded in the field of psychology with the aim of measuring behavioural intention and performance.	– Attitude – Subjective norm
2	Davis (1989): Technology Acceptance Model (TAM) – Hinged on the TRA, utilises two variables to explain factors influencing adoption and use of a technology.	– Perceived Usefulness (PU) – Perceived Ease of Use (PEOU)
	Venkatesh and Davis (2000): Technology Acceptance Model 2 (TAM2) – adapted from the TAM to include more variables.	– Subjective Norm – Experience – Voluntariness – Image – Job Relevance – Output Quality – Result Demonstrability
3	Davis et al. (1992): Motivational Model (MM) – from the field of psychology to explain behaviour towards technology adoption and use.	– Extrinsic Motivation – Intrinsic Motivation
4	Ajzen (1991): Theory of Planned Behaviour (TPB) by) – extends TRA by including one more variable to determine intention and behaviour.	– Attitude – Subjective norm – Perceived Behavioural Control
5	Taylor and Todd (1995): proposes a model that comes as a result of the TAM and TPB (C-TAM-TPB).	– Perceived Usefulness – Perceived Ease of Use – Attitude – Subjective norm – Perceived Behavioural Control

6	Triandis (1980): adjusts the Model of PC Utilization (MPCU) by Thompson et al. (1991) predict PC usage behavior.	– Social Factors affect perceived consequences (Complexity, Job-Fit, Long-Term Consequences of Use) – Facilitating Conditions – Habits
7	Moore and Benbasat (1991): adapts the Innovation Diffusion Theory (IDT) by Rogers (1962) to information systems innovations – done by combining five attributes from Rogers' model and two additional constructs.	– Relative Advantage – Compatibility – Complexity – Observability – Trialability – Image* – Voluntariness of Use* – Two additional constructs
8	Compeau and Higgins (1995): applies the Social Cognitive Theory (SCT) from Bandura (1986) to determine the usage.	– Others' encouragement – Others' Use & Support – Self-Efficacy – Performance Outcome Expectations – Personal Outcome Expectations – Affect – Anxiety
9	Venkatesh et al. (2003): Unified Theory of Acceptance and Use of Technology Model (UTAUT) – integrates most of the above theories and models to measure user intention and technology usage.	– Performance Expectancy – Effort Expectancy – Attitude toward Using Technology – Social Influence – Facilitating Conditions – Self-Efficacy – Anxiety

6.4 Critique of Some of the Adoption Frameworks/Models

Although studied for over 30 years, the science of investigating the process of adopting new phenomena and its integration into the organisational business processes or individual lifestyles is still in its nascent stage (Sahin, 2006). This is because there is still no global consensus on what theoretical or conceptual underpinnings need to be utilised in any given scenario. As a result, different e-Government researchers and practitioners have come up with their own models commensurate to what aspect of technology adoption they are investigating.

Choosing the best-fit (if there is such a thing) amongst the existing technology adoption models to be used in a study depends on the understanding of the limitations of each of the given models available. The understanding of the limitations may culminate into how best to adapt a given model to measure e-Government adoption in a given environment. This may also help in choosing the best attributes of different models in order to come up with a comprehensive model commensurate to given contextual characteristic. Amongst the common technology adoption models, the TAM and the UTAUT have enjoyed wider usage amongst the Information System research community and these have correspondingly attracted a lot of criticism with various researchers outlining their limitations (Bagozzi, 2007; Park, 2009; Legris, Ingham & Collerette, 2003; Williams, Rana, Dwivedi, & Banita, 2011).

One of the pioneers of the TAM, Richard Bagozzi is leading the onslaught against it (the TAM) by advocating for a paradigm shift with regards to the TAM's applicability (Bagozzi, 2007). Bagozzi (2007) posits that the TAM lacks the potential contingent, contextual nuances that influence decision making with regard to newly introduced phenomenon. The TAM fails to account for the Information System process design ramifications and disregards the contextual societal forces that dictate technology adoption. It is thus fitting to posit that grounded adoption cannot only be explained from the 'individual user' perspective. It is important to note that adoption is influenced by the context, cultural setting and socio-economic standing of individuals in an area where technology is introduced. The TAM takes Information System as an independent entity in organisational dynamics and only considers the individual as the unit of analysis. It is worth noting that effervescent integration of technology in the e-Government realm largely relies on the interdependence between the technology, the organisational context, and the model utilised to manage the change.

Another limitation in the TAM can be seen in their limited prediction of adoption as it only accounts for 40–50 percent of technology user acceptance (Park, 2009; Legris, Ingham & Collerette, 2003). This is a clear-cut indication that there must be other inherent factors that may account for individual's motivation to adopt a given technology. For the TAM to make considerable sense, it needs to be integrated with other models which include both human and social change process variables.

The UTAUT is one of the models that has been largely referenced in the literature. What is not clear, though, is whether it is actually integrated into the methodology of the numerous studies referencing it or it is merely cited (Williams, Rana, Dwivedi, & Banita, 2011). Although the UTAUT is widely referenced, it should not be considered as the final authority that should be used for measuring technology adoption. The UTAUT posits that technology adoption can be investigated by the factors obtained from combining eight different models in any environment. Of course the prediction capacity is improved (to about 70%) but there is a higher likelihood that some of the factors in the UTAUT may be redundant in certain environments. Therefore, it is logically coherent to posit that no absolute technology acceptance model exists across heterogeneous technological, organizational and contextual settings. The study by Williams, Rana, Dwivedi, and Banita (2011) has shown that each environment contains unique contextual settings where the pre-defined factors may not adequately explain the technology adoption and anticipated usage.

Because of the limitation in the technology adoption models, chapters 7 and 9 of this book are devoted to discussing the principles that guide the development of e-Government frameworks and paradigms. These frameworks can be referenced as they contain guiding principles for designing e-Government projects.

6.5 Conclusion and Summary

This chapter has outlined and discussed the different stages of adoption and development of e-Government in different countries. The cases of failure or successful implementation of e-Government projects serve as lessons towards determining what should be considered when designing strategic initiatives to aid e-Government development.

The chapter discusses the overall different factors that mainly affect e-Government adoption. It has been ascertained that e-Government adoption mainly depends on the individual and organisational characteristics. These characteristics are usually unique according to different areas where e-Government is implemented. To model these different factors influencing engagement or non-engagement in e-Government, a couple of e-Government adoption models have been designed. These models have been utilised in empirical studies aiming at understanding the factors that aid or inhibit e-Government uptake. Four pioneer models (IDT, TRA, TAM and the UTAUT) are being discussed in this chapter. The other models that have been utilised in different studies are but a modification of these four pioneer models.

The chapter concludes by providing a critique of the common adoption models. The discussion of adoption frameworks or models that can be used in the e-Government realm is presented in Chapter 7.

Chapter 7
E-Government Technology Design Frameworks

7.1 Introduction

This short chapter brings out the fundamental concepts and frameworks that guide technological design of e-Government applications. This is important because it has been shown that tailor-made e-Government applications based on the local context are the ones that are likely to succeed. There is anecdotal evidence that points to the fact that the integration of technologies in public service business processes is the major cause of delayed affluent development of e-Government. Therefore, there is need to devote to understanding the inherent entities and attributes that define the integration of different e-Government technology platforms. In this regard, a significant portion of this chapter will be devoted to discussing technology integration frameworks and interoperability frameworks that guide e-Government implementation. The chapter discusses different forms of interoperability and highlights ways of how these can be used in the e-Government environment.

It is important to discuss the different technology platforms and articulate ways of how these can be used in the e-Government realm. Robust and responsive e-Government designs need to ensure that they are erected with full sense of scalability capabilities to ensure that as technology rapidly evolves through short lifecycles, e-Government design also needs to follow suit. As technology is the hallmark or key enabler of e-Government implementation, it is important that e-Government applications and/or solution evolve as technology evolves.

7.2 Technology Nuances for e-Government

E-Government is evolving at a lightning speed and therefore its different forms need to evolve as technology evolves. With the metamorphosis in the technology platforms and applications, e-Government applications can now be accessed through both conventional computing platforms and ubiquitous or pervasive platforms. Even in less developed economies, a majority of people can now access Internet applications using mobile platforms such as mobile phones, anywhere and at any time. Despite this being the case, there are still a lot of situations where people access information content from networked environments using traditional personal computers. This entails that e-Government should be designed in such a way that it is accessible using both conventional and ubiquitous platforms.

One of the core requirements for basic implementation of e-Government is that the different systems deployed in different government departments should 'talk-to-each-other' so that decisions made in one government unit may replicate throughout the public service value chains. The establishment of such a governance environment ensures that decisions are made using a unison voice and that these decisions are evidence-based. In order for the aforementioned to be achieved, appropriate system integration platforms need to be implemented with adequate reference to the local contextual characteristics. Successful implementation of e-Government system integration depends on understanding the different obstacles that may be present in any given environment. The main obstacles for integration of e-Government applications stem from technical (great variety of legacy systems already installed and running in government departments), semantic (difference in data/information standards) and human (adoption of interoperable solutions by government officers) issues (Saekow & Boonmee, 2009).

One of the core tenets of technology in e-Government design is the need to design seamless data flow amongst different standalone systems in different government departments. For this to be achieved, it is necessary to have highly integrated and interoperable systems that can seamlessly exchange data. Of late, research in designing interoperability frameworks has taken centre-stage in e-Government design and practice. Despite being predominantly looked at from the technical side, interoperability can also be an organisational issue (ownership, people and business processes). In any competitive e-Government design, the importance of requisite interoperability frameworks cannot be overemphasized. Therefore, the design of the interoperability strategy is a cornerstone for designing any e-Government information system (Jarrari, Deik & Farraj, 2009).

There are different definitions of interoperability: the Institute of Electrical and Electronics Engineers (IEEE) defines interoperability as the inherent capacity and ability of two independent information systems entities or components to exchange information. The ISO/IEC 2382–01 defines it as the ability for two or more systems to communicate and execute programs and thereby transfer data among various functional units where the user is expected to have little or no knowledge of what is happening behind the systems (Tschumperlin, 2009).

Many of the e-Government technology platforms have been based on eXtensible Markup Language (XML) architecture. The XML family consists of the XML documents and the schemas themselves. There are basically two types of XML documents: XML Instance Documents which contain the actual data, and XML Schemas which define allowable XML constraints. The schemas are further sub-divided into XML Document Schemas and XML Library Schemas (Tschumperlin, 2009). The successful design of e-Government applications should be based as much as possible on XML-based technologies because most technological solutions and applications are based on XML for easy interoperability.

According to Al-Khouri (2013), some of the common technological platforms for developing e-Government applications are:
- Cybersecurity & access control (such as WS-Security, SAML, XACML, KMIP, DSS & XSPA);
- office documents and smart semantic documents (such as OpenDocument, DITA, DocBook & CMIS); and
- Electronic commerce (including Service Oriented Architecture (SOA) and Web Services, such as BPEL, ebXML, WS-Reliable Messaging & the WS-Transaction standards)

Other technology standards with a view of complementing on efforts by OASIS have been produced such as the following (Al-Khouri, 2013):
- UBL and Business Document Exchange (for e-procurement);
- CAP and EDML (for emergency first-responder notifications); and
- LegalXML (for electronic court filing data).

Utilization of open-source software in the design of e-Government is now getting prominence (Butler et al., 2004; Sourouni et al., 2008; Jarrari, Deik, & Farraj, 2009; Al-Khouri, 2013). One of the widely-used open-source software has been the *Portable Knowledge Asset Development System* (pKADS) which is a desktop-based knowledge management system which aims to facilitate the sharing of knowledge in government and non-governmental organizations.

Sourouni et al., (2008) described the design of a Web portal with focus on thorough description of the application ontology and repositories for e-Government. The Web portal was developed using ASP.NET and the DBMS component was based on SQL Server 2005 and utilized HTTP compression filter to make optimal usage of the available bandwidth. Reviewing different e-Government ontologies, Sourouni et al., (2008) proposed an e-Government Knowledge Interoperability Ontology (eGKI) which is a two-layer ontology enveloping the knowledge management conceptualization into public service business processes. The eGKI was formalized using Web Ontology Language (OWL).

Meneklis et al., (2005) designed a Web Services based platform for e-Government, the eMayor platform, which was based on the ISO/RM-ODP standard which supports the integration of distribution, interworking, interoperability and portability of e-Government applications. It can be observed from the above paragraphs that the design of requisite e-Government is influenced by a variety of factors such as ontologies (which may take care of the context) and Web portals and Web Services being designed using different technologies to ensure that context is taken into consideration. Also coming up is the role of Open-Source systems and software and the issues that they bring on board to e-Government platform design.

For effervescent e-Government design, it is important to investigate the different facets of interoperability and discuss technologies which allow integration of different e-Government systems from different government departments. The heterogeneity of data in the public sector calls for the development of adaptive systems that are able to handle all types of data. Technology platforms and standards such as Rosetta Net (B2B data exchange standard), EDIFACT (Electronic Data Interchange for Administration, Commerce, and Transport), XML and Electronic Data Interchange (EDI) have enabled different government departments to exchange data through common interoperable systems (Muthaiyah & Kerschberg, 2008). Despite the existence of these technology solutions, including the Service Oriented Architecture (SOA) and Web Services, the problem of data handling given its heterogeneity, has not been resolved by e-Government. Therefore, there is need for researchers and practitioners to engage and find ways on how this can be resolved (Muthaiyah & Kerschberg, 2008).

E-Government interoperability enables seamless exchange of information across government departments. In many instances, the main technology frameworks guiding this have been the Government Interoperability Frameworks (GIFs) and the Enterprise Architectures (EAs). One of the most pronounced GIFs has been the European Union Interoperability Framework (EUIF) which is further discussed in the next section. The EUIF acts as a guideline for e-Government interventions at the member state level. Some of the e-Government design programs at country level include the following:

1. The Italian e-Government Architecture (SPCoop Enterprise Architecture) which follows a Service Oriented Architecture (SOA). It also uses the *Zinna*r ontology build from Object Role Modeling (ORM) notation. The Zinnar ontology is based on the Palestinian e-Government Interoperability which outlines the set of vocabulary (naming), semantics (meaning), structure and business rules with regards to the data exchanged and applications involved in the e-Government service;
2. The Estonian Semantic Interoperability Architecture (X-Road) is also based on the *Zinnar* ontology; and
3. The UK e-Government Interoperability Framcwork (c-GIF) which has the following basic components: the e-Government Metadata Standard (e-GMS) – which defines the elements, refinements and encoding schemes for creating e-Government metadata; the Integrated Public Sector Vocabulary (IPSV/

GCL) – vocabulary and encoding scheme for e-GMS; the Government Data Standards Catalogue (GDSC) – outlines the agreed set of core government data standards; XML Schemas – describing all the data in the e-Government environment (Jarrar, Deik, & Farraj, 2011).

Saekow and Boonmee (2009) designed an approach called 'interoperability Practical Implementation Support (IPIS)' which utilizes UN/CEFACTs Modeling Methodology (UMM) for modeling or specifying organisational business processes, UN/CEFACT CCTS as the semantic tool for data standardization or harmonization, and the XML Naming and Design Rules, and Recommendation 34.

Lee, Yee and Cheung (2009) have suggested that interoperability framework comprise two parts: 1) definitions of recommended technical specifications; and 2) frameworks data exchanges based on XML standards (Schema design and design guide and its applications). Requisite technology applications interoperability has been based on the XML Schema Design and Management Guide which posits that there are basically three dimensions of interoperability (Lee, Yee, & Cheung 2009).

- **Technical interoperability:** outlines what communication protocols and message formats needs to be utilised when one entity sends information to another in an e-Government environment. An example could be two applications processes agreeing exchanging data using a three handshake system that packets will be encoded in XML, defined using a specific XML Schema, XML Encryption (or Secure Socket Layer – SSL channel) and XML Signature, and packet sent via HTTP;
- **Data interoperability:** two communication entities agree on what data should be sent across their networking media and also clearly defining the format in which it should be sent. Another important roadblock to affective highly interoperable e-Government systems has been the issue of data interoperability. Data interoperability is concerned with how different systems exchange data and how to represent data for common understanding. There are different standards that guide the achievement of data interoperability and these should be consulted if it were to be achieved. For example, they may agree to utilize ISO 8601 standard; and
- **Process interoperability:** provides details on agreements on how business activities affect each other and how they should be integrated (functional integration). This can be achieved, for example, using SOAP V.1.1., WSDL v. 1.1., and UDDI v.2.

Ellis (2004) and Jarrari, Deik and Farraj (2009) distinguish four types of interoperability within the European Union *viz* **political interoperability** (political support for improved public services), **legal interoperability** (provision of European legal frameworks for data exchange among member states), **organisational interoperability** (definition of business goals and processes), **semantic interoperability** (applications' ability to precisely understand the exchanged information and re-engineering of business processes), and **technical interoperability** (covering technical issues such as need for open interfaces, middleware, accessibility and security services). Tschumperlin (2007) has submitted that apart from the four types of interoperability discussed above, there are also higher levels of interoperability such as syntactic interoperability (common protocols for sharing information such as XML syntax) and others such as Pragmatic, Dynamic, Conceptual, Legal, International interoperability.

Apart from the design, it is important to recognize that technology deployment and process re-engineering are some of the key success factors for successful e-Government. To this regard, the 'Salford Process Re-engineering method Involving New Technologies' (SPRINT) was designed to introduce programs to counter the risk and complexity of e-Government projects (Eddowes, 2004). SPRINT focuses on strategic business alignment and change management and is strongly influenced by the principles of business process re-engineering. Business process re-engineering entails the metamorphosis of a business setting to accommodate the emerging change in the customers' or stakeholders' tastes and/or demands. With regards to e-Government, it is a known fact that people are already used to traditional government setups where they have to visit a physical office in order for them to obtain a government service. Bringing ICTs in the government business processes entails that citizens can obtain public services ubiquitously anywhere and anytime. For this to be achieved, it entails that traditional government business processes have to be re-engineered given the introduction of ICTs, employees have to change their work attitudes so as to allow easier integration of technology into the government's business processes, and that there should be strategic alignment of business to ever-changing technology platforms and solutions. Therefore, the need for SPRINT in dynamic e-Government environments cannot be overemphasised.

Based on the SOA, Widodo et al. (2013) attempted to create an Enterprise Architecture Framework (EAF) as a basis for data integration and system interoperability for e-Government applications in Indonesia. The architecture described the anticipated government applications platform using the Web Services Description Language (WSDL) and in order to make applications and business process integration easier, suggested technical specifications for the Government Service Bus (GSB) which was realized using the Business Process Execution Language (BPEL). The major goal for designing this EAF was to come up with a scalable interoperable e-Government systems environment which could easily support Web Services. The SOA makes it possible for the heterogeneous technology applications to be distributed and therefore emphasises the need for integration and interoperability in the e-Government domain. Distributed technology such as CORBA, COM/DCOM, EJB, JAVA RMI was used to implement interoperability between applications.

During the design of e-Government systems, it is important to note the importance of including modelling of data interaction as one of the core attributes. Business Process Modelling Methodology is clearly defined by the XML Schema Design and extends the *ebXML Core Components Technical Specification* (CCTS) (UN/CEFACT 2003). This allows business analysts monitoring e-Government business processes to specify data elements and documents for a variety of models such as *Aggregate Business Information Entity* (ABIE), *Association Business Information Entity* (ASBIE) and *Core Component Type* (CCT) used for modelling singular or complex property in an object class (Lee, Hon, & Cheung, 2009). In designing computer information systems, heterogeneous phenomena are modelled in a class. A class is a general term representing a set of like terms. The object class is the 'container' which is described at the highest level of abstraction. Object classes have member variables defining characteristics or properties of the object class. Modelling is used to create mathematical, syntactical or semantic representations of a phenomenon in a real environment. The ABIE, ASBIE and CCT are therefore standard modelling platforms which may be utilised for modelling different e-Government phenomena. One of the approaches towards solving semantic interoperability is the design of semantically enriched Web Services. Muthaiyah and Kerschberg (2008) proposed an hierarchical repository which was based on two-part semantic mediation approach using Semantic Relatedness Scores (SRS) and Semantic Web Rule Language (SWRL) which are necessary for schema heterogeneity. This repository employed a rule-based engine that reads and executes SWRL rules (i.e. RacerPro) and utilised several tools such as Protégé (i.e. Ontology editor) and JESS (Java Expert Shell System (Muthaiyah & Kerschberg, 2008). The semantic Web technologies are being supplemented with a metadata registry based upon ISO/IEC 11179 standard. The ISO/IEC 11179 allows the maintaining of semantics and metadata independently.

Dombeu, Huisman and Szpak (2011) provide a framework that may be used to generate semantic model ontologies in OWL syntax that may be used to construct e-Government applications. In achieving this, they used an ontology editor – Protégé. On the ontology aspects, the Simple Knowledge Organisation System (SKOS), Resource Description Framework (RDF) vocabulary designed to represent terminologies, thesauri and classification schemes has been used extensively in applications development (Crichton, Davies, Gibbons, Harris, Tsui & Brenton, 2009).

The need for a drive by e-Government researchers and practitioners towards global technology approaches for designing e-Government applications is a very urgent matter. Efforts to design context-aware interoperability frameworks cannot be overemphasized as there is currently no global semantic model that would aid such efforts. Even at the technology level, some standards do not 'talk to each other'. An example includes the XML standards developed by OASIS UBL which are incompatible with the OASIS xNAL (Tschumperlin, 2009).

7.3 Advances in Technology Designs

The different technology specifications aimed towards open interoperable defined by common ontologies, schemas and meta-languages towards harmonizing heterogeneous e-Government applications as specified in e-Government Interoperability Frameworks (e-GIFs). The Organization for the Advancement of Structured Information Standards (OASIS) is an international forum that is mandated to spearhead development of e-Government technology specifications towards global technology models. OASIS is one of the largest and oldest global open data standards consortia, founded in 1993 as SGML Open. OASIS has over 5000 active participants representing about 600 member organizations and individual members in over 80 countries. The OASIS e-Government Technical Committee has been set up to promote the use of XML-based technologies (e.g. ebXML, Web Services, SOAP, Web Services) for e-Government applications design (Borras, 2004). OASIS concentrates on providing technology interventions and evolving e-Government technology design paradigms so that e-Government solutions are relevant at any one given time.

In order to achieve this, the following program domains are currently pursued by OASIS (Borras, 2004):

- Search Service Interoperability;
- EbXML Messaging for use within e-Government – produced a requirements document detailing compliance with government issues and how to integrate this with ebXML;
- Common Data Definitions – common definitions facilitating data exchange within processes as a basis for application integration (Borras, 2004);
- Use by governments of ebXML Registries – efforts towards coming up with common standards for governments' data dictionaries, XML schema repositories and other registries storing information of the technology components used in e-Government platforms;
- Use by government of the eprXML Standard – developed by the Norwegian Government, the eprXML Standards covers electronic processes and is used

is used to describe how data support can be organized in a unified and standardized manner (Borras, 2004);
- Semantic interoperability and business implementation guidelines – project ongoing to extend the XML syntactic interoperability capability into semantic interoperability (where systems are able to talk and understand each other);
- Workflow standards – to enable systems to underpin e-Services especially in cases where a government business process needs input from several departments (such as the vehicle fitness license issuing office needs to check with the police traffic department whether a particular customer was implicated in road mal practices such s over-speeding at any time); and
- Naming and design rules for XML Schemas – project aimed to define the Naming and Design rules for use in XML Schemas towards future data sharing across governments using networked distributed e-Government systems (Borras, 2004).

The European Union has come up with the European Interoperability Framework (EIF) which aims to guide the interoperability of government services at both the country level and across countries and organisational silos (Ellis, 2004). The European e-GIF was necessary so as to clear barriers that are caused by accessibility, multilingualism among European nations and promote secure applications using Open-Source standards and providing multilateral solutions.

The Minimum Information Interoperability Standards (MIOS) sets out the South African Government's policies and standards for achieving interoperability and seamless information flow across government as well as the wider public sector (Segole, 2010).

The MIOS provides a framework that outlines the principles needed for successful implementation of e-Government across government departments: these principles are as follows (Segole, 2010):
1. Management process – how to successfully integrate information systems across government departments;
2. Lobbying for a Government-Wide Enterprise Architecture (GWEA) framework which details the composition of the governance layer comprising best practices, policies and interoperability standards;
3. Stakeholder engagement as a fundamental objective towards success;
4. Outlining of minimum set of standards such as:
   - Drivers of interoperability – technical policies and standards necessary to achieve interoperability and seamless information flows across government departments; universal adoption of standards across government departments, adoption of XML as primary data interoperability

standard and use of XML Schema to support Web Services through Web Services Description Language (WSDL) based interfaces, etc.
   - Outlining of principles relating to networks (migration from IPv4 to IPv6), security (based on provisions of ISO 17799), e-mail (SMTP/MIME).
5. Principle statement relating to data interoperability (use of RDF, OWL and RSS for metadata framework; UML and XMI for exchange of information and system design modelling, use of Extensible Stylesheet Language (XSL) for data transformation).

Despite the positive promises of e-GIFs, it cannot go without mentioning that because of the multiplicity and diversity in the public sector, it is very difficult to realize complete e-Government applications integration (Charalabidis & Askounis, 2008). Successful e-Government design does not only focus on designing requisite e-Government applications but also aims to look at non-technical aspects. An example of a non-technology solution in e-Government projects has been the New Institutional Economics (NIE) which is aimed at delivering transformational change towards inciting workers and citizens to accept e-Government as a delivery platform (Elis, 2004). The NIE combines two theoretical approaches to economic organization i.e. Transactional Cost Economic (TCE) and Agency Theory (AT). Technology design or deployment cannot succeed without requisite Project Management strategy. In order to emphasize the role of Project Management in e-Governments, Sarantis, Charalabidis and Askounis (2011) outlined a goal-driven and knowledge-based framework to manage critical e-Government projects thereby emphasizing that technology is not all it takes to achieve competitive and sustainable e-Government design.

7.4 Future Prospects

With the emergence of smart or ubiquitous e-Government systems, there is need to come up with novel, robust, scalable and easy-to-adapt e-Government platforms. This can be achieved by utilizing the emerging technology platforms which have shown much promise. The emergency of open-source e-Government platforms, tools and software ensures that the different e-Government interventions throughout the world are designed with unison platforms. This entails that researchers and practitioners should consider investigating the future role of Open-Source software/systems in designing requisite e-Government solutions.

Another possible area for future research is to check the likely impact of regional e-Government interventions. For example, the European Union has done a lot in as far as enacting laws to support e-Government growth in its member countries is concerned. Not all these interventions may be appropriate to successfully supporting e-Government growth. For example, Baldoni et al., (2009) reported that a legal framework supporting e-Government in most European countries presents a major stumbling block for e-Government proliferation. Future research should delve deeper in understanding how such regional interventions should be designed.

7.5 Summary and Conclusion

This short chapter has provided a synopsis of what is going on at the world stage in as far as e-Government technological platform design is concerned. One of the fundamental principles for designing e-Government interventions and programmes that will create sustainable value is that there should be appropriately integrated e-Government systems. Integration is important because it ensures that the different systems across the organisation are linked and seen as one system. Although integration has been looked at from the technology side, it is important to note that it is also purely an organisational issue (ownership, people and business processes). Therefore, design of requisite integration platforms and frameworks should focus on both the technical and non-technical sides of design.

Despite quantifiable accomplishments on the technology front of e-Government, it is still evident that there is a lot of work that needs to be done if all the anticipated organization and individual benefits of e-Government were to be realized. Researchers and practitioners are implored to design requisite technology frameworks and models that can be used guide the design of e-Government in heterogeneous environments.

Chapter 8
Selected Cases of e-Government Implementation

8.1 Introduction

The previous chapter discussed the different principles that guide the design of technology platforms for e-Government applications. In order to relate to the technology principles discussed, it is important to provide some cases of e-Government from different countries in the world especially focusing on the less developed countries. This chapter intends to investigate the different approaches on the supply side and demand side of e-Government implementation. The supply side provides an inventory of what interventions have done to encourage proliferation of e-Government and the demand side provides the likelihood of adoption and usage of the available e-Government applications.

This chapter intends to share cases of failure or success of e-Government implementation. Discussing tangible success and failure cases of e-Government will accentuate the fact that careful thought need to be exercised if requisite e-Government programmes were to be implemented. The value of such a discussion is that it will appropriately contribute to forming the knowledge body and best practice of e-Government especially in less developed countries.

8.2 Current Status of e-Government Adoption Worldwide

Chapters 2 and 3 have outlined the different factors (for example, cultural, individual, and organisational factors) that may influence the success of e-Government implementation in any given area. In order to appreciate the different statuses of e-Government implementation and development in the world, this section probes the different maturity levels of e-Government implementation and interventions that have been taken to encourage faster penetration and adoption of e-Government applications. The following sub-sections discuss the level of development of e-Government in selected developed, developing and less developed countries.

8.2.1 America (North and South)

Two countries have been surveyed from the American continent to gain understanding of the different interventions Americans are putting in placing to advance the e-Government agenda. Generally, the e-Government institution is well advanced in Canada, the United States, and Brazil. The status of e-Government in other countries such as Chile, Mexico, and Argentina is also comparatively developed (Gil-Garcia et al., 2007:267; Lau, Aboulhoson, Lin & Atkin, 2008:88–100).

a) Canada

For some years, Canada was a leader of e-Government and is one of the first countries to have shown an unprecedented commitment towards developing user-centric e-Government interventions (Roy, 2006:257; Park, Lamontagne, Perez, Melikhova & Bartlett, 2009:145; Shareef et al., 2011:23). At the moment, many interactions between the government and the citizens (cf: www.canadians-canadiens.gc.ca), and non-citizens (cf: www.canadainternational.gc.ca) or businesses (cf: www.businessgateway.gc.ca) are online. In the 2010 e-Government survey, Canada is ranked third (with a score of 0.8448, out of a possible 1.00) of overall e-Government development (UN e-Government Survey, 2010:65).

Just like other e-Government implementation endeavours elsewhere, the Canadian e-Government agenda is riddled with challenges such as the multicultural barriers and bi-lingual status of Canada; with English and French being the main languages (Wang, Rosenberg & Lo, 2008:1411). To mitigate these and the various other barriers, the Government of Canada together with its co-operating partners has put in place measures aimed at ensuring fast track e-Government implementation (Shareef et al., 2011:22–23). The e-Government agenda is managed by a Chief Information Officer (CIO) with funding for e-Government provided by the central fund and supplemented by individual agencies. The Government On-Line (GOL), (cf: www.canada.gc.ca/main_e.html), is an initiative of the Federal Government of Canada (FGC) which has ensured that its public service delivery is accessible, has clear and understandable content in two languages, and provides an integrated portal as a single entry to government services.

The first e-Government initiatives in Canada started in 1994 when the Canadian Investment Fund was launched (Paré, 2002:2). This fund enabled leading-edge Canadian technology companies to improve the diffusion and innovation of technology. In the same year, the Community Access Program (CAP) was launched and was aimed at providing Canadians with cost-reasonable Internet access and empower them with relevant ICT skills literacy to participate in the information and knowledge-based economy which was in the making (Gurstein, 2003; Deibert, 2004:24). In 1997, the FGC launched the Canadian Foundation for Innovation which was mandated to develop the information and knowledge infrastructure easily accessible to all Canadians. Employing the VoiNet programme established in 1998 (Kearns, 2002:25), the FGC allocated more than 20 million Canadian dollars towards the provision of 10,000 voluntary organisations with access to computer equipment, network support, and Internet connectivity (Mills & Brail, 2004). There is also the 'smart communities programme' which aims to position Canada as a world leader in the development and use of ICTs for socio-economic development (Gurstein, 2003).

A study by Ipsos-Reid (Kumar et al., 2007:71) reveals that despite the major improvements in overall e-Government implementation in Canada, 70% of Canadians are still hesitant to submit confidential and personal information through online media. The study revealed that a majority of Canadians lacked trust in e-Government platforms thus contributing to Canada's realisation that there was need to put in place a Privacy Impact Assessment (PIA) Policy which outlines assessment processes for new or redesigned service raising privacy issues (Stiftung, 2002). Kumar et al., (2007:64) mention FGC's recognition of user perceptions which largely depend on their assurance of how secure their information is when they transact online, introduced a state-of-the-art security infrastructure called ePass. The FGC has also put in place Canada's Secure Channel (SC) which essentially comprises a collection of network infrastructure, operations, and security and authentication services supporting the e-Government project (Just & Rosmarin, 2005:1). The EKOS survey done in 2005 mentions that 74% of Canadians are confident that their information on e-Government platforms is secure. This culminates into increased engagement in e-Government applications by many citizens and businesses. As a result of these appropriate interventions, e-Participation (use of ICTs to participate in various socio-economic value chains) has increased. From the description of the above, it is evident that trust is one of most important pillars for success of e-Government applications.

b) Brazil

Brazil is one of the emerging countries with a dedicated e-Government agenda. During the 1990s, e-Government rapidly developed in Brazil especially at the institutional level (Chahin, Cunha & Joia, 2004:147; Ferrer & Santos, 2004). The e-Government agenda in Brazil is spearheaded by the Executive Committee on e-Government (CEGE), which is chaired by the President's Chief of Staff (*Ministro da Casa Civil*). CEGE's efforts are complimented by the Technical Committee on Knowledge and Strategic Information Management (CTGCIE). Brazil has a dedicated e-Government portal (cf: www.governoeletronico.gov.br) that allows appropriate interaction between the government and citizens or businesses.

In 2000, the Green Paper on e-Government *(Livro Verde)* outlined the roadmap for transforming Brazil into an information society, paving way for the federal government to provide services on the Internet via the *RedeGoverno* ('GovernmentNet') portal where more than 4,800 types of information are available (Takahashi, 2000:74). The portal also enables the provision of public services such as tax payment certificates, income tax declaration, registration for government suppliers, and follow-up of judicial processes. The e-Government agenda is being promoted by putting in place various standards such as the e-Government Standards for Interoperability (e-PING) which is an architecture that aims to define the minimal set of premises, policies and technical specifications for the regulation of ICT usage in major departments of the federal government.

Realising that political will is very important if e-Government implementation were to succeed, the e-*Brasil* project aims to raise awareness of the benefits of e-Development strategy amongst government leaders (Knight, 2007:1). Bertot, Jagger and McClure (2008:19) have ascertained that even though e-Government has reached some high levels of development, democratic participation of ordinary individuals is still relatively a new concept.

So far, the e-Government platform has been used in a variety of applications in Brazil such as: annual income tax declaration submission with over 96% of submissions through the Internet media (Leão, 2006), electronic voting (e-Voting) which has been used since 1988, information of all tender biddings and contracts awarded by the public sector (through the federal government e-Procurement portal), and promotion of 'digital inclusion' of marginal individuals and electronic democracy (e-Democracy). There is also a one-stop public services rendering shop which integrates the different levels of governments, hosts the public Internet access points (Telecentros), and e-Government laboratories which promote partnerships between governments and academic organisations (Leão, 2006).

Other initiatives to encourage e-Government development include a joint e-Government project with European institutions and Peru, the e-GOIA project (Leão, 2006; Hoepner & Mendes, 2007). With the commitment to encourage the adoption of e-Government applications in the framework of government to government (G2G) applications, a project was implemented to electronically link the Brazilian Central Bank and the Senate in a bid to encourage appropriate use of ICTs, collaboration and efficient knowledge management (Leão, 2006). Unfortunately, this project failed to reach its objectives. This project failed because there was no strategic planning at the beginning of the project on the development roadmap of e-Government in this regard (Leão, 2006). The technology solutions were dumped onto the business processes without necessarily understanding and taking into consideration the type of the employees and other stakeholders in the bank's environment. As a result, users did not understand and appreciate the full benefits of utilizing these systems and as such the deployed technology platforms became white elephants.

Generally, public administration in Brazil has adopted the use of ICTs in its day-to-day activities. In Santa André, for example, GIS technology is utilised in issuing building permits and inspections (Bertot et al., 2008). In the current e-Government dispensation, over 358 municipalities have websites or portals. Another e-Government application used in the city of Santa André is the implementation of an Integrated Public Health System (*SISP*) which aims to provide a quicker health public service to the general populace. The SISP is linked and integrated with the Federal Health System and the magnetic card of the National Health System (*SUS*). The Brazilian Integrated Financial, Budgetary and Asset Management System (*SIAFI*) is utilised to bring about transparency in the public sector and therefore contribute to combating corruption.

Kažemikaitienė and Bilevičienė (2008:192) ascertain that Brazil has now embarked on developing mobile government (m-Government) applications where e-Government is being implemented using mobile platforms. This is because of its rapidly growing mobile penetration. By introducing mobile government, it is anticipated that more citizens will be reached and they will be able to use e-Government.

The two cases discussed above of Brazil and Canada show that for e-Government to succeed, there is need for the government and co-operating partners to financially invest in e-Government systems. The cases have also shown that e-Government can be used in a variety of applications thereby improving efficiency of public service delivery and bringing a host of conveniences to a variety of users as hinted above.

8.2.2 Europe

Just as in the previous section, two countries are surveyed in Europe to ascertain the level of penetration of e-Government applications and correspondingly e-Government development. This section emphasizes the fact that Europe has a comparatively developed e-Government institutional, legal, and regulatory framework together with robust socio-infrastructure environment.

a) Sweden

Sweden has shown some commitments toward advancing the e-Government agenda. It is one of the most successful e-Government implementers of all the Nordic countries (Lind, Östberg & Johannisson, 2009:5). E-Government development in Sweden started with the launch of the Swedish e-Government strategy in 2009. The e-Government agenda is spearheaded by the Swedish e-Government Delegation. Axelsson and Lindblad-Gidlund (2009:4) posit that there are different priorities that are considered when authoring e-Government strategies, with some strategists giving greater weight to improving customer service (effectiveness) and others to streamlining processes or reducing costs. For the case of Sweden, it is evident to notice that ICT has been infused in almost all the traditional public administration value chains (Wihlborg & Palm, 2008:3).

Many initiatives are focused on the promotion of e-Government development in Sweden. In 2004, the Swedish government appointed the Government Interoperability Board (GIB) which aims to promote secure information exchange within the public administration and the citizens (Löfgren, 2008:344). The GIB has laid out the following guidelines: guidelines for government websites, guidelines for government use of certificates and electronic signatures and guidelines for user interfaces that meet legal requirements.

Sweden has generally had a rapid up-take of information technology for administrative purposes translating into improved administrative practices throughout the public service. E-Administration roll-out in Sweden started in the early 1970s (Lind et al., 2009:4). To improve the uptake of ICTs, Swedish parliament passed a policy that employees should purchase PCs via their employers at a considerably lower tax incentive (Lind et al., 2009:5). This initiative has indirectly promoted e-Access and e-Participation and has acted as motivation for citizens to access public e-Services under the umbrella term e-Government.

The case of Sweden shows that specific strategies have been put in place to encourage e-Government development. The specific strategies have culminated into e-Government rapidly developing in Sweden. This is evident that novel e-Government implementation involves strategically planning the roll-out of activities and implementation plans.

b) Greece

There are many interventions that have been put in place to encourage the proliferation of e-Government applications in Greece (Markellos, Markellou, Panayiotaki & Stergianeli, 2007:2). Many background initiatives have been discussed as Greece aimed to transform itself into an information society starting first with a strategy to reduce the digital divide which hampered e-Participation. Greece came up with a strategy for information society as early as 1995 (Markellos et al., 2007:7). The major aim of this was to reduce the digital divide and further promote the adoption of ICTs by a majority of the Greek firms. Greece's aim of becoming an information society was also aimed at increasing the number of people with access to ICTs and therefore to encourage electronic transactions with the general public. Greece's e-Government initiatives are now fully focusing on both vertical and horizontal integration aspects of public sector service provision.

One of the first programmes to encourage e-Government penetration in Greece was the *Kleisthenis* programme of 1994 (Votis, Alexakos, Vassiliadis & Likothanassis, 2008:133). This programme was mandated with the modernisation of public administration over a five year period (1994–1999). One of the major programme components of the *Kleisthenis* was to develop a system for electronic tax services (TAXISnet) and to create a national public administration network (pilot phase of *Syzeyxis*).

In 1997, a strategic plan for administrative reform was adopted which had the overall aim of restructuring the public administrative system and encouraging faster adoption of ICTs in government's business endeavours. This started with the establishment of a call center service via a general website (cf: www.gsis.gov.gr). Aiming to implement an IS strategy relevant and coherent to the desired establishment of an information society, an Operational Programme for Information Society (OPIS) was adopted in 2000 (Markellos et al., 2007:74). The implementation of the OPIS cut across all government departments and was integrated to the eEurope initiative and based on the conclusions of the Lisbon Summit of March 2000.

In 2001, a government network *Syzefxis* (Hahamis & Healy, 2005:187; Bouras, Gkamas, Papagiannopoulos, Theophilopoulos & Tsiatsos, 2009:395) was formed as a national Intranet for the Greek public sector with a capacity of connecting more than 1,700 public organisations throughout Greece. To further compliment data sharing amongst different organisations, a P2P between *Syzefxis* and the Hellenic Network for Research and Technology (GRNET) was first operational in 2006 (Markellos et al., 2007:74). This was complimented by allowing access to the Secured Trans-European Services for Telematics between Administrations (TESTA) network (IDABC e-Government Observatory, 2006), design and implementation of MAN networks, optical fibre ring infrastructures and a variety of broadband networks (Markellos et al., 2007:75).

Another initiative towards the information society was the implementation of the IKAnet (cf: www.ikanet.gr) which falls into two categories: Information Services and Transaction Services (Markellos et al., 2007:75). Call centres were also established for citizens to dial a four-digit telephone number where their requests were recorded for further action (Markellos et al., 2007:75). The tentative e-Government strategic approach for Greece was laid out in a white paper, namely 'Greece in the Information Society: Strategies and Actions' published in 1999 and updated in 2002. The ARIADNI (Development and Operation of the Main Information, Support and Interconnection System of Citizens Service Centre

– ARIADNI Offices) is one of the initiatives that aim at improving public administration services in regional and local administrations by allowing citizens and businesses to interact with them using ICTs. There is also the *Politeia* programme which aimed to improve the services that are being offered to the general public (OECD, 2004:6). The main objective of the *Politeia* programme is to source and recruit competent human resources that would appropriately use ICTs in financial management models, adopt modern methods of public administration and control, and ensure transparency prevails and corruption in the public service is reduced.

One of the most important and contemporary e-Government initiatives is the implementation of the 'Greek Digital Strategy' earmarked for implementation from 2006 to 2013 (Markellos et al., 2007:77). This strategy contains a comprehensive list (65 items) of priorities for implementation to encourage ICT and e-Government uptake in the greater Greek society (Greek e-Government Factsheet, 2007; Markellos et al. 2007:77). The overall coordination of all these e-Government initiatives is vested into the general secretariat for public administration and e-Government which was launched in 2006 (Markellos et al., 2007:77). The emerging trends of m-Government are now evident in Greece because of the faster growing mobile penetration (Karadimas, Papatzelou & Papantoniou, 2008:4).

Just like in the Americas, the two cases from Europe also detail the huge commitment for e-Government development from the government and other co-operating partners. Commitment of stakeholders therefore becomes a pronounced need for successful e-Government development. These studies are important in that analyzing them carefully; one can identify what needs to be e-Government designs and interventions. The studies specifically articulate what interventions and programmes were put in place to encourage e-Government development.

8.2.3 Asia

The Asian economic boom, especially with the tiger nations – South Korea, Singapore, Hong Kong-China, Malaysia – has brought about faster adoption of ICTs in almost all the socio-economic establishments. These countries are the world leaders in the Digital Opportunity Index (DOI) (Ok, 2011:326). DOI is published by the International Telecommunications Union (ITU) and is used to measure the degree of attainment of an information society in a given area. Singapore and South Korea are surveyed so as to highlight what initiatives have been put in place to position them as one of the world leaders in e-Government development.

a) Singapore

Singapore is one of the leading countries in as far as e-Government development is concerned amongst other developing and emerging countries (Rowley, 2011:55). The Government of Singapore has scored many successes in transforming the country into an information society with advanced usage of ICTs to participate in global socio-economic and business value chains. These successes are obtained from initiatives such as the investing of over S$1.3 billion to upgrade its online public services (Mimicopoulos, 2004:6). This initiative is a supplement of the e-Government Action Plan II (eGAPII), which is a follow-up to a similar programme (eGAPI) which was implemented at a cost of S$1.5 billion (Mimicopoulos, 2004:6)

The Roundtable Report (2002:1) outlined some of the basic e-Government services that have been implemented in Singapore. The Singapore e-Citizen portal (cf: www.ecitizen.gov.sg) allows Singaporeans to have access to over 1,600 e-Services mostly offered by the public institutions. This portal allows users to submit forms for application to job openings, voter registration, search for school information, and participate in discussions (e-Forums) with the government concerning some decision-making. The portal averages 3.1 million hits a month (Roundtable Report, 2002:1) thus substantiating the fact that a lot more people and businesses are involved in interacting with the government. With a view of ensuring ubiquitous access to government information, e-Services, a network of eCitizen Help Centres were established in 2001 (Mimicopoulos, 2004:5). The Singapore's Government Electronic Business Centre (GeBiz) of 2000 was set up to aid the government in its procurement (Web integrated e-Procurement) and tender activities with a goal of reducing corruption in the public procurement process (Mimicopoulos, 2004:8).

Tan, Pan and Cha (2008:30–34) outline the different e-Government interventions that have taken place in Singapore. In order to advance e-Government development, Singapore has designed strategic management initiatives for the use of ICTs in the public administration platforms called 'Government Infocomm Plans'. These plans are separated in different strata and have definite anticipated outcomes. The first strata (1980–1999) is the Civil Service Computerisation Program (CSCP); the second (2000–2003) is the e-Government Action Plan I; the third (2004–2006) is the e-Government Action Plan II; and the fourth (2006–2010) is the iGov2010 (2006–2010).

The CSCP was launched in response to the National Computerisation Plan (NCP) of the Singapore government to transform its government into an efficient and effective exploiter of emerging ICT applications. The e-Government Action Plan I, together with the Infocomm Development Authority of Singapore (IDA), was formed to '*develop Singapore into a global infocomm capital with a thriv-*

ing and prosperous e-economy and an infocomm-savvy e-society' (IDAS, 2006). The second initiative, e-Government Action Plan II, was a US$900 million ICT blueprint which aimed at transforming Singapore public service delivery into a networked government that provides integrated, accessible and value-adding e-Services to the people. The result of the eGAPII was the re-launch of the Singapore Government Online portal (cf: www.gov.sg) in 2004 and the integration of the three existing portals for the government (SINGOV), citizens (e-Citizens), and the business community (EnterpriseOne) to provide a more comprehensive e-Government service. These different strategic initiatives have contributed positively to the development of e-Government in Singapore and serve as lessons to other countries, or regions that are in the process of implementing e-Government.

Having realised that the supply and demand sides of e-Government must be in equilibrium for it to develop, the Government of Singapore is pursuing interventions to make sure that the *'digitally secluded'* are also given an equal chance of accessing e-Government content (Maioli, 2008:135; Helsper & Heynon, 2009:19). One of the programmes that have been pursued on this front includes the CARE programme of 2004 that provide training for businesses on how to take advantage of the e-Services available in the portal. This programme is also encouraging the adoption of ICTs by lowering the cost of acquiring (buying) computers at comparatively affordable rates to the general population. The CARE programme also aimed at educating users at self-service kiosks on how to effectively obtain value from e-Government applications. Users are also given chance to provide feedback on their e-Government usage experience.

The different government departments who may want to design their own websites are guided by a set of Web Interface Standards (WIS) which was established in 2004 defining frameworks for designing government websites. Another landmark initiative was the introduction of a Service-Wide Technical Architecture (SWTA) which is a technical framework of principles, standards, and guidelines on the use of technology components. The SWTA was introduced for the purposes of facilitating inter-operability and information sharing across government agencies and other line ministries. The SWTA is part of a broader Singapore Government Enterprise Architecture (SGEA), a blueprint whose main aim is to achieve complete business process and information interoperability in the public sector by 2007 (Escobar, 2007).

The most recent initiative is the Igov2010 programme which has continued the work that was accomplished by eGAPII to another level. This initiative aims to bring diversity in the type of users accessing e-Government applications. The Singapore case has shown that there is much commitment from the government and other stakeholders in promoting e-Government development. It follows that stakeholders' involvement when drawing e-Government is sought (Rowley, 2011:53).

b) South Korea

South Korea is currently the world leader in e-Government development (UN e-Government survey, 2012). This country has shown impressive growth in ICT usage and innovation and has accomplished much in taking its rightful place in the information society and correspondingly establishing itself as a KBE (Lee & Gibson, 2002:302). Korea has highly matured ICT penetration which is currently the world's highest per capita Internet and mobile penetration (Kim, Kelly & Raja, 2010:13). Many initiatives have been implemented to place Korea at a competitive edge of ICT adoption and usage within its various socio-economic frameworks. Lee, O'Keefe and Yun (2001:83) posit that Korea has a steadily privatised and fully liberalised ICT sector anchored on deregulated market principles. On the policy front, the Korea Ministry of Information and Communication (MIC) pushes for high-speed ICT infrastructure development and encourages massive utilisation of ICT in various socio-economic value chains of the Korean economy.

Realising that building a proper information society begins with bridging the digital divide so that ICTs are easily accessed and used, Korea has kept intensifying its efforts to bridge the digital divide by putting in place a people-oriented and inclusive information society (Seo, 2011). Because of such initiatives, as of 2005, over 12 million people had access to broadband Internet and over 72% of the population were regular Internet users (Seo, 2011).

Other substantial and tentative initiatives have been implemented in Korea in a view to bridge the digital divide and encourage global access to ICTs by all the citizens regardless of status. The varying digital divide interventions in Korea were implemented in the framework of public-public-partnership (PPP) frameworks where the private sector (non-governmental organisations, private business entities, civil society, citizens) co-operated with the government. The PPP consisted of over 679 individual members from various sectors of the economy. Seo (2011) articulates some of the major interventions put in place by the PPP arrangements in Korea: In 1997, a high speed information infrastructure project was embarked on. This was the beginning of an Internet era which marked the beginning of e-Commerce services. The initiatives for digital excellence continued around 1999 when the government and co-operating partners embarked on establishing the 'Cyber Korea 21' programme which focused on digital mobile migration and mobile Internet service.

In 2002, the 'e-Korea Vision 2006' was launched and this laid the foundation of e-Government and initiated the world's first IMT-2000 service (third generation, 3G) wireless technology for higher data rates between mobile phones and base antennas. Further in 2004, a handful of the initiatives such as the Broadband Convergence Network (BcN) implementation plan, u-Sensor network and IPv6 Master plans were drawn and implemented (Menon, 2011:19–34). This enabled e-Commerce transactions to surge to several millions of dollars. The year 2005 was the beginning of the digital convergence era which saw the launch of terrestrial and satellite digital multimedia broadcasting (DMB) services. In 2006, there was transition towards the ubiquitous (pervasive) world. This was cemented by the establishment of the 'u-Korea Master Plan', launch of commercial services such as BcN, WiBro, and HSDPA. These interventions saw a surge in ICT access by ordinary citizens and the country being ranked tops in the world using the DOI criterion (Seo, 2011). The diversity of these ICT interventions in a bid to encourage e-Government development have had long-term benefits as over 60% of Korea's public service delivery is now executed online (West, 2010; Seo, 2011).

Noh (2009) outlines further initiatives towards e-Government development in Korea as follows: from 1987 to 1997, the legal and regulatory framework was put in place. This included the Computer Network Act of 1986 and the Informatisation Promotion Act of 1995. From 1998 to 2002, the Korea Information Infrastructure (KII) project was established and the legal framework included the Digital Divide Act of 2001, the Knowledge Resource Management Act of 2000, and the e-Government Act of 2001. From 2003 to 2007, there was active promotion of the ICT industry countrywide. This saw the implementation of 31 e-Government roadmap projects in 2003, implementing of broadband IT Korea Vision 2007, and the BcN plan of 2004 (Menon, 2011:26).

A Master Plan strategy (IT839 Strategy) was implemented in 2007 and aimed to achieve digital excellence and replication of an ICT-ready industry in all towns of Korea. The IT839 strategy was hinged on encouraging the implementation and usage of the following services: WiBro, DMB (terrestrial/satellite), intelligent and ubiquitous Home Network, Telematics, RFID-based, W-CDMA, terrestrial D-TV, and the Internet telephony (VoIP). Tentatively, a total of 101 laws, including the Electronic Signature Act and Online Digital Contents Industrial Promotion Act have been enacted for appropriate development of the IT industry in Korea. Most of these ICT innovations are being utilised in the context of e-Government.

The Korean experience provides a case where utilisation of ICT in various socio-economic sectors such as in education (e-Learning) was speedily adopted due to the cultural acceptance of the ICT usage (Kim, 2002:49). This positively impacted on the ICT diffusion process. Parents and pupils related to ICTs as a medium of education which had much potential for a promising future and therefore encouraged and facilitated its adoption.

In general, Korea's journey to e-Government has been as follows:

- Stage 1 (mid 1980s to mid 1990s) – establishment of 'Korea Information Infrastructure' project.
- Stage 2 (mid 1990s to late 1990s) – enactment of the framework act for information promotion in 1995 and the formation of the national plan for information promotion, and evolution to full scale e-Government.
- Stage 3 (2001 onwards) – acceleration of efforts for e-Government implementation with establishment of a special committee on e-Government. During this time, national e-Government projects are being actively rolled out.

The stage-by-stage development of e-Government in Korea substantiates the fact that e-Government development passes through distinct stages before it finally matures into being adopted widely in various socio-economic platforms. The different initiatives implemented in Korea and the step-by-step e-Government development further provide insight to this study on e-Government development in less developed countries that there is need for a concerted effort from multiple stakeholders and does not happen overnight.

8.2.4 Africa

Apart from a few countries such as Mauritius, South Africa and Egypt, there have generally not been many dedicated e-Government interventions on the continent of Africa, and there has correspondingly been low usage of ICT in government public service delivery platforms. This section explores the different e-Government interventions that have been done in South Africa and Mauritius and presents the current status of e-Government development in these countries.

a) Mauritius

Mauritius is the leader of e-Government Readiness and implementation on the African continent (UN e-Government Survey, 2010:48; Asiimwe, 2010:26; Rorissa & Demissie, 2010:5). Mauritius' strength lies in its ability to implement an integrated Web portal which is relatively interactive, (cf: www.gov.mu), allowing an array of sophisticated transaction-based services to static information to different e-Government stakeholders and users (Capurro & Britz, 2010:31–33); and a relatively high Human Development Index (0.800) and an adult literacy rate of 84.4% (Fosu & Mwabu, 2010:3; Wolff, Chong & Auffhammer, 2011:854). Mauritius' e-Government implementation has steadily developed because of government's desire to transform it into a Cyber island and transcend towards putting in place an information-based society where interactive ICT platforms are readily available for citizens and businesses to readily interact with the government (e-Government Initiatives, 2005; Pudaruth et al., 2010:416). Also, there is a strong will from the private sector thus e-Government is implemented effectively using the public-private-partnership (PPP) model.

Some of the most visible e-Government projects implemented have been the Contribution Network Project (CNP) which is a government-to-business (G2B) initiative of the Ministry of Finance. The CNP allows large employers to pay tax electronically (Vencatachellum & Pudaruth, 2010). In 2001, the e-Government Task Force was set up to spearhead the e-Government mandate in Mauritius (Vencatachellum & Pudaruth, 2010). E-Government Initiatives (2005) details the specific programmes that were implemented in a bid to promote e-Government development as follows: set up of the Government Online Centre (GOC) infrastructure at the Ebene Cybercity; unveil the e-Government Master Plan for the Civil service and set up the Government Web Portal; appointment of Chief Information Officers (CIOs) within individual ministries; set up of a Central IT Committee (CITC) at the Prime Minister's Office; and set up of a CIOs Council (Chauhan & Singh, 2011:16). To account for appropriate change management initiatives, a training programme targeting 5000 civil servants was set up in 2002 to provide the necessary IT-related training; introduced the e-Government Interoperability Framework (e-GIF) which sets out the technical policies and specifications to achieve interoperability and information coherence across the public service (Chauhan & Singh, 2011:11).

Just like Korea discussed above, Mauritius has shown a lot of commitment in advancing the e-Government agenda by financing and providing the technical support to the e-Government initiatives. Specifically, the e-Government task force has been able to achieve the following towards the overall e-Government agenda:
- Set up the Government Online Centre (GOC) to create a 'connected Government' for better online communication (the GOC also hosts the Government Portal).
- Established the Government Intranet System (GINS) to enable different agencies, departments and line ministries to integrate their services, share information and collaborate in the G2G e-Government framework.
- Set up community access points in Post Offices; computerised the back office applications in Ministries and Departments; introduced information security standards (ISO/IEC 17799) in the Civil Service in a view to provide the overall guidelines on the security of information systems.
- Set up an IT Security Unit at the Ministry of Information Technology and Telecommunications to inter-alia assist government departments to implement security standards and to carry out audit of Information Security Management Systems (ISMS).

- Prepared an ICT Manual for the civil service to provide a comprehensive set of guidelines, standards and procedures with regard to ICT implementation.
- Introduced Web standards document that outlined how context should be displayed on e-Government websites in Mauritius.

The institutional framework is thus largely evident looking at the aforementioned interventions that the Government of Mauritius has put in place. Regarding the legal framework, the government introduced the ICT Act of 2001 (cf: telecomit.gov.mu/download/ictact.pdf) which lays out the institutional and procedural guidelines for the regulation and democratisation of ICT-related matters. To combat cybercrime, the Computer Misuse and Cybercrime Act of 2003 (cf: telecomit.gov.mu/download/misuse.pdf) was formulated with the aim to repress criminal activities on the cyberspace and any criminal activities that may be perpetrated through computer systems. The Data Protection Act of 2004 protects the privacy rights of individuals regarding developments of techniques used for capturing, transmitting, manipulating, recording, or storing data relating to individual persons (Vencatachellum & Pudaruth, 2010; Chauhan & Singh, 2011:16).

The e-Government master plan of 2003 lined up a set of strategies and action plans for the implementation of e-Government in Mauritius (Chauhan & Singh, 2011:11–13). The specific recommendations coming of this, and which have been implemented to advance the e-Government agenda, included the following:
- There was need to set up a National Information Infrastructure (NII) to enable the public to have online access.
- Need to introduce Public Key Infrastructure (PKI) to provide additional security across e-Government applications.
- Need to investigate the possibilities of implementing multi-channel technologies in the context of e-Government services; and the establishment of Government Online Center (GOC).

It is worth mentioning that these state-of-the-art e-Government interventions come at a cost which takes a lot of commitment and dedication especially from a resource-constrained country from Africa (Evans & Yen, 2005:360–361; Bertot, Jaeger & Grimes, 2008:139–142; Lin et al., 2011:271). Therefore, Mauritius has shown that is adequately dedicated to advance its e-Government agenda. Stakeholder dedication in implementation strategies aimed at developing the e-Government institution is a cardinal point when a country intends to provide public services through ICT platforms.

b) South Africa

In addition to Mauritius, South Africa (SA) is one of the countries in Africa that has also achieved some considerable strides in promoting global ICT usage in its public service platforms (Basaruddin, Nawi, Shukor, Jusoff, Jahari & Saleh, 2010:114; Capurro & Britz, 2010:27). South Africa has massively invested in ICT infrastructure such as optical fibre networks and promoting ICT skills amongst its citizens who are the major consumers of e-Government services (Capurro & Britz, 2010:29; Kaisara & Pather, 2011:212). Just before hosting of the World Cup 2010, the authorities saw it necessary to put in place more robust and appropriate ICT infrastructures. These infrastructures are now are correspondingly contributing towards encouraging faster adoption of ICTs.

South Africa is a huge country spanning a total area of about 1,219,090 square kilometres and a population of just over 48 million people. Of these, 8.4% are active Internet users. South Africa is an economic power of Africa producing over 25% of the continent's GDP (DTI, 2009). With such huge socio-economic potential, it is expectant that South Africa should lead initiatives to improve public service delivery such as e-Government.

Some of the notable e-Government initiatives that have been put in place include e-Filing, a tax service used by the Southern African Revenue Service – SARS (Kaisara & Pather, 2008); the Cape Gateway portal presented in three languages – English, Afrikaans and iXhosa (cf: www.capegateway.gov.za/eng/) which offers transparency in public service delivery by offering all government information online; and the Judicial Inspectorate of Prisons, the South African Department of Correctional Services and the Home Affairs National Information System (HANIS) where citizens can access birth and death registration forms online (E-Business Handbook, 2005).

Commitments have been shown by co-operating partners such as the government and the private sector to transform SA into an information society. Some of the notable initiatives have been the Electronic Communications and Transactions Act of 2002 which came up with an e-Strategy especially hinged on developing a world class telecommunications infrastructure; and the putting together of a presidential National Council on ICTs directly answerable to the president of the country. All the e-Government interventions and vision are entrenched onto SA's Vision 2014 (Farelo & Morris, 2006:3).

In order to facilitate the implementation of the different e-Government applications, huge investments have been injected into putting up the National Information Infrastructure Backbone (NIIB) which is a public service network providing the necessary connectivity of e-Government applications (Kaisara & Pather, 2011:212). The e-Government projects are reflected in the national budgets showing the commitment that the government has towards the growth of the e-Government institution. Other initiatives include the Gologanang initiative which is coordinated by the DPSA with private sector sponsorship to provide cheap e-Access for public servants (Kaisara & Pather, 2011:213). E-Participation is promoted by the establishment of multi-purpose community centres which aim to take government services to the people through e-Centres and public information terminals (PITs).

On the legal framework, it is felt that the user should be protected as much as possible from any online bullying by other users or psychological disadvantaging by other users or some of the providers of the e-Government content. Some of the notable policies include: the Electronic Communications Transaction Act of 2002, Minimum Information Security Standards (MISS), the Law Commission Issue Paper on Privacy Public Service Act, and the Handbook on Minimum Interoperability Standards (MIOS). The Electronic Communications Act, formerly the Convergence Bill, aims to transform SA's telecommunications industry into a more competent, competition-oriented industry with multiple players.

Despite main relevant interventions that have been put in place to promote the proliferation of e-Government in South Africa, there are also many challenges that have been faced (Naidoo, 2004:139; Singh, 2007). Implementing an electronic strategy is one such challenge which is further complicated by the language and cultural diversity of the people of SA (Naidoo & Van Jaarsveldt, 2004:2). Another challenge that has been evident for a long time has been the lack of willingness of the government departments and businesses to conduct business online due to lack of a predictable legal environment governing these online transactions. Fortunately, there is hope in this regard as some acts of parliament regarding the same are slowly being implemented with much dedication. Further, most of the websites exist as information silos without due integration with other public services offered by other departments (Du Preez, 2009).

Naidoo (2004:138–144) and Singh (2007) have also highlighted other challenges facing e-Government implementation as follows: lack of clear guidelines on the legal barriers regarding the development of electronic models. In this regard, Chapter 7 above comes in handy; lack of proper educational and training endeavours sorely devoted to the promotion of e-Government; lack of dedicated change management programmes aimed at reducing the lack of preparedness by government institutions, consumers and the business community; and lack of clear plans to manage the negative socio-economic impacts resulting into job losses because of introduction of ICTs in major government business processes replacing the human resource capital.

c) Other e-Government Initiatives in Africa

Apart from South Africa and Mauritius, other African countries such as Ghana, Mozambique, Uganda, Kenya, Tanzania, and Botswana are at the very first stages of implementing e-Government. The e-Government interventions in most of the African countries are being made possible with the help of donor funding. For example, in Mozambique, the Italian government helped with the laying out of much of the e-Government background and strategy (Mabila, Mboane & Mondlane, 2010:13,30) and the UNDP has been supporting the Provincial Digital Resource Centers (CPRDs) which aim at becoming ICT hubs to cater both for access/connectivity as well as information and networking services to local communities (Mabila et al., 2010:6).

From the cases presented above, it is evident that the e-Government institution is slowly being adopted in Africa and several other parts of the world. It has also been stated in the above discussion that successful implementation of e-Government demands consented and well-coordinated efforts from several actors such as the government, private sector/businesses, citizens and civil society organisations. These different stakeholders should buy-in to the idea of e-Government in the first place if they were to support it.

8.3 Distinct Cases of Failure of e-Government Applications

Having looked at largely what have been successes, to a less or more extent, of e-Government applications (brought about by government affluent and appropriate interventions), this section looks at some examples of e-Government interventions that have largely been considered as failures. The discussion of failure cases is important in order to appreciate the impact of different factors on e-Government implementation and presents an opportunity where a balanced analysis of factors influencing e-Government development is presented. This is further presented as input in the development of the conceptual e-Government adoption framework for less developed countries and identifies the major important constructs of an appropriately designed e-Government strategy.

8.3.1 Gambia

One of the failure cases of e-Government have been that of The Gambia. Gambia implemented an e-Government project which had shown a lot of potential on the onset but eventually failed because of lack of strategic sustainability plans for its implementation. Sander, Bell and Rice (2005:135) present three cases of failure of

ICT projects in the republic of The Gambia (TG) which is a typical least developed country (LDC). These projects were implemented in the realm of e-Government as the Government of TG progressively started introducing the use of ICTs in its government departments with funding from donor countries. This section presents two case studies from TG of failure of e-Government implementation and discusses what where the major factors that led to these projects to fail.

a) The Personnel Management Information System

The Personnel Management Organisation (PMO) is the headquarters of the Human Resource (HR) responsible for managing the entire human resource base in TG's public service administration (Sander, Bell & Rice, 2005:151). The PMO maintains huge sets of information for a total of approximately 11000 full-time civil servants, and further handles all the human and/or career development perspectives of all the civil servants (Sander et al., 2005:138). Apart from purely HR duties, the PMO also liaises with the Accountant General's department on payroll issues. With these huge responsibilities of the PMO, it was thought that the use of ICTs in its daily activities, in the framework of e-Government, was desired at all costs. This is a case of back-end e-Government applications sorely targeted at improving efficiency in the public service delivery value chains. To achieve Excellency in personnel information management, the Personnel Management Information System (PMIS) was designed and installed around 1998–1999. This system remained under-utilised until the early 2000s when its active implementation was sought by the PMO. The PMIS was implemented with the help of a grant from the United Kingdom Department for International Development (DfiD). The usage of this system amongst the civil servants was low because they did not have adequate trust in the system itself (Sander et al., 2005:139).

The PMIS' immediate task was to transfer all the data held by the paper-based filing system (P-file data) into the electronic records in the database (Sander et al., 2005:139). The original 1998–1999 database did not give provision for storing or referencing any of the correspondence transactions (such as between PMO and the civil servant on such matters as promotions, career changes, or disciplinary matters). The system was based on four or five Personal Computers (PCs) linked using a P2P network and housed in a special air-conditioned office. The database was implemented as a conventional relational database scheme using Microsoft™ Access™ (Sander et al., 2005:140). The system, including staff, was initially known as the Human Resources Information System (HRIS) but later renamed the PMO Management Information System (PMIS) to align it with the EMIS, HMIS and other planned Gambian government management information systems' schemes.

The implementation of the PMIS started with the PMO staff travelling around the country visiting every civil servant at their place of work, explaining the issue, and getting them to complete the questionnaires. The following were some of the problems that arose from serious discrepancies between the PMIS and P-file data as follows:
- There was difficulty in verifying the information provided by civil servants on some topics as many did not have copies of relevant correspondence.
- The accuracy of the information inputted by Data Clerks was not checked for consistency.
- There were no crosschecks that were made comparing the information gathered on the forms with that on the corresponding P-files.

The operational procedures within PMO were never changed to make use of the PMIS database; paper files continued to be used for all PMO's work. Information regarding the P-files was accurate compared with PMIS data which was unreliable. Because of this and other reasons too numerous to mention, the PMIS was not adopted even to record the largely non-static employee information as civil servants frequently changed roles. The PMIS also showed numerous data access problems. The following reasons contributed in rendering the overall PMIS system useless:
- No training or explanation had been provided to the PMO staff outside HRIS on what a database might be used for and there was no guidance on what information the PMIS contained.
- Since the PMIS was only installed on five work stations located in one room (the HRIS office) whereas the PMO general staff were located in different locations, obtaining data by a general PMO staff was somewhat difficult. This is because they had to come to the HRIS office and ask the PMIS staff to obtain the information they needed.
- Generally, the employees working on the PMO were overworked and too busy to take some time off to visit HRIS so that they can learn how to use the PMIS. The general feeling was that staff had no understanding, let alone interest in the capabilities of the PMIS system. This was due to their propensity to resist change.

The PMIS stayed dormant for a period of 2 to 3 years before being revamped to live up to its expectations (Sander et al., 2005:140). These three years were actually a failure of this project and this came about principally from two causes: 1) the aid agency (DfiD) did not understand the operational – human and physical – environment in which the PMIS system was operated, and 2) the intended beneficiaries were unaware of how this system could be employed in a more useful manner to ease the difficulties encountered in their day-to-day activities. To reverse this failure of the project, the following interventions were put in place:

- Regarding the planned system updates, it was suggested that there should be acquisition of additional PCs / terminals so that they are placed at selected staff desks and linked to the PMIS core so that there could be easier access to information.
- PMO staff are being trained on how to use the PMIS by showing them what information the PMIS holds, how to extract it and how to utilise it in their work.
- Integrated the PMIS into simple day-to-day PMO operations. The other desired suggestion to improve the operations of the PMIS was to integrate it with the various existing systems in the public administration establishment so as to encourage G2G applications.

From this case study, distinct factors have been identified on what led to the failure of this e-Government initiative. Some of the factors identified are resistance to change by the public service employers, lack of technical or social buy-in by different users, lack of adequate ICT skills to effectively use different e-Government platforms, lack of trust in the e-Government platforms, and lack of a clearly-defined strategic implementation plan. The contextual environment in TG may be very similar to many environments in the less developed countries.

b) The Health Management Information System

TG's Department of State for Health and Social Welfare (DoSH&SW) is responsible for providing the general health care to the people. Most of the delivery of health care has been implemented at the community level. Secondary and tertiary services are provided by 4 hospitals and approximately 40 health facilities with more than 500 health posts at the primary level (in conjunction with the private sector health providers). Most of the DoSH&SW offices have been equipped with necessary ICT infrastructure throughout the country. This was made possible using funding acquired from donations from the donor community or funded by donor agencies such as World Health Organisation (WHO) and/or purchased using credit from the World Bank. The first initiative of a Health Management Information System (HMIS) was funded by the African Development Bank (ADB).

The ABK was responsible for the funding of the Participatory Health Population and Nutrition Project (PHPNP), which was initially a 5 year project but extended subsequently. PHPNP included HMIS as part of its Capacity Building and Policy Development programme. The HMIS was a comprehensive system with the following components: Health Indicator System (key health indicators information); Finance and Accounting Information System (financial activities of DoSH&SW); and the Maintenance Information System (information regarding the management and repair of various medical equipment, vehicles and facilities throughout DoSH&SW).

However, despite the HMIS being promising, it was a failure project. The critical issues linked to their perceived failures (and the suggested remedies for the HMIS to succeed) were identified as detailed in Table 8.1 below.

Table 8.1: Mitigation of failure of HMIS implementation.

Reason for failure	Remedy suggested
HMIS was a complicated and large system which had other systems such as FAIS embedded into it	Limit the scope – narrow the focus to the original requirements by implementing only three out of the eight core components identified in the HMIS policy
The sustainability of the system was not taken into consideration to a greater extent	Focus development of a solid core foundation on which the system was built to ensure its sustainability
Centralisation of the HMIS	Need for de-centralisation so that the HMIS could also be housed into divisional offices and build divisional capacity by providing the divisional staff with ICT training and installing essential ICT infrastructure
Evidence of departmental silos negatively impacting on departmental integration	Need to develop and establish the core infrastructure for HMIS that would enable inter-departmental communication, collaboration and co-operation
Lack of adequately trained human resource	Need to have competent IT developers or train some so that they can largely participate in the HMIS applications; also train the health personnel on how to interact with the basic HMIS system cores and on data analysis techniques
Unreliable power supplies consistently bringing damage to the systems	PHPNP to acquire necessary protective equipment (including UPSs, Voltage Regulators and fused Power Strips), establishment of long-term maintenance strategy and anti-virus software for sustainability

(Partially sourced from DoSH&SW, 2002)

Table 8.1 above has identified the different problems that were identified which directly contributed to the failure of HMIS implementation. The remedies are the initiatives that were implemented by co-operating partners and stakeholders on how to mitigate the impact of the identified reasons on overall implementation of the HMIS. Apart from these general reasons for failure, there were specific reasons that negatively impacted on HMIS implementation in Gambia. As detailed by Sander et al., (2005), the specific issues that led to the failure of the HMIS in The Gambia are the following:

- There was lack of high level support for ICT activities.
- Donors were generally unable to assess need before committing to implementing the HMIS (systems were installed as part of a worldwide effort without due consideration to their relevance to the country and caused serious disruption to the running of the health care system in general).
- There was lack of sustainability plans especially in as far as maintenance is concerned; inadequate basic education on the usage and basic functionality of the system (and lack of adequate IT trained personnel to maintain the system for sustainability).
- There was inadequate basic technical infrastructure including persistent power and water unavailability.
- There was lack of national capacity to acquire licensed software for HMIS applications.

The above two cases have brought out the major factors that have affect adoption of ICTs in the public service in Gambia. Given that the ICT contextual environmental in African countries is more or less similar to each other, these factors can be found in most of the African countries. The articulation of the different factors that influence successful e-Government implementation outlined above may help other less developed countries come up with carefully-designed e-Government implementation. In essence, it is important to note that despite countries' classification as developing countries, they may have different contextual settings with different cultures. Therefore, appropriate e-Government designs are those that reference experiences in similar environments but the final stimulus for design approach is done by local contextual characteristics.

8.3.2 India

In Asia, India serves as a country that has some of its major e-Government projects fail. Studying the factors that lead to failure of these projects in India may serve as further insights in understanding the multi-dimensional factors that affect e-Government implementation in less developed countries. Kumar and Best (2006:1–12) present a case study exploring the impact and sustainability of e-Government services in Tamil Nadu, India. The discussion centers on the adoption of village Internet facilities in the framework of the e-Government program. A total of 12 kiosks were included in this study. These kiosks offered the following e-Government services: birth certificates, death certificates, income certificates, community certificates, petitions of grievance to government officials, and old age pensions. E-Government services started in November 2001, peaked up to almost full potential by September 2002, and virtually stopped in December 2002. This project failed because it did not attract adequate political and administrative support to remain institutionally viable. Major factors identified for this failure were mainly centered on people, management, cultural, and structural barriers. The major factors for failure accentuate the fact that the multi-dimensional nature of e-Government entails that its success depends on multiple factors drawn from various socio-economic domains.

This project, named SARI, was a collaborative venture of several organisations including the Indian Institute of Technology (IIT), Madras; Berkman Center for Internet and Society, Harvard University Law School; Georgia Institute of Technology; I-Gyan Foundation; and n-Logue Communications Pvt Ltd (Kumar & Best, 2006:2). Using Wireless-in-Local Loop (WLL), Internet connectivity was provided to the local community in Internet kiosks using a self-sustained business model with cost recovery through service charges. Using written orders (issued in 2001), this project started on a solid ground with appropriate institutional partnerships with the government. This partnership allowed kiosks to send electronic applications for various e-Government services, and established a coordinating mechanism for monitoring such applications.

The SARI project has shown that initially, the kiosks had succeeded in delivering e-Government services to their communities but subsequently failed. The following were the major factors that led to the failure of this project:

- There were difficulties in obtaining timely and adequate responses from the district offices to the applications sent from the kiosks. This was motivation enough for citizens to revert to the traditional government systems where public services are accessed by physically visiting the government office and using paper systems.
- The government officials were not adequately trained to accept this new mode of governance and those who had acquired some knowledge after some time were frequently shifted to other locations.
- There was lack of sustained and effective public leadership, commitment and institutionalisation of the e-Government endeavours.
- There was no sustainable coordination and monitoring of the project (such as the subsequent stopping of the monthly coordination meetings between

the district administration and the private project partners for evaluating and monitoring the e-Government services).
- Lack of appropriate stakeholder involvement (confining consultation with the government administrative set up and leaving out the private project partners at the local level and the local elected representatives (at the village and district office levels).
- The shift in the existing power relations in the kiosks (some district and village level officials perceived the implementation of e-Government through the kiosks as a threat to their role, authority, and influence in the community if they were to lose their traditional contact with the villagers applying for these services).

A cursory analysis of the reasons for failure of the SARI project reveals that multi-dimensional factors may impact on e-Government development.

8.3.3 Lessons learnt from failed e-Government projects

A look at the case studies of e-Government project implementation in both The Gambia and India reveals some common oversights that e-Government designers fail to incorporate into their design frameworks. It is important that these oversights be incorporated into the e-Government agenda of any country that intends to implement e-Government. It is important to note that comparing the reasons that lead to failure of e-Government projects are almost identical regardless of whether the project was implemented in Africa or not. The following are some of the factors that impact on e-Government implementation:
- **Technology:** Despite being touted as the key enabler for successful implementation of e-Government, Information Technology (IT) was not a factor to determine the failure or success of project implementation; technology on its own was a mute factor in aiding any meaningful adoption of e-Government. Management of technology to allow sustainability was what the actual problem was. Technology management prowess is important in any e-Government implementation environment because it concerns technology integration strategies into the various business processes of the public service infrastructure. This was the case both in India and the Gambia.
- **ICT infrastructure problems severely affected project implementation:** The Gambia had lack of reliable power and telephone services which directly impacted on the implementation of the overall programme. In the rural areas of India, this problem was recurrent.

- **Culture and contextual conditions:** understanding cultural and contextual differences is cardinal to the implementation of any e-Government project. Both in the case of The Gambia and India, it was observed that there was basically poor quality of the education system, immature management context, and underdeveloped ICT infrastructures were totally ignored when the two e-Government interventions were designed. Also, robust training programmes were not put in place to ensure project recipients fully understand and appreciate the ramifications of the project.
- **Project sustainability plans:** In general, project cases in both The Gambia and India did not put in place long-term sustainability plans. The Gambia projects were implemented by a funding organisation over a fixed period of time excluding all the running costs such as hardware and software maintenance costs, telephone and Internet charges, cost of consumables such as paper, printer cartridges and backup media, and salaries required for retention of technical staff. There was a lack of dedicated e-Government endeavours to pursue sustainable funding such as engaging in PPP, vertical and horizontal funding mechanisms, and reliance on private owned ICT infrastructures. In the case of India, there were no responsive monitoring and evaluation endeavours to ascertain the evolving impact of e-Government which could otherwise contribute to project sustainability.
- **Lack of appropriately designed change management programmes:** existing staff in the public administration are afraid that their roles might be taken over by technology so do nothing to accelerate the e-Government agenda. In the case of India, many leaders were not aware of e-Government and it therefore came as a shock when they were implored to employ ICTs in their day-to-day work activities.
- **Suitable local individuals:** Severe lack of suitable local individuals for identification so that they may be trained as technical staff to further maintain e-Government system development as requirements evolve over time.
- **Local infrastructure:** Lack of appropriate local infrastructure (such as lack of reliable power supply, computer maintenance companies, availability of software development personnel) poses a threat to proliferation of e-Government applications.

So far, this chapter has discussed the different factors that may aid success or failure of e-Government. It is important to be in cognizance with these factors and include them in any e-Government agendas. This is very important as it is a direct input into any e-Government implementation roadmaps. The sections above have presented the success and failure projects of e-Government at a very high level of abstraction.

8.4 Detailed Case Study for e-Government Implementation: Zambia

According to the latest statistics, Zambia is one of the Least Developed Countries (LDC) with a population of just over 12 million people (Internet World Statistics, 2010). The country has been ruled using a one-party participatory democracy since 1964 but changed this political system to plural democracy (multi-party democracy) in 1991. Zambia has a moderately developed ICT infrastructure with some optical fibres in existence in most of the major towns, and robust ICT sector institutional, legal and regulatory frameworks. With a relatively developed democratic institution, Zambia is better placed to engulf e-Government which promotes participatory decision and socio-economic inclusiveness of marginal individuals.

Many of the e-Government development initiatives in the third world and emerging countries have been seen to be failing in one aspect or the other. This is because in most of the cases there is no linkage between the design and the actual reality culminating from the political, social, ICT infrastructure, and economical system of the environment in which it is implemented (Coates & Nikolaus, 2010:137–161). In addition, it is evident that most e-Government initiatives in developing countries fail because they are pursued from the highest level of political abstraction and citizens are not properly educated about its value (Coates & Nikolaus, 2010:137–161) and hence find it very difficult to appreciate the benefits that e-Government has to offer. For some of the countries where the citizens do not trust the traditional government system and have no confidence in local politicians, it becomes even more difficult for them to trust a government which is executed through a virtual environment. In order to understand the different facets and hidden intricacies of e-Government, there is need to discuss a detailed Case Study for e-Government in a less developing world context. This section discusses e-Government implementation in Zambia looking at the supply side (interventions put in place in order to encourage e-Government proliferation) and the demand side (readiness and willingness of individuals and businesses to engage in e-Government).

In Zambia, e-Government implementation is at the nascent stage where global interventions are being put in place. Although the e-Government institution is not fully developed, Zambia follows a model where e-Government is being rolled out rapidly to the anticipated consumers simultaneously with the interventions being put in place. Therefore, it is suffice to mention that e-Government implementation has not matured to any appreciable extent (Coates & Nikolaus, 2010:137–161). However, there are signs that, at the individual level, e-Government may develop further. For example, most commercial banks (such as First National Bank (FNB), Zambia National Commercial Bank (ZANACO), and Finance Bank) have introduced online banking where customers can access their accounts anywhere and anytime.

Further, there are chances that e-Government, once properly implemented, can further move Zambia on the road to effective and sustainable development and consolidate its young democracy (Coates & Nikolaus, 2010:137–161). Not only that, as detailed in Chapter 2, successful implementation of e-Government brings about seamless streamlining and integration of government business processes from different organs and ensures reduction in the cost to service delivery.

For the e-Government framework in Zambia, the following are some of the major motivations (Habeenzu, 2010:28):

- Pursuit to overcome administrative barriers and red tape that is available in government departments.
- Desire to simplify business processes in the public service delivery value chains.
- Build institutional capacity and reduce opportunities for the occurrence of corruption.
- Promoting transparency in business operations (pilot institutions included Zambia Revenue Authority, Ministry of Lands and Department of Immigration).

8.4.1 Supply Side of e-Government Implementation in Zambia

In order to encourage the proliferation of e-Government in Zambia, some interventions have been or are being put in place. In a bid to improve operational efficiency and effectiveness, the Government of Zambia has embraced a number of ICT projects and applications such as e-Government earmarked for improvement of information management in the public sector.

The commitment of the Zambian government in advancing e-Government can be seen in its commitment to align it to previous and current overall governance programmes. For example, e-Government is seen as a beacon in advancing the overall agenda of government because it can reach individuals and businesses anywhere at any time (ubiquitous in nature). With this in mind, e-Government has been closely linked to the Public Service Reform Programme (PSRP) which has been implemented from 1993 and aims to improve the quality, efficiency and effectiveness of overall public service delivery. One of the major cornerstones in improving public service delivery has been the acknowledgement that there is need to overhaul the entire business processes (re-engineering). Re-engineering business processes is being done with the help of the Public Service Capacity Building Project (PSCAP) which also aims to support PSRP.

E-Government is being incorporated into the PSCAP so that it hinges well to the overall agenda of the PSRP. For example, one of the PSCAP components is 'Financial Management, Accountability and

Transparency' to which the IFMIS is part. In short, all the different building blocks of e-Government are being implemented in the framework of PSCAP.

The International records Management Trust (IRMT, 2007) provides a summary of some of the major interventions which kick-started the ongoing interventions for the advancement of e-Government as listed in Table 8.2 below.

Table 8.2: Information Management Interventions in Zambia.

Date	Intervention	Anticipated impact
2006	Launch of public service management project	Aims to right size the public service, and to implement the pay and performance management reforms that the Government had pursued since 1993
2007	Introduction of a computerized human resource and payroll system	Towards better control of the establishment, improve information handling, eliminate loss of vital information and improve work flow processes
2007	Launched ICT policy	Among others, to support permeating of e-Government and information systems in the public sector
2007	Introduction of the Payroll Management and Establishment Control (PMEC) system	Improve information flows between the central Public Service Management Division, ministries, departments, regional and district offices, and the Ministry of Finance
2007	Integrated payroll management system with Integrated Financial Management Information System (IFMIS).	strengthen payroll integrity
2007	Implementation of the integrated Public Management Establishment Control (PMEC) System	To control the abuse prevalent in an older system that had resulted in ghost workers on the payroll and unapproved allowances being awarded to employees
2003	Computerization of the Customs system at the Zambia Revenue Authority through the Automated SYstem for CUstoms Data (ASYCUDA), (Nkamba, 2011)	Aim for improving internal efficiencies and provide value-adding business options in the revenue collection business.
2008	Introduction of the Zambia Immigration Management System (ZIMS)	Introduction of the Electronic Passport System and electronic Visa application system

The initiatives shown in Table 8.2 were conceived with the understanding that their effective implementation will culminate into improved information management practices in the public service.

This will in turn positively impact on the quality of the public service delivery. Despite the initiatives outlined in Table 8.4, the empirical study has shown that lack of appropriate access to information systems is a major bottleneck in the e-Government development in Zambia and entails that citizens cannot effectively participate in the various socio-economic frameworks. It is evident from the literature review that there is paucity in the ICT infrastructure in Zambia may be responsible for low Internet and information accessibility by the citizens. In order to address the infrastructure problem, government parastatals and other private entities have joined hands to put in place the requisite ICT infrastructure needed for appropriate information access and management thereof. The following are some of the notable projects for infrastructure development in Zambia:

- The Zambia Telecommunication Company (ZAMTEL) has erected, at a cost of USD48 million, a fibre optical network which spans a distance of 1,913 kilometers meant to provide faster data transmission and increased bandwidth in information interchange.
- The Copperbelt Energy Company (CEC) with approximately 700 kilometres of optical fibre network targeted to improve internal communication and increased bandwidth.
- The Zambia Electricity Supply Company (ZESCO) offers a fibre optical network dubbed 'FibreCom.
- Broadband network' for transmission of electrical energy, as a communication medium for data transfer and carrying Internet traffic for video, voice, and so forth. This network covers a distance of approximately 1,700 kilometres from Sesheke to Lumwana through Livingstone, Lusaka and the Copperbelt. Upon completion, this network will cover approximately 3,000 kilometers.
- There are efforts by ZESCO and ZAMTEL to link their fibre optical networks to the Eastern Africa Submarine Cable System (EASSy) which is since operational. EASSy was the first submarine cable to be operational and serving multiple countries in Africa. Since Zambia is landlocked, tapping from the possibilities of this cable involves passing the cable through neighbouring countries such as Tanzania and Malawi. This further increases the cost of accessing the services that this cable has to offer.
- Introduction of government Local and Wide Area Network based on ring topology fibre networks and Very Small Aperture Terminal (VSAT) technology to encourage seamless inter-organ service integration, improve internal communication, and improve bandwidth.

- Establishing appropriate and vibrant information systems and corresponding e-Government building blocks such as the Integrated Financial Management Information System (IFMIS) Project, Payroll Management and establishment Control Project, the Justice Case Management System Intelligent human resource information systems, and Payroll Management and Establishment Control Project.
- Other private entities such as Realtime Zambia has commissioned its independent end-to-end fibre project enabling corporate entities to link via fibre to the rest of the world through the SAT3 undersea cable. The SAT3 is the submarine cable in the Atlantic Ocean targeting countries along the western coast of Africa. The EASSy is the submarine cable in the Indian Ocean and targeting service data needs of countries along the eastern coast of Africa. These two cables are accessed by landlocked countries depending on proximity.

In promoting universal access, one of the interventions executed has been the liberalisation of the international gateway in an effort to bring down access costs. The recent (in the year 2010) liberalisation of the international gateway has significantly resulted in tariff reductions in as far as access to the Internet and usage of ICTs is concerned. Further, in pursuit of promoting and facilitating faster growth in Internet penetration, the government ushered in the new licensing regime under the ICT Act of 2009 and expects operators to extend Internet services to all parts of the country using broadband technologies. This has culminated into mobile operators' provision of Internet access through mobile phones resulting into tremendous increase in people (over 600,000) accessing the Internet through mobile gadgets.

8.4.2 Demand Side of e-Government Implementation in Zambia

This case study is informed by both primary and secondary data. Secondary data is gathered using extensive literature and document reviews on the status of e-Government development in Zambia. In particular, papers by Weerakkody et al., (2007:484–505), and Coates and Nikolaus (2010:137–161) are being extensively referenced to understand the current status of e-Government development in Zambia. The primary data was gathered in the empirical study: the pilot study and the main study. The empirical study further contained both interviews and questionnaire-type data collection methods. The questionnaire contained both open and closed-ended questions enabling it to collect both qualitative and quantitative data therefore emphasising the mixed methods approach that was utilised in the study.

The targeted sample size was 721 people. The data collection instrument in the form of a questionnaire included open-ended questions that did not restrict the respondent on how he or she should fill in the questionnaire regarding his or her opinions on any pre-defined phenomenon. Closed-ended questions were asked with options out of which a respondent was mandated to choose one or more of them relating to his experience about a phenomenon under investigation (Wilson, 1996; Saunders et al., 2002). Data was collected with the objective to gain primary data, that is, to have an original source of raw data without any interpretation, synthesis or analysis which represents a position on a specific matter (Cooper & Schindler, 2001). A total of 411 people participated in this study. The research participants were drawn from different sectors in Zambia including the following: government ministries, parliament, the private sector and civil society, the Zambia ICT Authority (ZICTA), staff at the University of Zambia, and the general public. The study utilised both quantitative and qualitative methods in investigating the same phenomenon in a study. For example, in this study, the Mahalanobis distance is analysed using two approaches: observation of the scatter plot showing the distances between the different cases in the data set, and the Mahalanobis distance shown by the residual statistics.

The study targeted businesses with potential to utilise e-Government applications and individuals who potentially had the requisite ICT education and skills to engage in e-Government applications. To be included in the study, it was necessary that a target participant be at least 16 years old and have completed some form of higher education and/or ICT education to be conversant with basic ICT usage. This is because it was assumed that citizens with such characteristics may likely use the Internet and therefore potential to engage in e-Government. Only participants from the towns of Kitwe, Lusaka and Livingstone were included in the study. These specific towns were chosen because they all lie along the line of rail where major interventions (such as erection of robust fibre optics) have been implemented by various ICT stakeholders from both the public and private sectors. Further, each of these towns has a population of over one million people and so it was easy to reach the targeted research participants.

Table 8.3 below shows the biometric data of the participants. It is evident that most of the participants have basic and tertiary education substantiating the likelihood to engage use e-Government services.

Table 8.3: Characteristics of participants.

Parameter	Subject (N = 408)
Age (mean, range)	26-49, 16-70
Gender (male, female, missing)	220, 164, 24
Race/ethnicity (African, other)	338, 21
Native language (English, Bemba, Tonga, Nyanja, others)	16, 121, 93, 77, 102
Education (PhD, Masters, Bachelors, other)	87, 22, 128, 172
Employment status (employed, unemployed)	312, 97

As mentioned previously, the total number of questionnaires that were returned and accepted for analysis in the main empirical study was 408. Using the Kaiser-Meyer-Olkin (KMO) measure to test sampling adequacy, the number of participants in this study shows that it is greater than 0.5 in all the cases and therefore adequate for appropriate statistical analysis. The KMO test was conducted on all the questions in the questionnaire to determine the sample adequacy. In the main study, a total of 721 questionnaires were distributed to potential study participants. Only 411 questionnaires were returned for analysis and eventually 408 questionnaires were included in the final analysis, representing a 57% overall response rate.

8.4.3 Questions and Responses Counter

Table 8.4: Awareness of e-Government initiatives in Zambia.

		Not at all aware
E-Government websites of the Lusaka City Council and other government agencies in Zambia.	Count	129
	Row N%	32.3%
The benefits of using Zambian e-Government websites.	Count	108
	Row N%	27.2%
Educational/training programs about the overall features of Zambian e-Government websites.	Count	138
	Row N%	34.5%
Government campaigns/advertisements encouraging the use of e-Government websites in Zambia.	Count	169
	Row N%	42.3%

This section presents the actual (*voet-stoed* ('as is')) data collected in this study showing the questions asked and the responses counter and perceptions on each of the questions. Please note that not all questions are shown here and the ones shown are for reference purposes only. The tables show how many people attempted a given question and in what category they answered a particular question. For example, in Question 9.2 of the questionnaire which aimed to investigate the general awareness of e-Government initiatives in Zambia, Table 8.4 below shows the specific responses from the respondents.

In summary, the respondents posited the following regarding e-Government development in Zambia:

- Generally, half of the respondents indicated that they have the requisite skills necessary to use a computer efficiently and have the adequate ICT skills to effectively use e-Government websites. Despite this being the case, the survey has shown that usage of e-Government applications is low with only 27% of the respondents acknowledging that they use e-Government applications and the rest absconding.
- A total of 49% of the respondents indicated that they were not at all aware of any e-Government services in Zambia. Only 30% indicated they were moderately or slightly aware and the rest indicated that they were fully aware of e-Government services in Zambia.
- Regarding reliability of information on the e-Government websites, over 61% of the respondents indicated that it is not reliable; 69% of the respondents indicated that there are no policies in place to protect the user in the online environment and 84% of the respondents indicated that there are no security policies stated on the e-Government websites. Further, 84% of the respondents

Slightly aware	Somewhat aware	Moderately aware	Fully aware	Total
66	90	38	38	399
16.5%	22.6%	9.5%	9.5%	100%
67	74	50	50	397
16.9%	18.6%	12.6%	12.6%	100%
86	70	31	31	400
21.5%	17.5%	7.8%	7.8%	100%
72	65	23	23	400
18.0%	16.3%	5.8%	5.8%	100%

mentioned that they would not allow the government to share their information with other sites or be stored in a central repository. This will have direct implications on the seamless service integration desired by e-Government applications.
- Over 50% of the respondents agreed that lack of readily available Internet access, affordable Internet, non-availability of appropriate and readily accessible ICT infrastructure, non-availability of native language options, lack of awareness campaigns and lack of appropriate end-user support directly contribute to low development of e-Government in Zambia.
- As can be seen from Table 8.4 above, a majority of the participants agreed that they are ready to continue using e-Government applications if appropriate interventions are put in place for it to become reliable.

The study utilises inferential statistics which require that, for appropriate statistical inferences to be obtained, there is a need for the data set to follow the Gaussian normal distribution. For this reason, this study utilises the multivariate normality testing procedure to test for normality. The data set utilised in this research showed some abnormality when analysed using the Kolmogorov-Smirnov and the Shapiro-Wilk normality test. It was thus necessary that data transformation (data screening) be administered to correct the negative skewness and remove the outliers (i.e. extreme values of observed variables that can distort estimates of regression coefficients) from the data set.

In essence, residual scatter plots (essentially utilised to check atypical cases) were utilised to check the following:
- **Normality:** the residuals should follow the general Gaussian normal distribution. A normal distribution presents a good model for assessing random phenomena and, with reference to the central limit theorem, posits that when the sample size gets large, some of the sample statistics behave as if they are normally distributed variables.
- **Linearity:** the residuals should have a straight-line relationship with predicted dependent variable scores.
- **Homoscedasticity:** variance of the residuals about the predicted dependent variable scores should be the same for all the predicted scores.

All the variables such as ICT infrastructure, Perceived Usefulness (PU), Perceived Ease of Use (PEOU), trust, language and content were tested for normality to determine whether they confirm to the general Gaussian distribution which shows data normality. For references' purposes, the following shows the distribution obtained from the data set on ICT infrastructure. It should be noted that most of the data from the empirical study follow the same characteristics as 'ICT infrastructure'.

Multivariate regression analysis was done in order for this research to draw out appropriate statistical inferences. The inferences included in the final analysis were arrived at after comparing the various results obtained using multiple statistical analysis methodology. For example, in determining the number of factors to include in the proposed e-Government model, both restricted Exploratory Factor Analysis (EFA) and Principal Component Analysis (PCA) were utilised as statistical approaches. The factors used in the analysis are as follows:

ICT_infra = *ICT infrastructute;*
PEOU = *Perceived Ease of Use;*
PU = *Perceived Usefulness;*
Comp_SE = *Computer self-efficacy;*
Actual_Usage = *Actual usage of e-Government applications; and*
Cont_Usage = *continuous usage of e-Government applications*

The above statistical procedures ensured that the emerging analysis from this study was highly statistically relevant and acceptable. In order to understand what factors influence e-Government adoption at the individual level, the TAM was used as the main theoretical lens. With a goal of getting more insight on the demand side of e-Government in Zambia, a total of seven hypotheses were subjected to statistical testing using multiple regression analysis. For the purposes of this book, detailed statistical procedures have been dropped to ensure a logical flow of content.

8.5 Testing Hypotheses

The hypotheses were subjected to rigorous statistical testing to establish their validity and impact on the continuance usage of e-Government applications and correspondingly e-Government development in Zambia.

Perceived ease of use of e-Government websites will positively influence the perception of usefulness of e-Government websites and applications.

[Hypothesis 1]

To test Hypothesis 1, several tests were done; the first one being regression analysis using the square root of PU after the cases with large residuals (outliers) were removed. Regression was then performed using the logarithmic value of 'PU' and this was utilised to analyse the data set. The descriptive statistics of the PEOU and the PU data set are shown in Table 8.5 below.

Table 8.5: Descriptive statistics of the PEOU and the PU data set.

	Mean	Std. Deviation	Number of Respondents
Log_PU	.2794	.14943	401
PEOU	3.1004	.78930	377

Using Pearson's correlation, Table 8.6 shows that there is some correlation, although not a substantial one (-0.317) between the dependent and independent variable with higher statistical significance. All requested variables on PEOU have been entered and the Log_PU is the dependent variable. Table 8.6 below shows the correlation between the dependent and independent variables, PU and PEOU, respectively.

Table 8.6: Correlations between PU and PEOU

		Log_PU	PEOU
Pearson Correlation	Log_PU	1.000	-.371
	PEOU	-.371	1.000
Sig. (1-tailed)	Log_PU	.	.000
	PEOU	.000	.
N	Log_PU	401	377
	PEOU	377	377

It can also be seen from Table 8.6 above that the number of respondents (N) who attempted questions with the measured variables was more than 377 and therefore enough to establish validity of the statistical procedures. Table 8.7 below shows the R square value which details the predictive value of PEOU on PU. R squared is the proportion of variation in the dependent variable explained by the regression model. R squared equals the coefficient of determination. This value determines how much of the variation in one variable is due to the other variable. R square is .137 which entails that the prediction capacity of the regression model obtained from this data set entails that 13.7% of the variation in the outcome is determined by the predictor variable.

Table 8.7: Model Summary predictive value of PEOU on PU.

Model	R	R Square	Adjusted R Square	Std. Error of the Estimate
1	.371[a]	.137	.135	.13897

Table 8.8 below presents the analysis of variance. It can be seen that the contribution of PEOU on the overall variance of Log_PU is statistically significant at 0.001 level. The values of R squared range from 0 to 1. Small values indicate that the model does not fit the data well. The sample R squared tends to optimistically estimate how well the models fit the population.

Table 8.8: Analysis of Variance.

Model		Sum of Squares	Df	Mean Square	F	Sig.
1	Regression	1.153	1	1.153	59.702	.000[a]
	Residual	7.243	375	.019		
	Total	8.396	376			

a. Predictors: (Constant), PEOU
b. Dependent Variable: Log_PU

A regression analysis, predicting Log_PU from PEOU, was highly statistically significant with the F statistics, $F(1) = 59.702$, $p < .001$. Table 8.9 below is utilised to calculate the regression equation and establish the predicting capacity of the model. It can be observed that the t values associated with the Log_PU scores is significant at the same level the F statistics was. The regression equation for this case is:

$$Log\_PU = 0.497 - 0.070\ PEOU \qquad \textbf{[Equation 1]}$$

Table 8.9: Predicting capacity of the model.

Case Number	Std. Residual	Log_PU	Predicted Value	Residual
-------- 44	-3.071	.00	.4267	-.42674

Dependent Variable: Log_PU

The residual statistics (highlighted in Table 8.0 below) confirmed that the Mahalanobis distance has an acceptable value for one independent variable and does not exceed the Chi-square critical value for 1 degree of freedom which is 10.828.

Table 8.10: Residuals Statistics[a].

	Minimum	Maximum	Mean	Std. Deviation	Number of Respondents
Predicted Value	.1461	.4267	.2794	.05538	377
Stud. Deleted Residual	-3.141	2.481	.000	1.012	377
Mahal. Distance	**.016**	**7.081**	**.997**	**1.454**	**377**

a. Dependent Variable: Log_PU

To demonstrate the validity of the results obtained above, the following three figures (Figure 8.1, Figure 8.2, and Figure 8.3) show the charts to prove that the data set, to a greater or lesser extent, followed the Gaussian normal distribution and that the normal (probability-probability) P-P plot of regression standardised residual with Log_PU as the standardised residual dependent variable.

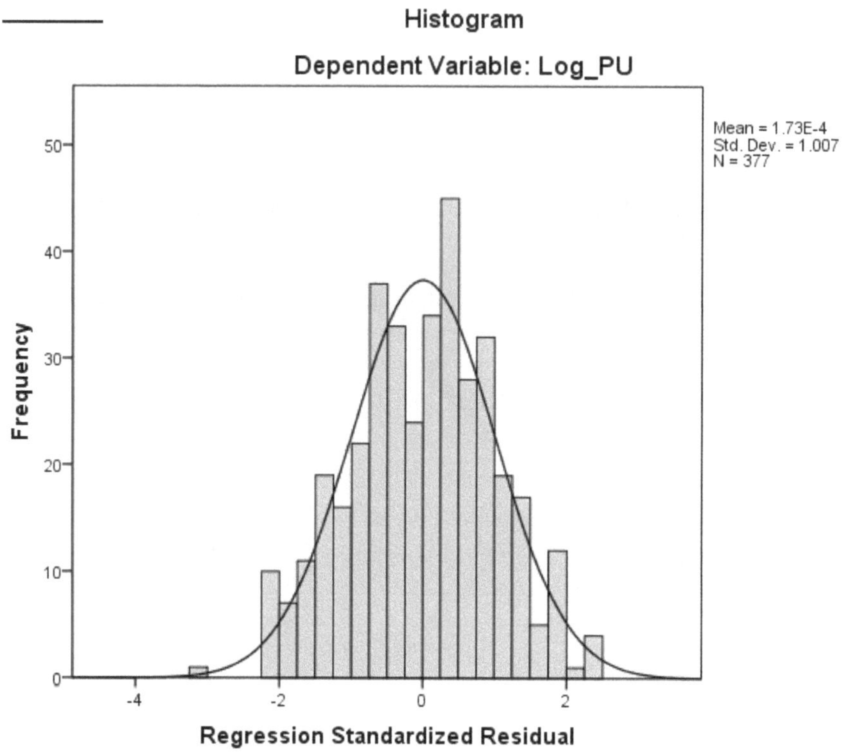

Figure 8.1: Gaussian normal data fit of PU on PEOU.

From Figure 8.1 above, it is evident that although the data set does not follow a complete fit of the Gaussian distribution, only small straits lie outside the cone-shaped figure shown. This demonstrates that the data follows normality to some appreciable extent.

The following figure, Figure 8.2, shows the P-P plot for standardised residue of PU on PEOU. Figure 8.2 shows the linearity in the data set. From the two immediate figures above, it can be observed that the data set does not substantially diverge from normality and therefore the results obtained from the analysis are highly valid.

The scatter plot of the distances between the different cases in the data set shows no defined shape. This confirms that Mahalanobis distance does not exceed the Chi-square critical value for 1 degree of freedom which is 10.828, confirming the value that was earlier obtained using the residual statistics. This fact is supported by the dispersion shown on the scatterplot obtained from this data set as shown in Figure 8.3.

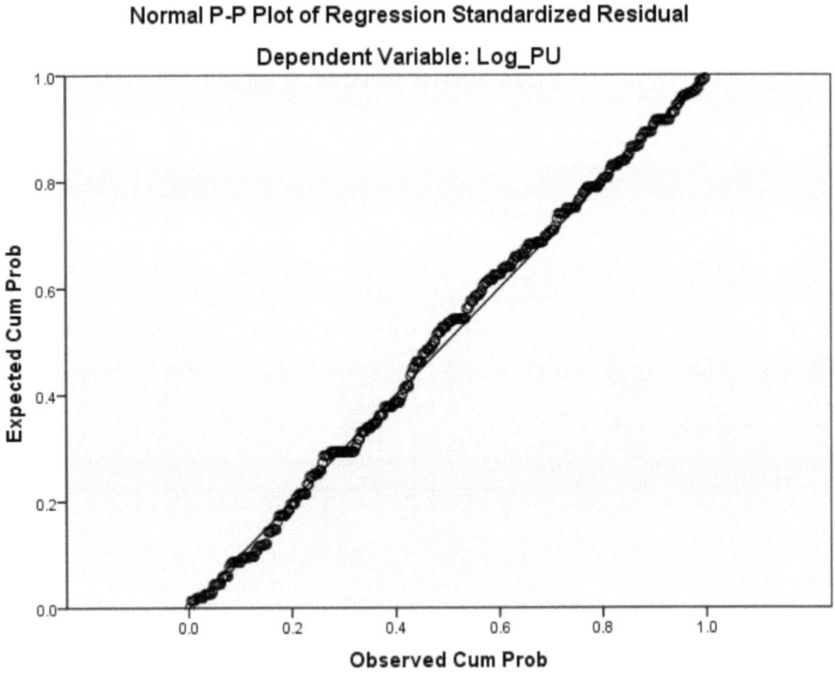

Figure 8.2: P-P plot for standardised residue of PU on PEOU.

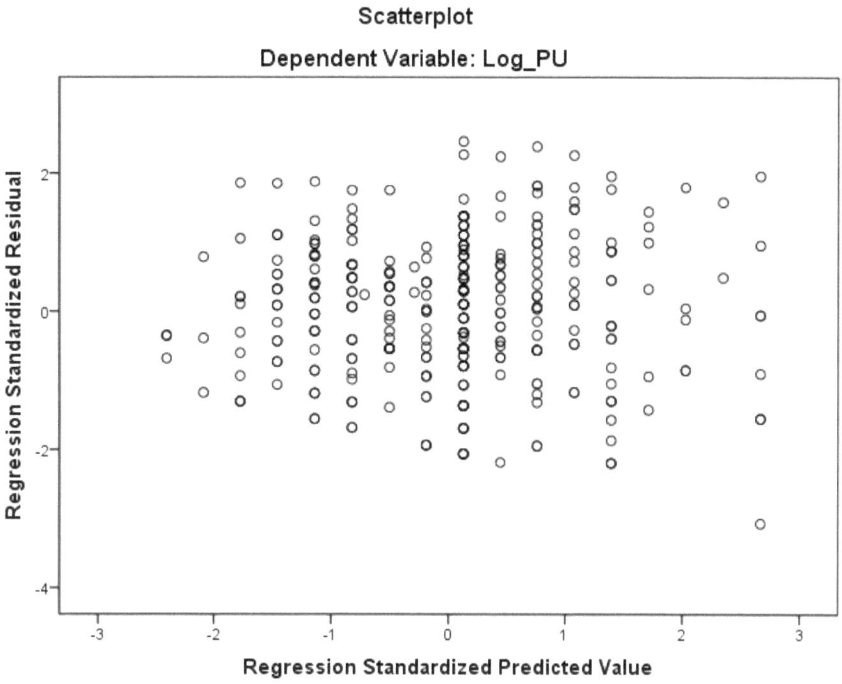

Figure 8.3: Scatterplot of the Mahalanobis distance of PU on PEOU.

Conclusion on H1: From the statistical results shown above, it is evident that PEOU of e-Government websites positively influences the PU of e-Government websites and applications in Zambia. This relationship should, therefore, be considered in the proposed conceptual framework of e-government adoption in Zambia.

> *Perceived usefulness of e-Government websites will positively influence citizen's adoption (actual usage) of e-Government websites and applications.*
>
> **[Hypothesis 2]**

The statistical tests for Hypothesis 2 were done using the same procedure as with Hypothesis 1 above. The first testing case involved regression testing utilising the original variables in the data set. The second test involved finding regression after taking the logarithmic values of both variables and after having excluded case number 247. The third case involved checking the regression on the data set without case 247. Also not included in this analysis were cases 271 and 306 because of having Mahalanobis distances that exceed the Chi-square critical value for 1 degree of freedom which is 10.828. From Figure 8.4 below, it can clearly be seen that the data set utilised in the analysis follows linearity.

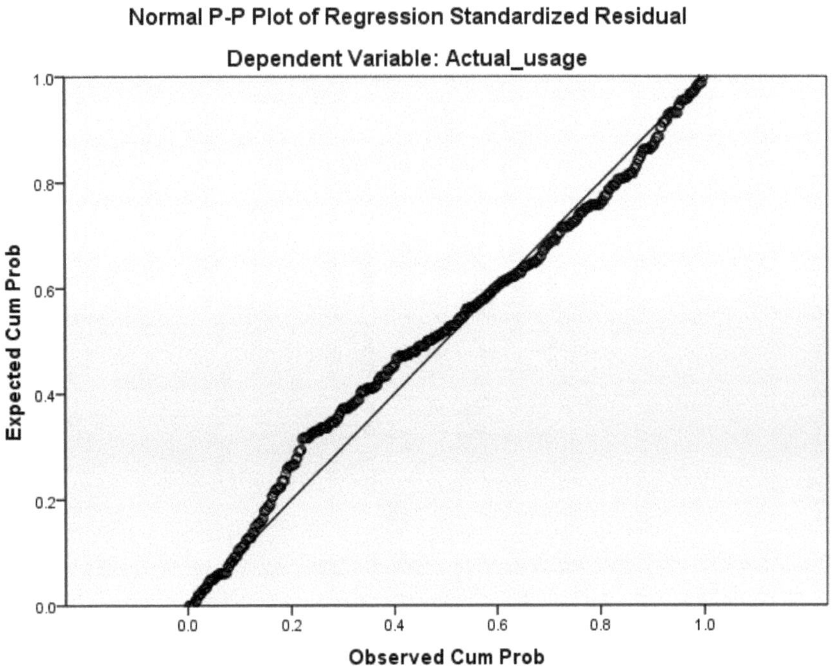

Figure 8.4: P-P plot for standardised residue of actual usage on PU.

Conclusion on H2: Because e-Government has not been globally deployed in the government departments in Zambia, and partly due to lack of affluent awareness campaigns, PU of e-Government applications was not evidently mentioned by the study participants. Therefore, at the current stage of e-Government development in Zambia, the study cannot state with confidence that PU will directly impact on positive adoption of e-Government applications. This has been evidenced by the non-linearity in the data set as shown in Figure 8.3 and Figure 8.4 above. Looking at the strong correlation in the coefficients in the Pearson's Correlation matrix and the higher statistical significance ($p<0.001$) and the acceptable value of R^2 at 24.6% the study posits that at higher maturity levels of e-Government implementation, it is possible that PU could have a direct positive impact on PEOU and correspondingly e-Government adoption.

Perceived ease of use (usability) of e-Government websites will positively influence citizen's adoption of e-Government websites and applications.

[Hypothesis 3]

Using Pearson's correlation, the first test involved using the original variables in the data set and showed very visible non-linearity. The second test carried on the data set showed considerable linearity and correlation (although not a substantial one – 0.238) between the dependent and independent variable with higher statistical significance (0.001). All requested variables on PEOU have been entered and the log. Log_Actual_Usage is the dependent variable.

R^2 value for this test is .238 which entails that the prediction capacity of the regression model obtained from this data set entails that 23.8% of the variation in the outcome is determined by the predictor variable.

A regression analysis, predicting Log_PU from PEOU, was highly statistically significant with $F(1) = 22.591$, $p < .001$. Using casewise diagnostics, case 242 was excluded from the analysis because it has a standard residual value above the norm. It can be observed that the t values associated with the Log_PU scores is significant at the same level the F statistics was. The regression equation for this case is:

$$Log\_Actual\_Usage = 0.358 - 0.041\ PEOU \qquad \textbf{[Equation 2]}$$

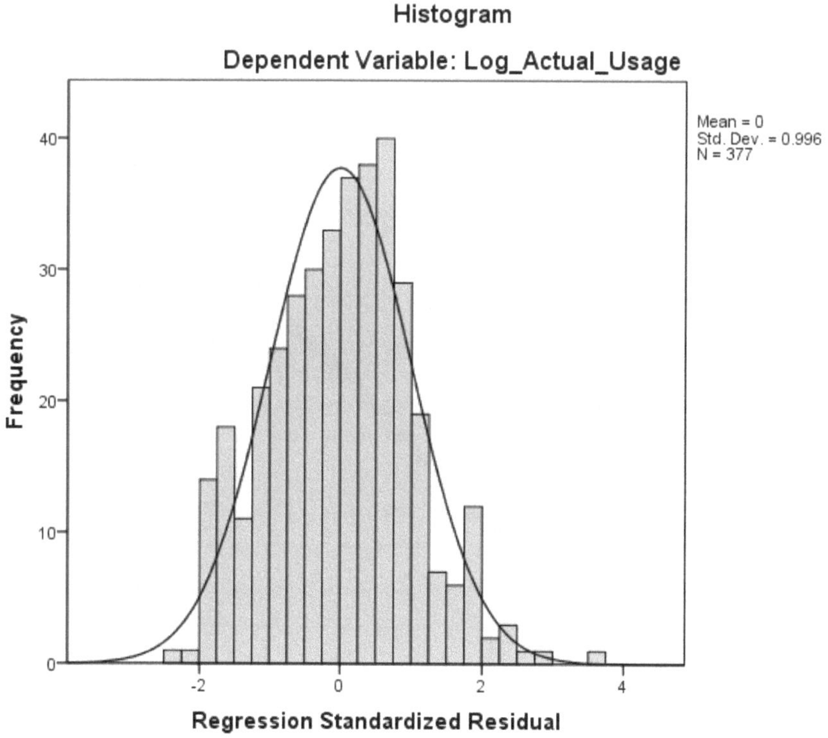

Figure 8.5: Gaussian normal data fit of actual usage on PEOU.

The residual statistics shown below confirmed that the Mahalanobis distance has an acceptable value for one independent variable and does not exceed the Chi-square critical value for 1 degree of freedom which is 10.828.

To demonstrate the validity of the results obtained above, the following figures show the charts to prove that the data set followed, to a greater or lesser extent, the Gaussian normal distribution and that the normal (the probability-probability) P-P plot of regression standardised residual with Log_PU as the standardised residual dependent variable (cf: Figure 8.5 and Figure 8.6).

It is evident from Figure 8.6 that the data set shows a lot of normality because most of the data plotted makes it into the conical shape drawn. Figure 8.7 shows the P-P plot for standardised residue of Log_Actual_Usage on PEOU to demonstrate the linearity in the data and correspondingly how reliable the analysis obtained from this data can be. From these two figures it can be observed that the data set observes normality and linearity; therefore, the results obtained from the analysis are highly valid.

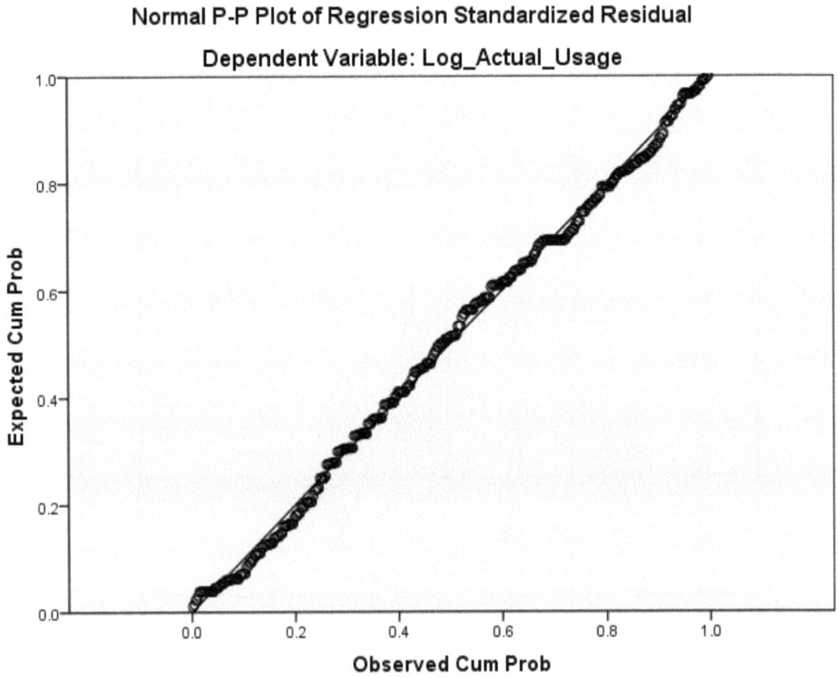

Figure 8.6: P-P plot for standardised residue of actual usage on PEOU.

Conclusion on H3: PEOU will positively influence citizens' adoption of e-Government services. This, therefore, is shown in the proposed conceptual e-Government adoption model for Zambia.

> *Appropriate ICT infrastructure and lower costs to access the basic ICTs impacts positively on usability and correspondingly on perceived ease of use (PEOU).*
> **[Hypothesis 4]**

Similar to the above, statistical tests were done without case 249 in the first test because its residual value lied outside the accepted values as per the casewise diagnostics; second test using the transformed variables to logarithmic values; and the third test using original variables (used for analysis). This test carried on the data set showed considerable linearity and correlation (although not a substantial one – 0.113) between the dependent and independent variable with higher statistical significance (0.001). All requested variables on ICT infrastructure have been entered and the log. PEOU is the dependent variable.

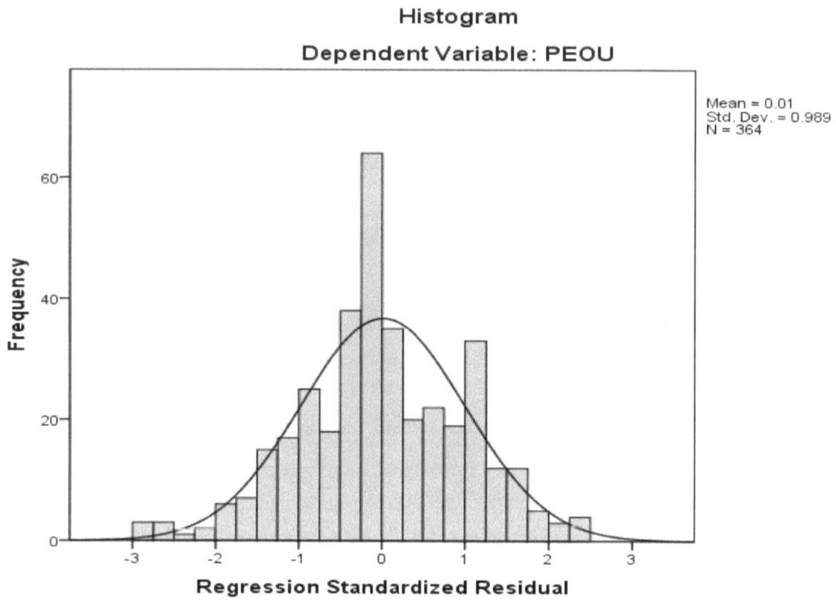

Figure 8.7: Gaussian normal data fit of PEOU on ICT infrastructure.

R^2 value for this test is .13 which means that the prediction capacity of the regression model obtained from this data set entails that 13% of the variation in the outcome is determined by the predictor variable.

A regression analysis, predicting Log_PU from PEOU, was highly statistically significant with $F(1) = 4.708$, $p < .01$. It can be observed that the t values associated with the Log_PU scores is significant at the same level the F statistics was. The regression equation for this case is:

$$PEOU = 2.369 + 0.166\ ICT\_infra \qquad \textbf{[Equation 3]}$$

The residual statistics shown below confirmed that the Mahalanobis distance has an acceptable value. The following figures show the P-P plot of regression standardised residual with PEOU as the standardised residual dependent variable.

Figure 8.8 below, shows the P-P plot for standardised residue of PEOU on ICT infrastructure.

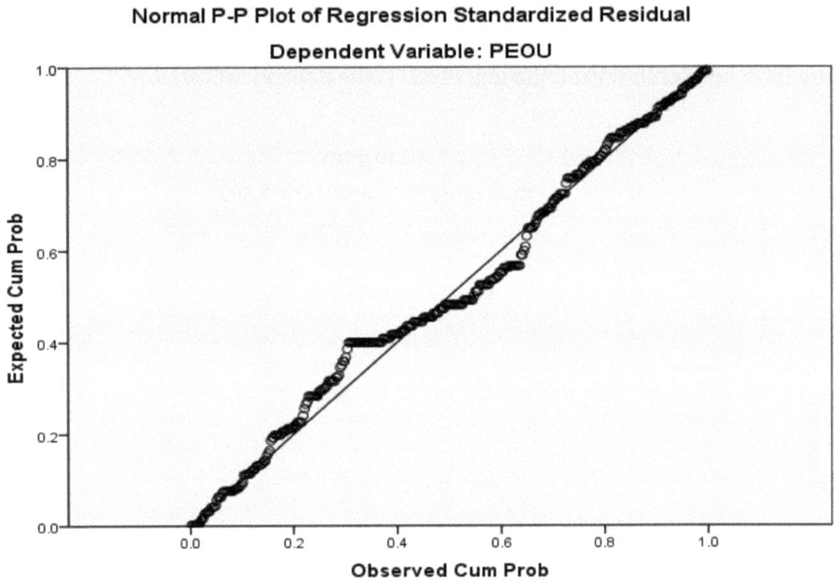

Figure 8.8: P-P plot for standardised residue of PEOU on ICT infrastructure.

Conclusion on H4: The existence of ICT infrastructure and low costs alone cannot positively influence the PEOU of e-Government services. This essentially entails that the existence of robust ICT infrastructure cannot alone influence the positive adoption of e-Government service.

Trust directly influences engagement or non-engagement in e-Government applications. **[Hypothesis 5]**

Using casewise diagnostics, case 247 and 242 were eliminated in one of the tests; in the second test, the regression of Actual Usage on Trust was done using the original variables; and in the third case, regression was done using transformed variables (utilised in the analysis). Correlation in the third case was 0.288 (positive but non-substantial correlation) with strong statistical significance (0.001). Log_Actual_Usage is the dependent variable.

R^2 value for this test is .083 which entails that the prediction capacity of the regression model obtained from this data set entails that 8.3% of the variation in the outcome is determined by the predictor variable.

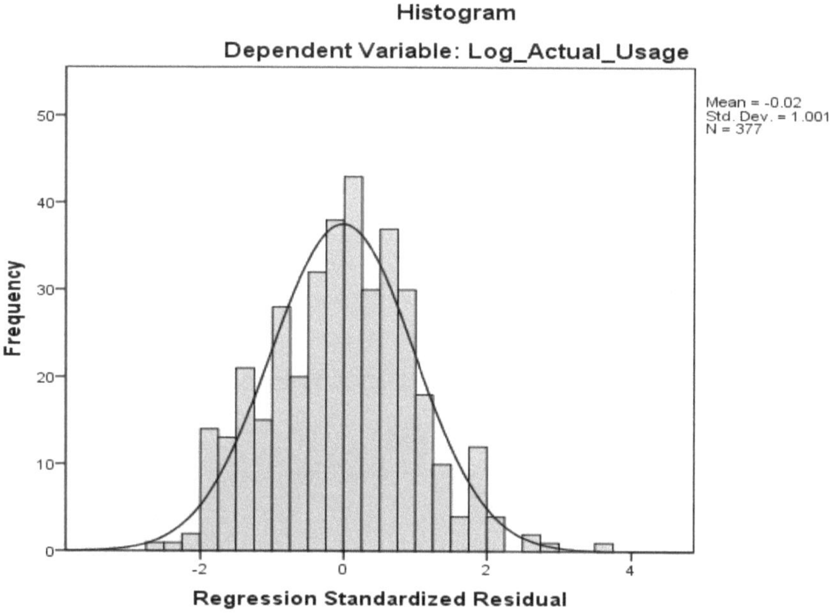

Figure 8.9: Gaussian normal data fit of trust on actual usage.

A regression analysis, predicting Log_PU from PEOU, was highly statistically significant with $F(1) = 33.835$ $p < .001$. It can be observed that the t values associated with the Log_PU scores is significant at the same level the F statistics was. The regression equation for this case is:

$$Log\_Actual\_Usage = 0.381 - 0.050\ Trust \quad \textbf{[Equation 4]}$$

The residual statistics shown below confirmed that the Mahalanobis distance has an acceptable value. The following figures demonstrate graphically the linearity of the data set on the measured variables.

Figure 8.9 has shown that the almost all the data set lies inside the Gaussian curve and therefore shows that it follows normality. There is one point, however, that is way outside the curve and this may be a case for outliers. Figure 8.10 shows the linearity of the data set.

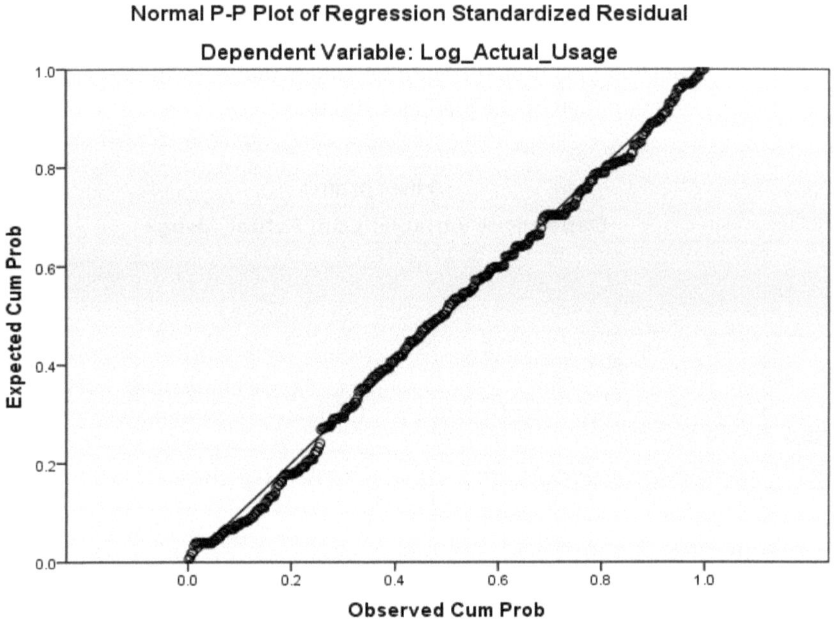

Figure 8.10: P-P plot for standardised residue of trust on actual usage.

It can be shown that the data set follows linearity and normality to a greater extent. Therefore, the results obtained from this data set are highly valid.

Conclusion on H5: Despite low predictive value of the regression model (R^2 value), trust (both in ICT platforms and the government) has a direct influence on engagement of citizens and businesses in e-Government applications.

The level of computer self-efficacy will impact on the actual use of an e-Government system by an individual. **[Hypothesis 6]**

As above, the regression of Actual Usage on Computer Self-efficacy was done using original data set and the transformed (logarithmic) variables. The later was used in the analysis and yielded a correlation value of 0.367 and strong statistical significance (0.001). All requested variables on the logarithmic value of Computer

Self Efficacy (Log_Comp_SE) have been entered and the log. Log_Actual_Usage is the dependent variable.

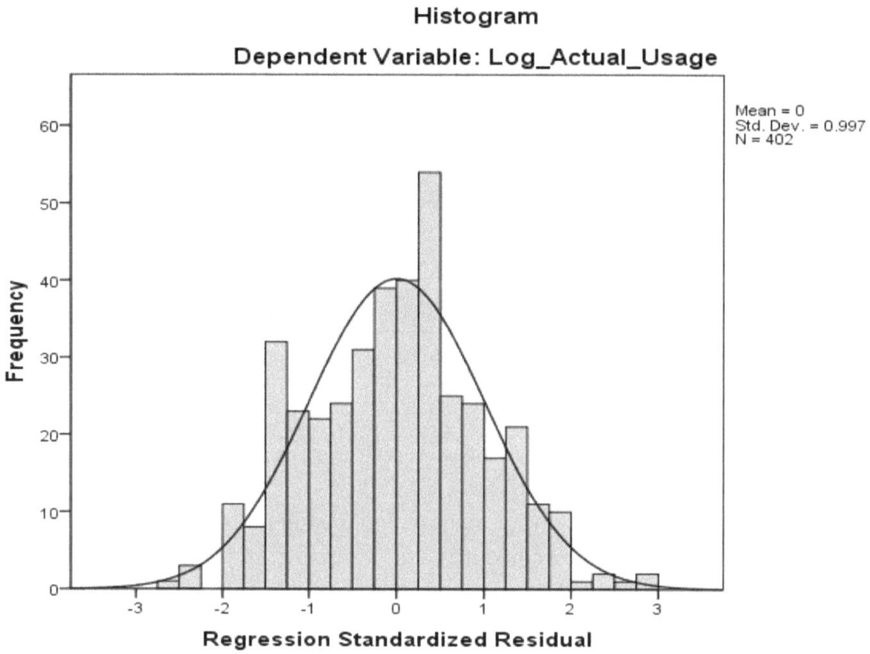

Figure 8.11: Gaussian normal data fit of actual usage on computer self-efficacy.

R^2 value for this test is .135 which entails that the prediction capacity of the regression model obtained from this data set entails that 13.5% of the variation in the outcome is determined by the predictor variable.

A regression analysis, predicting Log_PU from PEOU, was highly statistically significant with $F(1) = 62.161$, $p < .001$. It can be observed that the t values associated with the Log_PU scores is significant at the same level the F statistics was. The regression equation for this case is:

$$Log\_Actual\_Usage = 0.161 - 0.280\ Log\_Comp\_SE \qquad \textbf{[Equation 5]}$$

The residual statistics shown below confirmed that the Mahalanobis distance has an acceptable value. The following figures demonstrate the linearity in the data set utilised for this analysis.

Figure 8.12 below, shows the linearity of the data set after taking the regression of the standardised residual with actual usage as the dependent variable.

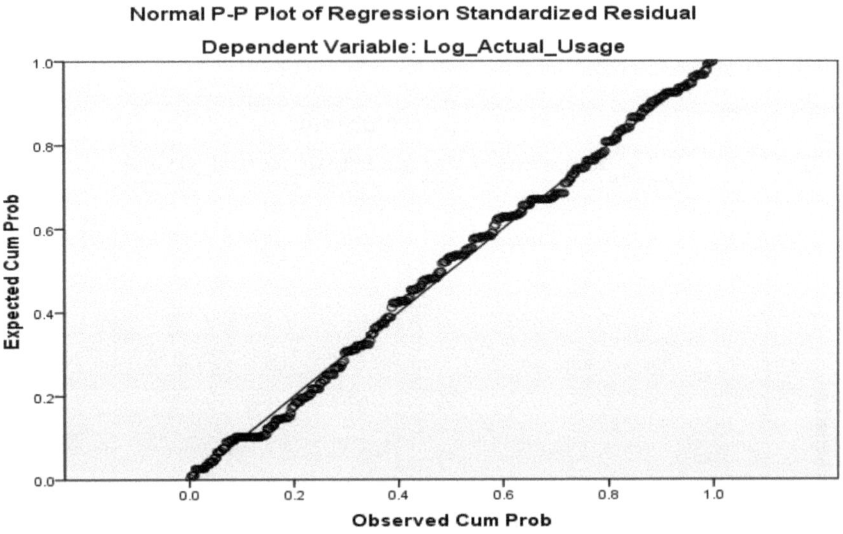

Figure 8.12: P-P plot for standardised residue of actual usage on computer self-efficacy.

The three figures immediately above have demonstrated that the data set utilised in this particular test follows linearity and normality and therefore, it is anticipated that valid results will be obtained from the analysis.

Conclusion on H6: An individual's level of computer self-efficacy will positively influence his or her involvement in the utilisation of e-Government services.

> *Positive ICT developments will facilitate actual usage and correspondingly continuance usage of e-Government applications.* **[Hypothesis 7]**

As above, the regression of Continued Usage on Actual Usage was done using several approaches. In the first case, the test utilised transformed variables without involving the cases 247, 145 and 271 as per the results of the casewise diagnostics. The case utilised for analysis involved using the logarithmic values of the Actual Usage. Regression was at -.276 and statistically significant at level 0.001. All requested variables on Log_Actual_Usage have been entered and the log. Cont_Usage is the dependent variable.

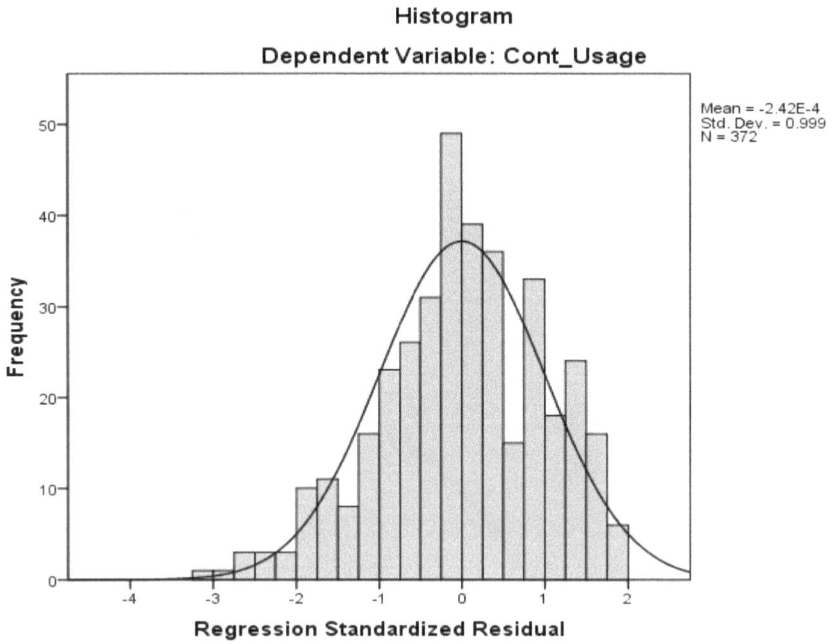

Figure 8.13: Gaussian normal data fit of continuance usage on all other variables.

R^2 value for this test is .076 which entails that the prediction capacity of the regression model obtained from this data set entails that 7.6% of the variation in the outcome is determined by the predictor variable.

A regression analysis, predicting Log_PU from PEOU, was highly statistically significant with $F(1) = 30.559$ $p < .001$. It can be observed that the t values associated with the Log_PU scores is significant at the same level the F statistics was. The regression equation for this case is:

$$Cont\_Usage = 4.438 - 1.382\ Log\_Actual\_Usage \qquad \textbf{[Equation 6]}$$

The residual statistics shown below confirmed that the Mahalanobis distance has an acceptable value. The following two figures show the linearity and normality of the data set (cf: Figure 8.13 and Figure 8.14).

Figure 8.14 shows the linearity in the data set.

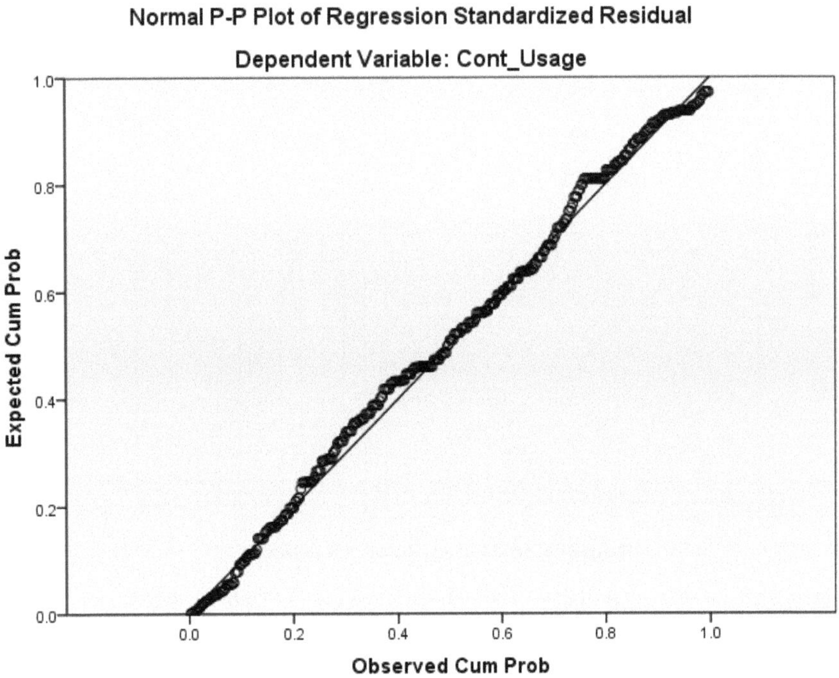

Figure 8.14: P-P plot for standardised residue.

The two figures above both demonstrate the validity of the data set utilised in this analysis.

Conclusion on H7: Positive ICT developments and actual continuance usage will culminate into positive continuance usage of e-Government applications.

> *Appropriate ICT infrastructure coupled with higher perceived ease of use (PEOU) will culminate into improved overall perceived usefulness (PU).*
> **[Hypothesis 8]**

The regression of PU on PEOU and ICT Infrastructure has been done with both original and transformed variables (logarithmic value forced on ICT infrastructure and PU to eliminate skewness); the latter being utilised in the analysis. Correlation is at -0.371 (PEOU) and 0.19 (Log_ICTInfra) with high statistical significance (0.001) and (0.01). All requested variables on Log_ICTInfra and PEOU have been entered and the log. Log_PU is the dependent variable.

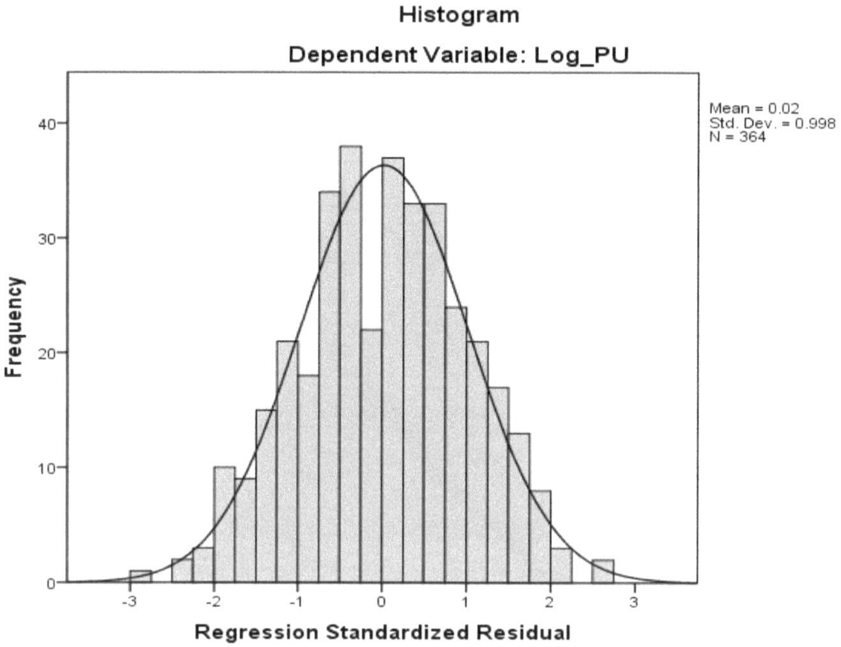

Figure 8.15: Gaussian normal data fit of PU on PEOU and ICT infrastructure.

R^2 value for this test is .162 which entails that the prediction capacity of the regression model obtained from this data set entails that 16.2% of the variation in the outcome is determined by the predictor variable.

A regression analysis, predicting Log_PU from PEOU, was highly statistically significant with $F(1) = 34.902$, $p < .001$. It can be observed that the t values associated with the Log_PU scores is significant at the same level the F statistics was. The regression equation for this case is:

$$Log\_PU = 0.457 - 0.067\ PEOU + 0.172\ Log\_ICTInfra \qquad \textbf{[Equation 7]}$$

The residual statistics shown below confirmed that the Mahalanobis distance has an acceptable value. The figure following shows the linearity in the regression used in the data set used in the analysis (cf: Figure 8.15).

Figure 8.16 below, shows the linearity in the data set used in the analysis.

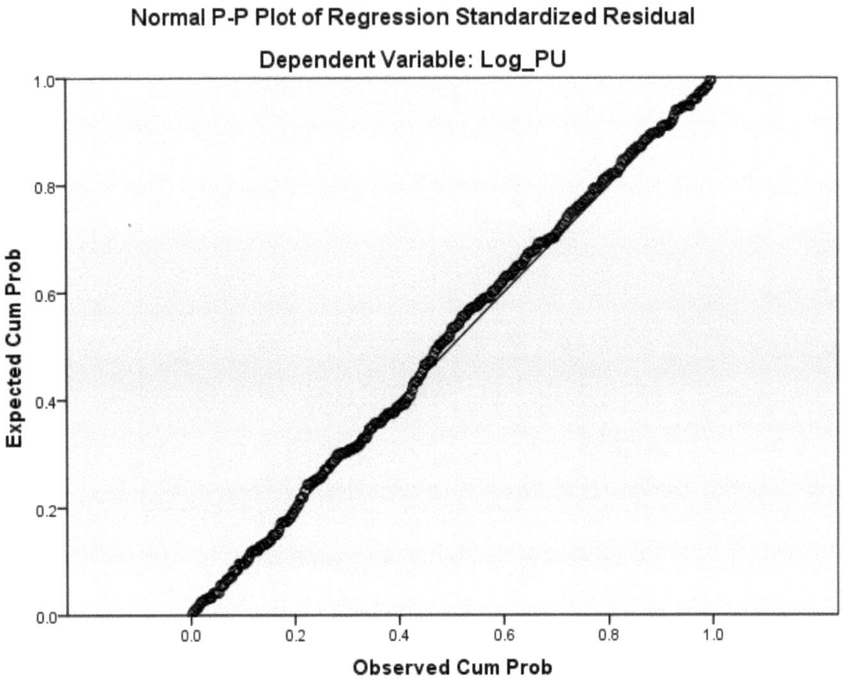

Figure 8.16: P-P plot for standardised residue of PU on PEOU and ICT infrastructure.

Conclusion on H8: Appropriate ICT infrastructure coupled with higher PEOU will culminate into improved PU for the case of Zambia's e-Government development.

Now that the regression analysis has been done on the individual hypotheses, the next section investigates the regression of CU on all other transformed variables; and the regression of Continuance Usage on ICT Infrastructure, Perceived Ease of Use and Computer Self-efficacy.

8.6 Regression of CU on All Other Variables

The regression of Continuance Usage (CU) on all other variables has been done using two cases: with original variables from the data set and excluding case 145 with anomalies as per the casewise diagnostics, and with Log_ICTInfra, PEOU, Log_PU, Log_Actual_Usage, Log_Comp_SE and Trust. The latter case has been utilised in the analysis. Correlations are at -0.404 (Log_ICTInfra), 0.250 (PEOU), -0.176 (Log_PU), -0.259 (Log_Actual_Usage), -0.254 (Log_Comp_SE) and 0.172 (Trust) with high statistical significancy (0.001). All requested variables on Log_ICTInfra, PEOU, Log_PU, Log_Actual_Usage, Log_Comp_SE and Trust have been entered and the log. Note that CU is the dependent variable.

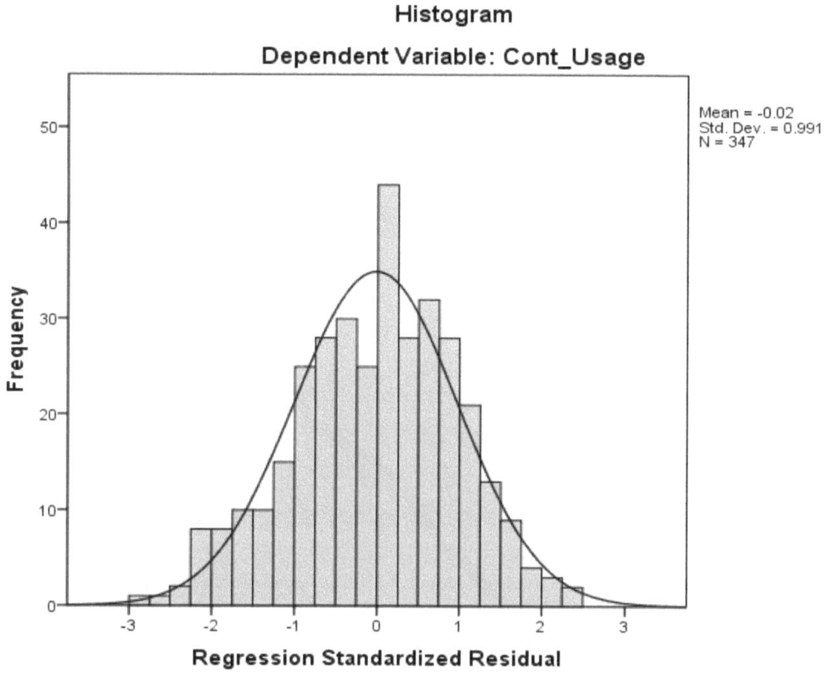

Figure 8.17: Gaussian normal data fit of CU on all other variables.

R^2 value for this test is .231 which entails that the prediction capacity of the regression model obtained from this data set entails that 23.1% of the variation in the outcome is determined by the predictor variables.

A regression analysis, predicting Log_PU from PEOU, was highly statistically significant with $F(1) = 17.652$, $p < .001$. It can be observed that the t values associated with the CU scores are significant at the same level the F statistics was. The regression equation for this case is:

$$CU = 4.030 - 1.668\,x_1 + 0.137\,x_2 + 0.046\,x_3 - 0.176\,x_4 - 0.511\,x_5 + 0.042\,x_6$$

[Equation 8]

$$
\begin{aligned}
\textit{Where } x_1 &= Log\_ICTInfra \\
x_2 &= PEOU \\
x_3 &= Log\_PU \\
x_4 &= Log\_Actual\_Usage \\
x_5 &= Log\_Comp\_SE \\
x_6 &= Trust
\end{aligned}
$$

The residual statistics shown below confirmed that the Mahalanobis distance has an acceptable value. On the next page Figure 8.17 and Figure 8.18 show the linearity in the regression used in the data set used in analysis.

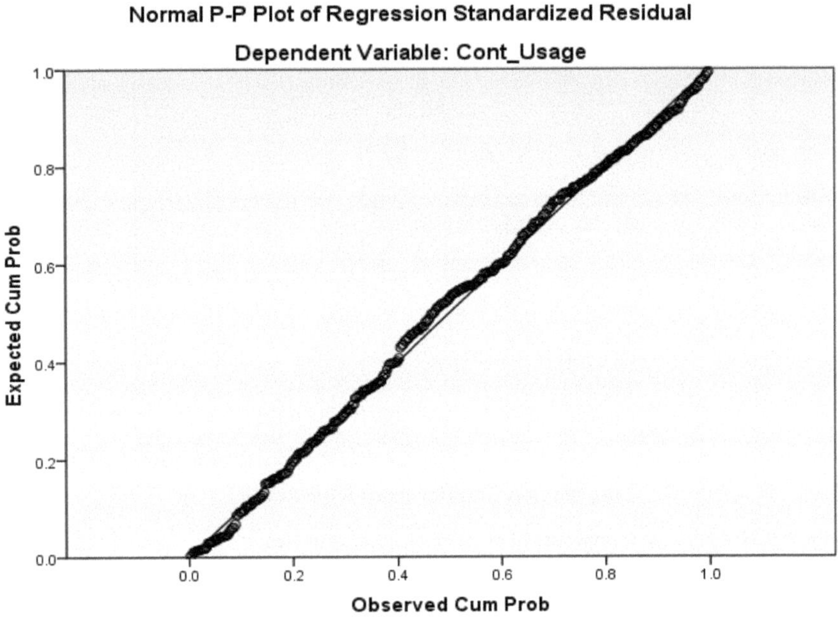

Figure 8.18: P-P plot for standardised residue of CU on all other variables.

Figure 8.19 above, shows the linearity in the data set. From the analysis of the impact of the different individual factors on continuance usage which directly represent the sustainable development of e-Government, the study concludes that each of the factors has an impact on CU. This has been demonstrated in the analysis of the individual hypotheses in this study. In this regard, it can be seen that the factors investigated in this study only contribute partial variance (with 23.1% predictability value). This is testimony that e-Government depends on many factors to thrive thereby further accentuating its multi-dimensional nature. It is worth noting that the empirical results in this study show minimal predictability value owing to the fact that e-Government has not been commercialised in Zambia at the moment.

8.6.1 Anticipated Interventions for e-Government Proliferation

In the only open-ended question in the questionnaire, the respondents were asked what needs to be in order to encourage e-Government proliferation in Zambia. The participants in the study identified several interventions that need to be put in place in order to facilitate fast track e-Government development in Zambia. The suggestions emanating from this study are grouped according to the following sub-headings:

a) ICT Infrastructure

- There is need for acute investments in the ICT infrastructure (such as erecting appropriate backbone infrastructures and networks for promoting broadband and Internet penetration).
- Need to promote citizens' and businesses' global accessibility of relevant and affordable devices to promote wider usage of e-Government applications.

b) Awareness

- Anticipated consumers should be made aware of the benefits and opportunities that can be amassed from appropriate and efficient use of e-Government applications.
- Common information platforms such as radios and the television (through discussion programmes or advertisements in form of commercials) should be encouraged. In some cases, community outreach programmes or workshops should be organised to enable people at the community level to appreciate and buy-in the idea of e-Government.
- There is need to organise meetings with stakeholders such as Non-Governmental Organisations (NGOs) and the civil society communities and all consumers of government services and brainstorm about challenges that they may likely encounter as they engage in e-Government and identify interventions on how to rectify them.

c) ICT Literacy

- There is need to promote grassroots ICT education at the lower primary school level. For example, computer literacy courses should be embedded into the general curricula.
- At the community level, elderly people and other citizens who do not have the privilege of accessing ICTs should be encouraged to enroll in community ICT education programmes where the cost of attending such course is borne by the government and other e-Government partners.

d) Back-end Competencies

- There is need to train more people who with ICT (technical) and managerial competencies so that they timely develop and manage e-Government applications;
- There is need to ensure timely update of content on the websites as new information emerge.
- There is need to have appropriate and adequate political will for the cause of e-Government. Politicians should be made to understand the critical role that e-Government plays in their governing endeavours in the contemporary world setup;
- There is need to put in place an office sorely responsible for coordinating e-Government implementation and provide affluent front-end support to e-Government consumers.
- A national data base of all residents of Zambia needs to be maintained in electronic form and should be accessible to all government institutions. This will ease the flow of information between organisations relating to people. For example, there can be process integration between the revenue office (Zambia Revenue Authority – ZRA) and the police department to apprehend tax defaulters.
- It is important to have each department manage its own website and provide content that may be appealing; for example, youths would be interested in information such as available vacancies in government departments, how to access government sponsorship for education, and infotainment.
- Government should subsidize cost of ICTs.
- There is need for the government to strive to have all the major government services online: for example, application for national registration cards, passports and entry into tertiary education procedures should be put online.

e) ICT Market Proliferation

- There is need to reduce tax on imported ICTs components to encourage more people and businesses to own ICT gadgets (such as computers, mobile phones and Personal Digital Assistants (PDAs)) and correspondingly be better placed to access e-Government applications.
- ICT vendors should be exempted from huge tax payments so that they are encouraged to import a variety of ICT gadgets to help citizens and businesses to access e-Government applications.

f) Local Context Dynamics

- E-Government applications should be designed in such as way that even people in remote parts of the country are accorded an opportunity to access them. For example, rural e-Institutions such as telecentres should be opened to enable rural inhabitants have access e-Government services. Backbone infrastructures should reach all corners of the country so that rural inhabitants can access e-Government applications even using mobile phones.
- Since Zambia has 72 languages, it is important that e-Government content on the websites should also be presented in the major local languages to promote global access to e-Government applications.
- There is need to promote wider-scale Internet penetration in tandem with tele-density and mobile phone-penetration for long-term e-Government success. The government should further provide or establish and help run community information centres by equipping them with the necessary ICT gadgetry so that citizens can easily access e-Government services.

8.7 Contextual Challenges of e-Government implementation in Zambia

The development of the ICT sector in Zambia is happening at comparatively faster rate. In 2005, Zambia had no online presence but started implementing e-Government systems in the last quarter of 2005 (UN e-Government Report, 2008:23). Despite this development, there has been slow growth of e-Government development in Zambia. This may be because of several barriers which this study aims to uncover. Preliminary scan of the e-Government environment in Zambia (by way of few verbal interviews and literature reviews) suggest that the basic barriers of e-Government implementation are evident in Zambia. As e-Government initiatives either fail or succeed (Saxena, 2005:498; Yildiz, 2007:652), in any environment where e-Government is implemented there are issues and challenges that either aid or inhibit the development of e-Government. The following list provides the most common factors that impact on e-Government implementations. Some of these factors may be the ones preventing rapid growth of e-Government implementation in Zambia.

a) Leadership Failures

Lack of visionary leaders may hamper the growth of e-Government implementation (Suinat, 2007). It is evident that slow and patchy progress to e-Government can result from a lack of adequate leadership during any stage in the initiation, implementation, promotion and ongoing support of e-Government systems maturity models. Currently, the study found out that Zambia does not have an e-Government office or persons sorely dedicated to advance the e-Government agenda. Further, the policy framework for e-Government is not in place. For example, in the 2006 ICT policy, e-Government is only mentioned in one small paragraph less a paragraph.

b) Poor Technical Design

Lack of interoperability among different ICT platforms and poor technical design delay the faster uptake of e-Government systems (Ralyte, Jeusfeld, Backlund, Kuhn & Arni-Bloch, 2008:757; Vernadat, 2010:141–143). Difficult-to-use interfaces to e-Government services exemplify the kinds of practical flaws that can become serious operational obstacles to uptake and adoption of e-Government systems. Zambia shows that requisite technical (and/or ICT) infrastructure is not there to support appropriate e-Government development.

c) Workplace and Organisational Inflexibility

Organisational inflexibility can limit the realisation of efficient change management programs which facilitate faster adoption of e-Government systems (Al-Shehry, Rogerson, Fairweather & Prior, 2006:7; Modinis, 2007). Inflexibility can also slow the response to make necessary changes in public administration practices, processes and organisational structures to allow them to be better able to make appropriate effective use of electronic networking capabilities. The Zambian public service is riddled with a lot of unnecessary red tap which has made the flow of government transactions very slow. Most of the government departments are not willing to erase the traditional organisational structures to adopt emerging trends.

d) Financial Inhibitors

Lack of adequate financial capital to foot the costs of implementing and developing e-Government, together with inappropriate cost/benefit analysis approaches, can limit the flow of investment at the levels necessary to support future e-Government implementation and innovation (Al-Shehry et al., 2006:15). In most of the African countries, the e-Government initiatives are financed by donors who mostly do a one-off payment. Such kind of e-Government initiatives are hard to sustain and in most cases are prone to fail. Since Zambia is a third world country, it cannot afford to finance most of the expensive e-Government applications.

e) Digital Divides and Choices

Limitation in access to ICT infrastructure and lack of ICT skills can limit and fragment uptake and adoption of e-Government systems (Yonaz & Boonstra, 2007:175–176). If the user needs of potential e-Government users are overlooked, this can translate into limited uptake and adoption. It is evident that the digital divide is evident in Zambia looking at the disparity amongst the citizens in the access to ICTs and to information.

f) Poor Coordination

For any e-Government implementation to succeed, it is desired that there is appropriate coordination and harmonisation paradigms to support and foster novel e-Government systems implementation (Ebrahim & Irani, 2005:596; Pudjianto & Hangjung, 2009:3). Lack of coodination can limit the establishment of appropriate e-Government networks and services that cut across organisational, governance, administrative and geographic boundaries.

g) Lack of Trust

Lack of trust in ICT frameworks inhibits levels of usability (Thorbjornsen et al., 2002:18; Tassabehji & Elliman, 2006:9). Security and privacy concerns reduce trust in electronic networks and a general distrust of government can undermine confidence and up take of e-Government. For the Zambian context, trust in ICT applications is a far-fetched dream as most of the citizens do not trust the government because of politicians' lack of adherence to their promises.

These categories presented here present a skeleton of the visible barrier peaks: they are tied to a multitude of more specific barriers that are relevant at different governance, institutional and jurisdictional levels, and may be unique for any given location. The local context largely determines what kind of barriers a location is going to have.

Apart from the challenges mentioned above, one of the main issues confronting successful e-Government implementation is that of legal frameworks. The legal dimensions of e-Government barriers underpin the seven barrier categories mentioned above.

8.8 General Barriers to e-Government Implementation

Having a closer look at the success and failure cases of e-Government implementation together with the detailed Case Study of Zambia, it is evident to note the common straits of barriers. These barriers have a direct impact on the adoption and uptake of e-Government systems. It is important to further note that these barriers are almost the same regardless of the contextual characteristics of the environment in which e-Government is implemented.

a) Authentication and Identification

This refers to the situations concerning 'user identity management'. This is a crucial e-Government concept that arises when the online service provider (e.g. a government department or ministry) needs to check the identity of an online user (NOVOSEC, 2008). The authentication procedure mostly involves establishing or confirming whether a person or other entity (e.g. a business), is *bona fide*, genuine and authentic thereby establishing or confirming the identity of a person. These processes can become barriers if they are too cumbersome, tedious, costly or insecure.

b) Intellectual Property Rights (IPR)

Intellectual property rights (IPR) and copyright laws (in form of patents or whatever) protect innovations that can apply to many electronic services provided by governments, and therefore limit interactions between different players in the e-Government environment (Goel & Tripathi, 2007:2–5). This can affect the exchange of e-Documents and digital multimedia (e.g. video) or the protection of databases, software and other e-Services and e-Products. This can constrain or block the sharing of certain digital contents, for example, through charges that exacerbate digital divides.

c) Liability

At least one person should embrace responsibility of all repercussions that come out of exchanging digital content in both an online and offline environments (Minow, 2010). In two-way and interactive electronic relationships between government, businesses and citizens, there is a need for a considered division of responsibility regarding damages resulting from a malfunction in the process or from inaccuracies in the information involved.

d) Privacy and Data Protection

It is important that people should have rights to protect their data when they involve in any of the e-Government applications. Rights relating to privacy and the protection of personal data should be included in a wide range of legislation (Minow, 2010). As these issues are at the heart of many types of e-Government development, systematic and detailed consideration must be given to addressing them in ways that do not impair the achievement of e-Government goals.

e) Public Administration Transparency

The openness of government activities and deals installs confidence in its dealings by the general public. Wide availability of public sector information and the openness of democratic processes (for example, e-Consultations, online forums) are key elements in promoting public administration transparency to help build trust in government in general, and e-Government in particular. The issue of Freedom of Information (FOI) legislation is a key mechanism for giving the public more access to government information.

Depending on the degree of complexity of the environment in which e-Government is implemented, there can be many barriers other than the ones mentioned here and these can complicate e-Government implementation. Therefore, this book posits that affluent e-Government design should take cognizance of the different barriers and contextual challenges that impact on e-Government implementation, and to be assure of existing design frameworks both with regards to technology and managerial perspectives.

8.9 Summary and Conclusion

This chapter has discussed the different e-Government projects done throughout the world with a special focus on less developed countries. It is evident that most governments relate to e-Government with the seriousness it deserves out of the realization that it positively impacts on the efficiency and effectiveness of the public service delivery. The chapter has outlined the major barriers and challenges that impact on e-Government development.

In order to comprehend the heterogeneous factors that impact on e-Government, Understanding the inherent factors that influence e-Government in any given environment is important to designing context-aware e-Government interventions which will be able to evolve as technology and consumers' need evolve.

Chapter 9
E-Government Development Paradigms

9.1 Introduction

Given the multi-dimensional nature of e-Government which is marked for implementation in heterogeneous environments as outlined in the previous chapters, it is important to note that there is need to have carefully considered e-Government development plans and design frameworks to inform the implementation plans. This chapter, therefore, intends to highlight the different e-Government implementation paradigms and technology/management frameworks that have been employed in informing e-Government implementation in heterogeneous environments. It is not logically coherent to assume that e-Government design frameworks for similar environments will be homogeneous. This is because areas in the same environmental domains may have locally inherent characteristics which differentiate their environmental setups. The frameworks discussed in this chapter act as reference points for e-Government design and implementation by outlining minimum principles.

The different frameworks discussed in this chapter are mostly concentrating on understanding the organisational aspects of technology deployment and integration into the various business processes. As articulated in Chapter 6, it is worth noting that technology adoption in any environment happens at two levels: the organisational and individual level. Therefore, explaining adoption at these two levels is done with the help of different conceptual and theoretical frameworks. At the organisational level, there is need for the Information and Communication Technologies (ICTs) to be assimilated and integrated into the existing and future business processes of the government department or unit. At the individual level, there is need for the acceptance and continuance usage of technology. This can only be achieved if an individual acknowledges the benefits of technology in lessening the burden of the workload.

The chapter highlights e-Government design principles and basics that need to be observed if meaningful e-Government development is to be achieved. Principally, the chapter discusses the e-Government adoption models and highlights the different e-Government design and implementation frameworks. The pivot of this chapter is the discussion of the different e-Government Interoperability Frameworks (e-GIFs) informing e-Government implementation in both the developed and less developed countries. The motivation of this chapter is that the different frameworks and models discussed herein may be used as reference points to guide e-Government implementation especially in less developed countries.

NOTE that the discussion of technology platforms was initiated in chapter 7 where the different forms of interoperability were started.

Because e-Government implementation is very resource intensive, the need for standards with regards to management approaches and technologies cannot be overemphasized.

9.2 E-Government Design Frameworks

E-Government's success depends on organisation's environment and the strategies utilised to achieve ICT integration into the already-existing business processes (Al-Rashidi, 2010). The e-Government Interoperability Framework (e-GIFs) are a roadmap of technical and non-technical attributes of e-Government need to be rolled at various stages of the implementation cycle. The e-GIFs detail the minimum specifications that need to be followed when implementing e-Government.

As aforementioned in the previous section, the need for any e-Government to have e-GIFs cannot be overemphasised. This is because e-GIFs provide the managerial and technical fibre and roadmap for any successful e-Government development and is considered as the main issue to be addressed and a bedrock for designing responsive e-Government systems (Guijarro, 2010). The e-GIF provides the general guidelines on the policy, technical standards, and managerial dimensions on how to best implement e-Government in a given context (Raina, 2009). Further, the e-GIF aims to support interconnectivity of heterogeneous information systems dispersed all over the public service hierarchy (NICT, 2011). Therefore, this section highlights the desired functionalities and characteristics of any e-GIF.

Malinauskienė (2013) posits that the fact that e-Government is multi-dimensional complicates many efforts at the technology level to achieve a well-rounded e-Government implementation. An example is an effort to draw interoperability plans which demand multi-dimensional and local contextual characteristics. Given the aforementioned complexity, there is utmost need to study non-technological and technological issues with regard to e-Government interoperability. Appropriate interoperability conceptualisations and designs should ensure that contextual factors are taken into consideration and the heterogeneous dynamic, multi-dimensional and context-based organisational capabilities are not left unconsidered during the design. Further, affluent e-Government interoperability should be based on globally-agreed-upon standards (e.g. *national interoperability framework*) and architecture (e.g., the *national enterprise architecture*). Given the multi-dimensionality of e-Government, the enterprise architecture may take a multi-layer approach which looks at different levels of interoperability such as institutional, legal, semantic, technological and political as discussed in Section 9.3 below. E-Government standards are important because they bring about technology neutrality and provide open interfaces and platforms to facilitate vendor independence (Budhiraja & Sachdeva, 2002). The standards ensure that there is sanity in the e-Government implementation value chains and that interoperable 'middleware' are in place to achieve service platform integration.

Many researchers and practitioners have recognised the multi-dimensional nature of e-Government and have emphasised that design frameworks should incorporate this multi-dimensional understanding. Despite the fact that e-Government is implemented with various objectives, its fundamental essence has been that it should be citizen-centric (Shareef, Kumar, Kumar & Dwivedi, 2011). Therefore, the different attributes of e-Government are only supportive to the major objective towards citizen centricity. In this regard, the different forms of interoperability should devote to ensuring that the expectations of the citizens are met.

In order to understand technology implementation and adoption, as posited in the introduction of this chapter, one needs to distinguish between organisation/institutional and individual e-Government readiness. Investigating the likelihood of successful integration of technology into the different organisational business processes can only be achieved by understanding the different technology frameworks, their deployment strategies and conceptual/frameworks. Amongst the many theoretical and conceptual frameworks used to explain integration of technology, the following take precedence: the Institutional Theory, the Technology Enactment Framework, and the Technology, Organisation and Environment (TOE). These theoretical frameworks enable the investigation of the different factors that influence technology deployment in heterogeneous organisational contexts, in this case e-Government.

With regards to conceptualisation of e-Government interoperability, there is no consensus as to what basic and fundamental principles that should guide interoperability designs.

9.3 Interoperability and Process/Application Integration

A contemporary and desired e-Government system is one which harmonises all the different information systems utilised in the different government departments/units. A further anticipation is that such a system should be able to exchange information as desired. The aforementioned scenario can be achieved if the different business processes/applications are integrated using a common hardware or software platform such as a middleware. Process/applications integration can only be achieved if the systems are interoperable. Interoperability facilitates seamless interoperation of the different heterogeneous services offered by the government departments. The need for highly interoperable systems in e-Government environments is brought about by the need to have requisite information and data exchange services in order to ensure that unison decision-making is achieved (Furdík, Tomášek & Hreňo, 2011).

Although there are acute discussions around interoperability, it still remains one of the cardinal challenges for e-Government (Ojo, Janowski & Estevez, 2011). Further to the discussion in chapter 7, the various attributes of interoperability are discussed below (Feuerlicht & Cunek, 2011):

1. **Legal interoperability:** enacting laws that support the integration and authenticity of digital data as legal tender in public service platforms. For example, in the USA, the introduction of Information System of Data Boxes necessitated approval of Act 300/2008 (Digital agenda), and the Government Portal is supported by Act 365/2000 (Information systems in public administration). In Mauritius, for example, with the realisation that e-Government and ICTs usage in different socio-economic strata was on the rise, the government drew up the ICT Act of 2001 (cf: http://telecomit.gov.mu/download/ictact.pdf) which lays out the institutional and procedural guidelines for the regulation and democratisation of ICT-related matters. To combat cybercrime, the Computer Misuse and Cybercrime Act of 2003 (cf: http://telecomit.gov.mu/download/misuse.pdf) was formulated with the aim to repress criminal activities on the cyberspace and any criminal activities that may be perpetrated through computer systems. The Data Protection Act of 2004 protects the privacy rights of individuals regarding developments of techniques used for capturing, transmitting, manipulating, recording, or storing data relating to individual persons (Vencatachellum & Pudaruth, 2010; Chauhan & Singh, 2011:16).
2. **Organizational Interoperability:** need for re-alignment of the different organisational structures and processes in government units. For example, if one were to apply for a bank loan, the regulation may be that such an individual obtain clearance from the police that he/she does not hold criminal record, clearance from the central credit bureau that he/she does not owe other banks, etc. Such information need to be accessed at one point automatically without having to subject the individual hop from one department to another. To achieve such levels of service integration where all the services are accessed at one point, there is need to re-align existing structures of the different government units;

3. **Semantic-Level Interoperability:** different government departments with disparate information systems are endowed with data heterogeneity which presents problems in as far as data interchange is concerned. Therefore, the meaning of data exchanged needs to be resolved if favourable interoperability is to be achieved;
4. **Technical-Level Interoperability:** with the data standards pursued in order to achieve interoperability, technical interoperability focuses on technical specifications such as data exchange protocols (e.g. Simple Object Access Protocol (SOAP), Web Services Description Language (WSDL), secure Hypertext Transmission Protocol (HTTPS), Web Services, etc); and
5. **Information-level interoperability models:** need for models which ensure that information is easily and seamlessly shared among different government systems. Two basic models are discussed:
   a) **Document-Centric Interoperability Model:** involves shipping business documents between partner systems whose advantage is that the use of documents as basic artefacts do not call for technology platform compatibility as documents are transmitted as whole entities; and
   b) **Service-Centric Interoperability Model: with the help** of Service-Oriented Architecture (SOA) and Web Services, rely on well-defined interfaces which have the capability of implementing single business functions as Web Services.

In addition to the above models, there are also integration types at the lowest levels such as data integration. As posited in Chapter 7, data integration can be achieved using common standards such as XML, SOAP, Web Services (Budhiraja & Sachdeva, 2002).

Implementation of interoperability requires a clearly defined methodological framework that considers all the multi-dimensional attributes and facets of interoperable information systems. In addition, there are several challenges that need to be resolved when implementing interoperable services between government departments/units. Some of these challenges include standardization of data structure and semantics across all the public service value chains and business processes, specification of open technology interfaces with a clearly defined middleware to allow seamless interoperability, etc. In summary, the design of interoperability framework requires careful though referencing fundamental concepts in e-Government design and a careful analysis of the contextual setting.

Although acknowledging that technology is the main enabler of e-Government, when establishing interoperability frameworks, robust e-GIFs focus on enabling the business of government rather than investigating different technology approaches. The e-GIF performs the same function in e-Government as the

Road Code does on the highways. Driving would be excessively costly, inefficient, and ineffective if there were a need to agree on road rules each time one vehicle encountered another (Tucker & Miller, 2005). The same applies to e-Government.

Generally, any e-GIF architecture contains the following two entities: 1) framework detailing high-level statements, policies for technology design and implementation, management, implementation and compliance principles; and 2) the e-GIF registry which acts as a data dictionary. Diagrammatically, the e-GIF architecture can be presented as shown in Figure 9.1.

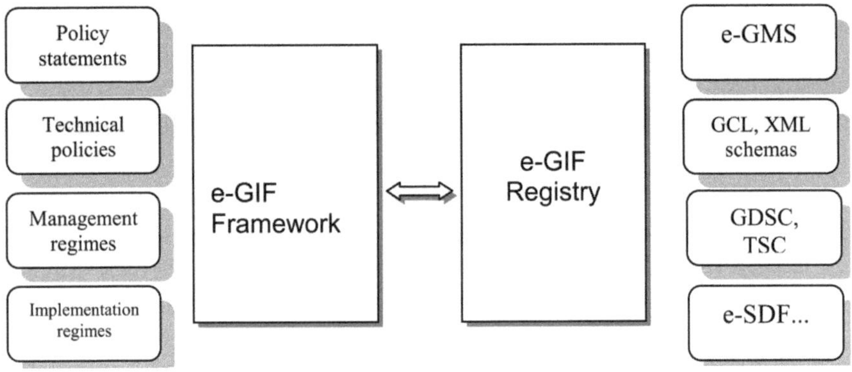

Key

e-GMS: e-Government Metadata Standard
GCL: Government Category List
GDSC: the Government Data Standards Catalogue
TSC: Technical Standards Catalogue
e-SDF: e-Services Development Framework

Figure 9.1: e-GIF Architecture.

Apart from a good interoperability framework, appropriate authentication framework is a crucial factor for successful implementation of e-Government (Prokopios, Dimitris, Stefanos, Costas & Mitrou, 2009).

9.4 E-Government Interoperability Frameworks Worldwide

Throughout the world, there are a lot of e-Government Interoperability Frameworks being developed. For example, e-GIFs have been designed in Afghanistan, Saint Lucia (NICT, 2011; Raina, 2009). Amongst the different countries, the USA, the European Union (EU), Australia, and the government of India are some of the countries that have well-developed e-GIF (Budhiraja & Sachdeva, 2002). Table 9.1 shows the characteristics and focus of different e-GIFs in different parts of the world. The table Highlights some of the interoperability frameworks and enterprise architectures that have attempted to address issues of integration, interoperability and act as both a managerial and technical blueprint (Tucker & Miller, 2005; Pankowska, 2008; Budhiraja & Sachdeva, 2002).

Table 9.1: E-Government Interoperability Frameworks.

Country	Name of framework/ architecture	Models/segments	Focus
USA	Federal Enterprise Architecture Framework (FEAF)	– Performance Reference Model – Business Reference Model – Service Component Reference Model – Technical Reference Model – Data Reference Model	To build a comprehensive business-driven blueprint to promote collaboration within and across government agencies
			Align agency capital investments to the standardized vocabulary, allowing interagency discovery, collaboration and interoperability.
			Define capabilities of discovering and sharing data and services across disparate systems and vendors.
Brazil	e-PING architecture – Standards of Interoperability for Electronic Government		defines a minimum group of assumptions, policies, and technical specifications to regulate ICTs for e Government interoperability.
			Defines the interoperability paradigm for the federal government
New Zealand	The e-Government Interoperability Framework (e-GIF) Version 3.3	– Standards – Policy – Resources	is a set of policies, technical standards, and guidelines.

Australia	Australian Government Interoperability Framework	– Business Process Interoperability Framework (BPIF) – Australian Government Architecture Reference Model v.1.0 (AGA) – Performance Reference Model (PRM): – Data Reference Model (DRM) – Technical Reference Model (TRM)	addresses the information, business process and technical dimensions of interoperability
			sets the principles, standards and methodologies that support delivery of integrated and seamless services
			Provides guidelines for agency's transition to networked operations
			Identifies gaps and overlaps in the investment intentions of agencies
Hong Kong	The Interoperability Framework (IF)		defines a collection of specifications to facilitate interoperability.
			Defines technical and data standards to define interface across systems
			Articulate standards documents that define infrastructure architecture, conventions and procedures.
			Provides guidelines for on business-oriented specifications
India	India e-Governance Framework	– Program management related documents i.e. Project Management Plan (PMP), Software Requirements Specification (SRS), Software Design Document (SDD), User Manual (UM), and Test Plan (TP) – Record management, archival and retrieval	Provides continuity of services by the government, records and documentation
			Provides guidelines on preparation of RFP (Request for Proposals) i.e. functional, technical, and commercial specifications, legal specifications including Service Level Agreements (SLAs)

Malaysia	Malaysian Government Interoperability Framework (MyGIF)		Covers the following five interoperability areas: interconnection, data integration, information access, security and metadata
Saudi Arabia	Yesser Framework For Interoperability (YEFI)		Specification of semantics; Data integration.
			Interoperability; Market support: Scalability; Openness; Integration approach; Specification of all technology standards relevant to the integration.
United Kingdom	United Kingdom e-Government Interoperability Framework (e-GIF)	Contains the e-GIF .registry,	Sets out the government's technical policies and specifications for achieving interoperability
German	German Standards and Architectures for Interoperability	Standards and Architectures for e-Government Applications (SAGA)	Identifies the necessary standards, formats and specifications, sets forth conformity rules and updates these in line with technological progress
Denmark	Danish e-Government Interoperability Framework		Descriptions and recommendations of selected standards, technologies and protocols, which might be used and supported in relation with the implementation of e-Government in Denmark
Ghana	Ghana Government Enterprise Architecture (GGEA)		Improves interoperability in the practical application of ICTs for government's business processes.

Apart from the e-GIFs designed for the countries shown in Table 9.1, other countries elsewhere have put in place dedicated e-GIFs in a bit to jump onto the e-Government implementation bandwagon. For e-Government to be embedded into the organisation's business processes, there is need for process re-engineering or '*structure metamorphosis*'. Mutula (2013) reports that e-Government is still in its nascent stage in Southern Africa. The need for most African countries to further restructure their public bureaucracies in response to the demands of the information society cannot be overemphasised (Asogwa, 2013).

E-Government strategies in less developed countries have most been informed by theories and experience of the developed countries (Chen, Chen, Huang & Ching, 2006; Maumbe, Owei & Alexander, 2008). Realising this discrepancy, less developed countries have started designing e-Government specifications and implementation roadmaps based on global e-Government trends. For example, the Mozambique eGIF4M service delivery architecture which will serve as the basis for interoperation of data, systems, and processes. The architecture is based on Government Service Bus (GSB) and follows the standard SOA (service-oriented architecture) and Event-Driven Architecture (EDA) approaches. In another development, in order to encourage global usage of ICTs at different levels of the socio-economic infrastructure and the general reduction of poverty, the Common Market for Eastern and Southern Africa (COMESA) has come up with a Regional Information Communications Technology Support Programme (RICTSP). In this regard, it can be seen that successful implementation of e-Government may also positively impact on the reduction of poverty (COMESA 2008).

Existence of a requisite Digital 21 ICT strategy as a blueprint to ensuring that different ICTs are integrated into the different business processes in Hong Kong. Further and specifically, the Hong Kong e-Government Interoperability Framework (HKeGIF) outlines the different standards and technical specifications towards the realisation of e-Government interventions (Lee, Yee & Cheung, 2009). The HKeGIF aims to ensure that there is technical, data, and process interoperability to realise affluent e-Government implementation (Lee, Yee & Cheung, 2009). To aid e-Government design, Widodo, Istiyanto, Wardoyo, and Santoso (2013) proposed an Enterprise Architecture Framework (EAF) for interoperability and data integration on e-Government applications combining the approach of Service Oriented Architecture (SOA) and Event Driven Architecture (EDA).

The different efforts exhibited by different countries, both developed and less developed, confirm that the need for careful design of e-Government implementation specifics and roadmap cannot be overemphasised. Other than the e-GIFs the e-Government Implementation Frameworks outline clear roadmaps on how e-Government can be implemented.

9.5 e-Government Implementation Frameworks

Chen, Chen, Huang and Ching (2006) proposed an e-Government implementation framework that emphasises the need to ensure that implementation approaches are defined by the contextual characteristics in the area where e-Government is implemented. This framework recognised the following as cardinal factors to e-Government implementation: network access, infrastructure development, resources and IT support, citizen utilisation of the Internet, existence of a networked economy, network policy which outlines ICT adoption and use in different socio-economic hierarchies including culture and society factors impacting on technology acceptance.

Trusler (in Traunmüller, 2003) pronounced the challenges being met in South Africa's e-Government drive as a result of gaps in anticipated outcomes and what is currently obtaining on the ground. The current 10-year implementation framework covers six stages as follows: information provision; two-way transactions; multi-purpose portals; personalized portals; clustering of services; and comprehensive corporate transformation. Based on Network Actor Theory (NAT), Trusler (2003) proposed a more pragmatic implementation framework which actively references the current contextual setting of the environment in South Africa.

Rahman and Rajon (2012) proposed a framework for implementing e-Government aimed at maximum utilization of existing infrastructure. Their framework aimed to ensure the e-Government implementation drive derived maximum returns. In this regard, the implementation framework and principles ensured that there were value prepositions at all the stages of the e-Government implementation cycle.

The above three different cases show that any robust and responsive e-Government implementation endeavour should be informed by a defined framework which outline the principles to be followed in any one given case. These principles are defined by the contextual characteristics of the area in which e-Government is going to be implemented.

9.6 Conceptual and Theoretical Frameworks/Models

Further to foregoing discussions, it is important to note that contextual e-GIFs or any implementation roadmap needs to be designed with a careful reference to a framework or model. The frameworks or theories discussed in this section mainly aim to discuss factors influencing technology integration into organisation's business processes and structures. This takes account of the fact that adoption frameworks and models have already been discussed in Chapter 6 of this book.

Further, the quest to understand the inherent factors that affect e-Government penetration at the organisational level is very important as it is the start-point of any successful e-Government implementation. In this regard, it is important to note that failure of e-Government is as a result of lack of understanding of the correlation between different factors such as technologies, information use, organizational factors, institutional arrangements, and socio-economic contexts (Luna-Reyes & Gil-García, 2013).

To understand the different factors that influence technology adoption at the organisational level, many e-Government researchers have utilised the technology-organization-environment (TOE) framework (Zhu, Xu & Dedrick, 2003; Arpaci, Yardimci, Ozkan & Turetken, 2012; Muafi, Gusaptono, Effendi & Charibaldi, 2012). The genesis of the TOE is the common belief that the structure of any organisation is defined by its surrounding environment needs. The following the major attributes of the TOE:

1. **Technology** – How does technology impact on the adoption process? The heterogeneous technology have a huge impact on whether individuals and/or business utilise e-Government applications. Some of the technology that citizens have may not be compatible with the given e-Government solutions. In essence, the technology aspect of the TOE probes whether the technology platforms that citizens have at their disposal make it easy to access e-Government applications.
2. **Organisation** – provides a thorough description of the organisational characteristics such as firm size, structure, management structure complexity, degree of organisational structure flexibility, available human resource base and competence levels, complexity of both internal and external business processes, etc. Further, the technology aspect of the TOE probes the flexibility of the structure of the organisation in assimilating new and emerging technologies in its business processes. By so doing, it probes the degree of flexibility in the different organisational dimensions such as the willingness of employees to adopt technology.
3. **Environment** – the definition of the environment in which the organisation does its business, competitors, industry domain, rules and regulation, and relationships with other players in the environment such as the government.

The three different aspects of the TOE present opportunities and constraints to technology integration into the organisational structures and should therefore be carefully probed when designing e-Government development roadmaps.

As aforementioned, several studies have investigated technology encapsulation at an organisational level using the TOE. For example, Zhu, Xu and Dedrick (2003) used the TOE *framework for assessing e-Business at the firm level.* The TOE looks at three attributes of a firm that may influence the rate of adoption of technology and integration into the existing business processes: technology options/platforms, organisational context, and the environment. In another instance, using the TOE, Arpaci, Yardimci, Ozkan and Turetken (2012) carried out a detailed review of the different studies that investigated organisational adoption of technologies. The TOE is integrated with other models to try as much as possible to understand the inherent factors that impact on e-Government adoption (Muafi, Gusaptono, Effendi & Charibaldi, 2012).

Another theoretical framework, the Institutional Theory, has been used in many instances to measure the behaviour of different institutional entities and therefore their propensity to accept new phenomenon such as technology. The Institutional Theory investigates the deeper aspects of the social order by considering the different rules, norms and routines which act as authoritative guidelines for social behaviour (Scott, 2004). There are many studies that have applied institutional theory in e-Government research especially in as far as understanding the hidden traits and the factors affecting adoption of ICTs at an organisational level is concerned (Hassan & Gil-Garcia. 2009).

Because e-Government needs to be designed with the local context in mind, the institutional theory recognises the importance of context and helps appreciate influences of various factors in technology selection, design, implementation and use. Institutions are recognised as entities or social structure that confine behaviour of individuals. The complexity of an organisation with regards to implementing e-Government cannot be overemphasised. To demonstrate the complexity of any organisational setting, Humes & Reinhard (2007) posit that there are cognitive, normative and regulative structures and activities that define behaviour in an organisational or institutional setup.

Further, Fountain (2001) proposes the Technology Enactment Framework (TEF) which is deeply rooted in institutional theory recognising the intersections between institutions, bureaucratic structures, and information technologies. Within these different entities of the TEF, there are inherent factors impacting on technology adoption mostly hinged on the local contextual characteristics.

9.7 Closer look at Zambia's Case

To appreciate the complexity of e-Government development in a developing world context, the following section presents the proposed e-Government implementation framework for Zambia. The proposed framework may be relevant to other developing countries with similar contextual characteristics as those depicted in Zambia. Therefore, requisite and responsive e-Government implementation can be achieved. Note that this section does not go deeper into the methodology aspects as this is devoted to Chapter 10. The proposed framework paves way for the design of a robust e-GIF for Zambia. As aforementioned, an appropriate e-GIF in any environment is one that takes into considering all the technical and non-technical multi-dimensionalities of e-Government. In this regard, there is need to consider all the possible aspects of the supply and demand sides of e-Government. The supply side includes all the interventions done in the realm of encouraging e-Government proliferation and the demand side includes anticipated users' (citizens and businesses) perspectives on e-Government adoption and usage.

The theoretical framework utilised in the Case Study is premised on the Davis' 1989 TAM model which identified PU and PEOU as the core factors influencing adoption of a technology. The study measures the 'Behaviour Intention to Use (BIU)' which is the stimulant for actual usage of e-Government services. It is easy to note that the BIU to use e-Government services is supported by the ICT available platforms. In this case, a majority of the participants have alluded to the fact that availability of appropriate ICT infrastructure coupled with adequate perception levels of PU and PEOU will positively influence the uptake of e-Government. The study identified several additional factors to the original TAM model such as Computer self-efficacy, limited literacy levels, trust in both e-Government platforms and the government, low cost to access Internet, and availability of local language options as one of the factors that influence citizens' and businesses' engagement in e-Government services. However, some of these factors did not make it for inclusion in the proposed model owing to low variance caused by their regression models on the final predictability of Continuance Usage (CU) of e-Government applications. The conceptual e-Government adoption model for Zambia is shown in Figure 9.2 below.

Although e-Government implementation is still in its infancy in Zambia, Figure 9.2 has shown that the adoption trends are influenced by the common factors as reported in the TAM model. The only difference is that the R^2 is a bit low for all the variables and correctively the predictive capacity of the regression equation and model. This may be attributed to the fact that the implementation of e-Government has not reached its full potential in Zambia and this has a direct implication on the citizens' perception of e-Government in general and correspondingly their willingness to engage in e-Government.

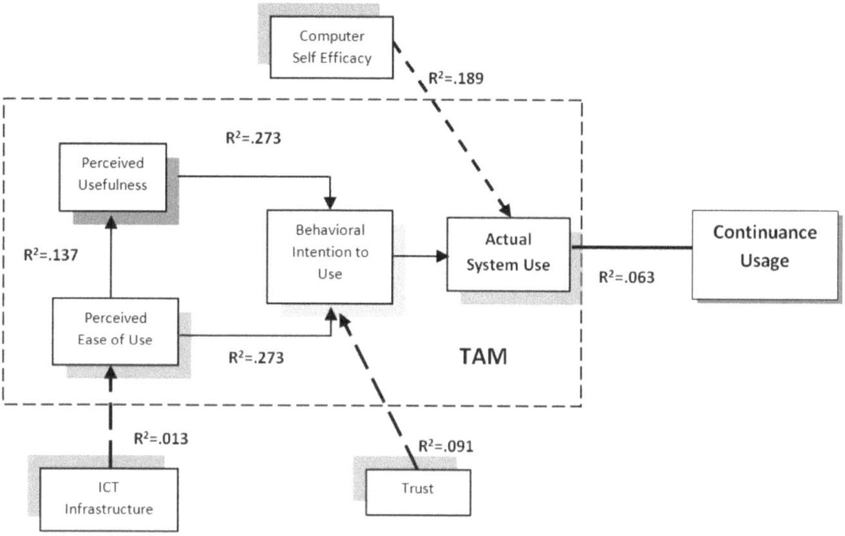

Figure 9.2: Proposed conceptual e-Government adoption model (e-Government consumers).

A closer look at the literature and documents analysis with regards to the status of e-Government development in Zambia, it is clear that there are inherent gaps that need to be bridged if e-Government implementation were to be a success in Zambia. For example, there is limited capacity on the part of the government establishment in as far appropriate development of technical e-Government applications and its management, thereof, is concerned. Simply put, as been highlighted above, robust e-Government implementation involves a fine balance between the technical and socio-economic or managerial dispositions. This balance can be provided for in the e-Government design frameworks by incorporating the e-Government interoperability framework (e-GIF) which provides detailed specifications on the socio-economic/managerial and technical feasibility and principles for e-Government implementation. As aforementioned, the e-GIF is a roadmap for the continuous monitoring and sustainability of the relevancy of the different e-Government applications to the consumers by providing frameworks which allow the applications to be modified or scaled up (scalability) as technologies evolves and new applications or computing paradigms come on the scene. This is called process re-engineering. Process re-engineering should not be a one-off endeavour but should be anchored to the e-Government strategy that is under development. Process re-engineering should be embedded into the e-GIF (to be developed) for Zambia and should form part of the monitoring and evaluation framework for sustenance of e-Government applications. The proposed e-GIF in the context of Zambia is presented in the next section.

9.8 Proposed e-Government Strategy Design Framework

As aforementioned, the bedrock of effective and sustainable e-Government development strategy lies in its capacity to strike a balance between the supply and the demand side of e-Government. The e-GIF aims to outline the synthesis and integration of technology-centric and the socio-economic centric e-Government solutions. In essence, a robust e-Government strategy should contain the following attributes:

1. The institutional, regulatory and legal frameworks should appropriately be in place; and should be able to give comprehensive statements regarding e-Government and give legal recognition to the blueprint e-Government strategy in place.
2. There is need to incorporate change management plans on the overall government culture and practice and encourage public service business process re-engineering. This should include be guided by the Aristotelian questions "what, how, where, who, when and why". The change management plan should be a continuous plan that should be embedded into the all core clusters of the overall e-Government strategy.
3. Consider the relationship of national culture (Khalil, 2011) and propensity to change and device ways on how to best go around it. For example, different ethnic groupings should be consulted and their input considered in designing robust change management programs and paradigms to accommodate e-Government even in remote areas and at the local levels of governance.
4. Design a context-aware e-GIF which should be considered as the cornerstone of the e-Government strategy. The e-GIF should be wary of all the effects of the supply and the demand side aspects of e-Government implementation. This should be designed in such as way that it is the main evaluation and monitoring tool of e-Government down its implementation cycle.
5. The e-GIF should consider both the technical and managerial aspects of the e-Government institutional framework.

Based on the common principles of the e-GIFs discussed above, the following aspects on the technical side should be considered:

1. Establishment of a wider Government Intranet System (GINS) which is responsible for interconnection of Governmental bodies. This will make it possible for the different databases hosting citizens' and businesses' information, and the different e-Government applications to be integrated.
2. Encouraging a culture of easy-to-use e-Government designs to allow global access by the general consumer base.

3. Putting in place a Public Key Infrastructure (PKI) for security and authentication of e-Government applications.
4. Putting in place an Enterprise Application Integration (EAI) infrastructure to provide the much-desired interoperability of e-Government applications.

The following aspects of the socio-economic/managerial side should be considered when designing e-GIF:

1. A list of competencies of individuals (such as Information Managers, Business Intelligence Specialists, Database Managers) who should be mandated to manage all information resources generated by e-Government applications.
2. List of guidelines that should inform back-end e-Government applications managers on what to do on what circumstances.
3. List of procurement guidelines for e-Government technical infrastructure and applications, and any software.
4. List of strategies and approaches to be utilised in e-Government consumer support.
5. Expectations (and do's and don'ts) of the e-Government project management team.
6. A list of guidelines of strategies that should be employed in managing different sets of data and information according to their security ratings and type (such as bio data and personal information).
7. List of business intelligence strategies aimed for capacitating government workers and correspondingly facilitating efficiency (value for investments) and effectiveness of public service delivery frameworks.
8. Provision for cyber laws, e-Signatures, and procedures for cybercrime prevention and therefore protection of the user in the cyber space.
9. A separate policy from the national ICT policy, dubbed the e-Government policy to outline the detailed specifics for anticipated e-Government development and implementation.
10. Need to embedded robust marketing strategies for e-Government application in the strategy to promote global buy-in of the would-be consumers.
11. Inclusion of local context-relevant information content in all the major languages;
12. Ensure availability of relevant, adequate and appropriate human resource base and e-Government champions to advance the e-Government development agenda.
13. Put in place appropriate funding models (such as self-financing from revenue charged from accessing e-Government services or utilisation of the Public Private Partnership (PPP) for ICT infrastructure roll-out (and e-Readiness

interventions and plans) and sustainability of e-Government implementation. The e-Government strategy in place should draw ways on which funding models to use with reference to the local context conditions.
14. There should be plans to up the ICT literacy skills for the general population. As mentioned in Chapter 6, this can be done by introducing ICTs educations as part of the general curricula of the lower primary school level.
15. Deliberate policies and plans should be in place to encourage universal access of e-Government applications and e-Participation.

The items listed above are some of the building blocks that should be considered for successful e-Government implementation. Note that the above list is not exhaustive but serves to give guidelines on pertinent issues that should be considered when designing a robust e-Government model.

The empirical study conducted in Zambia showed that favourable e-Government implementation is dependent on many factors. In order to ensure that all the heterogeneous factors are included in the e-Government design and implementation, there is need to design an e-GIF informed by the local context. Figure 9.3 shows the proposed e-Government strategy design framework which emanated from the careful analysis of the different dimensions of e-Government in Zambia. This framework can be used to discern the different constructs that should be considered when designing any strategic e-Government roadmap. The detailed specifics and constructs can be seen on the figure itself.

The proposed framework for e-Government strategy development outlines the synthesis of the socio-economic/managerial and technical sides of e-Government implementation. The factors that impact on e-Government have been subdivided into those that are targeted at facilitating the 'organisational and institutional e-Government readiness' and the 'individual and business motivation factors or individual e-Readiness parameters' as posited in Chapter 4. The socio-economic perspectives are hinged on the kind of project management strategies and approach that would be employed in advancing the e-Government agenda and the change management plans in place. Further, the cost and financing models (for example the PPP approach discussed in chapter 10) to be employed define the socio-economic/managerial aspects of e-Government implementation. The technical perspectives are defined by the monitoring and evaluation strategies to be employed (such as the kind of business process re-engineering to be employed) and the detailed specifications outlined in the e-GIF.

It is worth noting that the actual strategies to be employed at each node of the proposed framework very much depend on the characteristics of the local environment. The framework is proposed to serve as a guideline for the design of the actual e-Government development strategy. Further, the framework has outlined the building blocks for successful e-Government implementation.

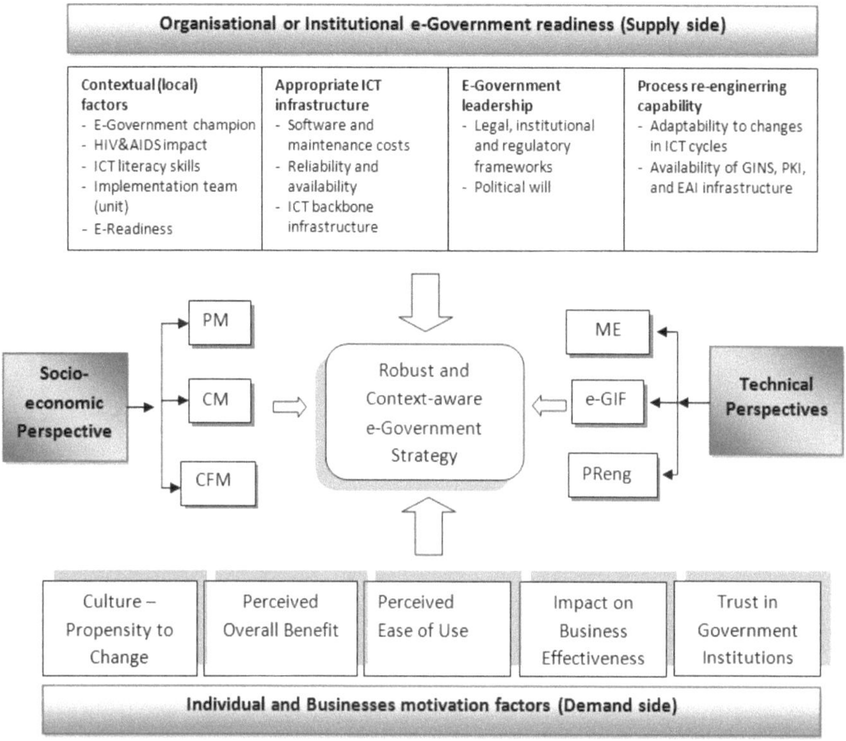

Key to Figure 9.3
e-GIF: e-Government Interoperability Framework
CFM: Cost and financing Models (such as PPP)
CMgt: Change Management Plan
ME: Monitoring and Evaluation Strategy
PM: Project Management
PReng: Process re-engineering

Figure 9.3: Proposed framework for e-Government strategy development.

9.9 Conclusion and Summary

This chapter has outlined the major principles that are used for designing e-Government interventions and implementation. The chapter has highlighted the major principles guiding integration of heterogeneous information systems, business processes and e-government application in the public service environment. Further, the chapter provides a list of some of the approaches utilised in designing e-GIFs in different countries of the world. The essence of highlighting the different e-GIFs is to highlight the fact that many countries, including the less developed ones, have realized the importance of designing e-GIFs as blueprints for e-Government implementation. The chapter ends by drawing results from a case study on Zambia which outlines the real environment intricacies involved in designing e-GIF.

The chapter recognizes the fact that there are several design frameworks and models which have attempted to provide guidelines on how to appropriate design the technical and non-technical aspects of e-Government. However, it is worth mentioning that the major principle that should guide design of e-GIFs is that there should be adequate reference on the local contextual characteristics whilst not forgetting the globally accepted principles on both the technical and non-technical aspects of e-Government.

Chapter 10
Methodology and Practical Perspectives for e-Government Research and Practice

10.1 Introduction

In recognizing the fact that research informs practice, it is importance to ensure that correct and methodologically sound research is done. If wrong conclusions emanate from research, it is logically coherent to assume that even e-Government practice will be flawed. Therefore, with a view of reducing on the percentage of e-Government projects that fail, this research probes the methodological ramifications utilised by different e-Government researchers and practitioners to investigate the proliferation and integration of e-Government into the different socio-economic strata.

One of the key debate topics in e-Government research and practice has been around understanding the ramifications of the different methodologies utilised in assessing e-Government development, impact or penetration in a given area. As can be seen from Chapter 5 and 6 of this book, many e-Government researchers and practitioners have taken heterogeneous methodological approaches investigating different factors that affect e-Government development. Many other researchers and practitioners have continued singing the rhetoric that 'e-Government is still in its nascent stage therefore its conceptual foundations and frameworks/models are still inexistence'. The lack of globally-accepted e-Government conceptualisations should be a concern to all e-Government stakeholders but should not be an excuse as to not delve deeper into designing context-aware methodological approaches or theoretical frameworks.

In order to contribute effectively to the methodology discussion of e-Government, this chapter intends to bring out the inherent entities with regards to measuring any aspects of e-Government. The chapter presents a synoptic overview of the different methodological approaches have been utilised in both developed and less developed countries with regard to measuring e-Government. The complexity of e-Government methodology is further pronounced because of the multi-dimensional nature of e-Government.

Generally, e-Government research has been meet with methodological inconsistencies and weakness both in scope and usefulness in understanding the full gamut of e-Government (McCurdy & Cleary, 1984). Further, it is not difficult to observe that most studies excessively utilise qualitative methods with higher degrees of Case Studies and non-empirical research. The need for empirical research cannot be overemphasised because such research has the potential to generate original theories and frameworks and/or models that are going to be key reference points with regards to implementation.

10.2 Research and Practice Focus

E-Government research and practice has mostly been devoted to understanding the likelihood of technology adoption at the individual level. The thinking has been that individual acceptance and usage of technology points to success of e-Government implementation. What has been lacking are a set of serious enquiry with regards to other facets of e-Government implementation such as organisational and managerial attributes of e-Government implementation. With this lack of research on e-Government enquiry, the general practice of e-Government research has correspondingly resulted into many projects failing. It is worth mentioning that the correlation between research and practice in e-Government implementation is pronounced. Therefore, it can be posited that the start point in successful e-Government research is defining appropriate methodology.

Appropriate e-Government research should show the heterogeneity in its methodological approaches given the multi-dimensional nature of e-Government. This means that a different methodology appropriately fitting the given aspect of e-Government should be employed at any given time. It is also appropriate to investigate e-Government phenomenon from multiple vantage points by utilizing more than two methodological approaches to investigate a given phenomenon of e-Government.

In order to appreciate which methodology to use to understand the different aspects of e-Government so that appropriate interventions are employed on the supply side (implementation side), there is need to understand the inherent attributes of what are called 'the four pillars of e-Government implementation'. These four pillars are as follows:

1. Need for requisite Information and Communication Technology (ICT) infrastructure;
2. Leadership to manage e-Government implementation at the various stages of its development projectile;
3. Organisational and individual readiness paradigms; and
4. Availability of responsive, context-aware institutional, legal and regulatory frameworks.

The basic questions guiding the choice of methodologies in answering the four questions above may be the following:

1. Since ICTs are a main enabler for e-Government, careful enquiry needs to be done before any interventions are put in place. For example, the following are some of the questions that may need to be asked to ensure that context-aware e-Government interventions are put in place:
   - Which technologies are best suited to implement specific e-Government solutions in a given area? (context-aware e-Government solutions – deployment of technologies that suit the local contextual characteristics)
   - What type of technologies are largely being accessible by the majority of the citizenry and business entities (do they access Internet using conventional means i.e. using immobile personal computers at Internet cafes or access Internet on mobile platforms (e.g. on mobile phones) ubiquitously)?
   - What are the local culture perceptions with regards to accessing government information and services online?
   - What is the anticipated lifecycle of a given technology considering the current short lifecycles of technology adoption?
   - How to design e-Government technology infrastructure so that a common, open middleware that allows technology gender neutrality?
   - How to design robust e-Government systems that can easily exchange information?
   - How to design scalable e-Government systems?
   - Which e-Government Interoperability Framework to use to achieve system integration?
2. What is the available leadership cadre to drive e-Government implementation? This general question may be followed by the following specific areas of enquiry:
   - Are there enough information management specifics to ensure that there is sanity in the e-Government environment?
   - Are there adequate technical specialists to ensure that development of context-aware and evolving e-Government applications is sustained?
   - Are there adequate business specialists to ensure that the business and funding aspects of e-Government implementation are always addressed?
   - Are there politicians who have the political will to continue investigating in e-Government in order for it to remain current?
   - Are there adequate monitoring and evaluation specialists to continuously assess the impact of e-Government down the implementation cycle?
3. What are the different organisational and individual readiness scenarios?

   What conceptual or theoretical frameworks guide e-Government at the organisational/institutional and individual levels?

   - What are the contextual characteristics influencing e-Government readiness at the organisational or individual levels?
   - Does the public service arrangement allow easy integration of ICTs into its business processes?
   - Are organisational policies and culture in support of enveloping new interventions in the public service delivery frameworks? (organisational behavior)
   - Are organisational structures flexible enough to allow new interventions? (susceptibility to change)
   - Are individuals endowed with requisite ICT skills, computer self-efficacy, see the need, etc. to engage in e-Government?
4. Are there responsive, context-aware institutional, legal and regulatory frameworks?

It is very clear that the above sets of questions cannot be investigated using a homogeneous approach. Therefore, the need for multiple methods in investigating e-Government cannot be overemphasized.

10.3 Methodology of Research

There are different research paradigms that are being utilised in e-Government research. Some of the prominent ones have been the positivist, interpretive, and the critical perspective (Chen & Hirscheim, 2004; Myers, 1997). Focus of e-Government research have mostly been devoted to understanding the willingness of individuals to adopt e-Government or the assessment of the availability of requisite ICT infrastructure, policy frameworks and the leadership cadre to drive e-Government implementation. Essentially, the focus has therefore been techno-centric; government-centric; citizen-centric (Grönlund, 2010; Sahroui, 2007). The knowledge frameworks utilised in the investigation of e-Government have been the following: theory-based; framework-based; model-based; schema-based; concept-based; category-based (Heeks & Bailur, 2007).

In addition to the general issues being investigated in e-Government as articulated in section 10.2 above, the major focus of e-Government research has been the following:

1. E-Government design and implementation: understanding Information Technology (IT) artefacts and platforms, which of these are suitable for a targeted population? How to integrate the heterogeneous Information Systems (IS) in the public service? Which are the IT/IS development frameworks informing e-Government practice?

2. What are the determinants and processes of technology adoption at both the organisational and individual levels? What the inhibiting factors (problems) with regards to technology adoption?
3. What are the evaluation frameworks of e-Government implementation at different levels of the socio-economic hierarchy? What are the context-specific success or failure factors of e-Government implementation?
4. What instruments/frameworks or assessments are used to measure the impact of e-Government on socio-economic strata?

The different focuses of e-Government research and practice can be seen in Figure 10.1 below.

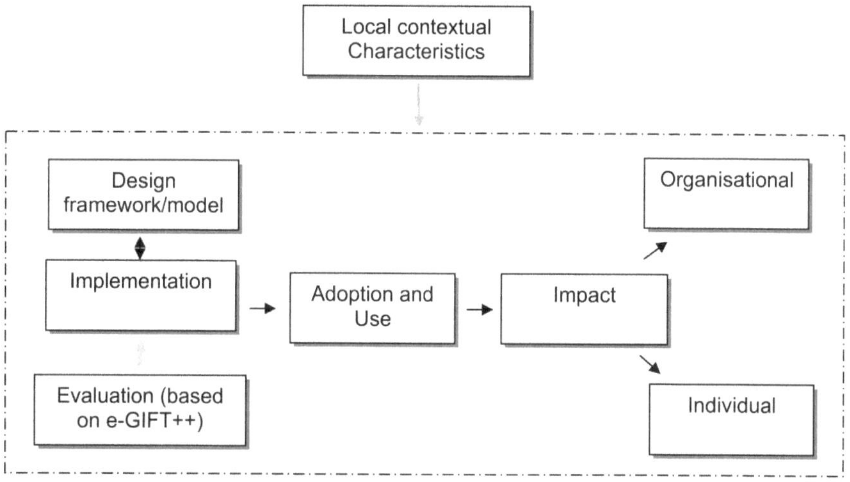

Figure 10.1: Areas under the ambit of e-Government research and practice.

Figure 10.1 shows the key research and practice nodes of e-Government. As can be seen, the start-point of e-Government implementation is when the different interventions are being designed. The design culminates into a well-articulated e-GIF for a specific location. The impending implementation is then done based on the recommendations and articulation of the principles mentioned in the e-GIF. Thereafter, adoption and use and correspondingly the impact of e-Government manifests at both the organisational/institutional and individual levels. Therefore, any assessment of e-Government impact can be done at both the institutional and individual levels.

10.4 E-Government and Multi-dimensional Methodological Inclination

This section intends to outline the multi-dimensionality of e-Government and highlight how this characteristic of e-Government influences methodology or enquiry approach in understanding penetration of ICTs in public service delivery frameworks. Because of its nature and the many factors that simultaneously impact on e-Government, there is need to utilize multiple methods to investigate similar phenomena in the e-Government realm. In order to understand the general methodology and research trends with regards to e-Government, the following paragraph discusses the Pasteur's quadrant which outlines the different paradigms in research innovation. This discussion is important because it outlines the different aspects of methodology in e-Government environments. The next paragraph highlights the different classification methods of research types according to Pasteur's quadrant defined by Stokes (1997:10).

Stokes (1997), in his book entitled '*Pasteur's quadrant: Basic science and technological innovation*', recognises two basic types of research: one is 'basic research' which refers to theoretical or experimental investigation to advance scientific knowledge where immediate practical application is not a direct objective. This type of research aims at generating knowledge with major emphasis on the theoretical perspective. Another type is 'applied research' which focuses on experimental investigation with much reference to existing knowledge for practical perspectives. In agreement with Stokes (1997), Tushman and O'Reilly III (2007:769) posit that research can be undertaken both as a quest for basic knowledge and understanding (rigor) and with considerations of use (relevance) such as in solving a particular problem. Some research can be done to understand a particular phenomenon with no intention for any specific use (such as Neils Bohr's discovery of the atomic structure); done for applied uses (such as Edison's invention of phonograph); and some research is done both out of a quest for knowledge and desire to apply the findings (such as Pasteur's development of microbiology). These different research types are presented in Figure 10.2 below.

In Figure 10.2 above, the upper left, first quadrant shows Niels Bohr's research which focus on investigating the atomic structure only for the purposes of generally seeking knowledge about the atomic phenomenon. The sterile quadrant (lower left) shows the type of research which researchers, especially in universities and research institutions do to return tenure or their position. In most of the cases, this type of research does not have any clear goals of seeking knowledge for application in real-life situations. The Edison's quadrant (lower right) presents pure applied research which aims at using existing knowledge to create applications for use. Pasteur's quadrant (upper right) presents a synthesis for furthering knowledge on a specific subject and how this knowledge can be used to come up with applications. With the different research types, it is clear that the most relevant quadrant is the Pasteur's quadrant because of its synthesis approach.

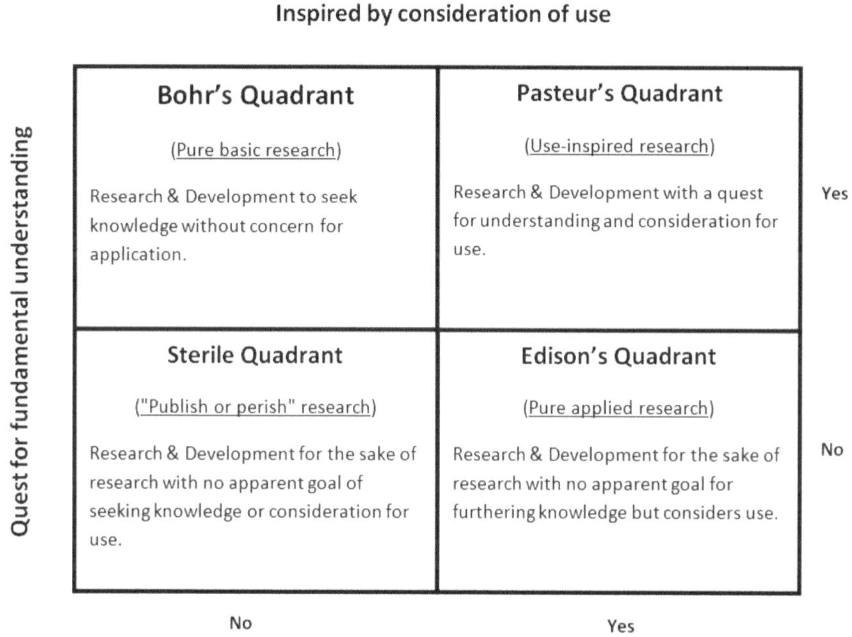

Figure 10.2: Research classification quadrants (Stokes, 1997:73; Barnard, 2007:125).

As outlined by Rowley (2004:208), Pasteur's research quadrant posits that good research has the following characteristics:

- Research contributes to existing knowledge
- Research has a clear purpose or research question
- Research is objective and reliable
- Research addresses the issues of:
  - Access (to people, organisations, or data)
  - Politics (internal)
  - Ethical conduct (with reference to privacy, confidentiality and transparency).

In order to ensure that the characteristics of Pasteur's quadrant are fulfilled, and given the multi-dimensionality of e-Government research, there is need to utilize the Mixed Methods Research (MMR) approach. Mixing of the research methods and approaches is done at all the stages of the research cycle. For example, both the qualitative and quantitative can be used for data collection approaches, and the analysis of the collected data may be done using multiple methodological approaches.

The MMR approach has no global definition at the moment and researchers are at liberty to define it as they deem fit provided that its fundamental characteristics and nature are preserved (Ngulube et al., 2009:106). Fidel (2008:265) posit that there is, at the moment, no shared understanding of what constitutes MMR. Despite this being the case, there are common traits on which researchers on methodology agree upon. For example, Johnson, Onwuegbuzie and Turner (2007:123) define MMR as a 'type of research in which the researcher or team of researchers combine elements of qualitative and quantitative research approaches (for example, use of qualitative and quantitative view points, data collection, analysis, inference techniques) for the broad purposes of breadth and depth of understanding and corroboration'. Agreeing with this concept, Bazeley (2008:133) posit that mixed methods, in the context of research paradigm terminology, has 'developed currency as an umbrella term applying to almost any situation where more than one methodological approach is usually used in combination with another, but not essentially, involving a combination of at least some elements drawn from each of the qualitative and quantitative approaches to research'. These definitions are not mutually exhaustive on their own when employed in a research study, and as such there exists other forms of defining the mixed method approach. For example, triangulation, that is the combination of quantitative and qualitative research methods, is also considered as part of MMR.

Triangulation has been defined as a combination of two or more data collection techniques, methodological approaches, investigators, or theoretical perspectives (Kimchi, Polivka & Stevenson, 1991:365). Triangulation makes it possible for researchers to capture a more comprehensive, holistic and contextual portrayal of a research process (Polit & Hungler, 1995). Methodological triangulation is done to seek 'convergence, inconsistency and contradiction by investigating a research question from different vantage points' (Ngulube et al., 2009:107). Methodological triangulation can also refer to either data collection methods or research designs (Lincoln & Guba, 1985). It can further refer to a combination of quantitative and qualitative methods with an indication of a paradigmatic connection (Barbour, 1998:355). Triangulation is employed primarily in qualitative research.

There are distinct differences between triangulation and MMR (Ngulube, 2010:255). Triangulation employs 'mixing' at a methodological or application level (i.e. collecting, analysing and interpreting data) and seeks convergence, whereas in MMR, 'mixing' is done at all phases of the research process, including the philosophical assumptions and the research question (Teddlie & Tashakkori,

2009:4). In this study, triangulation has been used at all stages of the research process, such as 'sources triangulation' (investigating the e-Government phenomenon using multiple sources), data collection methods triangulation, and data analysis triangulation; culminating into complete utilisation of the MMR approach. This is in conformance to O'Cathain, Murphy and Nicholl (2007:148) who showed that MMR can be defined as mixing different methods at the different stages in a study process in relation to design, sampling, analysis, and interpretation.

The investigation of the research problem from different vantage points ensures that the MMR approach is utilised at all stages of the research process in this study. E-Government studies have attempted to utilize multiple methods in order to minimise 'deficiencies and biases that may stem from any single method' (Mitchell, 1986:19), thereby creating a research environment where cross-method triangulation – both qualitative and quantitative data collection methods are utilised in the same study (Boyd, 2000:461). Cross-method triangulation employs both participant interviews and questionnaires as data collection platforms.

Theoretical triangulation as applied in e-Government research involves the testing of multiple hypotheses in the examining of the e-Government adoption phenomenon. This is in conformance with Denzin (1970:236) who defined theoretical triangulation as the intent to conduct a study with multiple lenses and questions in mind to support or refute findings. Data-analysis triangulation is combining two or more methods of analysing data. In line with Kimchi et al., (1991:364–366), many e-Government studies have used different statistical techniques to determine and analyse the different data sets obtained from the research and validate the hypotheses and data gathering instruments.

For any qualitative research, a hypothesis is not desired before the research is commissioned whereas in quantitative research, a hypothesis is required before any research endeavors can be commissioned. Golafshani (2003:597), quoting from Hoepfl (1997), posit that researchers who use quantitative research employ quantitative measures to test hypothetical generalisations. This is exactly the case in this study. Qualitative methods are generally more flexible and allow greater spontaneity and adaptation of the interaction between a researcher and the research participant. Salant and Dillman (1994:81) and Golafshani (2003:600) emphasise the major advantage of qualitative methods for exploratory research, namely, using open-ended questions accords the participants an opportunity to respond in their own words rather than forcing them to choose from fixed responses. For these reasons, some e-Government studies employ MMR which applies multiple research methods, both quantitative and qualitative. The major difference between the quantitative and qualitative methods is that the quantitative method applies deductive reasoning and in the qualitative method reasoning is inductive (Lawley, 1999:132; Wood & Welch, 2010:57).

Other e-Government studies have used concurrent MMR, as clarified by Ngulube et al., (2009:107) where data is collected 'using both qualitative and quantitative procedures simultaneously (for example, administering a questionnaire which has both closed-ended and open-ended questions)'. MMR is 'research in which the investigator collects and analyses data, integrates the findings, and draws inferences using both qualitative and quantitative approaches and methods in a single study or program of inquiry' (Tashakkori & Creswell, 2007:4). As stated by Ngulube et al., (2009:106), the rationale for using the MMR approach is to ensure that the research questions are answered holistically, there is significance enhancement where the interpretation of the data obtained is enriched, and there is elimination of inherent biases (from data sources, researchers, and methods) that may be evident when only one method is used. With strong references to other researchers, the rationale for utilising methodological pluralism in the form of MMR in e-Government research cannot be over-emphasised as shown in the following cases:

- To explore the belief that the quality of any study can be improved because the inherent biases, limitations, and weaknesses that may be eminent when only one methodological approach is utilised are counterbalanced, or in other cases, compensated for (Fidel, 2008:265).
- Enrichment of the researcher's interpretation of the data.
- Participant enrichment, i.e. increasing the number of participants in the study (Collins, Onwuegbuzie & Sutton, 2006:76). Participants who cannot be reached by one methodological approach can be reached using another methodological approach.
- Instrument validity and reliability – in this case, pre-testing and piloting the data collection instruments before full row-out in the study (Collins et al., 2006:89).
- Assessing the reliability of interventions and programmes that have been put in place to encourage e-Government development.

This ensures that the findings are consistent with what unfolds on the ground. The use of the MMR approach enables e-Government research to explore the research objectives from different vantage points. Having different vantage points, affirmed by Ngulube et al., (2009:109), assists in achieving higher validity and reliability of research results. The findings from a one quantitative component enrich the qualitative component (and vice versa), which is in agreement with what is posited by Ngulube et al., (2009:114).

The major differences between quantitative and qualitative research are summarised in Table 10.1 below.

Table 10.1: Comparisons between quantitative and qualitative research approaches.

	Quantitative	Qualitative
General framework	Seeks to confirm hypothesis about phenomenon	Seeks to explore phenomena
	Instruments use more rigid style of eliciting and categorising responses to questions	Instruments use more flexible, iterative style of eliciting and categorises responses to questions in a more presentable manner
	Uses highly structured methods such as questionnaires, surveys, and structured observation	Uses semi-structured methods such as in-depth interviews, focus groups, and participant observation
Analytical objectives	To quantify variation	To describe variation
	To predict causal relationships	To describe and explain relationships
	To describe characteristics of a population	To describe individual/case experiences and to describe group norms
Question format	Close-ended	Open-ended
Data format	Numerical, i.e. obtained by assigning numerical values to responses	Textual, i.e. obtained from audiotapes, videotapes and field notes
Flexibility in study design	Study design is stable from beginning to end	Some aspects of the study are flexible, for example, the addition, exclusion, or wording of particular interview questions
	Participant responses do not influence or determine how and which questions researchers ask next	Participant responses affect how and which questions researchers ask next
	Study design is subject to statistical assumptions and conditions	Study design is iterative, that is, data collection and research questions are adjusted according to what is learnt

The combinational use of qualitative and quantitative research methodologies ensures that interpretation and understanding of complex reality of a given situation is guaranteed. Powell (2006:9) posit that quantitative data helps researchers to understand the processes involved in achieving pre-defined objectives, but does not explain the difficulties that may be experienced in exploring a certain context.

In order to appreciate the use of requisite methodologies in e-Government research, the next section presents a Case where assessment of e-Government development is done.

10.5 Further Look at the Zambia Case Study

Chapter 9 showed the case study on Zambia's e-Government at the highest levels of abstraction without going deeper into the methodological aspects. This section concentrates on the methodology utilised in investigating e-Government development in Zambia. Understanding the methodology tenets employed in the Zambia Case Study may reveal the methodological nuances that may be critical in the design of any e-Government study. Therefore, e-Government developers are counselled to observe the critical tenets used in the Zambia's case to appreciate what it takes to design an appropriate e-Government study.

In order to assess the level and potential of e-Government development in Zambia, a mix of methodological approaches were employed. This was because it was understood that e-Government is a multi-dimensional phenomenon which depends on multiple factors. This research was informed by both the primary and secondary data collected during the research process. Secondary data was gathered using extensive literature review and document analysis concerned with the status of e-Government development in Zambia. In particular, papers by Weerakkody et al., (2007:484–505), and Coates and Nikolaus (2010:137) were extensively referenced to understand the status of e-Government implementation in Zambia. The primary data was gathered in the empirical part of this study which included two parts: the pilot study and the main study. The primary data are basically original sources of raw data without any interpretation, synthesis or analysis which represents a position on a specific matter (Cooper & Schindler, 2001). The objectives of the pilot study were two-fold: 1) to investigate the appropriateness, validity and feasibility of the data collection instruments and approaches; and 2) to understand the supply side of e-Government in Zambia by pursuing a comprehensive literature review and document analysis. This was followed by the empirical study which further contained both interviews and questionnaire-type data collection methods.

Prior to the main survey, in accordance with the advice of Creswell, (1994:78–80), a systematic pilot study was done to test the face validity and reliability, and improve the questions and test the respondents' comprehension and clarity. Yin (2003:236) explains that reliability aims to minimise the errors and biases in the study, and Luk (2009:598) adds that validity aims to collect true and authentic data which can be observed empirically and subjected to objectivity. The Research Assistants who collected the data in the pilot study phase were given introductory letters about the research; they had copies of the ethics adherence document from the University of Johannesburg, and were given a brief summary of the objectives of the research.

The pilot study comprised two major components: the empirical study and document reviews. High-level interviews with six e-Government experts at different times were conducted in the initial phases of the empirical research. The empirical research employed interviews and questionnaires as data collection methods. The questionnaire contained open and closed-ended questions enabling it to collect both qualitative and quantitative data. Open-ended questions do not restrict the respondent on how he or she should fill in the questionnaire regarding his or her opinions on any pre-defined phenomenon and does not contain pre-determined categories of answers or possible options (Wilson, 1996:94–120). On the other hand, closed-ended questions come with many options out of which a respondent is mandated to choose one or more of them relating to his experience about a phenomenon under investigation (Salant & Dillman, 1994:83; Saunders et al., 2002:324). In accordance with Creswell's (1994:126) definition of MMR, this approach taken in the current study is considered as a mixed methods approach and was carried out throughout the empirical research. Given a brief discussion of what methodology was employed in this study, the next few paragraphs will elaborate on the concept of 'methodology' and what it entails as a research component.

In essence, 'methodology' is a series of procedures and strategies used in a study to obtain and analyse data (Doordan, 1998:86). Other definitions, although along the same axis, have also emerged in literature. For example, Adams and Schvanneldt (1995:234) define methodology as a set of techniques used by researchers to carry out an enquiry; emphasising that a research process systematically gathers information to describe, explore, explain or predict a phenomenon of interest. Within the design stage of this study, there was also a task of defining the sampling criteria and the sample frame. The sample frame includes a list of the population from which a sample (i.e. a cohort representative of the population) is to be taken, whereas sampling is the process of selecting research participants from the sample frame. Merriam (1998:60) has defined sampling as the process used in selecting a research site, time, people and events in field research. Le Compte and Preissle (1993:69) posit that sampling involves choosing a representation of individuals and subsets making up the population from which results could be generalised. The quality of any sampling technique depends on the sample frame, sample size or unit. Sample, explains Fowler (1993:105), is a subset of the population serving as the reference group for drawing inference about population.

Within the confines of qualitative and quantitative data collection approaches, sampling is classified either as probabilistic or non-probabilistic. Probabilistic sampling is where each member of the population has an equal chance of being selected. The extent of bias (i.e. the extent to which a sample might differ from the population) in selecting the participants is reduced. Sampath (2005:69) has outlined several types of probability sampling mechanisms including simple random sampling (where potential research participants have equal chance of being randomly selected from a given sample frame), systematic sampling (similar to simple random sampling despite the sample being selected systematically), and stratified sampling (sample frame subdivided into homogeneous groups with similar characteristics such as gender, age, and education). Contrary, non-probabilistic sampling employs techniques where the bias cannot be determined as research participants have no equal chance of being selected for inclusion in the study. Sampath (2005:72) describes non-probabilistic sampling to include convenience sampling (inexpensive exploration of the truth by selecting a convenient sample), purposive sampling (sample chosen with specific purpose in mind targeting one pre-defined group), quota sampling (research first identifies strata of the sample list and how they are presented in the population), and snowball sampling (utilised when desired sample characteristic is rare).

In its qualitative data collection approaches, this study utilises purposive sampling where the participants have been grouped according to the desired information that has been targeted to be collected, and relevant to particular research questions. The general aspects of e-Government development were solicited from individuals and businesses. The level of policy development in support of e-Government applications and the level of ICT infrastructure development were solicited from policy makers and heads of parastatals using the interview approach. The size of the samples was not fixed beforehand but was determined at a point of theoretical saturation (when no new data brings further insights to the research questions). A special form of purposive sampling, termed 'quota sampling' was utilised in this study. The major difference between purposive and quota sampling is that in the latter, the number of participants (with characteristics – age, place of residence, gender, class, profession, marital status, etc.) to be included in the study was decided at the study design stage. This has made it possible for people with necessary expertise and exposure to be targeted (such as this study's target of academic staff at the University of Zambia), right from the beginning of this study. For example, it would not make sense to go about asking everyone on the streets about the policies that are in place for e-Government development in Zambia as not everyone has knowledge on the same level.

Because of the nature of this study, probabilistic sampling was not considered as it would unnecessarily complicate the study in obtaining the permutations needed to choose the sample population. Probabilistic sampling uses random selection with each unit drawn with known probability (Yamane, 1967:135) or with a non-zero chance of being selected in the sample (Raj, 1972). This type of sampling starts with deciding on the population of interest and then establishing a frame (listing) of all the units of that chosen population and implies the researcher knows the exact possibility of selecting each member of the population (Keppel, 1991:311; Doherty, 1994:2). This was not the case in the current study, which entailed quota sampling and utilised non-probabilistic sampling techniques. It enables the study to have an opportunity to select a sample according to the researcher's convenience. The chance for a member of a targeted population to be selected and included in the study is unknown. The limitation of the non-probabilistic samples is that the results obtained from such a survey cannot be generalised statistically. Hernon (2009:2) posits that although non-probability sampling techniques do not involve random selection and lack representativeness, inherently it does enable researchers to draw inferences about a particular phenomenon being studied despite the fact that such inferences are limited to the sample itself. Thus, in the case of this study, the results can be theoretically generalised. This study set out to bring about the theoretical fundamentals that may be used as reference regarding the adoption of e-Government in Zambia. In order to do this required a systematic research approach.

This study closely followed the appropriate research processes with due reference to the local context. The research process includes comprehensive literature reviews in the research proposal stage and throughout the study cycle; the identification of the research problem with reference to the gaps between the supply and demand sides of e-Government in as far as e-Government development in Zambia is concerned; establishing the research methodology; understanding the general research limitations; collecting and analysing evidence; developing conclusions; and presenting the recommendations in the form of research findings. These steps are in conformance with the research process detailed in a book by Remenyi, William, Money and Swartz (1998:32).

The research process utilised in this study is illustrated in Figure 10.3 below and is explained next.

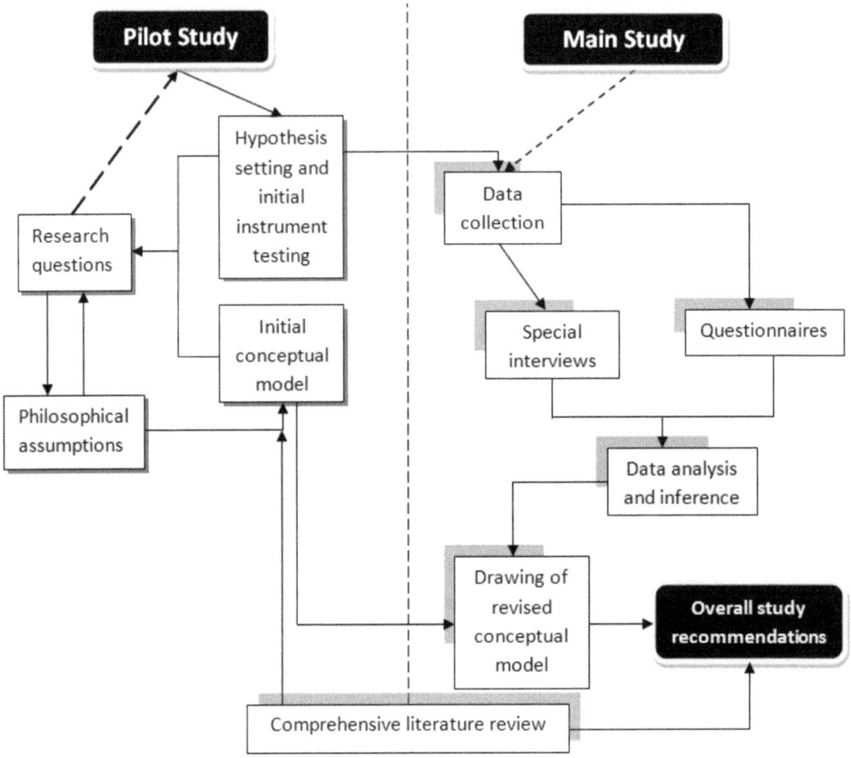

Figure 10.3: Study design and research process.

The research process included a series of steps in order to accomplish the objectives of the study. Figure 10.3 above shows the major components of the research process which are principally sub-divided into the pilot phase and the main study. The pilot phase was mainly aimed at establishing the feasibility of the study, refining the research idea, establishing the reliability and validity of the research instruments, and determining the common barriers to e-Government implementation in general. It was also aimed at conceptualizing the preliminary e-Government adoption model, and testing the viability and appropriateness of the data collection instruments. The main study comprised further literature review, data collection, analysis and presentation of the revised conceptual e-Government adoption model.

Regardless of perfect research design, a study that does not take research ethics into consideration is bound to be criticized. An overview of the ethical principles that were employed in this research follows. These principles have enabled the researcher and assistants to observe and respect the interest of the research participant cohort.

This research utilizes the fusion of quantitative and qualitative research approaches – termed Mixed Methods Research (MMR). Although it has been used at all stages of the research process, the qualitative approach has been used extensively in the pilot study to establish the feasibility of this study at the proposal level. The quantitative approach was used at the empirical research stage which aimed to capture data constructs detailing e-Government development at the micro levels of the Zambian society. Mixed methods formed the main methodological approach for this research. Figure 10.4 below shows a snapshot of the research motivation and process.

The research process shown in Figure 10.4 shows a step-by-step research process. This is in conformance with Yin (1997:27–35) who posited that any research design should ultimately have a logical sequence that connects a study's initial research questions, literature review and the empirical study to its conclusions.

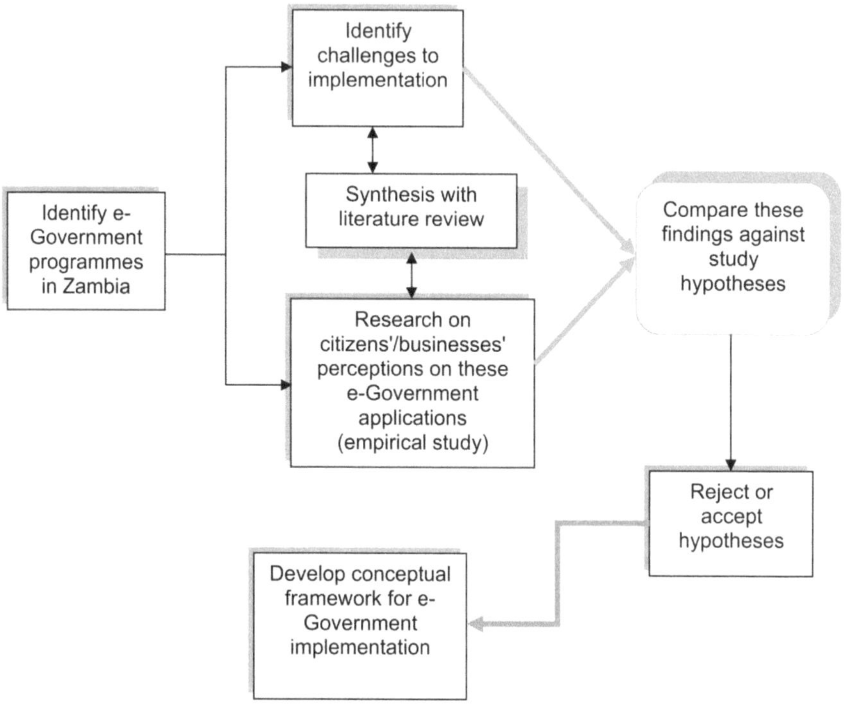

Figure 10.4: Snapshot of research motivation and process.

The following list of principles based on the Code of Ethics of the American Anthropological Association (1998) was observed by the researcher and implemented in this study:

- Informants were made aware of the aims of the investigation as clearly as possible.
  - Informants had the right to remain anonymous.
  - Questions asked were not insulting or embarrassing.
  - Participants were guaranteed that their dignity or privacy was not going to be infringed upon at any point of the research process.
  - There was no exploitation of informants for personal gain as all the research participants participated in this research voluntarily.
  - Any risks of participating in this research were highlighted.
- The researchers were implored to observe the following rights of individuals participating in the research:
  - The informant or subject has consented to the research without coercion; and that the questions posed are not insulting or embarrassing.
  - The informant has been explained to that he or she can withdraw participation at any point of the research and that participation is strictly voluntary.
  - Confidential matters that could embrace the participant or place the participant in a false or compromising position in respect of authorities are handled circumspectly.
  - The privacy and wishes of informants are respected, i.e. anonymity of the informant is maintained if required.
  - The informant is informed as fully as possible as to the aims and possible implications of the research.

These principles were mentioned on all the data collection instruments that were utilised in this research. The following section discusses the research model employed in this study and outlines the different factors that may possibly influence the engagement or non-engagement of individuals in e-Government applications.

The study employed a synthesised model to guide its research. The reasoning behind this model is based on Davis' 1989 technology acceptance model (TAM) and the influence of community informatics which is largely seen to be influencing adoption or non-adoption of technology (Mutula, 2010:1). Community informatics may be defined as an emerging conceptualisation, often called electronic community networking or community-based technologies, concerned with principles and norms related to ICTs with a core focus on the personal, social, cultural or economic development of, within and by communities. The different hypotheses tested in this study were aligned with the principles of community informatics. The conceptualisation of this research in this regard is shown in Figure 10.5 below.

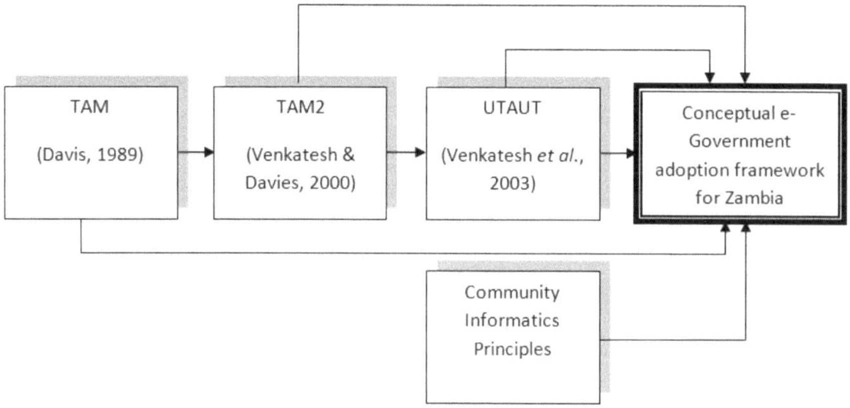

Figure 10.5: Fundamental research models and anticipated conceptual model.

Figure 10.5 above depicts how the anticipated conceptual e-Government adoption model for Zambia is premised on the original TAM by Davis (1989), the TAM2 (Venkatesh & Davis, 2000:188), the UTAUT model (Venkatesh et al., 2003:426), and community informatics. In order to have a well-informed e-Government research, the hypotheses need to be conceived with careful reference to the local context. Using the hypotheses conceived with careful reference to Zambia's contextual characteristics, Figure 10.6 below shows the expanded view of the research model.

Figure 10.6 above shows the expanded view of the research model presented in Figure 10.5 and presents the interaction between the hypothetical assertions and other factors that impact on technology adoption as presented in earlier models of the TAM and the UTAUT. The solid lines in Figure 10.6 show what has been observed from the earlier models in literature. The dotted lines represent the factors of e-Government adoption that are closely investigated in this study, with the anticipation of potential value.

The interdependence between the various factors in the research model requires some explanation in order to comprehend how the different hypotheses impact on overall e-Government adoption; and also to understand how the analysis of the data collected was approached. To this extent, Figure 10.7 shows the interdependence among the different factors in the research model employed in this study. For example, the factor Perceived Ease of Use (PEOU) acts a intermediary between the independent factor, ICT infrastructure and the dependent factor, Perceived Usefulness (PU). Thus, the relationships amongst the different factors in the model require attention on how these relate and impact on e-Government adoption and development as a whole. In any appropriate e-Government study design, these relationships amongst the dependent, intermediate and independent factors need to be clearly understood.

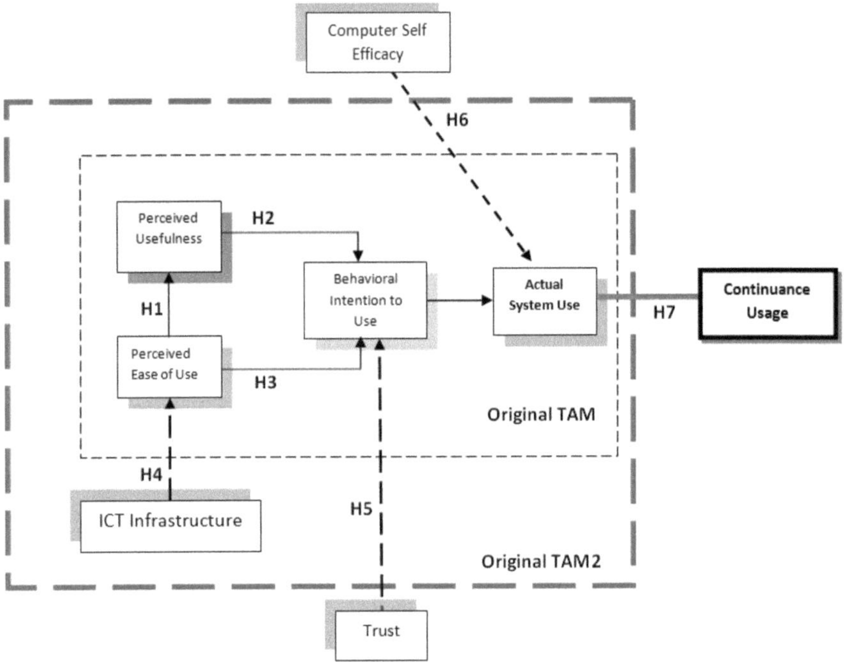

(H=Hypothesis)

Figure 10.6: Expanded view of the research model utilised in this study.

An understanding of the factors that influence individuals and businesses to engage in e-Government is cardinal to designing appropriate e-Government adoption models. As already articulated, both individual and organisational factors highly impact on e-Government uptake and adoption. It is thus necessary to know what these factors are, and important to form a clear understanding of the different technology adoption models.

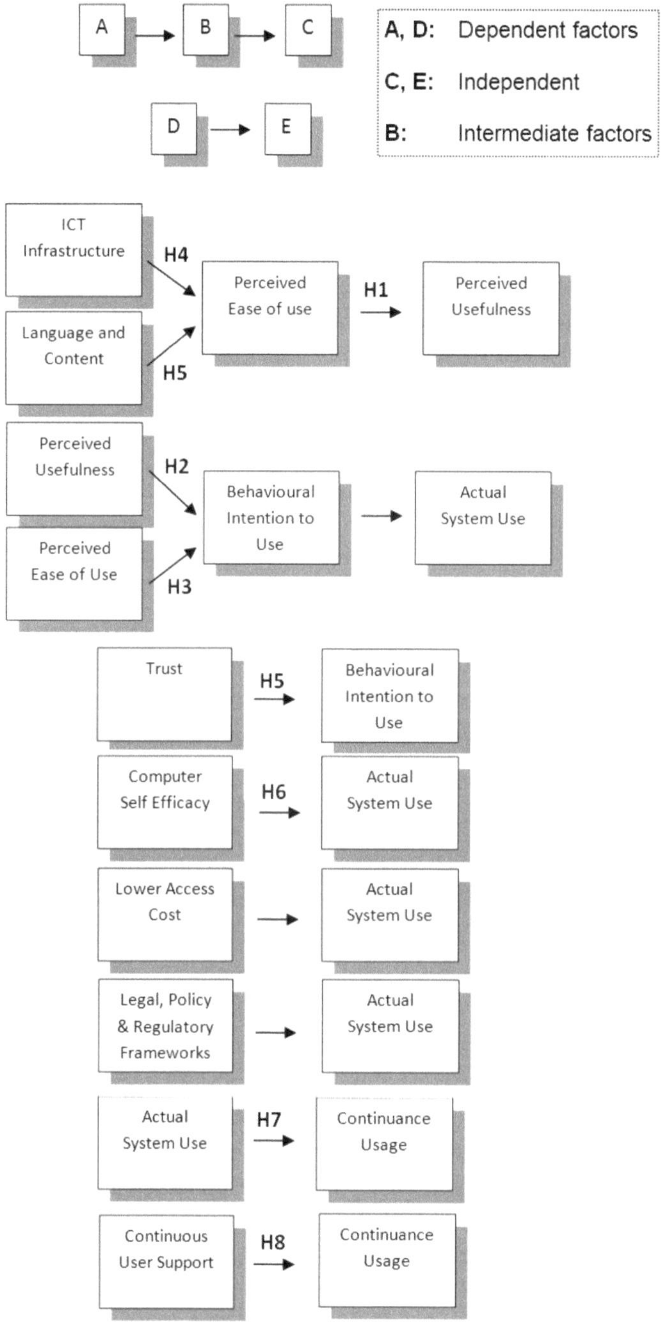

Figure 10.7: Interdependence among different factors in the research model.

Several authors (for example, Warkentin et al., 2002:158) have pointed out that data security, accessibility and perceived confidentiality influence individual adoption of e-Government to a greater extent. Titah and Barki (2006:35) have suggested that apart from organisational factors, individual beliefs of citizens have a significant influence on the adoption of e-Government services. With strong reference to the Davis' technology acceptance model of 1989, it is known that individual beliefs such as perceived usefulness (PU) and perceived ease of use (PEOU) have been considered as the dominant factors that influence the intention to adopt or use the technology in a business to consumer (B2C) model (Warkentin et al., 2002:157). Heeks and Santos (2009:3) presented a study where they outlined some perspectives on the adoption of public sector innovations – 'one that understands adoption as based on the behaviour of individual actors set within a contextual framework'. Their motivation came from the fact that e-Government faces low usage rates and stated that there exists huge gaps between designers and adopters. In their study, they employed case research to study the practice-based problem of e-Government where it was thought that the experiences of the actors are important and the context of action is critical (also cited in Benbasat, Goldstein & Mead, 1987). Their study identified different factors that affect the role of the designers (as principals) and adopters (as agents) in as far as e-Government development is concerned. The findings by Heeks and Santos (2009:1) are premised on PU and PEOU, which are the major constructs of the TAM. The TAM has been used by many researchers to test the adoption of technology in diverse ICT environments.

TAM's testing in different parts of the world has proved that it is one of the most reliable and easier models that can be utilised to explain individual's intention of adoption of a technology. It has also proved in yielding statistically reliable results in high quality research endeavours (Moon & Kim, 2001:217–218). Specifically, TAM has been used to explain users' initial intention to engage and use a technology. Furthermore, there are instances when it has been used to predict long term intention of citizens to use a technology. Venkatesh and Davis (2000:186), Kim and Malhotra (2005:741–742) have demonstrated, in their longitudinal studies, that PU and PEOU are one of the most important ingredients and determinants of citizen's intention to engage in a technology. The incorporation of the TAM, TAM2, and the UTAUT adoption models aim to present the different factors that affect the adoption of a technology. Chapter 2, Chapter 3 and Chapter 4 of this thesis have shown that the different factors affecting e-Government adoption are well documented.

10.6 Statistical Analysis

The data that has been collected in this research has been subjected to standard multiple regression analysis. The first point of analysis has been testing the reliability of the questionnaire in a pilot study conducted prior to full commencement of this research. On the research, the different reliability tests have been done to ascertain what factors and constructs should be included in its final version. The questionnaire was content-validated to establish whether it can capture data that may answer all the research questions in the study. The questions utilised in the interviews were also tested on 3 people to establish whether they can easily be comprehended by the potential respondents. Reliability was tested using the Reliability coefficient which is "the *correlation coefficient* between the two sets of scores scores" (Polit & Beck, 2004: 417). All the necessary statistical analysis was done with the help of the Statistical Package for Social Sciences (SPSS) programme.

The case study utilised a variety of statistical procedures on the data set to arrive at the proposed e-Government adoption model. The study utilised multivariate analysis to have correlation with the multiple methods utilised in the data collection. To achieve this analysis as distinct to univariate analysis, it was a requirement that the data set in this study follow a multivariate normal distribution. Any e-Government assessment endeavour may consider utilizing the following methodological approaches:

1. If the study utilises multivariate analysis, there are pre-procedures that need to be done to prepare the data from the empirical study for the main study. This is important to ensure that the data is ready for multiple regression analysis and that no fake and statistically inconsistent results are obtained. In order to achieve that, the following may need to be done:
   - The adequacy of the sample size was checked.
   - Checked for multicolinearity and singularity.
   - Checked for outliers.
   - Checked for normality, linearity, homoscedasticity and independence of the residuals.
2. In assessing e-Government development and the factors that influence its successful implementation, some of the statistical testing that may be used to identify the multi-dimensional factors include the following:
   - The Kaiser-Meyer-Olkin (KMO) test may be used to measure the sampling adequacy of the population of the participants in the study. If the value of the KMO test was more than 0.5, it means the study sample is statistically adequate. This is important as the results can be relied upon to appropriate inform policy and e-Government implementation.

- The Shapiro-Wilk Test which tests for normality (i.e. tests the hypothesis and whether the data set under scrutiny follows a normal distribution) may be utilised to check if the data set includes a great proportion of outliers. Outliers may influence the dataset to produce negative research results.
- On all the measured items and data sets, the Bartlett's Test of Sphericity should be administered to test the null hypothesis that the correlation matrix is an identity matrix (all diagonal elements are 1 and all off diagonal elements are 0). This test measures the reliability of the dataset to produce statistically acceptable results.
- Factor analysis (to re-confirm reliability and face validity of the questionnaire) using the restricted Exploratory Factor Analysis (EFA) methodology at 0.005 level of significance. If the dataset yields negatively skewed data distributions, data transformation is therefore necessary to remove negative values. This test is done to ascertain reliability of the research results.
- The restricted EFA was done in unison with Principle Component Analysis (PCA) using Principal Axis Factoring as the extraction methodology and Promax with Kaiser Normalisation (with *eigenvalues* at 1) as the rotation (oblique) methodology. This test checks which factors may have significant impact on e-Government right at the pre-processing stage.
- Komolgorov-Smirnov and Shapiro-Wilk test for normality may be utilised to test for the reliability and validity of the dataset. If negative values in the results exists, this calls for data transformation using the Log10 (6-X) to remove the negative skewness.
- Hierarchical Multiple Regression analysis (ANOVA) may be implemented on the individual hypotheses to ascertain whether they hold or can be rejected. These sets of tests will be enough to determine the inherent factors influencing e-Government development in a given area when multi-variate analysis. The use of multivariate analysis and the Mixed Methods Research paradigm is recommended because of the heterogeneous factors that impact on e-Government development.

One of the statistical procedures that was extensively utilised was factor analysis using the Exploratory Factor Analysis (EFA) and Principal Component Analysis (PCA). Both EFA and PCA are used in factor analysis which is a procedure that basically aims to examine how the underlying constructs influence the responses on a number of measured variables. Factor analysis measures the strength of the relationship between each factor and each observed measure by providing a platform through which the pattern of correlations (or covariances) between observed measures can be observed. It also helps in the determination of the features that are most important when classifying a group of items. PCA reduces data dimensionality by performing a covariance analysis between factors, making it suitable for analysing data sets in multiple dimensions (DeCoster, 1998). EFA aims to discover the nature of the constructs influencing the responses in a number of measured variables. In factor analysis, the number of factors to be retained is similar to the number of the positive *eigenvalues* of the correlation matrix.

In this case study, in testing for reliability, a detailed statistical approach was performed on the data set from the 408 research participants. The approach was basically a stepwise process incorporating a mix of statistical approaches so as to determine which factors to include in the model to appropriately achieve reliability in the parameter estimates of the proposed adoption model. To begin with, factor analysis was performed on the correlation matrix obtained from computation of the collected data set to estimate communalities; else, the PCA was performed on the data set to extract the unities (using Principle Axis Factoring coupled with Promax rotation with Kaiser Normalisation) in diagonal of the correlation matrix. This enabled the study to obtain factor loadings and/or scores that determined what factors need to be included or excluded in the adoption model.

Given the foregoing discussion, the importance of appropriate methodology in e-Government research and practice cannot be overemphasized.

10.7 Summary

This chapter has presented the methodological nuances of e-Government implementation. The chapter accentuates the fact that since e-Government is a multi-dimensional phenomenon, its methodological aspects should also employ a multi-dimensional approach to appropriately investigate inherent factors impacting on its development. The chapter started by highlighting the need for carefully-thought methodologies when investigating e-Government and then outlining the different characteristics of these methodological approaches.

In the given case study, a mix of methodological approaches has were employed. Specifically, the research utilised the mixed methods research approach at the all the stages of the research process. MMR entails that triangulation is done at all stages of the research process. The MMR approach has been utilised in this study so that validation is done at all stages of the research cycle. It follows that at the data collection level, both quantitative and qualitative data collection approaches were utilised. Prior to actual data collection, the questionnaire was subjected to pilot testing to establish reliability and construct validity of the research instruments. In its qualitative data collection approaches, the study utilises purposive sampling where the participants are grouped according to the desired information targeted to be collected, and relevant to a particular research question. Data collection and analysis, as well as the mixing of quantitative and quality approaches were done concurrently. Purposive sampling was complimented by quota sampling. This has made it possible for people with necessary the expertise and exposure to be targeted, right from the beginning of the study. Coupled with quota sampling, this study utilises non-probabilistic sampling techniques.

The lesson obtained from the given case study is that methodological aspects of any e-Government assessment are defined by the contextual setting where the study is undertaken. Therefore, there is need for a thorough understanding of the context in which e-Government is to or is being implemented. Further, appropriate e-Government assessment involves carefully-thought methodological ramifications done to obtain multiple vantage points of a given phenomenon.

Chapter 11
E-Government Funding Models and Sustainability Frameworks

11.1 Introduction

In any e-Government implementation scenario, the cost incurred is one of the most critical factors for successful and effervescent e-Government development. Although the exact cost of e-Government implementation is unprecedented, it is known that the establishment of different facets of e-Government infrastructure costs a fortune. At a high level of abstraction, one may consider the following as some of the costs directly involved in e-Government conceptualisation, design, implementation and evaluation:

1. Insurmountable costs incurred to pay specialists or consultants involved in drawing the e-Government strategy, e.g. designing the e-Government Interoperability Framework (e-GIF);
2. Procurement of the different technology platforms to be utilised at the back-end and front-end e-Government implementation consoles;
3. Training of managerial and technical experts to drive the e-Government agenda. Technical experts are needed to develop context-aware e-Government applications. Managerial experts are needed to ensure that change is managed appropriately and that ICTs are embedded into the organization's business processes;
4. Cost of awareness campaigns and training for some of the civil servants and citizens; and
5. Cost of evaluating the impact of e-Government.

Because of the multi-dimensional nature of e-Government, most of these costs are further sub-divided making the whole e-Government implementing initiative very costly. The huge amounts of money devoted towards any e-Government implementation could have been utilised in other socio-economic development agendas. However, weighed against the many benefits of e-Government implementation as outlined in Chapter 2, the huge opportunity cost incurred in implementing e-Government against other socio-economic developmental programs is not as big as perceived. With the cognizance of the fact that most of the e-Government projects fail (Heeks, 2004), there is need to ensure that a careful thought is given to the funding models so that e-Government implementation endeavours do not fail on account of lack of funds at any stage of the implementation cycle.

It is worth noting that many of the less developed world countries have not jumped onto the bandwagon for e-Government implementation because of the substantial costs and capital needed to initiate e-Government implementation. The funding models discussed in this chapter may provide insights on how the less developed countries can fund their e-Government programs towards competitiveness and sustainability.

This chapter intends to highlight the different principles used in determining funding models for e-Government implementation in heterogeneous environments. The different responsive funding models are important because they go a long way in realizing e-Government sustenance even in the advent of changing technology and contextual environmental trends.

11.2 Background to e-Government Funding

The funding model utilised in e-Government implementation defines the likely levels of sustainability that any e-Government implementation can achieve. Rudimentary funding approach commensurate to the local contextual characteristics is important because it enables responsive funding paradigms that get advanced as technology and other cardinal e-Government success factors evolve.

The unending pressure on public service from both citizens and businesses to deliver responsive, accessible and convenient has culminated into enabling government institutions to move with speed in this information era. The unprecedented developments in technology further call for government services to be delivered ubiquitously at the convenience of the e-Government consumers. Governments are now expected to invest in robust ICT infrastructure in order to provide connected government. This drive towards the virtual governance models comes at a cost and this cost needs to be contained.

11.3 E-Government Funding Frameworks and Models

The need to have carefully-thought e-Government designs in developing countries with robust funding models for sustainability cannot be overemphasised (Chowdhury & Satter, 2013). The use of ICTs at various levels of the socio-economic structure ensures that citizens regardless of their status participate in the governance hierarchy (Islam, 2008).

The failure of many e-Government projects in developing countries has been attributed to copy-and-paste approach of the funding models adopted from the developed world. It is worth mentioning that funding models meant for the developing world may not be exact fit for all the less developed countries because of differences in contextual setting. For example, most countries in the developed world may have already put in place design features key to the success of e-Government such as favourable economic climate, responsive government policies and adaptive institutional frameworks, capital market environments, and the participation of the private sector in the socio-economic value chains (Giff & Coleman, 2003). These prerequisites for e-Government implementation may be at different stages of development in less developed countries. For the less developed countries without already-existing relevant ICT infrastructures and institutional setups to support e-Government implementation, the need for appropriate funding models is pronounced.

After the 2008 global economic meltdown, many governments around the world reduced spending on government programs. Therefore, governments around the world are interested in funding e-Government initiatives at minimal costs and emphasise that the funded e-Government interventions should create value to the general conceptualisation of government. This calls for careful design of e-Government funding models so that the cost is substantially reduced and sustainability attained.

In funding e-Government projects, countries have used heterogeneous approaches (Reeder & Pandy, 2009). The two common approaches have been the vertical approach (financial evaluation is done for a particular organisation or program) and the horizontal approach (financial evaluation done on a number of agency budget or cross-agency initiatives). These two funding approaches allow the government and other e-Government partners to ascertain the opportunity cost incurred in e-Government implementation. For example, in the vertical funding approach, it is possible to gauge whether impending ICT investments are worthwhile against other socio-economic development agenda. Government can decide whether it makes economical sense. For example, the government may weigh whether it creates value to procure and erect additional hospital infrastructure against erecting ICT infrastructure to support e-Government in a given context. The horizontal funding model aims to address the deficiency in vertical funding by encouraging pooling of resources.

Generally, the funding pools for e-Government interventions can be sourced from the government coffers or from the private sector. The emerging funding models show that funding expensive e—Government interventions and programmes cannot only be the preserve of government alone but that other socio-economic players should also jump onto the bandwagon. The general outline for e-Government funding is shown in Figure 11.1 below.

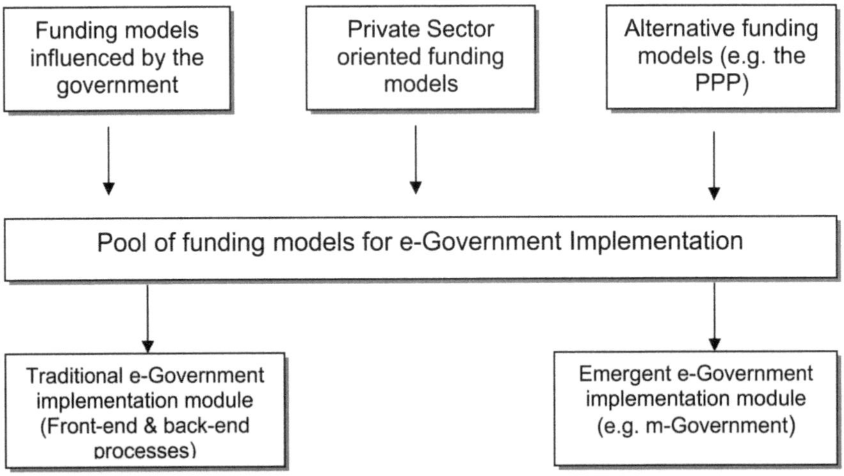

Figure 11.1: Pool for e-Government funding.

The emerging governance models are showing that governments should not be seen as vehicles for providing public services free of charge. Although not currently obtaining in most parts of the world, there is now a paradigm shift which demands that governments should be looked at, not only as public service providers, but as profitable business entities which do not depend on grants and taxes as the major sources of income (Giff & Coleman, 2003). If governments place themselves as profitable public business entities, the attainment of sustainability of their programmes, operations and competence may not be a far-fetched dream. In line with this paradigm shift, many investments in e-Government are done with the pretext that they will support one aspect of a government program. This is to ensure that the public service is not costly at the same time maintaining a certain level of efficiency. Given the aforementioned, the challenge in ensuring that e-Government programmes are self-sustainable cannot be overemphasised (Shehadi, Khoury, Kassatly & Lamaa, 2013). Further, the importance of responsive funding models for e-Government to foster sustainability cannot be ignored (UN, 2004).

Building on to what has been posited above, in as far as sustainable implementation of e-Government is concerned, a self-funded model is desired which charges small transaction fees for a number of services. The money generated from the fees can be used to reimburse private partners who bankrolled the initial investments in procuring ICT infrastructure in a PPP arrangement. Further, the money can be used for paying for ongoing maintenance, upgrades and development of new e-Government service applications and solutions. The main advantage of such a model is that the government integrates ICTs into its governance value chains without straining state budgets and overlooking other pertinent developmental projects.

E-Government infrastructure financiers are interested in the anticipated gains/benefits they can obtain from investigating. They are mostly interested in what financial returns they will generate and what products are likely to come out. E-Government can also be financed from the national budget – the approach used by many of the less developed countries, special grants (one-off), user fees, or non-government financing from the private sector such as loans, bonds or capital investment (Giff & Coleman, 2003). It is worth mentioning that for the less developed world countries, many of these funding models may not suffice as the financial markets are not developed to that extent. Some of the possible e-Government funding options:

1. Obtaining funding from the budgets of the line ministries. Each ministry becomes responsible for erecting and managing its own e-Government infrastructure. The only disadvantage of such a model is that the level of development of e-Government initiatives in the different ministries will be disparate. Therefore, their capabilities will also be not uniform further complication e-Government system integration.
2. Forge partnerships between government and donor agencies. An example could be the use of the proceeds from "Tied Aid Financing" to purchase e-Government ICT infrastructure components from donor country(ies) or send government workers to train in donor country(ies).
3. Government can pool e-Government resources. For example, regional e-Government initiatives can have a funding component embedded into them. The resources shared cannot be strictly money but other non-monitory items such as sharing of experiences and human resources. An example is the Nordic Trust Fund for governance in Africa.
4. Special e-Government taxation. A general tax can be introduced in all the socio-economic transactions so that individuals and businesses foot the bill for e-Government implementation.
5. Government can negotiate low interest loans from banks to finance e-Government interventions

The traditional model for e-Government funding has been that governments are expected to pay all the costs (Shehadi, Khoury, Kassatly & Lamaa, 2013). The emerging funding models entail that e-Government implementation should be self-sustaining. The following presents the different approaches to self-sustaining e-Government implementation:

1. Using the Public-Private-Partnership (PPP) model – private entities (Non-Governmental Organisations, micro financing) jumping onto the bandwagon of funding e-Government with possibilities of coming up with requisite scenarios where e-Government consumers pay a minimal fee for accessing the services. The PPP funding model has shown a lot of promise in both less developed and developed world countries such as the USA and India;
2. Access bonds (e.g. community bonds), leasing and implementing universal service fees;
3. Using Open data platforms – governments publish data collected over the years and encourages companies and individual entrepreneurs to develop value-added services and new services and applications which could in turn fund e-Government endeavours. Since this data will be published periodically, it means companies and entrepreneurs that periodically pay for this service will continuously contribute to e-Government;
4. Encouraging private entities to take advantage of the advertising space on e-Government platforms at a fee. This funding model may work well in a developed world context where the economy is appropriately developed; and
5. Encouraging private companies or organisations to use already developed e-Government platforms such as e-Payment channels for a fee.

Giff and Coleman (2003) have identified the following as environmental features or factors that influence what funding models/frameworks to use in a given environment:
1. Economic setting of the given environment
2. Government policies and other relevant supporting infrastructure
3. Organisational or institutional culture; and
4. Human resource base.

The articulated ways of funding alternatives, although not mutually exclusive, make e-Government implementation self sustaining. The other benefits of such an approach are that they may create jobs, encourage sprouting of new businesses, encourage mass adoption of technology platforms, etc.

11.4 Implications and Future Work

Although a lot has been achieved in the e-Government research, it is evident that more needs to be done to produce theoretical and conceptual frameworks that would guide how the emerging forms of e-Government such as mobile government would be implemented and funded. The understanding is that if research remained stagnant, the current theoretical and conceptual frameworks would then become obsolete

On another front and in agreement with Kim et al., (2007), future research should seek to formulate more generalized explanations as to why certain sequences lead to certain outcomes, or more specifically, why certain interventions during the different stages of ICT diffusion (maturity stages), lead either to success or failure of e-Government implementation. Future research should also aim to investigate the importance of efficient monitoring and evaluation of e-Government application so as to understand value of e-Government in a given context and therefore suggest frameworks for context aware e-Government designs, and what appropriate project management techniques should be utilised for any one specific context.

Future research should also aim to understand the socio-political conceptualisations and connotations revolving around successful implementation and development of e-Government. This is because many studies on e-Government have focussed on techno-managerial underpinnings of e-Government which look at successful e-Government implementation being shaped by balancing only the demand and supply side of e-Government. The understanding of successful e-Government implementation based only on maintaining equilibrium of the demand and supply side presents a narrow-minded view of the multi-dimensional factors that impact on e-Government.

11.5 Summary and Conclusion

This study has outlined the different e-Government funding and sustainability approaches in different e-Government environments. Some of the funding principles include the involvement of the Public Private Partnership's (PPP) model in financing e-Government applications for sustainability; need for informed design of monitoring and evaluation strategies and initiatives; and need to consider context-aware e-Government adoption models during the design process..

Chapter 12
Contemporary and Future Research and Practical Directions

12.1 Introduction and Background

This book has so far discussed the different aspects of e-Government carefully outlining the different facets of its multi-dimensional nature. It is clear that any e-Government strategies or implementation frameworks should take note of this multi-dimensionality and be informed by referring to the local contextual characteristics in the area in which it is implemented. Given that the fundamental conceptualisations for e-Government implementation the core e-Government practice attributes have been clearly articulated, this chapter discusses the current and future research and practical directions.

Therefore, this chapter discusses and highlights the different contemporary developments with regards to e-Government conceptualisation and outlines the future research and practical prospects. Discussion of possible research opportunities (Future trends and m-Government issues) is important because it will provide a snapshot in the design and practice of e-Government in both emerging and developed countries.

12.2 The Future Outlook of Public Service

The traditional public service is slowly transcending towards placing itself at the competitive edge so as to address restraints and delve towards process-oriented public administration for improved services. Despite global held conception that the existence of an innovative government is only paradoxical, competitiveness in public service delivery lies in government's innovative capacity and responsiveness to changes in external environments (Teofilovic, 2009). Governments that need to be competitive, efficient and innovative have identified e-Government as a pragmatic tool that unleashes opportunities in the information and knowledge society (Potnis & Demissie, 2002).

It is not a hidden fact that technology, the main enabler of e-Government, has a short lifecycle. The implication of this short lifecycle is that some of the e-Government applications may become obsolete and no longer be accessible on technology platforms with time. Therefore, this calls for e-Government to put in scalable and evolving application designs that retain their currency as technology evolves towards more advanced variants. With the emerging technology metamorphosis, there are many forms of e-Government sprouting up. One of the common emerging forms of e-Government is mobile government (m-Government). M-Government has take precedence even in less developed countries owing to the rapid diffusion of mobile technologies. The possibilities brought about by m-Government include availing itself as a ubiquitous platform which facilitates convergence of many different aspects of IT applications.

The rapid change in technology platforms for e-Government, the ever-changing socio-economic value chains and the rapid adoption of mobile technologies for user convenience entails that the traditional understanding of e-Government is let go of. E-Government now presents itself as a multi-disciplinary undertaking which cannot be investigated or understood from one vantage point (*see* Chapter 10). With these recent developments and complexity in the technology and socio-economic value chains, there is need to highlight the current and future developments in the e-Government domain.

12.3 Convergence of e-Government Applications

Because of the emergence of heterogeneous variants of technology platforms, there are several emerging technology applications. Researchers have been working round the clock to ensure that there heterogeneous technology platforms are able to talk to one another. One of the direct outcomes of technology convergence in the e-Government realm is the emergence of the mobile government (m-Government), which is the access of government services on mobile devices, has shown a lot of potential considering the rapid growth of mobile penetration in Africa and the world at large. M-Government is the convergence of wireless devices and e-Government applications and essentially aims to bring mobility to e-Government applications (Du Preez, 2009; Zefferer, 2011:8). Thus, it is right to state that m-Government is a subset of e-Government. A simple, layman and formulaic definition of convergence is that convergence involves the joining of two or more things together to form one thing.

M-Government is a complimentary subset of e-Government as it uses ICTs to provide public services by offering anytime, anywhere, by anyone functionality to all e-Government users. Moon (2010:100) defined m-Government as public administration endeavours to provide public services to employees, businesses, and non-profit organizations through the use of wireless communication networks and mobile devices such as pagers, Personal Digital Assistants (PDAs), cellular phones, and their supporting systems. M-Government takes advantage of the IEEE 802.11 standard which has made it possible for many wireless applications (such as GSM enabled Internet) to be realized. Such advances in technology and their faster adoption justify a move towards m-Government (Kushchu & Kuscu, 2003:1–12; Moon, 2010:102). It is worth mentioning that m-Government will not eventually replace e-Government but is complementally to, and comes as an additional value to e-Government.

There are many benefits attributed to m-Government. For example, law enforcement agents (such as policemen) on patrol can adequately communicate with station commanders anytime and anywhere (Kushchu & Kuscu, 2003:4). This may enable appropriate and real-time information management of crimes, accidents and other issues concerning the general public.

Just as e-Government, there are different drivers of m-Government applications. The major forces influencing m-Government is the technological infrastructure and the subsequent advances in mobile telecommunications. The technology changes are divided into three major categories: ‘mobile device penetration; convergence of wired Internet and wireless telecommunication networks; and the move towards 3G services and higher data transfer rates (Kushchu & Kuscu, 2003:3). Mobile device penetration has grown rampantly from about 14% (850 million people) of the world population in 2001 brought about by de-regulation and GSM communications to over 4 billion in 2009 with Africa recording the fastest growth (The Guardian, 2009). Already, currently there are more than 5 billion mobile device users (BBC, 2010). The growth in mobile penetration has correspondingly resulted in the emergence of mobile Internet. It is estimated that by the end of 2010, there will be more than 1 billion mobile Internet users (AccuraCast, 2010). The future of m-Government applications looks promising given the emerging new mobile technologies on the market.

As aforementioned, with the rapid adoption of mobile technologies in developing countries, implementing m-Government shows a lot of potential given the huge costs incurred when implementing e-Government. M-Government does not require the expensive ICT infrastructures that may be needed in traditional e-Government applications. It is worth noting that mobile use penetration is higher in less developed countries than in developed countries. This justifies the need for less developed countries to delve towards m-Government so that a majority of its citizens and businesses can engage in the wide e-Government conceptualisation (Asiimwe & Bhuiyan, 2010).

The following are some of the many possibilities realised using m-Government:

1. Access of Location-Based Services (LBS) – working in combination with GPSs, LBS and Interactive Voice Response (IVR) technologies, mobile devices are able to decode the location of nearby baking services such as an Automated Teller Machine (ATM), access information regarding traffic conditions,

ascertaining the exact location of an approaching train or bus, congestion management, alternative routes, etc.;
2. Facilitating of learning in pervasive and virtual environments;
3. Facilitating m-Voting – use of mobile technologies to participate in mobile processes;
4. Enabling mobile agriculture (m-Agriculture) – use of mobile platforms (mobile phones, etc.) to provide up-to-date information to the farmers regarding market statistics, weather forecasts, best farming practices, recommended prices of farm produce, disaster alerts, etc.;
5. Facilitating mobile health (m-Health) – online consultations, remote diagnosis, etc.; and
6. Facilitating m-Payment for information and services – digital wallet (m-Cash): mobile platforms as means for proprietary cash systems, and GSM banking systems;

12.4 Future Technologies and Impact on Governance Practices

As mentioned earlier, technology has a short life-cycle. Therefore, it is right to assume that the future metamorphosis of technology platforms and domains will correspondingly have an impact on the mode of e-Government. As shown in Figure 4.2 in this book, future e-Government maturity will delve towards international interoperability. This is a scenario where national e-Government systems will have regional interoperable platforms and ontologies already defined to facilitate system integration. With the changing technologies, e-Government modes/forms will change and will therefore impact on the way governance is executed. Table 12.1 below shows the promising trends in technology and anticipate impact on the governance hierarchies.

These technologies and the emerging ones not articulated in Table 12.1 will dictate how development projectile of e-Government. In this regard, e-Government researchers are implored to focus on coming up with research models and interventions (respectively) which will inform the emerging forms of e-Government implementation.

Table 12.1: Emerging Technologies and Governance impact.

Technology	Technology characteristic and potential impact
Personal Digital Assistant	Limited application by government departments in policing and health care sectors.
	Enhances communication and organisation capabilities of information resources and therefore changes the information power balance.
	PDA technology is mature with huge potential to be deployed on a large scale by the government.
Mobile phones	Existing technology with full potential for use as a communication medium
	Technology is mature and potential to be deployed on a large scale, e.g. in m-Government
Wearable computing devices	Mainly applied in the defence sector
	Technology relatively immature but with huge potential for further development and possible deployment by government departments.
Robotics	Existing technology applied on a large scale in entertainment and automobile industry.
	Has potential to encourage shift in tasks, roles and processes. Has potential to be deployed on a large scale in future.
Intelligent agents	Existing technology mainly used in the defence sector.
	Has potential to be deployed on a large scale in governance value chains in future.
Sensor technology	Existing technology solution used by governments for governments for surveillance purposes.
	Stimulate a shift in roles, tasks and processes. Technology is relatively mature and can be used by government on a commercial level.
Natural Language Processing Systems	Mainly used in telecom industry, is in existence and maturing at a steady rate.
	Has potential to be deployed on a larger scale by government in policing, social security and healthcare sector.
RFID	Existing, mature technology largely used in retail industry.
	Has potential to be deployed in government departments for tracing and trailing purposes.

Biometrics	Exiting technology utilised by governments for identification purposes.
	Can be used on a large scale in government departments to check time employees check in and check out of work, among other uses.
WiMax	Existing technology deployed in trials in most of the cases.
	Strengthens mobility and access to information simultaneous, therefore can be deployed in government departments to encourage pervasive access to government information and services.
Social software	Mature, existing technology (mySpace, Hi5, Facebook, Badoo, etc.).
	Government can deploy this technology to target timeless communication with individuals or groups of citizens/businesses.
Semantic technologies	Existing technology mainly found in the private sector.
	Has huge potential to be deployed on a large scale.
GRID	Mature technology predominantly utilised in the research sector.
	Enables new forms of usage of available computer resources and therefore can be used on large by government departments to foster efficiency.

12.5 Future Transformation in Government

The previous section has highlighted some of the existing and potential directions in which technology will go and the potential of such technologies being utilised in governance value chains. Since e-Government is very dependent on technology as the main enabler, it follows that future variants and forms of e-Government will be defined by emerging technologies. The emerging open, interoperable and converged technology platforms may shift the information power balance from government to the citizens presenting scenarios where citizens may '*call the shots*' with regards to desired public service quality.

Table 12.2 shows some of the emerging trends in e-Government given the emerging robust technologies.

It can be observed from Table 12.2 that the possibilities that emerging technologies will bring forth are imaginable in as far as opening up government is concerned. With the possibility of divergence usage of the emerging e-Government models, it is clear that attempts to understand the actual role of e-Government on governance has to be continuously investigated.

Table 12.2: e-Government and the emerging technology landscape.

Governance factor	Technology characteristic	Technology platforms
Transparency	– Individuals empowered with personal medial tools and the social media which are highly networked (netizens) – Provoke risk-averse behaviour in government departments and promote innovation	– Community sensor networks – Personal mobile video casting
Privacy/Ethics	– Intelligent e-Government to manage highly sensitive bio data – Citizens will participate in key decisions ubiquitously at anytime.	– Biometrics, ambient technologies, biotechnology, sensor networks, mobile platforms
Accountability	– Technology will provide traceability in the actions made by public officers.	– Next generation Intelligent Workflow Systems
Transparency	– Decisions made in all government business processes will be made public.	– Personal Mobile Video casting. Community and business operated sensor networks
Enforcement	– Citizens will be traceable and therefore made it easy for enforcement of statutes and laws, e.g. real-time vehicle monitoring system will reduce traffic violations.	– GPS 2.0, biometrics, RFID. – Wearable ICTs.
Networked and intelligent government	– Need for common pools of knowledge and consistent interpretation across all government departments. – E-Government systems will learn and observe trends in the information they process.	– Artificial intelligence, the semantic web. – Pervasive and Alternative – Reality gaming.

Because of the rapid penetration of mobile technologies in less developed countries, m-Government has shown as one of the contemporary e-Government variants that can possibly thrive. The next section presents cases highlighting the potential of m-Government implementation in less developed world contexts.

12.6 M-Government Initiatives

The possibility of implementing m-Government in a less developed country context is achievable as demonstrated by Trimi and Sevrani (2010) who carried out a qualitative study on m-Government development in Albania. Albania has a very poorly developed democratic institution with undeveloped ICT infrastructure brought about by 50 years if autocratic rule. Their study posited that m-Government implementation may be the way forward in less developed countries with poorly developed ICT infrastructures and political institutions. Therefore, despite its many goal being to improve efficiency and competitiveness levels in the public service delivery, e-Government also positively impacts on the democratic setup in a given area.

The realisation of m-Government implementation can be seen in the following cases:

1. South Korea uses m-Government in various socio-economic frameworks as detailed by Campbell and Im (2012) in the following scenarios:
   a) With approximately 7,600 buses serving over 5 million people a day, mobile applications are used to check the exact location of the next bus. Each bus is fixed with a GPS device which reads its exact locations and transmits to the sensor database nodes at each of the bus stops.
   b) The Korea Expressway Corporation has developed an application that shows real-time traffic and highway congestion information. Motorists and other citizens in need of traffic information can access such information using platforms on Apple's iOS and Google's Android smartphone operating systems.
2. Realising the potential of mobile platforms such as mobile phones and tablets as ubiquitous information management platforms owing to their internet access capacity, Malawi government has started pushing for mobile government (m-Government). Some of the few mobile applications include the Esoko application (agriculture market information via SMS), RapidSMS, VillageReach and FrontlineSMS (all in the health sector), Banki Mmanja, Bank Ponseponse and M0626 (all in the banking sector), etc. (Mtingwi & Van Belle, 2012).

Comparatively, m-Government is a promising platform for e-Government applications because consumers can use m-Government using mobile gadgets anytime, anywhere and does not involve erection of huge ICT infrastructures. Therefore, m-Government is a convenience to both government (supplier) and citizens and businesses (consumers).

12.7 Future Issues in m-Government

Active e-Government research has been in progress since the mid 1990s with researchers from diverse disciplines taking part. The first generation research focussed on establishing the contours of the relationship between government and citizens brought about by the rapid usage of ICTs in public service delivery frameworks (Dawes, 200Y). The organisational aspects of e-Government and the complex heterogeneous social contexts were not adequately considered. With the rapid developments in ICTs and its integration into the different socio-economic setups, e-Government takes different forms. In this regard, there is utmost to encourage research enquiry that delves deeper into the emerging forms of e-Government. Robust research entails that there will be good reference points for e-Government practice.

Currently, there is a huge debate as to whether e-Government is an academic discipline or a more broadly based field of enquiry, or in other instances, whether it will simply be absorbed and embedded into traditional disciplines. The truth of the matter is that e-Government has transcended the theoretical and practical realms as can be seen in its quest to move shoulder-to-shoulder with technology advancements. Therefore, e-Government Research should be clearly linked to the practice of governance competitiveness.

Because e-Government is in its nascent stage, it has not been adequately analysed at the theoretical level. This has can be seen from lack of theoretical frameworks/models solely targeting the understanding of e-Government proliferation. Therefore, there is need for an independent research domain which is solely devoted to developing the theoretical frameworks/models to guide contemporary and future e-Government development. The lack of theoretical frameworks is further complicated by the fact that e-Government keeps changing into new forms which further need theoretical frameworks on how they can be appropriately integrated into socio-economic establishments. Therefore, future research paradigms should not be confined to a given set of research goals/topics but should be guided by the general principle of expectation of generating new knowledge useful to government.

Much research and best-practice sharing of experience has focused on national e-Government interventions without necessarily bringing out the inherent factors that influence e-Government development. In this regard, e-Government research at the local government level is lacking. There is utmost need for research at this level because the local government is the basic level of e-Government implementation (Löfstedt, 2005).

The e-Government research agenda should be investigator-driven so its multi-dimensional perspectives are reflected into the research paradigms. There is need to draw the e-Government research agenda that takes into consideration the multi-disciplinarily and multiple research domains (e.g. e-Democracy, e-Participation, e-Administration, e-Health, e-Justice, m-Voting, etc.) (Löfstedt, 2007). Given the heterogeneity in the literature on e-Government research domain and the lack of a clear defined research agenda, there is need for researchers and practitioners to exchange notes on what matters most in as far as successful e-Government implementation is concerned (Bolívar, Muñoz & Hernández, 2010).

There has been limited research aimed at understanding the impact of e-Government in less developed countries (Weerakkody, El-Haddadeh, Sabol, Ghoneim & Dzupk, 2012). Impact studies are very important because they articulate the fit of a given approach against wider expectations. Given the fast changing contextual settings in e-Government environments, it is important that researchers and practitioners engage to articulate the various impacts of e-Government (and its variant emerging forms) on the soci0-economic setup.

Further research in e-Government should possibly use combined approaches to investigate e-Government from multiple vantage points. An example could be the use of the Artefact Approach and the Social Systems Design Approach or the utilisation of the institutional theory and the Technology Enactment Framework as theoretical/conceptual basis for e-Government research.

Despite showing potential for revitalising e-Government efforts, m-Government applications have their own issues and disadvantages. The challenges predicted by Lanwin (2002) still hold even today. These challenges are most centred on development of m-Government applications, privacy and security. These include:
- **Infrastructure development**: both physical (technology, equipment, and network) and 'soft' (institutional arrangements and software developed for m-Government such as PacketWriter, Pocket Blue, and Pocket Rescue) infrastructure must be present for m-Government to flourish.
- **Payment infrastructures**: building trustworthy systems where consumers of various e-Government services can send their credit card information using a mobile device or over the Internet in the framework of m-Government.
- **Privacy and security**: fear of citizens over their mobile phone numbers being traced when accessing e-Government services, and fear of messages being intercepted and eavesdropped. Othman and Mokdad (2010:310) provided a framework for enhancing data security in ad hoc networks based on multipath routing. This framework can be a milestone in as far as security is concerned in m-Government environments.
- **Accessibility**: the success of m-Government applications partly depend on the number of concurrent users for a given service.
- **Legal setup**: availability of the law of fair information practices which detail rights of data subjects (citizens) and the data holders (government), and how the users are generally protected in the m-Government environment.
- **Compatibility**: how to deal with technical difficulties regarding compatibility of mobile systems with the existing e-Government systems.

With the faster development of technology, it is right to make a prognosis that m-Government applications will be implemented in various socio-economic platforms for a considerable period of time. Therefore, m-Government presents a very good opportunity for digital inclusion of everyone regardless of status given the faster mobile penetration worldwide.

12.8 Issues in e-Government Practice and Implementation

There are several issues that need to be addressed if e-Government, and its emerging variants, were to be successfully implemented. The following points briefly discuss the common factors that need to be looked at carefully and considered in any e-Government design frameworks:

1. Privacy and security issues need to be addressed (Kumar & Sinha, 2007). Consumers can only comfortably engage in e-Government if their privacy and security issues are guaranteed. Acceptable levels of security and privacy entail that e-Government's consumers' information will not be compromised in any way or used to disadvantage the consumer.
2. There is need to find ways of bridging multi-cultural and multi-lingua barriers. E-Government content should be presented in a language understandable by majority of the anticipated e-Government users. In less developed countries, in addition to official languages, it is recommended that e-Government content is also presented in local languages.
3. Interventions should be put in place in order to allow consumers trust the e-Government institution. Trust can be in government (an efficient, less corrupt government is one which can easily be trusted), e-Government trust (trust that accessing public services through ICTs is the same as in traditional governance settings), process-based trust (belief that ICT-enabled business processes will deliver the anticipated service), etc.
4. Ensuring that the right interoperability strategic is put in place given emerging technology convergence. Government systems should be able to seamless share information.
5. Need for a strategy on how to implement laws and policies pertaining to e-Government, and
6. Designing strategies to ensure that e-Government is available and accessible to everyone regardless of socio-economic status.

Once the factors outlined here have been included in the design interventions, there are high chances that e-Government can thrive.

12.9 Conclusion and Summary

This short and concluding chapter has outlined the future prospects of e-Government and outlined pointers that should be considered in the implementation of e-Government programmes. There are many challenges related to e-Government implementation of its ever changing forms and variants brought about by short life-cycles of technology and other socio-economic factors.

The need for robust e-Government implementation plans cannot be overemphasised in this era where competitiveness is at the centre of any socio-economic endeavour. The traditional government setups demanded that public institutions provided their services free of charge to the citizens and businesses. The contemporary understanding is that public organisations should provide services at a minimal cost to the recipients to ensure that to offset the money spent in setting up the public infrastructures to remain competitive. Further, e-Government needs to respond to the changing trends in its environment and be responsive to the customers' tastes. The USA realised these different dynamic aspects of e-Government and ensured that the e-Government institution develop faster than anticipated especially at the local government level ((Holden, Norris & Fletcher, 2003).

Because of changing technology platforms and contextual settings of the heterogeneous socio-economic hierarchies, e-Government is now changing its forms in order to remain competitive. For example, with rapid penetration and adoption in less developed countries, e-Government consumers now use m-Government platforms. The lack of requisite theoretical and conceptual frameworks with regards to the emerging forms of e-Government is a big concern. There are a lot of future works that need to be pursued as articulated in this chapter.

The future of e-Government implementation in its various evolved forms shows promise as long as context-aware strategies and interventions are put in place. This book theorises that context-awareness is the bedrock of designing responsive e-Government interventions, particularly in less developed countries.

Chapter 13
Conclusion

This book has highlighted the different conceptual and fundamental principles that are overlooked in most cases when implementing e-Government. The Case Study, drawn from a developing world context, accentuates the need for a carefully-thought e-Government design with full reference to the local context. The thesis of the book is that e-Government design and implementation should be informed by the local contextual setup culminating into context-aware e-Government implementation. In addition, e-Government design should not ignore the globally accepted fundamentals from the global e-Government body of knowledge.

In this book, the importance of e-Government on the governance hierarchy has been articulated and pronounced. E-Government provides benefits on both the government (e.g. reduction in the cost of public service delivery, increasing efficiency levels, etc.) and the consumers (accessing anticipated public services timely and ubiquitously, etc.). With the emerging funding models, it is evident that governments are now pressured to be innovative and be self-sustaining, requiring the public services to be responsive to the opportunities and changing experiences offered by emerging technologies.

A careful analysis of the chapters presented in this book reveals the following:

- There is a paradigm shift in the public service where it is slowly becoming mandatory for government departments to deploy ICTs in their business processes and utilise Knowledge Management practices for them to remain competitive.
- Government departments are implored to be responsive to changing technology landscapes and citizens'/businesses' behaviour patterns so that they remain relevant in contemporary competitive business environments;
- E-Government designs should be informed by the local context (e.g. the e-GIF, which is one of the first steps towards robust e-Government implementation, should be informed by the socio-economic setup of the area). Some of the attributes of the local contextual setting may be the following: availability of requisite human resource base to develop responsive e-Government applications and to draw strategic deployment and management scenarios (e.g. based on citizens' ICT skills, trust in governance, general perception to technology, etc.); economic muscle of the area – are they able to procure state-of-art technology solutions to be used in the e-Government realm? etc.

- E-Government design should incorporate robust funding models whose choice depends on the area in which e-Government is implemented.
- There is need to design strategic interventions to ensure e-Government is streamlined into the different government business processes.
- The design of e-Government should be cognizant of the fact that technology has a short life-cycle and therefore the emerging forms entail that e-Government has to change with time as well.

This book is, therefore, a germane and timely resource that can guide future research and practice for the emerging e-governance models. Although the guidance in this book is as comprehensive and thorough as our present understanding permits, further empirical testing of the frameworks and/or models emanating from the main case study should be a focus for future research endeavours.

Appendix 1

Definitions of e-Government

ADF IV (2004)

E-Government is one of the ingredients to strengthening the democratic process and institution, productivity of the public service, citizen participation through ICT platform on different national development issues, and facilitates social inclusion.

Backus (2001)

E-Government is the transformation of the business of the government; including processes, operations, and transactions; which are driven primarily by effective use of ICTs.

Bwalya (2010)

E-Government is the use of ICTs to promote interaction amongst different players (government, citizens, and businesses) in the socio-economic hierarchy to promote participatory decision-making, reduction of corruption, facilitating easier and efficient public service delivery, electronic voting (e-Democracy) and social inclusiveness.

Bhatnagar (2004)

E-Government is loosely used to describe the legacy of any kind of use of information and communication technology within the public sector and represents the use of the Internet to deliver information and services by the government.

Coleman (2006)

E-Government as the combination of electronic information-based services (e-Administration) with the reinforcement of participatory elements (e-Democracy) to achieve the objective of 'balanced e-Government'.

Council of Europe

The concept of e-Governance includes the use of electronic technologies in three areas of public action:

- relations between the public authorities and civil society
- functioning of the public authorities at all stages of the democratic process (e-Democracy)
- the provision of public services (electronic public services)

Curtin et al., (2004)
E-Government runs wide across all aspects of government, deep within the core of every governmental entity, and will inevitably be a transforming agent for government and governance.

Finger & Pecaud (2003)
E-Government brings about socio-economic development opportunities by opening up new channels and platforms for accessing government, and contemporary systems for organising and managing information and public services.

Grönlund, (2002)
E-Government involves not only a profound transformation in the way government interacts with the governed but also the reinvention of its internal processes and organisation. It concerns both internal and external use of IT, for internal administration as well as for external services.

Gartner Group
E-Government involves optimisation of public service delivery frameworks, encouraging ordinary citizens from the constituency to participate in governance, and provides a platform where internal and external relationships can be transformed though appropriate use of technology such as the Internet and new media.

Kumar et al., (2007)
E-Government is the delivery of improved services to citizens, businesses, and other members of the society through drastically changing the way governments manage information.

Lenk &Traunmüller (2000)
E-Government is a powerful guiding vision for the transformation which governments must adapt to over the next years. E-Government is the term that reflects the use of ICT in public administration to change structures and processes of government organisation.

McClure (2000)
E-Government refers to government's use of technology to interact with different stakeholders such as citizens, business partners, employees and other agencies and provide them with various government information services.

Mehrtens et al., (2001)
E-Government involves a paradigm shift where traditional methods of governance, of using paper-and-file approaches in managing government businesses, are transformed to using ICTs instead of paper.

Michel (2005)
E-Government, together with e-Administration and e-Governance, is the final result of the digitisation digitisation process of public service delivery systems.

Moon & Norris (2005)
E-Government is delivering government information and services through ICTs.

Muir & Oppenheim (2002)
E-Government as the delivery of government information and services online through the Internet or other digital means.

United Nations
E-Government is defined fairly broadly as the use of ICT, and its application, by the government for the provision of information and public services to the people.

USA Federal Government
E-Government is the use of information technologies (such as wide area networks, the Internet, and mobile computing) for the purposes of exchanging information and services with different stakeholders such as citizens, businesses and other arms of governments.

US e-Government Act of 2002
Section 3601 states that e-Government involves the use of information technologies to to improve access to governmment information and services to the general public, government agencies and businesses, and encourage improvements in public service delivery frameworks including effectiveness, service quality, efficiency, and transformation.

Riley (2003)
E-Government refers to 'government' as a superstructure that deals with decisions, rules, implementation and outputs of its policies; whereas 'governance' refers to functioning based on processes, goals, performance, coordination and outcomes.

Zweers & Planqué (2001:92)
E-Government entails to provide or attain information, services or products produced by government agencies through ICTs at any given moment or place (ubiquitous or pervasiveness) with a view of value creation for all the participants.

Lenk & Traunmüller (2001: 64)
E-Government involves the collection of four perspectives of governance based on citizens, processes, co-operation and knowledge management through appropriate and effective mainstreaming of ICTs in their specific domains.

Sheridan & Riley (2006)
E-Government refers to the structure that is responsible for electronic service delivery, electronic workflow, electronic voting and electronic productivity.

Siftung (2002)
E-Government ushers in a paradigm where adoption of usage of ICTs usage by ordinary or marginal citizens and businesses has potential to transform the generation and delivery of public services by public institutions.

Tassabehji & Elliman (2006)
E-Government has the potential to enhance the decentralisation reforms by bringing decision-making closer to the doorsteps of ordinary citizens by collaborative reasoning made possible with the use of ICT.

Webopedia
E-Government refers to any government functions or processes that are carried out in digital form over the Internet. Local, state and federal governments essentially set up central Websites from which the public (both private citizens and businesses) can find public information, download government forms and contact government representatives.

World Bank (2003)
E-Government involves government agencies' use of information technologies (such as Wide Area Networks, the Internet, and mobile computing) with a view of transforming the way it relates with ordinary citizens, business entities and other government agencies.

Yildiz (2007)
E-Government refers to the use of ICTs by public administration to create a networked structure for; interconnectivity, service delivery, efficiency, effectiveness, transparency, and accountability.

Appendix 2: Research Questionnaire

Please answer the following questions by ticking (✓) the relevant block or writing down your answer in the space provided.

Your responses will remain anonymous. Your co-operation is highly appreciated.

EXAMPLE of how to complete this questionnaire:

What is your age?

If you are **42** years old, you would answer this question as follows:

16 – 21	22 – 25	26 – 35	36 – 49
1	2	3	4✓

SECTION A: Biographical Information

This section aims to obtain background or biographic information.

Question 1: What is your current age?

Please select only **one** option:	16 – 21	22 – 25	26 – 35	36 – 49	50 – 59	60 – older
	1	2	3	4	5	6

Question 2: What is your gender?

Please select only **one** option:	Male	Female
	1	2

Question 3: What is your native language?

Please select only **one** option:	English	Bemba	Chewa (Cinyanja)	Tonga, Lozi	Kaonde, Lunda	Other (specify)
	1	2	3	4	5	6 ....

Question 4: What is your race/ethnicity?

Please select only **one** option:	African	Asian	Indian	European	African American	Latino	Other (specify)
	1	2	3	4	5	6	7 ....

Question 5: What is the highest level of education you have completed?

Please select only **one** option:	High School	Certificate	Diploma	Bachelors Degree	Masters Degree	Doctoral Degree	Other (specify)
	1	2	3	4	5	6	7 ....

Question 6: What is your current employment status?

Please select only **one** option:	Employed (Full-time)	Employed (Part-time)	Employed (Contract basis)	Self-employed
	1	2	3	4
	Unemployed (Seeking employment)	Unemployed (not seeking employment – e.g. retired)	Employer (Owner of a company or business enterprise)	Other (specify)
	5	6	7	8 ....

SECTION B: Behaviour / Usage of the Internet

This section of the questionnaire explores your experience and usage of the Internet which may give an indication on e-Government applications usage.

Question 7: How familiar are you with the use of a computer?

Please indicate your **experience** with the use of a computer:	*Tick (✓) where appropriate*				
	Very untrue	Untrue	Neutral	True	Very true
1) I have the necessary experience to use a computer efficiently.	1	2	3	4	5
2) I have the necessary skills to use the Internet.	1	2	3	4	5
3) I have adequate ICT skills in using e-Government websites.	1	2	3	4	5
4) I feel confident working on the computer even if there is no assistance available.	1	2	3	4	5

SECTION C: E-Government Status

This section intends to obtain your opinion/perception on the general status of e-Government in Zambia and ascertain what should be done to encourage its development.

Question 8a: Do you use e-Government websites and applications?

Please select only **one** option:	Yes	No
	1	2

Question 8b: If you use e-Government services, which websites do you use?

Please select **all** that apply:	Zambia State House	National Assembly of Zambia	Lusaka City Council	Zambia Revenue Authority	Zambia ICT Authority
	1	2	3	4	5

Question 8c: If you use e-Government services, please name the services you use.

Please name **any** e-Government services you use:	....

Question 9: What is your view on the general status of e-Government?

9.1 In your opinion, do you think the benefits of engaging in e-Government have adequately been explained to stakeholders and potential users (citizens and government workers)?

Please select only **one** option:	Yes	No
	1	2

9.2 To what extent are you aware of e-Government initiatives in Zambia?

Please indicate your level of **awareness** of each of the following:	***Tick (✓) where appropriate***				
	Not at all aware	Slightly aware	Somewhat aware	Moderately aware	Fully aware
1) E-Government websites of the Lusaka City Council and other government agencies in Zambia.	1	2	3	4	5
2) The benefits of using Zambian e-Government websites.	1	2	3	4	5
3) Educational/training programs about the overall features of Zambian e-Government websites.	1	2	3	4	5
4) Government campaigns/advertisements encouraging the use of e-Government websites in Zambia.	1	2	3	4	5

9.3 Given a chance to use technologies that would allow access to Zambian e-Government platforms, how important do you consider the following applications?

Please indicate how **important** each of the following e-Government applications are/would be to you:	***Tick (✓) where appropriate***				
	Not important	Low importance	Neutral	Important	Extremely important
1) Retrieval and printing of online forms.	1	2	3	4	5
2) Use of interactive online forms (i.e. completing and sending government forms online).	1	2	3	4	5
3) Participation in online discussions and forums.	1	2	3	4	5
4) Information search for government services.	1	2	3	4	5
5) Electronic applications e.g. passports and national registration cards.	1	2	3	4	5
6) Communicating with parliamentarians through email.	1	2	3	4	5
7) Payment of bills to utility companies.	1	2	3	4	5
8) Paying tax online (e.g. through www.zra.org.zm).	1	2	3	4	5
9) Accessing and reading policy documents from the government websites.	1	2	3	4	5
10) Electronic voting (e-Voting).	1	2	3	4	5
11) Making online payments to government organisations.	1	2	3	4	5
12) Online tendering and procurement (e-Procurement).	1	2	3	4	5
13) Company and/or car registration.	1	2	3	4	5
14) Electronic procurement and e-Tendering.	1	2	3	4	5
15) Finding information about employment opportunities (recruitment searches).	1	2	3	4	5

Please indicate how **important** each of the following e-Government applications are/would be to you:	*Tick (✓) where appropriate*				
	Not important	Low importance	Neutral	Important	Extremely important
16) Banking and financial services (e-Banking).	1	2	3	4	5
17) Formal online education or training activities (e-Learning).	1	2	3	4	5
18) Other (please specify)	1	2	3	4	5

9.4 To what extent do you agree on the usefulness or value of e-Government applications listed below?

Please indicate your level of agreement to the **value** of e-Government applications:	*Tick (✓) where appropriate*				
	Strongly disagree	Disagree	Neutral	Agree	Strongly agree
1) Using e-Government websites enables/could enable me to accomplish tasks more quickly.	1	2	3	4	5
2) Using e-Government websites allows/could allow me to easily obtain government information.	1	2	3	4	5
3) The results of using e-Government websites are apparent to me.	1	2	3	4	5
4) Using e-Government websites can reduce queuing time.	1	2	3	4	5
5) Having an e-Government website means my business with government is not limited to regular business hours.	1	2	3	4	5
6) It is quicker to obtain service through Government websites than through traditional government services.	1	2	3	4	5
7) E-Government websites give a wider choice of interactions with different functions compared to interactions with the physical government office.	1	2	3	4	5

8) Using e-Government websites is more costly than visiting the government office.	1	2	3	4	5
9) Using e-Government websites can reduce travelling expenses.	1	2	3	4	5

9.5 In your opinion, what relationship exists between language and access to e-Government applications?

Please indicate your level of agreement on the role of **language** in accessibility of e-Government:	*Tick (✓) where appropriate*				
	Strongly disagree	Disagree	Neutral	Agree	Strongly agree
1) Availability of native language (mother tongue) options on the e-Government website could make performing tasks easier.	1	2	3	4	5
2) Availability of native language (mother tongue) options on the e-Government website could encourage me to engage in e-Government more actively.	1	2	3	4	5
3) Without the native language (mother tongue) options, I cannot perform my tasks on the website.	1	2	3	4	5

9.6 To what extent do you agree with the ease of use of e-Government websites?

Please indicate your level of agreement on the **ease of use** of e-Government websites:	*Tick (✓) where appropriate*				
	Strongly disagree	Disagree	Neutral	Agree	Strongly agree
1) It is easy to login to e-Government websites.	1	2	3	4	5
2) Getting the required information from e-Government websites is easy.	1	2	3	4	5
3) It is easy to complete a transaction via an e-Government website.	1	2	3	4	5
4) The organisation and structure of e-Government websites is easy to follow.	1	2	3	4	5

Question 10: In terms of trusting e-Government transactions, privacy and security, to what extend would you agree with the following statements?

Please indicate your level of agreement on issues of **trust** involving e-Government:	*Tick (✓) where appropriate*				
	Strongly disagree	Disagree	Neutral	Agree	Strongly agree
1) Information on e-Government websites is reliable.	1	2	3	4	5
2) E-government websites guarantee that its information is accurate.	1	2	3	4	5
3) Doing business via the e-Government website is more reliable than making a physical visit to a government office.	1	2	3	4	5
4) The government sends a clear message that it will take full responsibility for any breach of security during interaction/ transaction at the website.	1	2	3	4	5
5) Policies exist to protect users of e-Government websites.	1	2	3	4	5
6) It is safe to conduct a financial transaction e.g. entering credit card details, on the e-Government website.	1	2	3	4	5
7) The security policy is clearly stated on e-Government websites.	1	2	3	4	5
8) I would give permission to government to share my personal information with other sites.	1	2	3	4	5

Question 11: To what extent would you agree that the potential barriers (listed below) delay the wide-scale usage of ICTs within government departments?

Please indicate your level of agreement on the **significance** of potential e-Government **barriers:**	*Tick (✓) where appropriate*				
	Strongly disagree	Disagree	Neutral	Agree	Strongly agree
1) Lack of readily available Internet access points.	1	2	3	4	5
2) Lack of affordable Internet access points.	1	2	3	4	5
3) Lack of services relevant to the local context.	1	2	3	4	5
4) Lack of user-friendly e-Government platforms.	1	2	3	4	5
5) Lack of availability of ICT infrastructure.	1	2	3	4	5
6) Risk of information to end up in hands of unauthorised individuals.	1	2	3	4	5
7) Fear of change on part of the customer and/or government staff.	1	2	3	4	5
8) Limited ICT skills on the part of the customer.	1	2	3	4	5
9) Limited ICT skills on the part of government employees.	1	2	3	4	5
10) The customers limited experience in interacting with ICT platforms and the Internet.	1	2	3	4	5
11) Non-availability of native language (mother tongue) option on the website which could help the customer to perform tasks better.	1	2	3	4	5
12) Lack of protection of the end-user in the online environment.	1	2	3	4	5
13) Lack of awareness campaigns on the benefits of engaging in e-Government.	1	2	3	4	5

14) Lack of appropriate end-user support.	1	2	3	4	5
15) Other (please specify)	1	2	3	4	5

Question 12: In your opinion, what level of priority do the ICT developments listed below have in encouraging meaningful e-Government development in Zambia?

Thinking of how you use/would use e-Government applications, please indicate which, if any, of the following ICT developments should be **prioritised** to enhance your usage:	*Tick (✓) where appropriate*				
	Not a priority	Low priority	Neutral	Priority	Essential priority
1) Faster broadband network connectivity.	1	2	3	4	5
2) Faster wireless network connectivity.	1	2	3	4	5
3) More affordable connectivity.	1	2	3	4	5
4) Increased network security and data protection.	1	2	3	4	5
5) Greater range of the latest ICT devices and platforms.	1	2	3	4	5
6) More affordable devices.	1	2	3	4	5
7) Greater interoperability of ICT devices and platforms across all government departments.	1	2	3	4	5
8) Increased seamless usage of broadband or wireless services across all government departments.	1	2	3	4	5
9) More local content on government websites.	1	2	3	4	5
10) More foreign content on government websites.	1	2	3	4	5
11) More interactive applications.	1	2	3	4	5
12) Increased development of ICT professionals.	1	2	3	4	5

13) Increased awareness of public about ICT usage in the context of e-Government.	1	2	3	4	5
14) Other (please specify)	1	2	3	4	5

Question 13: To what extent will you engage/continue to engage with e-Government?

Please indicate your intention to **continue engaging** in e-Government websites:	***Tick (✓) where appropriate***				
	Strongly disagree	Disagree	Neutral	Agree	Strongly agree
1) In future, I will not hesitate to use e-Government websites.	1	2	3	4	5
2) In future, I will consider e-Government websites to be my first choice to do business with the government.	1	2	3	4	5
3) I intend to increase my usage of e-Government websites.	1	2	3	4	5

Question 14: Do you have any suggestions for improving e-Government in Zambia?

Please write your suggestions in the block below:
....
....
....
....
....

Thank you for your time in answering this questionnaire.

Bibliography

Abrahams, L., and Goldstuck, A. (2010). *The state of e-development in South Africa: A view from the end of the first decade of the 21st century*. LINK Public Policy Paper No 11, July 2010. Wits University: Johannesburg.

Abramsom, M., and Morin, L. (2003). *E-Government 2003*. Rowman and Littlefield, 40–48.

Abrahams, L., and Newton-Reid, L. (2008). *e-Governance for Social and Local Economic Development: Gauteng City Region perspective*. LINK Public Policy Research Paper No 9:1–47. Wits University: Johannesburg.

AccuraCast (2010). 1 Billion Mobile Internet Users by 2010, Accessed April 3, 2014. http://www.accuracast.com/news/mobile-7471/1-billion-mobile-internet-users-by-2010/.

Adams, G.R., and Schvanneldt, J.D. (1985). *Understanding Research Methods*. New York: Longman.

ADF IV. (2004). Fourth African Development Forum, Governance for a Progressing Africa, 11–15th October 2004, Addis Ababa, Ethiopia, Accessed April 3, 2014. http://213.55.79.31/adf/adfiv/adf_4_report_final_sml.pdf

Aichholzer, G. (2010). Scenarios of e-Government in 2010 and implications for strategy design. *Electronic Journal of e-Government*, 2(1):1–10.

Ajzen, I. (1991). The theory of planned behaviour. *Organisational Behaviour and Human Decision Processes*, 50(2):179–211.

Ajzen, I. (1988). *Attitudes, personality, and behaviour*. Milton-Keynes, England: Open University Press, and Chicago, USA: Dorsey Press.

Al-adawi, Z., Yousafzai, S., and Pallister, J. (2005). Conceptual model of citizen adoption of e-Government. In: *The Second International Conference on Innovations in Information Technology*, September 26–28, 2005 Dubai, UAE, Accessed April 3, 2014. http://citeseerx.ist.psu.edu/viewdoc/download?doi=10.1.1.92.2165&rep=rep1&type=pdf

Al-Gahtani, S.S., Hubona, G.S., and Wang, J. (2007). Information technology (IT) in Saudi Arabia: Culture and the acceptance and use of IT. *Information and Management*, 44:681–691.

Al-Khouri, A.M., Al-Mazrouie, N.M., and Bommireddy, M. (2010). A Strategy Framework For the Risk Assessment And Mitigation For Large E-Government Projects. *International Journal of Managing Value and Supply Chains*, 1(2), 36–43.

Al-Khouri, M.A. (2011). An innovative approach for e-Government transformation. *International Journal of Managing Value and Supply Chains* , 2(1):22–43.

Al-Omari, A., and Al-Omari, H. (2006). E-Government readiness assessment model. *Journal of Computer Science*, 2(11): 841–845.

Al-Omari H. (2006). E-Government architecture in Jordan: A comparative analysis. *Journal of Computer Science*, 2(11): 846–852.

Al-Otaibi, M.B., and Al-Zahrani, R.M.(2009). Electronic Commerce in the Kingdom of Saudi Arabia. Accessed: http://faculty.ksu.edu.sa/DrRasheed/My%20Publications/Ecommerce_in_KSA.pdf (Accessed 3 April 2014).

Al-Rashidi, H. (2009). Examining Internal Challenges to E-Government Implementation from System Users Perspective. In: *European and Mediterranean Conference on Information Systems, April 12–13 2009, Abu Dhabi, UAE*, Accessed April 3, 2014. pdf

Al-Shafi, S., and Weerakkody, V. (2009). Understanding citizens' behavioural intention in the adoption of e-government services in the state of Qatar. In: *European Conference on Information Systems, Verona, Italy, Accessed* April 3, 2014. http://is2.lse.ac.uk/asp/aspecis/20090134.pdf

Al-Shehry, A., Rogerson, S., Fairweather, B., and Prior, M. (2006). The motivations for change towards e-Government adoption: Case studies from Saudi Arabia. In: *e-Government Workshop '06 (eGOV06), September 11, 2006, Brunel University, West London, UB8 3PH*, Accessed April 4, 2014. http://workspace.unpan.org/sites/internet/Documents/UNPAN033536.pdf

Ali, M., Weerakkody, V., and El-Haddadeh, R. (2009). The Impact of National Culture on E-Government Implementation: A Comparison Case Study. In: *Proceedings of the Fifteenth Americas Conference on Information Systems, San Francisco, California August 6th–9th 2009*, Accessed April 3, 2014. http://www.researchgate.net/publication/49402273_The_impact_of_national_culture_on_e-government_implementation_A_comparison_case_study/file/9fcfd50f840c5b0de8.pdf

Almarabeh, T., and AbuAli, A. (2010). A General Framework for E-Government: Definition Maturity Challenges, Opportunities, and Success. *European Journal of Scientific Research*, 39(1):29–42.

Alsaghier, H., Ford, M., Nguyen, A., and Hexel, R. (2009). Conceptualising Citizen's Trust in e-Government: Application of Q Methodology. *Electronic Journal of e-Government*, 7(4): 295–310.

Althoff, S. (2004). Point, Click, Elect should voting be that easy? *Boston Globe* (Boston, MA), March 7, p.26.

American Library Association (1989). American Library Association Presidential Committee on Information Literacy, Final Report, p.1. Chicago: American Library Association, 1989.

Anandarajan, M., Igbaria, M., and Anakwe, U.P (2002). IT acceptance in a less-developed country: a motivational factor perspective. *International Journal of Information Management*, 22:47–65.

Andersen, K.V., and Henriksen, H.Z. (2006). E-Government maturity models: Extension of the Layne and Lee model. *Government Information Quarterly*, 23(2):236–248.

Andrykowski, M., Beacham, A., Schmidt, J., and Harper, F. (2006). Application of the theory of planned behaviour to understand intentions to engage in physical and psychosocial health behaviours after cancer diagnosis. *Psycho-Oncology*, 15 (9):759–771.

Anttiroiko, Ai-V., and Malkia, M. (2006). *Encyclopedia of digital government*. Hershey, PA: Idea Group Reference (IGI) Publishing.

Arlotto, P.W., and Oakes, J.L. (2003). *Return on Investment: Maximizing the Value of Healthcare Information Technology*. Healthcare Information and Management Systems Society, Chicago, Illinois, 1–74.

Arpaci, I., Yardimci, Y.C., Ozkan, S., and Turetken, O. (2012). Organizational adoption of information technologies: a literature review. *International Journal of e-Business and e-Government studies*, 4(2), Accessed April 3, 2014. http://www.sobiad.org/eJOURNALS/journal_IJEBEG/arhieves/2012_no2_new/ibrahim_arpaci.pdf

Arora, E. (2011). Knowledge management in public sector. *Journal of Arts Science and Commerce*, 2(1):166–171.

Asiimwe, E, N., and Lim, N. (2010). Usability of Government Websites in Uganda. *Electronic Journal of e-Government*, 8(1):1–12.

Asiimwe, E.N., and Shakhawat, M.H.B. (2010). Contemporary Research on Mobile Government. In: *Scandinavian Workshop on e-Government (SVEG), 27–28 January 2010, Orebro*

University, Sweden, Accessed April 14, 2014. http://www.mgovworld.org/libra/mgovernance/papers/contemporary-research-on-mobile-government.pdf

Asogwa, B.E., and Azikiwe, N. (2013). Electronic government as a paradigm shift for efficient public services: Opportunities and challenges for Nigerian government. *Library Hi Tech,* 31(1), 141 – 159.

Avila, A. (2009). Underdeveloped ICT areas in Sub-Saharan Africa. *Informatica Economică,* 13(2):136–146, Accessed April 2, 2014. http://revistaie.ase.ro/content/50/016%20-%20Avila.pdf

Axelsson, K., and Lindblad-Gidlund, K. (2009). E-Government in Sweden: New Directions – Editorial. *International Journal of Public Information Systems*, 2:31–35.

Azab, N.A., Kamel, S., and Dafoulas, G. (2009). A suggested framework for assessing electronic government readiness in Egypt. *Electronic Journal of e-Government,* 7(1):11–28.

Backus, M. (2001). E-Governance and developing countries , Introduction and examples, . *IICD Research Brief,* Vol. 1. The Hague, the Netherlands, Accessed April 3, 2014. http://editor.iicd.org/files/report3.doc.

Bagozzi, R., Wong, N., Abe, S., and Bergami, M. (2000). Cultural and situational contingencies and the theory of reasoned action: Application to fast food restaurant consumption. *Journal of Consumer Psychology*, 9(2):97–106.

Bagozzi, R.P. (2007). The Legacy of the Technology Acceptance Model and a Proposal for a Paradigm Shift. *Journal of the Association for Information Systems,* 8(4), 4, Article 12, Accessed April 2, 2014. http://www.eduneg.net/generaciondeteoria/files/2007-bagozzi.pdf

Baker, E., Al-Gahtani, S., and Hubona, G. (2007). The effects of gender and age on new technology implementation in a developing country: Testing the theory of planned behavior (TPB*). Information Technology and People*, 20(4): 352–375.

Bamberg, S. (2006). Is a residential relocation a good opportunity to change people's travel behaviour? Results from a theory-driven intervention study. *Environment and Behaviour,* 38(6): 820–840.

Banerjee, P., and Chau, P.Y.K, (2004). An evaluative framework for analysing e-Government convergence capability in developing countries. *Electronic Government,* 1(1):29–49.

Barbour, R.S. (1998). Mixing qualitative methods: Quality assurance or qualitative quagmire? *Qualitative Health Research*, 8(3):352–361.

Barnard, Z. (2007). Online community portals for enhanced alumni networking. Unpublished doctoral thesis. University of Johannesburg.

Basaruddin, S., Nawi, A.S.A., Shukor, N.S.A., Jusoff, K., Jahari, N.A., and Saleh, H. (2010). Influencing Factors for Effective Community ICT Hubs. *World Applied Sciences Journal*, 11(1):114–117.

Baum, C., and Maio, D. (2000). *Gartner's four phases of e-Government model.* Gartner's group.

Baumgarten, J., and Chui, M. (2009). E-Government 2.0, Accessed April 2, 2014. http://www.mckinsey.com/insights/public_sector/e-government_20

BBC. (2010). Over 5 billion mobile phone connections worldwide. Accessed: http://www.bbc.co.uk/news/10569081 (Accessed 3 April 2014).

Bazeley, P. (2008). Mixed methods in management research. In: Thorpe, R. and R. Holt, R (eds). *The SAGE dictionary of qualitative management research*. London: Sage, 133–136.

Bedi, A.S., Manda, D.K., Nafula, N.N., and Kimalu, P.K. (2001). The Decline in Primary School Enrolment in Kenya. Draft KIPPRA Discussion Paper, Accessed April 3, 2014. http://www.sp.uconn.edu/~wwwciom/DPNO14.pdf

Bedi, K., Singh, P.J., and Srivastava, S. (2001) government@net: *new governance opportunities for India*. New Delhi: Sage.

Bekkers, V., and Moody, R. (2010). Visual events and electronic Government: What do pictures mean in digital government for citixen relations? Accessed April 3, 2014. http://ac.els-cdn.com/S0740624X11000554/1-s2.0-S0740624X11000554-main.pdf?_tid=a3e71192-bbd5-11e3-9882-00000aacb361&acdnat=1396601380_d08e6548db412f18a98a44a67a48072a

Bélanger, F., and Carter, L. (2008). Trust and risk in e-Government adoption. *Elsevier Journal of Strategic Information Systems*, 17:165–176.

Benbasat, I., Goldstein, D., and Mead, M. (1987). The case research strategy in studies of information systems. *MIS Quarterly*, 11(3):369–386.

Bertelsmann Foundation (2002). Balanced e-Government: E-Government – Connecting efficient administration and responsive democracy, Accessed April 3, 2014. http://www.eamericas.org/documentos/BertelsmanFoundationeGov02.pdf

Bertot, J.C., Jaeger, P.T., and Grimes, M. (2010). Using ICTs to create a culture of transparency: E-Government and social media as openness and anti-corruption tools for societies. *Government Information Quarterly*, 27(3):264–271.

Bertot, J.C., Jaeger, P.T., and McClure, C.R. (2008). Citizen-Centered E-Government Services: Benefits, Costs, and Research Needs. In: *The Proceedings of the 9th Annual International Digital Government Research Conference: 137–142. Montreal, Canada, May 18–21, 2008.*

Bhatia, S. (2001). E-Asean e-Readiness Assessment. Presented at the workshop on *The Internet in South East Asia, Bangkok, Thailand, 21 to 23 November 2001*. Accessed April 3, 2014. http://www.itu.int/asean2001/documents/pdf/Document-28.pdf

Bhatnagar, S. (2003). E-Government and access to information, *Global Corruption Report* 2003, 24–32. Transparency International, Accessed April 3, 2014. http://unpan1.un.org/intradoc/groups/public/documents/apcity/unpan008435.pdf

Bhatnagar, S.C., Rao, T.P., Singh, N., Vaidya, R., and Mandal, M. (2007). Impact Assessment study of e-Government projects in India. Center for e-Governance, Indian Institute of Management, Ahmedabad, Accessed April 3, 2014. http://www.iimahd.ernet.in/egov/documents/impact-assessment-study-dit.pdf

Bhatnagar, S.C. and Singh, N. (2008). Assessing the Impact of E-Government: A Study of Projects in India. *Information Technologies and International Development*, 6(2):109–127.

Billon, M., Marco, R., and Lera-Lopez, F. (2009). Disparities in ICT adoption: A multidimensional approach to study the cross-country digital divide. *Telecommunications Policy*, 33:596–610.

Braaksma, B. (2004). A million hits won't get you far: information literacy and the engaged citizen. In: Oliver, E. Lynn and Sanders, Larry. (eds). *E-Government reconsidered: renewal of governance for the knowledge age*. Regina, Sask.: Canadian Plains Research Center. 151–160.

Brewer, P., Chandra, G., and Hock, C.A. (1999). Economic Value Added (EVA): Its uses and limitations, *SAM Advanced Management Journal*, 64, 4–10.

Bridges.org. (2005). Comparison of e-readiness assessment models and tools (updated), Accessed April 2, 2014. http://ictlogy.net/bibliography/reports/projects.php?idp=333

Bolívar, M.P.R., Muñoz, L.A., and Hernández, A.M.L. (2010). Trends of e-Government Research. Contextualization and Research Opportunities. *The International Journal of Digital Accounting Research*, 10, 87–111.

Bouaziz, F. (2008). Public Administration Presence on the Web: a Cultural Explanation. *The Electronic Journal of e-Government*, 6(1):11–22.

Bouras, C., Gkamas, A., Papagiannopoulos, J., Theophilopoulos, G., and Tsiatsos, T. (2009). Broadband municipal optical networks in Greece: A suitable business model. *Telematics and Informatics*, 26:391–409.

Boyd, C.O. (2000). Combining qualitative and quantitative approaches. In: P.L. Munhall and C.O. Boyd (Eds.), *Nursing research: A qualitative perspective,* 2nd ed., 454–475. Boston: Jones and Bartlett.

Boyle, B., and Nicholson, D. (2003). E-Government in New Zealand. In Curtin, Gregoy. G., Sommers, Michael. H. and Vis-Sommer, Veronika. (eds). *The world of e- government.* New York: The Haworth Political Press. 89–105.

Budhiraja, R., and Sameer, S. (2004). E-Readiness Assessment (India), Accessed April 2, 2014. http://www.indiaegov.org/knowledgeexchg/ereadiness_Assessment.pdf

Bui, T.X., Sankaran, S., and Sebastian, I.M. (2003). A framework for measuring national e-readiness. *International Journal of Electronic Business,* 1(1):3–22.

Bwalya, K.J. (2009). Factors affecting adoption of e-Government in Zambia. *The Electronic Journal on Information Systems in Developing Countries (EJISDC),* 38:1–13.

Bwalya, K.J., and Healy, M. (2010). Harnessing e-Government Adoption in the SADC Region: a Conceptual Underpinning. *Electronic Journal of e-Government,* 8(1):23–32.

Bwalya, K.J., Du Plessis, T., and Rensleigh, C. (2011). Setting the Foundation for e-Democracy in Botswana: An Exploratory Study of Interventions. In: Cropf, R., and Krummenacher, W.S. (Eds.). *Information Communication Technologies and the Virtual Public Sphere: Impacts of Network Structures.* Information Science Reference, Hershey, New York, 229–241.

Caldow, J. (2001). Seven E-Government Leadership Milestones. In: *Vision and Revision.* IBM Corporation: Institute for Electronic Government, Accessed April 3, 2014. http://gcc.uni-paderborn.de/www/wi/wi2/wi2_lit.nsf/a9d9ba5440dfda62c1256bc900519bf1/0d9f71d1c010d5ccc1256af400640ab0/$FILE/egov_milestones.pdf

Campbell, J., and Im, T. (2012). Beyond ubiquity: Mobile government, theory and practice, KAPA conference at Seoul National University, Accessed April 3, 2014. http://www.kapa21.or.kr/english/files/1-3-3Jesse%20Campbell.pdf

Capgemini analysis. (2007). The User Challenge, Benchmarking the Supply of Online Public Services, 7th measurement, Accessed April 3, 2014. http://www.epractice.eu/files/media/media1673.pdf

Capurro, R., and Britz, J.B. (2010). In search of a code of global information ethics: The road travelled and new horizons. *Ethical Space: The International Journal of Communication Ethics,* 7(3):28–36.

CDTI *see* Center for Democracy and Technology, and InfoDev

Center for Democracy and Technology, and InfoDev. (2002). *The E-Government Handbook for Developing Countries.* The World Bank Group.

Centrone, F., Goia, A., and Salinelli, E. (2007). Demographic processes in a model of innovation diffusion with dynamic market. *Technological Forecasting and Social Change,* 74(3):247–266.

Chahin, A., Cunha, M.A., Knight, P.T., and Pinto, S.L. (2004). *egov.br – A próxima revolução brasileira. São Paulo*: Financial Times Prentice Hall/Pearson Education do Brasil.

Chandler, S., and Emanuel, S. (2002). Transformation Not Automation. *Proceedings of 2nd European Conference on E-Government,* St Catherine's College Oxford, UK, 91–102.

Chau, P.Y.K. and Hu, P. J-H. (2002). Investigating healthcare professionals' decisions to accept telemedicine: An empirical test of competing theories. *Information and Management*, 39:297–311.

Chauhan, R. and Singh, A. (2011). Generalizing Meta-Data Elements: Global Scenario and Indian Perspective. *Journal of Administration and Governance*, 5(1).

Chen, Y., Chen, H. M., Ching, R. K. H., and Huang, W. W. (2006). E-Government Strategies in Developed and Developing Countries: An Implementation Framework and Case Study. *Journal of Global Information Management*, 14(1), 23–46.

Chen, Y., Chen, H. M., Ching, R. K. H., and Huang, W. W. (2007). Electronic government implementation: A comparison between developed and developing countries. *International Journal of Electronic Government Research*, 3(2), 45–61.

Chêne, M. (2008). Overview of Corruption in Zambia, Accessed January 19, 2014. http://www.u4.no/helpdesk/helpdesk/query.cfm?id=184.

Chikanta, H.R.H.C., and Mweetwa, F. (2007). The Need for Information and Communications Technologies in Rural Areas, LinkNet – 2007, Accessed April 3, 2014. http://www.share4dev.info/kb/documents/4782.pdf

Chismar W., and Wiley-Patton, S. (2003). Does the extended technology acceptance model apply to physicians. In: *Proceedings of the 36th Hawaii International Conference on System Sciences (HICSS'03), January 6–9, 2003, Big Island, Hawaii, USA.* Accessed April 14, 2014. http://citeseerx.ist.psu.edu/viewdoc/download?doi=10.1.1.97.9056&rep=rep1&type=pdf

Cho, Y. H., and Choi, B. (2004). E-Government to combat corruption: The case of Seoul metropolitan government. *International Journal of Public Administration, 27*(10):719–735.

Choi, D. (2003). Policy and Knowledge Economy Development National ICT Strategy, E-Policy and Knowledge Economy Development, DESA-UNITAR Diplomacy Seminar 2002 25 June 2003 Rome, Italy, Accessed April 3, 2014. http://unpan1.un.org/intradoc/groups/public/documents/un/unpan012237.pdf

Choudrie, J., and Dwivedi, Y.K. (2004). Towards a Conceptual Model of Broadband Diffusion. *Journal of Computing and Information Technology – CIT*, 12(4):323–338.

Chowdhury, Z.H., and Zaidi, A.K.M. (2013). Citizen Perspective E-Governance Model for Developing Countries: Bangladesh Context,. *American Journal of Modeling and Optimization*, 1(3): 43–46.

Center for International Development (CID). (2000). Readiness for the Networked world: A Guide for the developing Countries, Accessed April 2, 2014. http://cyber.law.harvard.edu/readinessguide/guide.pdf

Coates, N., and Nikolaus, L. (2010). Zambia and e-Government: An Assessment and Recommendations. In: Maumbe, B. (Ed.). *E-Agriculture and E-Government for Global Policy Development: Implications and Future Directions.* Hershey, PA: IGI Global, 137–161.

Code of Ethics of the American Anthropological Association. (1998), Accessed April 2, 2014. http://www.oswego.edu/Documents/wac/Dens%27%20Awards,%202013/Kirby,%20Samantha.pdf

Collins, K., Onwuegbuzie, A.J., and Sutton, I.L. (2006). A model incorporating the rationale and purpose for conducting mixed-methods research in special education and beyond. *Learning Disabilities: A Contemporary Journal*, *4*(1): 67–100.

Codagnone, C. (2008). The Future of e-Government: Supply and demand trends and needs, Delivered by RSO/Sineura within the Study, 'Future technology needs for future e-Government Services' for the European Commission, DG Information Society, e-Government Unit, Milan, Italy, Accessed January 31, 2014. http://ec.europa.eu/information_society/activities/egovernment/funding/results/ docs/d2_needs_and_trends_analysis_report.pdf

Coleman, S. (2006). *African e-Governance-Opportunities and Challenges*, University of Oxford, Univ. Press.

Coleman, S., and Kaposi, I. (2009). New democracies new media what's new? A study of e-Participation projects in third-wave democracies, Accessed April 3, 2014. http://www.ega.ee/files/Coleman_handbook.pdf

Colvin, C.A. and Goh, A. (2005). Validation of the technology acceptance model for police. *Journal of Criminal Justice*, 33:89–95.

Common Market for Eastern and Southern Africa (COMESA). (2008). Regional Information and Communication Technology Support Programme (RICTSP), COMESA Regional e-Government Framework, February, 2008. Accessed April 3, 2014. http://programmes.comesa.int/attachments/article/78/COMESA%20Regional%20e-Gov%20Framework.pdf

Consulting and Audit Canada. (2004). Consulting and Audit Canada, *Transformation for the digital age: The development of Botswana's National ICT policy*. Preliminary report for consultancy for the formation of a national information and communication technology policy technical bid (1–81). Government of Canada, Toronto.

Cooper, R.D., and Schindler, S.P. (2001). *Business Research Methods, 7th Edition*. McGraw-Hill, New York.

Creswell, A.M. (2006). The role of public return on investment assessment in government IT projects. In: *ACM International Conference Proceeding Series*. New York: ACM. 151:379–380.

Creswell, W.J. (1994). *Research design: Qualitative and quantitative approaches*. SAGE publications, London.

Crichton, C., Davies, J., Gibbons, J., Harris, S., Tsui, A., and Brenton, J. (2009). Metadata-Driven Software for Clinical Trials. In: *Proceedings of the 2009 ICSE Workshop on Software Engineering in Health Care (SEHC '09). May 18–19, 2009, Washington DC, USA*. Accessed April 3, 2014. http://www.cs.ox.ac.uk/people/jeremy.gibbons/publications/consort.pdf

Crump, B.J. (2005). E-Government, community and social inclusion: A New Zealand case study. 816–820. In: *IADIS International Conference e-Society 2004*. July 16–19, 2004, Avila, Spain. Accessed April 3, 2014. http://unpan1.un.org/intradoc/groups/public/documents/apcity/unpan039458.pdf

Compaine, B (Ed.). 2001. *The Digital Divide: Facing a Crisis or Creating a Myth?* Cambridge, MA: MIT Press.

Computer System Policy Project (CSPP). (1998). Readiness Guide for Living in the Networked World, Computer systems Policy project, Accessed April 3, 2014. http://www.broadband.wv.gov/research/Documents/Strategies%20-%20Tools/CSPP%20Guide%20for%20Living%20in%20a%20Networked%20World.pdf

Computer System Policy Project. (2000). The CSPP Readiness Guide for Living in the Networked World. *Journal of Purchasing and Supply Management*, 11(5–6):252–259.

Csáki, C., and Gelléri, P. (2005). Conditions and benefits of applying decision technological solutions as a tool to curb corruption within the procurement process: The case of Hungary. *Journal of Purchasing and Supply Management, 11(5–6)*, 252–259.

Dada, D. (2006). E-Readiness for Developing Countries: Moving the Focus from the Environment to the Users. *The Electronic Journal on Information Systems in Developing Countries (EJISDC)*, 27(6):1–14.

Dawes, S.S. (2009). Building the Next-Generation Digital Government Infrastructures: Governance in the digital age: A research and action framework for an uncertain future. *Government Information Quarterly,* 26(2), 257–264.

Davis, F.D. (1989). Perceived Usefulness, Ease of Use, and User Acceptance of Information Technology. *MIS Quarterly*, 13(3): 319–339.

Davis, F.D., Bagozzi, R.P., and Warshaw, P.R. (1989). User acceptance of computer technology: A comparison of two theoretical models. *Management Science*, 35(8):982–1003.

De Cannière, M.H., De Pelsmacker, P., and Geuens, M. (2009). Relationship Quality and the Theory of Planned Behavior models of behavioral intentions and purchase behaviour. *Journal of Business Research*, 62(1):82–92.

DeCoster, J. (1998). *Overview of Factor Analysis,* Accessed April 4, 2014. http://www.stat- http://www.stat-help.com/factor.pdf

Dehning, B., Richardson, V.J., and Zmud, R.W. (2003). The value relevance of announcements of transformational information technology investments. *MIS Quarterly,* 27(4):637–656.

Deibert, R.J. (2004). E-Democracy: Current Trends and Future Prospects, A Report to the Panel on the Role of Government. Accessed April 4, 2014. http://www.law-lib.utoronto.ca/investing/reports/rp19.pdf

Deloitte. (2004). Citizen Advantage™: Enhancing economic competitiveness through e-Government, *The second of a two-part series on IT value in the public sector.* Accessed April 3, 2014. http://unpan1.un.org/intradoc/groups/public/documents/apcity/unpan022639.pdf

Deloitte and Touche. (2001). The citizen as customer. *CMA management*, 74(10):58.

Denzin, N.K. (1970). *The research act: A theoretical introduction to sociological methods.* Chicago: Aldine.

Department of Trade and Industry. (2009). *South Africa: Geared for growth*. Pretoria: Government of South Africa.

Department of Economic and Social Affairs. (2003). World public sector report 2003: e-Government at the crossroads, New York: United Nations, Accessed April 3, 2014. http://unpan1.un.org/intradoc/groups/public/documents/un/unpan012733.pdf

DESA *see* Department of Economic and Social Affairs.

Dimitrova, D., and Chen, Y. C. (2006). Profiling the adopters of e-Government information services: the influence of psychological characteristics, civic mindedness, and information channels. *Social Science Computer Review,* 24(2):172–188.

Dinev, T., Hu, Q., and Goo, J. (2005). User Behaviour toward Preventive Technologies – Examining Cross-cultural Differences between the United states and South Korea. In: *Proceedings of the 13th Annual Cross-Cultural Research in Information Systems Conference (CCRIS 2005). December 10. Las Vegas, NV. USA,* Accessed April 14, 2014. http://www.researchgate.net/publication/229014149_USER_BEHAVIOR_TOWARD_PREVENTIVE_TECHNOLOGIESEXAMINING_CROSS-CULTURAL_DIFFERENCES_BETWEEN_THE_UNITED_STATES_AND_/file/60b7d52150cc05d9d6.pdf

Dishaw, M.T., and Strong, D.M. (1999). Extending the technology acceptance model with task-technology fit constructs. *Information and Management*, 36:9–21

Dobnikar A., and Nemec, Z. (2007). e-Government in Slovenia. *Informatica*, 31:357–365.

Doherty, M. (1994). Probability versus Non-Probability Sampling in Sample Surveys. *The New Zealand Statistics Review,* 21–28.

Dombeu, J.V.F., Huisman, M., and Szpak, Z. (2011). A Framework for Semantic Model Ontologies Generation for E-government Applications, Paper presented at ThinkMind // ICDS 2011, The Fifth International Conference on Digital Society. 152–158.
Doordan, A.M. (1998). *Research Survival Guide*, Lippincott, New York.
Dowling, M.P. (2001). Libraries, librarians, and library associations in the United States in 2001: Making a difference in the knowledge age. *IFLA Journal*, 27(3):133–412.
Dos Santos, B., and Sussman, L. (2000). Improving the Return on IT investment: The Productivity Paradox. *International Journal of Information Management*, 20:429–440.
DoSHandSW. (2002). Health Management Information System Policy, Department of State for Health and Social Welfare, Accessed April 4, 2014. pdf
DTI *see* Department of Trade and Industry
Du Preez, J. (2009). Assessing the m-Government readiness within the provincial government Western Cape., Unpubublished Masters Degree thesis – University of Stellenbosch, Accessed April 2, 2014. http://scholar.sun.ac.za/bitstream/handle/10019.1/3292/Du%20Preez,%20J.pdf?sequence=1.
Dutta, S., and Mia, I. (2010a). GICT for Sustainability, Accessed April 2, 2014. http://www.itu.int/wsis/implementation/2010/forum/geneva/docs/publications/GITR%202009-2010_Full_Report_final.pdf
Dutta, S., and Mia, I. (2010b). *The Global Information Technology Report 2009–2010: ICT for Sustainability*. World Economic Forum, Geneva, Switzerland. Accessed March 11, 2014. http://www3.weforum.org/docs/WEF_GITR_Report_2010.pdf.
Dwivedi, Y. K., and Weerakkody V. (2007). Examining the Factors Affecting the Adoption of Broadband in the Kingdom of Saudi Arabia. *Electronic Government: An International Journal*, 4(1):43–58.
E-Business Handbook. (2005). *The 2005 review of innovation at work in South African business*. An IT web informatica Publication. Cape Town. South Africa. Creda Communication.
Ebrahim, Z., and Irani, Z. (2005). E-Government adoption: architecture and barriers. *Emerald Business Process Management Journal*, 11(5):589–611.
Eddowes, L.A. (2004). The Application of Methodologies in e-Government. *Electronic Journal of e-Government*, 2(2):115–126.
E-Government Initiatives. (2005). E-Government Initiatives 2000–2004, Accessed April 3, 2014. http://www.gov.mu/portal/goc/telecomit/files/e-gov%20initiatives.pdf
Escobar, H.M. (2007). E-Government architectures, technical and political situation in Latin America, Accessed April 2, 2014. http://www.eclac.org/ddpe/publicaciones/xml/7/28647/W129.pdf.
Esteves, J., and Joseph, R.C. (2008). A comprehensive framework for the assessment of e-Government projects. *Government Information Quarterly*, 25:118–132.
EU Report. (2007). E-Government Progress in EU27+: Reaping the Benefits Progress Report, e-Government Unit, DG Information Society and Media, European Commission, September 2007, Accessed April 3, 2014. http://ec.europa.eu/information_society/newsroom/cf/document.cfm?action= display&doc_id=391&ei=j_FQTuqFAse2hAfF6JDVBg&usg=AFQjCNHSTUZS89y5e1uCXWWUjl2wU6mjmw.
Evans, D., and Yen, D.C. (2005). E-Government: An analysis for implementation: Framework for understanding cultural and social impact. *Government Information Quarterly*, 22:354–373.
Fang, Z. (2002). E-Government in Digital Era: Concept, Practice, and Development. *International Journal of the Computer, the Internet and Management*, 10(2):1–22.

Feller, J., Finnegan, P., and Nilsson, O. (2010). Open innovation and public administration: transformational typologies and business model impacts. *European Journal of Information Systems,* 20: 358–374.
Ferrer, F., and Santos, P. (2004*). E-Government – o governo eletrônico no Brasil.* São Paulo: Saraiva.
Ferro, E., Carratta, T., and Dadayan, L. (2006). ROI Analysis in e-Government Assessment Trials: The Case of Sistema Piemonte. In: *Proceedings of the 5th international conference on Electronic Government (eGov06), Krakow, Poland, September 4–8, 2006.* Wimmer, M.A., Scholl, H.J., Grönlund, A., Andersen, K.V. (Eds.), Springer Verlag: Berlin.
Fidel, R. (2008). Are we there yet? Mixed methods research in library and information science. *Library and Information Science Research,* 30:265–272.
Finger, F., and Pecaud, G. (2003). From e-government to e-governance? Towards a model of e-governance, *Electronic Journal of e-Government,* 1: 1–10.
Fisher, H. (2008). Hosting the FIFA 2010 Soccer World Cup: The South African Service Delivery Dilemma. Paper presented at: *2008 CAPAM Biennial Conference,* Accessed April 3, 2014. http://www.capam.org/_documents/paper.fisher.pdf
Fishbein, M., and Ajzen, I. (1975). *Belief, attitude, intention, and behaviour: An introduction to theory and research.* Reading, USA: Addison-Wesley.
Farelo, M., and Morris, C. (2006). The Status of E-government in South Africa, Accessed April 3, 2014. http://researchspace.csir.co.za/dspace/bitstream/10204/966/1/Farelo_2006_D.pdf
Flannery, B., and May, D. (2000). Environmental ethical decision-making in the U.S. metal-finishing industry. *Academy of Management Journal,* 43(4):642–662.
Fortunati, L. (2008). Rethinking Social Inclusion. Abstract of paper offered for: *Prato CIRN 2008 Community Informatics Conference: ICTs for Social Inclusion: What is the Reality?* Accessed March 29, 2014. http://stoa.usp.br/schwartz/files/1135/6404/prato2008abstracts.pdf
Fosu, A.K., and Mwabu, G. (2010). Human Development Research Paper 2010/08 Human Development in Africa, Accessed April 2, 2014. http://hdr.undp.org/sites/default/files/hdrp_2010_08.pdf.
Fowler, F. J. (1993). *Survey Research Methods.* Sage Publications, London.
Gauld, P., Goldfinch, S., and Horsburgh, S. (2010). Do they want it? Do they use it? The 'Demand-Side' of e-Government in Australia and New Zealand. *Government Information Quarterly,* 27:177–186.
Gefen, D., and Straub, D.W. (2000).The Relative importance of Perceived ease of use in IS adoption: A Study of e-Commerce Adoption. *Journal of the Association for Information Systems,* 1:1–28.
Gefen, D., and Straub, D.W. (1997). Gender differences in the perception and use of e-mail: An extension of the technology acceptance model. *MIS Quarterly,* 21:389–400.
Georg, E., and Harald, H. (2010). National Innovation Policies, Globalisation and the Asian Challenge, Accessed March 28, 2014. http://papers.ssrn.com/sol3/papers.cfm?abstract_id=1710613.
Georgiadis, C.K., and Stiakakis, E. (2010). Extending an e-Government Service Measurement Framework to m-Governement Services. In: *Ninth International Conference on Mobile Business, 2010, 9th Global Mobility Roundtable,* 432–439. Accessed April 14, 2014. http://ieeexplore.ieee.org/stamp/stamp.jsp?tp=&arnumber=5494837

Gerster Consulting. (2008). ICT in Africa: Boosting Economic Growth and Poverty Reduction. 10th meeting of the African Partnership Forum, Accessed April 3, 2014. http://www.gersterconsulting.ch/docs/ICT-Africa_Report_final_engl.pdf

Giff, G., and Coleman, D. (2003). Funding Models for SDIs: Are they Applicable in Emerging Nations? In: *9th EC GI & GIS Workshop, ESDI Serving the User, Coruña, Spain, 25–27 June 2003*, Accessed April 14, 2014. http://www.ec-gis.org/Workshops/9ec-gis/papers/funding_giff.pdf

Gil-García, R.J., and Pardo, T.A. (2005). E-Government success factors: Mapping practical tools to theoretical foundations. *Government Information Quarterly*, 22(2):187–216.

Gil-Garcia, J.R., and Martinez-Moyano, I.J. (2007). Understanding the evolution of e-Government: The influence of systems of rules on public sector dynamics, *Government Information Quarterly*, 24(2):266–290.

Gillmore, M., Archibald, M., Morrison, D., Wilsdon, A., Wells, E., Hoppe, M., Nahom, D., and Murowchick, E. (2002). Teen sexual behaviour: Applicability of the theory of reasoned action. *Journal of Marriage and Family*, 64(4):885–897.

Godse, V., and Garg, A. (2007). From E-Government to E-governance. Foundation of E-Government. Computer Society of India, Accessed April 3, 2014. http://www.csi-sigegov.org/1/2_313.pdf

Goel, G., and Tripathi, R. (2007). E-Government Approach to Management of Intellectual Property in Indian Folklore, Accessed April 1, 2014. http://www.csi-sigegov.org/1/32_383.pdf

Golafshani, N. (2003). Understanding reliability and validity in qualitative research. *The Qualitative Report*, 8(4):597-606, Accessed April 2, 2014. http://www.nova.edu/ssss/QR/QR8-4/golafshani.pdf

Golubeva, A.A. (2007). Evaluation of regional government portal on the basis of public value concept: Case study from Russian Federation. In: *ICEGOV '07:* Proceedings of the 1st international conference on Theory and practice of electronic governance, Macao, 10–13 December 2007. Accessed April 20, 2014. http://dl.acm.org/citation.cfm?id=1328139

Gonzalez, E.T. (2007). Policy transfer in the Philippines: Can it pass the localisation test. *Journal of Administration and Governance*, 2(1):1–10.

Gonzalez, P., Adenso-Diaz, B., and Gemoets, L.A. (2010). A cross-national comparison e-Government success measures: A theory-based empirical research. In: *Americas Conference on Information Systems (AMCIS) 2010 Proceedings*, Accessed April 1, 2014. http://aisel.aisnet.org/cgi/viewcontent.cgi?article=1356&context=amcis2010

Grandon, E.E., and Pearson, J.M. (2004). Electronic commerce adoption: An empirical study of small and medium U.S. businesses. *Information and Management*, 42:197–216.

Greek e-Government Factsheet. (2007). European Communities, Accessed April 4, 2014. http://www.epractice.eu/files/media732.pdf

Grönlund, Å. (Ed.). (2001). *Electronic Government: Design, Applications, and Management.* Hershey, PA: IDEA Group Publishing.

Grönlund, Å., Andersson, A., and Hedström, K. (2005). NextStep e-Governemnt in developing countries – Report D3: Suggestions for projects within the SPIDER area of interest, Accessed April 2, 2014. http://citeseerx.ist.psu.edu/viewdoc/download?doi=10.1.1.106.2557&rep=rep1&type=pdf .

Guardian *The*. (2009). Nice talking to you mobile phone use passes milestone, Accessed April 1, 2014. http://www.guardian.co.uk/technology/2009/mar/03/mobile-phones1.

Guijarro, l. (2007). Interoperability frameworks and enterprise architectures in egovernment initiatives in Europe and the United States. *Government Information Quarterly, 24, 89–101.*

Guijarro, U. (2010). Frameworks for fostering cross-agency interoperability in e-government initiatives, In: H.J. Scholl (Ed.), *E-government: Information, technology, and transformation*, 17, 280–300. M.E. Sharpe: Armonk.

Gupta, M. P., and Jana, D. (2003). E-government evaluation: a framework and case study. *Government Information Quarterly,* 20(4), 365–387.

Gupta, P., and Vasishta, P.K. (2008). An Approach for e-Government Project Assessment, Accessed April 3, 2014. http://www.csi-sigegov.org/1/22_318.pdf

Gurstein, M. (2003). Effective use: A community informatics strategy beyond the Digital Divide, *First Monday – Journal of the Internet,* 8(12), Accessed April 2, 2014. http://firstmonday.org/article/view/1107/1027 .

Guy, M. (2003). Public Management, In: J.E. Shafritz (ed.), *Defining Public Administration*, 161–168. Western Press.

Habeenzu, S. (2010). Zambia ICT Sector Performance Review 2009/2010: *Towards Evidence-based ICT Policy and Regulation, 2, Policy Paper 17/2010,* Accessed April 2, 2014. http://www.researchictafrica.net/publications/ICT_Sector_Performance_Reviews_2010/Vol%202%20Paper%2017%20-%20Zambia%20ICT%20Sector%20Performance%20Review%202010.pdf

Hafkin, N.J. (2009). E-government in Africa: Progress made and challenges ahead, Accessed April 4, 2014. http://unpan1.un.org/intradoc/groups/public/documents/un/unpan033526.pdf

Hahamis, P.J., and Healy, M. (2005). E-Government in Greece: Bridging the gap Between Need and Reality. *The Electronic Journal of e-Government,* 3(4):185–192.

Hanafizadeh, P., Hanafizadeh, M.R., and Khodabakhshi, M. (2009). Taxonomy of e-readiness assessment measures. *International Journal of Information Management,* 29(3):189–195.

Hamel, J-Y. (2010). ICT4D and the Human Development and Capability Approach: The Potentials of Information and Communication Technology. Human Development Research Paper 37, Accessed April 2, 2014. http://hdr.undp.org/sites/default/files/hdrp_2010_37.pdf

Hansen, T., Jensen, J.M., and Solgaard, H.S. (2004). Predicting online grocery buying intention: a comparison of the theory of reasoned action and the theory of planned behaviour. *International Journal of Information Management,* 24(6):539–550.

Hargreaves, I. (2011). Digital opportunity: A review of intellectual property and growth, Accessed April 2, 2014. http://www.ipo.gov.uk/ipreview-finalreport.pdf

Hassan, S., and Gil-Garcia, J.R. (2009). Institutional Theory and E-Government Research, Accessed April 2, 2014. http://www.systemdynamics.org/conferences/2009/proceed/papers/P1310.pdf

Haris, R. (2006). Policies, Programmes and Projects for e-inclusion. Meeting of Eminent Experts on Information, Communication and Space Technology for Development – Preparation for the Third Ministerial Conference on Space Technology Applications for Sustainable Development in Asia and the Pacific, 3–4 August 2006, Bangkok, Accessed April 2, 2014. http://e.unescap.org/icstd/SPACE/documents/EMINENT%20EXPERTS%202006/Presentations/Harris-How%20to%20design,%20manage%20and%20operate%20programmes.pdf

Hawamdeh, S. (2005). E-Government and Economic Development, *The Role of NII and ICT, World summit of the information society, Tunis 2005,* Accessed April 3, 2014. http://www.hawamdeh.net/WSIS%20egov%20Presentation.pdf

Heeks, R. (2004). eGovernment for development: What is eGovernment? Accessed April 2, 2014. http://www.egov4dev.org/success/definitions.shtml .

Heeks, R. (2003a). Achieving Success/Avoiding Failure in e-Government Projects. IDPM, University of Manchester, Accessed April 3, 2014. http://www.egov4dev.org/success/sfdefinitions.shtml.

Heeks, R. (2003b). Most e-Government-for-Development Projects Fail: How Can Risks be Reduced? *iGovernment Working Paper Series*, Paper no. 14, Accessed April 15, 2014. http://unpan1.un.org/intradoc/groups/public/documents/NISPAcee/UNPAN015488.pdf

Heeks, R. (2002). E-Government in Africa: Promise and Practice, Accessed April 3, 2014. http://www.africainfoethics.org/pdf/2009/Heeks_conference_documentation.pdf

Heeks, R., and Santos, R. (2009). Understanding Adoption of e-Government: Principals, Agents and Institutional Dualism. *iGovernment Working Paper Series,* Accessed April 4, 2014. http://www.sed.manchester.ac.uk/idpm/research/publications/wp/igovernment/documents/iGWkPpr19.pdf

Helbig, N. C., Gil-Garcia, J.R., and Ferro, E. (2005). Understanding the Complexity in Electronic Government: Implications from the Digital Divide Literature. In: *AMCIS 2005 Proceedings.* Paper 139. Omaha, Nebraska, USA, August 11–14, *2005,* Accessed April 1, 2014. http://aisel.aisnet.org/amcis2005/139.

Helsper, E., and Eynon, R. (2009). Digital natives: where is the evidence? *British Educational Research Journal,* 1–18, Accessed April 3, 2014. http://eprints.lse.ac.uk/27739/1/Digital_natives_(LSERO).pdf

Hermana, B., and Silfianti, W. (2011). Evaluating E-Government Implementation by Local Government: Digital Divide in Internet Based Public Services in Indonesia. *International Journal of Business and Social Science*, 2(3):156–163.

Henriot, P.J. (2007). Good Governance for Sustainable Growth." Presented at the German World Bank Forum on "Africa on the Rise", Berlin 2007, Accessed April 3, 2014. http://www.jctr.org.zm/index.php?option=com_joomdoc&task=cat_view&gid=56&Itemid=76&limitstart=20.

Hernon, P. (2009). Procedures: Research design, Editorial. *Library and Information Science Research,* 31:1–2.

Hiller, J. S., and Bélanger, F. (2001). Privacy Strategies for Electronic Government. In: M. A. Abramson and G. E. Means (Eds.), *E-Government 200.*Lanham, MD: Rowman and Littlefield Publishers. 162–198.

HIPSSA Project. (2008). Support for Harmonization of ICT Policies in Sub-Sahara Africa, Accessed April 2, 2014. https://www.itu.int/ITU-D/projects/ITU_EC_ACP/hipssa/docs/HIPSSA_implementation_strategy_EN_090608.pdf.

Hoepner, P., and Mendes, M. (2007). EGOIA – Electronic GOvernment Innovation and Access, Accessed April 4, 2014. http://www.cgu.gov.br/ivforumglobal/pdf/petrahoepner-2.pdf

Hoffman, B.D., and Gibson. C.C. (2005). Fiscal Governance and Public Services: Evidence from Tanzania and Zambia. Department of Political Science, University of California San Diego, August, Accessed April 4, 2014. http://www.sscnet.ucla.edu/polisci/wgape/papers/9_GibsonHoffman.pdf

Holden, S.H., Norris, O.F., Fletcher, P.D. (2003). Electronic Government at the Grass Roots: Contemporary Evidence and Future Trends. In: *Proceedings of the 36th Hawaii International Conference on System Sciences (HICSS'03). January 6–9, 2003, Hawaii, US,* Accessed April 15, 2014. http://citeseerx.ist.psu.edu/viewdoc/download?doi=10.1.1.127.2491&rep=rep1&type=pdf

Holmes, D. (2001). *E-gov: e-business strategies for Government.* Nicholas Brealey Publishing, London,

Horst, M., Kuttschreuter, M., and Gutteling, J. (2007). Perceived usefulness, personal experiences, risk perception and trust as determinants of adoption of e-Government services in The Netherlands. *Computers in Human Behavior*, 23:1838–1852.

Hossan, C.G., Habib, W., and Kushchu (2006). Success and Failure Factors for e-Government projects implementation in developing countries: A study on the perception. EuroMGov, Accessed April 3, 2014. http://citeseerx.ist.psu.edu/viewdoc/download?doi=10.1.1.99.3572&rep=rep1&type=pdf

Howard, M. (2001). E-Government across the Globe: How will 'e' Change Government? Accessed March 26, 2014. http://www.gfoa.org/downloads/eGovGFRAug01.pdf

Hu, P., Chau, P., Liu Sheng, O., and Tam, K. (1999). Examining the Technology Acceptance Model Using Physician Acceptance of Telemedicine Technology. *Journal of Management Information Systems*, 16(2):91–112.

Hu, Y., Xiao, J., Pang, J., and Xie, K. (2005). A Research on the Appraisal Framework of e-Government Project Success. In: *Proceedings of the 7th International Conference on Electronic Commerce – ICEC 2005, Xian, China, August 15–17, 2005*, 532–538. Accessed April 20, 2014. http://dl.acm.org/citation.cfm?id=1089647

Huang, D.C, and Hu, Q. (2004). Integrating Web services with competitive strategies: The balanced Scorecard approach. *Communications of the Association for Information Systems*, 1(13):57–80.

Humes, L.L., *and* Reinhard, N. (2007). Institutionalization of an Information System through the Exercise of Power. In: *Proceedings of the 9th International Conference on Social Implications of Computers in Developing Countries, São Paulo, Brazil, May 2007*, Accessed April 15, 2014. http://www.ifipwg94.org.br/fullpapers/R0049-1.pdf

Hung, C-L, Chou, J, C-L., and Dong, T-P. (2011). Innovations and communication through innovative users: An exploratory mechanism of social networking website. *International Journal of Information Management*, 31(4):317–326.

IDABC e-Government Observatory (2006). European eGovernment News Roundup, Accessed April 2, 2014. http://selis.unipi.gr/selis/main/files/eGovNews.pdf

IDAS *see* Infocomm Development Authority of Singapore.

Ilie, V., Slyke, C.V., Green, G., and Lou, H. (2005). Gender differences in perceptions and use of communication technologies: A diffusion of innovation approach. *Information Resources Management Journal*, 18(3):13–31.

Infocomm Development Authority of Singapore. (2006). Singapore's e-Government Journey, Accessed March 14, 2014. https://www.ida.gov.sg/~/media/Files/Archive/News and Events/News_and_Events_Level2/20060530150726/eGovJourney.doc .

Im, L.L., Hong, S., and Kang, S.L. (2011). An international comparison of technology adoption: Testing the UTAUT model. *Information and Management*, 48(1):1–8.

Irani, Z., Al-Sebie, M., and Elliman, T. (2006). Transaction Stage of e-Government Systems: Identification of its Location and Importance. In: *Proceedings of the 39th Hawaii International Conference on System Science, January 4–7, 2006, Hawaii, USA. 4:* 82c, Accessed April 15, 2014. http://bura.brunel.ac.uk/bitstream/2438/4486/1/250740082c.pdf

Iribarren, M., Concha, G., Valdes, G., Solar, M., Villarroel, M.T., Gutiérrez, P., and Vásquez, A. (2008). Capability Maturity Framework for e-Government: A Multi-dimensional Model and Assessing Tool . In: M.A. Wimmer, H.J. Scholl, E. Ferro (Eds.), *Electronic Government: Lecture Notes in Computer Science, 5184*: 136–147. Springer-Verlag, Berlin.

Islam, M.M., and Ahmed, A.B.S (2007). Understanding e-governance: a theoretical approach. *Asian Affairs*, 29(4), 29–46.

Iqbal, M. S., and Seo, J.W. (2008). E-Governance as an anti-corruption tool: Korean cases. *Journal of Korean Association for Regional Information Society*, 11(2):51–78.

Iyer, L., Baqir, M. N., and Vollmer, T. (2006). A comparative analysis of E-government strategies. In: R. K. Mitra (Ed.), *E-Governance: Macro Issues*, 141–152. New Delhi: GIFT Publishing.

James, E.P. (2002). The supply side of the digital divide: is there equal availability in the broadband Internet access market? Accessed April 2, 2014. http://wp.econ.ucdavis.edu/02-5.pdf

Jarrar, M., Deik, A., and Faraj, B. (2011). Ontology-Based Data and Process Governance Framework – The Case Of E-Government Interoperability In Palestine. In pre-proceedings of the *IFIP International Symposium on Data-Driven Process Discovery and Analysis (SIMPDA'11), Campione, Italy. June 30, 2011*, 83–98. Accessed April 15, 2014. http://sesar.dti.unimi.it/SIMPDA2011/SIMPDA2011.pdf

Johnson, R.B., Onwuegbuzie, A.J., and Turner, L.A. (2007). Toward a definition of mixed research design. *Journal of mixed methods research*, 1(2):112–133.

Joia, L.A. (2004). Developing Government-to-Government enterprises in Brazil: a heuristic model drawn from multiple case studies. *International Journal of Information Management*, 24(2):147–166.

Jones, S., Irani, A., and Sharif, A. (2007). E-Government Evaluation: Reflections on Three Organisational Case Studies. In: *Proceedings of the 40th Hawaii International Conference on System Sciences, Accessed March 20, 2014*. http://ieeexplore.ieee.org/stamp/stamp.jsp?tp=&arnumber=4076584.

Joseph, K. J. (2002). Growth of ICT and ICT for Development: realities of the Myths of the Indian Experience. Discussion paper No. 2002/78. *UNU/ WIDER Conference, 10–11 May 2002, Helsinki,* Accessed April 15, 2014. http://www.wider.unu.edu/stc/repec/pdfs/rp2002/dp2002-78.pdf

Jupp, V., and Younger, M.P. (2004). A Value Model for the Public Sector. Accenture. Accessed http://www.accenture.com/SiteCollectionDocuments/PDF/hp_gov.pdf (Accessed 2 April 2014).

Just, M., and Rosmarin, D. (2005). Meeting the Challenges of Canada's Secure Delivery of E-Government Services. In: *Pre-Proceedings to 4th Annual PKI R&D Workshop: Multiple Paths to Trust, Gaithersburg, MD, April 2005,* Accessed April 15, 2014. http://middleware.internet2.edu/pki05/proceedings/preproceedings.pdf

Kaisara, G., and Pather, S. (2008). Evaluation of e-Government websites: A Batho Pele-aligned approach for e-service quality measurement. In: P A. van Brakel (Ed.), *Proceedings of the 10th annual conference on WWW applications*, Cape Town, 3–5 September 2008. Accessed April 15, 2014. http://www.zaw3.co.za/index.php/ZA-WWW/2009/paper/viewFile/156/19

Kamal, M.M., and Themistocleous, M. (2006). A Conceptual Model for EAI Adoption in an e-Government Environment. In: *European and Mediterranean Conference on Information Systems (EMCIS), July 6–7 2006, Alicante, Spain*, Accessed April 15, 2014. http://dspace.brunel.ac.uk/bitstream/2438/4018/1/EAI%20Conceptual%20Model%20-%20CRC.pdf

Kamal-Vaezi, S., and Bimar, H.S. (2009). Comparison of E-readiness assessment models, Full Length Research Paper. *Scientific Research and Essay*, 4(5):501–512.

Kao, L-J., Lu, C-C., and Chiu C-C. (2011). The training institution efficiency of the semiconductor institute programme in Taiwan—application of spatiotemporal ICA with DEA approach. *Journal of the Operational Research Society, 62(12): 2162–2172.*

Kaplan, R., and Norton, D.P. (1992). The Balanced Scorecard – Measures That Drive Performance. *Harvard Business Review*, 71–79.

Karadimas, N.V., Papatzelou, K., and Papantoniou, A.N. (2008). M-Government services in Greece. In: *Proceedings, 22nd European Conference on Modelling and Simulation*, Accessed April 4, 2014. http://www.scs-europe.net/conf/ecms2008/ecms2008%20CD/ecms2008%20pdf/ibs-ECMS2008_0135.pdf .

Karunasena, K., and Deng, H. (2010). Exploring the Public Value of e-Government: An Empirical Study from Sri Lanka. In: *23rd Bled eConference eTrust: Implications for the Individual, Enterprises and Society, June 20–23, 2010; Bled, Slovenia*, Accessed April 15, 2014. https://domino.fov.uni-mb.si/proceedings.nsf/0/89113f16ffd4e6e7c1257757003bfa7b/$FILE/21_Karunasena.pdf

Kažemikaitienė, E., and Bilevičienė, T. (2008). Problems of involvement of disabled persons in e-Government. Technological and economic development. *Baltic Journal on Sustainability*. 14(2):184–196.

Kearns, P. (2002). Towards the Connected Learning Society: An International Overview of Trends in Policy for Information and Communication Technology in Education, Accessed April 1, 2014. http://www.voced.edu.au/content/ngv9887 .

Keller, C., Hrastinski, S., and Carlsson, S.A. (2008). Students' Acceptance of E-Learning Environments: A Comparative Study In Sweden and Lithuania, In: Österle H, Schelp J and Winter R. Eds., *Proceedings of the Fifteenth European Conference on Information Systems*, 395–406, Accessed April 4, 2014. http://is2.lse.ac.uk/asp/aspecis/20070083.pdf

Kelly, G., Mulgan, G., and Muers, S. (2002). *Creating public value: An analytical framework for public service reform*. Strategy Unit, Cabinet Office, UK.

Keohane, R.O., and Nye, J.S. (2000). Introduction. In Nye, J.S. and Donahue, J.D. (editors), *Governance in a Globalization World*. Washington, D.C.: Brookings Institution Press.

Keppel. G. (1991). *Design and Analysis: A Researcher's Handbook*, 3rd edition, Prentice Hall.

Khalil, O.E.M. (2011). E-Government readiness: Does national culture matter? *Government Information Quarterly*, 28, 388–399.

Kijsanayotin, B., Pannarunothai, S., and Speedie, S.M. (2009). Factors influencing health information technology adoption in Thailand's community health centers: Applying the UTAUT model. *International Journal of Medical Informatics*, 78(6):404–416.

Kim, H. (2002). Predicting how ontologies for the Semantic Web will evolve. *Communications of the ACM – Special Issue of Ontological Engineering*, 45(2):48–54

Kim, Y., Kelly, T., and Raja, S. (2010). *Building Broadband: Strategies and Policies for the Developing World*. Global Information and Communication Technologies (GICT) Department, World Bank, Washington, Accessed April 4, 2014. http://siteresources.worldbank.org/EXTINFORMATIONANDCOMMUNICATIONANDTECHNOLOGIES/Resources/282822-1208273252769/Building_broadband.pdf

Kim, S., and Malhotra, N.K. (2005). A longitudinal model of continued is use: an integrative view of four mechanisms underlying post-adoption phenomena. *Management Science*, 51 (5):741–55.

Kimchi, J., Polivka, B., and Stevenson, J.S. (1991). Triangulation: Operational definitions. *Nursing Research*, 40(6):364–366.

Kitaw, Y. (2006). E-Government in Africa prospects, challenges and practices, Accessed April 4, 2014. http://www.friends-partners.org/GLOSAS/Global_University/Global%20University%20System/List%20Distributions/2008/MTI1948_05-27-08/E-Government_in_Africa%20copy.pdf

Klievink, B. and Janssen, M. (2009). Realizing Joined-up Government. Dynamic Capabilities and Stage Models for Transformation. *Government Information Quarterly*, 26(2): 275–284.

Knight, P. (2007). Knowledge Management and e-Government in Brazil. Paper prepared for the *Workshop on Managing Knowledge to Build Trust in Government, 7th Global Forum on Reinventing Government, 26–29 June 2007, Vienna, Austria,* Accessed April 15, 2014. http://unpan1.un.org/intradoc/groups/public/documents/unpan/unpan025989.pdf

Koh, C.E., and Prybutok, V.R. (2003). The Three Ring Model and Development of an instrument for Measuring Dimensions of e-Government Functions. *Journal of Computer Information Systems*, 33(3):34–39.

Koh, C.E., Prybutok, V.R., and Zhang, X. (2008). Measuring e-Government readiness. *Information and Management*, 45:540–546.

Kokkinaki, A. I., Mylonas, S., and Mina, S. (2005). E-Government Initiatives in Cyprus. E-Government Workshop '05, September 13 2005, Brunel University. West London, UK, Accessed April 29, 2014. http://www.iseing.org/egov/eGOV05/Source%20Files/Papers/CameraReady-25-P.pdf

Konde, V. (2007). What type of national ICT policies maximize ICT benefits? *African Technology Development Forum (ATDF) Journal*, 4(1):37–48, Accessed April 1, 2014. http://www.atdforum.org/IMG/pdf_what_ICT_policies_work_Konde.pdf

Koufaris, M. (2002). Applying the technology acceptance model and flow theory to online consumer behaviour. *Information Systems Research*, 13(2):205–223.

Kovacic, Z. (2005). The impact of national culture on e-Government readiness. *Information Science Journal*, 8:146–158.

Kumar, R., and Best, M.L. (2006). Impact and Sustainability of E-Government Services in Developing Countries: Lessons Learned from Tamil Nadu, India. *The Information Society*, 22:1–12.

Kumar, M., and Sinha, O. P. (2007). M-Government – Mobile Technology for E-Government. In: *Proceedings of the International Conference on E-government, India*, 294–301. Accessed April 15, 2014. http://workspace.unpan.org/sites/internet/documents/S4IN13%20M-Government%E2%80%93Mobile%20Technology%20for%20e-Government.pdf

Kumar, V., Mukerji, B., Irfan, B., and Ajax, P. (2007). Factors for successful e-Government adoption: a Conceptual Framework. *The Electronic Journal of e-Government*. 5(1):63–77.

Kumar, S.P., and Umashankar, C. (2010). E-Governance Applications for citizens- Issues and Framework. *International Journal on Computer Science and Engineering*, 2(7):2362–2365.

Kushchu, I., and Kuscu, H (2003). From E-Government to M-government: Facing the Inevitable. In: *Proceeding of European conference on E-Government* (ECEG 2003), 13–14 June, Como, Italy, Accessed April 15, 2014. http://citeseerx.ist.psu.edu/viewdoc/download?doi=10.1.1.113.2448&rep=rep1&type=pdf

Kraemer, K.L., and King, J.L. (2003). Information Technology and Administrative Reform: Will the Time After E-Government Be Different? Paper prepared for the *Heinrich Reinermann Schrift fest, Post Graduate School of Administration, Speyer, Germany,* Accessed April 4, 2014. http://unpan1.un.org/intradoc/groups/public/documents/APCITY/UNPAN022640.pdf

Kwon, H. (2000). A test of the technology acceptance model: the case of cellular telephone adoption. In: Proceedings of the *33rd Annual Hawaii International Conference on System Sciences, Big Island, HI, USA,* Accessed April 15, 2014. http://citeseerx.ist.psu.edu/viewdoc/download?doi=10.1.1.101.4295&rep=rep1&type=pdf

Lanwin, B. (2002). A Project of Info Dev and The Center for Democracy and Technology: The E-Government handbook for developing countries, Accessed April 4, 2014. http://www.cdt.org/egov/handbook/2002-11-14egovhandbook.pdf

Lau, T.Y., Aboulhoson, M., Lin, C., and Atkin, D. (2008). Adoption of e-Government in three Latin American countries: Argentina, Brazil and Mexico. *Telecommunications Policy*, 32(2): 88–100.

Lawley, E.L. (1999). Making sense of doctoral student attribution in library and information science, Accessed April 9, 2014. http://www.itcs.com/elawley/elldiss.pdf

Lawson-Body, A., and Miller, G. (2006). Investigating a theoretical foundation of e-Government performance: an exploratory study. *Journal of E-Business*, 5(2):76–97.

Layne, K., and Lee, J. (2001). Developing fully functional e-Government: a four stage model. *Government Information Quarterly,* 18(2):122–137.

Le Compte, M. and Preissle, J. (1993): *Ethnography and Qualitative Design in Educational Research*. London: Academic Press Inc.

Leão, P.A.S. (2006). E-Brasil: e-Development for Brasil and Its States. In: *Global e- Government for Developent Conference, University of Maryland, USA, 22–23 March 2006,* Accessed April 2, 2014. .

Lederer, A.L., Maupin, D.J., Sena, M.P., and Zhuang, Y. (2000). The technology acceptance model and the World Wide Web. *Decision Support Systems*, 29:269–282.

Lee, T.Y., Yee, P.K., and Cheung, D.W. (2009). E-government Data Interoperability Framework in Hong Kong. In: *Proceedings of the International Conference on Interoperability for Enterprise Software and Applications, Beijing, China, 21–22 April 2009*, 239 – 244. Accessed April 4, 2014. http://i.cs.hku.hk/~dcheung/publication/i-esa2009.pdf

Lee, J-W. (2010). 10 year retrospect on stage models of e-Government: A qualitative meta-synthesis. *Government Information Quarterly*, 27:220–230.

Lee, S.K., and Gibson, D.V. (2002). Towards knowledge-based economy in Korea: metrics and policy. *International Journal of Technology, Policy and Management, 2(3): 301–313.*

Lee, H., O'Keefe, B., and Yun, K. (2001). The Growth of Broadband Internet Connections in South Korea: Contributing Factors. *The Information Society, 9*:82–93.

Lee, J.H., Kim, H.J., and Ahn, M.J. (2011). The willingness of e-Government service adoption by business users: The role of offline service quality and trust in technology. Government Information Quarterly. *Government Information Quarterly*, 28:222–230

Lee, Y-C., Li, M-L., Yen, T-M., and Huang, T-H. (2010). Analysis of adopting an integrated decision making trial and evaluation laboratory on a technology acceptance model. *Expert Systems with Applications*, 37(2):1745–1754.

Legris, P., Ingham J., and Collerette, P. (2003). Why do people use information technology? A critical review of the technology acceptance model. *Information and Management*, 40(3):191–204.

Leitner, C. (2003). eGovernment in Europe: The State of Affairs. eEurope Awards, Eipascope, 3, Accessed April 4, 2014. http://aei.pitt.edu/5922/1/scop_3_5.pdf

Lenk, K., and Traunmüller, R. (2001). Broadening the concept of electronic government. In: Prins, J.E.J., Editor. *Designing E-Government.* Kluwer Law International: Netherlands, The Hague, 63–74.

Liang, H., Xue, Y., and Byrd, T. A. (2003). PDA usage in healthcare professionals: testing an extended technology acceptance model. *International Journal of Mobile Communications,* 1(4): 372–389.

Liker, J., and Sindi, A. (1997). User acceptance of expert systems: A test of the theory of reasoned action. *Journal of Engineering and Technology Management*, 14(2):147–173.

Lin, F., Fofanah, S.S., and Liang, D. (2011). Assessing citizen adoption of e-Government initiatives in Gambia: A validation of the technology acceptance model in information systems success. *Government Information Quarterly*, 28:271–279.

Lincoln, Y.S., and Guba, E.G. (1985). *Naturalistic inquiry*. Newbury Park, CA: Sage.

Lind, M., Östberg, O., and Johannisson, O. (2009). Acting out the Swedish e-Government action plan. *International Journal of Public Information Systems*, 2:37–60.

Lips, A.M.B., Eppel, E.A., Cunningham, A., and Hopkins- Burns, V. (2010). *Public Attitudes to the Sharing of Personal Information in the Course of Online Public Service Provision, Final Research Report*. Wellington, New Zealand: Victoria University of Wellington, Accessed April 17, 2014. http://e-government. vuw.ac.nz/summary_IRD.aspx.

Liu, J., Derzsi, Z., Raus, M., and Kipp, A. (2008). E-Government project evaluation: An Integrated framework. *Lecture Notes in Computer Science*, 5184:85–97.

Liu, B., Madhavan, R., and Sudharshan, D. (2005). DiffuNET: The impact of network structure on diffusion of innovation. *European Journal of Innovation Management*, 8(2):240–262.

Löfgren, K. (2007). The governance of e-Government: a governance perspective on the Swedish e-Government strategy. *Public, Policy and Administration*, 22(3):335–352.

Löfstedt, L. (2005). E-Government assessment of current research and some proposals for future directions. *International Journal of Public Information Systems*, Accessed April 2, 2014. http://www.ijpis.net/issues/no1_2005/IJPIS_no1_2005_p4.pdf .

Löfstedt, U. (2007). Public e-services research a critical analysis of current research in Sweden. *International Journal of Public Information Systems*, Accessed April 3, 2014. http://www.ijpis.net/ojs/index.php/IJPIS/article/view/44/40.

Luk, S.C.Y. (2009). The impact of leadership and stakeholders on the success/failure of e-Government service: Using the case study of e-stamping service in Hong Kong. *Government Information Quarterly*, 26:594–604.

Luna-Reyes, L.F., and Gil-García, J.R. (2011). Using Institutional Theory and Dynamic Simulation to Understand Complex E-Government Phenomena. *Government Information Quarterly*, 28 (3), 329–345.

Lytinen, K., and Damsgaard, J. (2001). What's wrong with the diffusion of innovation theory? In: *Proceedings of the 4th Working Conference on Diffusing Software Products and Process Innovations, Banff, Canada*, Accessed April 3, 2014. http://citeseerx.ist.psu.edu/viewdoc/download?doi=10.1.1.9.592&rep=rep1&type=pdf

Ma, L., Chung, J., and Thorson, S. (2005). E-Government in China: Bringing economic development through administrative reform. *Government Information Quarterly*, 22:20–37.

Mabila, F., Mboane, J.M.N., and Mondlane, A.I. (2010). *Mozambique ICT Sector Performance Review 2009/2010: Towards Evidence-based ICT Policy and Regulation. No 2, Policy Paper 16/2010*. Accessed March 13, 2014. http://www.researchictafrica.net/publications/ICT_Sector_Performance_Reviews_2010/Vol%202%20Paper%2016%20-%20Mozambique%20ICT%20Sector%20Performance%20Review%202010.pdf

Mahajan, V., Muller, E., and Bass, F. (1990). New product diffusion models in marketing: A review and directions for research. *Journal of Marketing*, 54(1):1–26.

Malinauskienė, E. (2013). Conceptual framework for context-based e-government interoperability development. *Socialinės technologijos; social technologies*, 3(1): 68–84

Mamelodi-Onyadile, C. (2008). E-Government in Africa progress made and challenges ahead, Accessed March 18, 2014, http://unpan1.un.org/intradoc/groups/public/documents/un/unpan033663.pdf

Mancinelli, E. (2008). E-Inclusion in the Information Society, Accessed April 4, 2014. http://www.ittk.hu/netis/doc/ISCB_eng/10_Mancinelli_final.pdf

Maio, A.D. (2003). Beyond ROI in e-Government: introducing the Public Value of IT. *IDA e-Government News*, European Commission, December 2003, Accessed April 4, 2014. http://www.epractice.eu/en/news/283733.

Maioli, C. (Ed.). (2008). E-Government and digital inclusion, *Prensas Universitarias de Zaragoza*, Accessed March 18, 2014. http://zaguan.unizar.es/record/4286/files/BOOK--2009-009.pdf

Marchewka, J.T., Liu, C., and Kostiwa, K. (2007). An Application of the UTAUT Model for Understanding Student Perceptions Using Course Management Software. *Communications of the IIMA*, 7(2): 93–104.

Markellou, P., Panayiotaki, A., and Tsakalidis, A. (2003). E-Government and Applications Levels. In: *Proceedings of IADIS Conference e-Society, June 3–6, 2003,Portugal*, 2:849–854, Accessed April 15, 2014. http://delab.csd.auth.gr/bci1/Panhellenic/58markellou.pdf

Markellos, K., Markellou, P., Panayiotaki, A., and Stergianeli, E. (2007). Current State of Greek e-Government Initiatives. *Journal of Business Systems, Governance and Ethics*, 2(3):67–88.

Marshall, G.W. and Stamps, M.B. (2005). Sales force use of technology: Antecedents to technology acceptance. *Journal of Business Research*, 58:1623–1631.

Martinsons, M.G., Davison, R.M., and Tse, D.S.K. (1999). The Balanced Scorecard: A foundation for the strategic management of information systems. *Decision Support Systems*, 25 (1):71–88.

Masrom, M. (2007). Technology Acceptance Model and E-learning. *In: Proceedings of the 12th International Conference on Education, Brunei Darussalam*, 21–24. Accessed April 15, 2014. http://eprints.utm.my/5482/1/MaslinMasrom2006_Techn.pdf

Materska, K. (2004). Librarians in the knowledge age. *New Library World*, 105(1198/9):142–148.

Matenga, C.R. (1998). Corruption: is it endemic in Zambia? Published on the Internet by the SAP – Project, Electronic Publications from the University of Zambia, Lusaka, Accessed January 28, 2011, http://www.fiuc.org/iaup/esap/publications/zambia/corruption.pdf

Maumbe, B.M., Owei, V., and Alexander, H. (2008). Questioning the pace and pathway of e-government development in Africa: A case study of South Africa's Cape Gateway project. *Government Information Quarterly*, 25: 757–777.

Mbeki, T. (2000). Keynote address of the President of the ANC to the National General Council, Accessed April 15, 2014. http://www.anc.org.za/show.php?id=2560 .

McClure, D.L. (2000). Statement of David L McClure, US General Accounting Office, before the subcommittee on Government Management, Information and technology, Committee on Government reform, House of Representatives, Accessed April 1, 2014. http://www.gao.gov/new.items/a200179t.pdf .

McConnell. International with World Information Technology and Services Alliance (WITSA). (2000). *Risk e-business: seizing the opportunity of global e-readiness*, Accessed April 3, 2014. http://www.witsa.org/papers/e-readiness.pdf

Mehrtens, J., Cragg, P.B., and Mills, A.M. (2001). A Model of Internet Adoption by SMEs. *Information and Management*, 39:165–176.

Menda, A. (2005). Successes and Challenges: E-Governance in Tanzania, Accessed April 3, 2014. http://www.tanzaniagateway.org/news/news/article.asp?ID=76.

Menon, S. (2011). Policy agendas for South Korea's broadband convergence network infrastructure project. *Journal of policy, regulation and strategy for telecommunications*, 13(2):19–34.

Merriam, S.B. (1998). *Qualitative Research and Case Study Applications in Education*. San Francisco: Jossey-Bass Inc.

Michel, H. (2005). E-Administration, e-Government, e-Governance and the Learning City: A typology of Citizenship management using ICTs. *The Electronic Journal of e-Government*, 3(4):213–218.

Mills, L., and Brail, S.G. (2004). New media in the new millennium: The Toronto Cluster in Transition. UToronto working paper series. Accessed February 11, 2013, http://www.utoronto.ca/isrn/publications/WorkingPapers/Working00/Mills00_NewMedia.pdf.

Mimicopoulos, M.G. (2004). *E-Government funding activities and strategies*. Department of Economic and Social Affairs, Division for Public Administration and Development Management, United Nations, New York.

Minow, M. (2010). *Policy considerations – what are the legal risks?* Accessed April 2, 2014. http://www.egovflorida.org/pdfs/E-GovernmentServicesinFloridaPublicLibraries-Final.pdf

Misra, D.C. (2007). Ten guiding principles for knowledge management in e-Government in developing countries. *First International Conference on knowledge Management for Productivity and Competitiveness*, New Delhi, 1–13, Accessed April 1, 2014. http://unpan1.un.org/intradoc/groups/public/documents/UNPAN/UNPAN025338.pdf

Mitchell, E.S. (1986). Multiple triangulation: A methodology for nursing science. *Advances in Nursing Science*, 8(3):18–26.

Modinis. (2007). *Breaking Barriers to e-Government: Overcoming obstacles to improving European public services*, Accessed April 1, 2014. http://www.inst-informatica.pt/servicos/informacao-e-documentacao/biblioteca-digital/gestao-e-organizacao/Deliverable_1b_Aug_16_2006.pdf.

Mohd-Suki, N., and Ramayah, T. (2011). Modelling Customer's Attitude Towards e-Government Services, *International Journal of Human and Social Sciences*, 6(1), Accessed March 28, 2014. http://mpra.ub.uni-muenchen.de/41601/1/MPRA_paper_41601.pdf.

Moon, M.J. (2010). Shaping M-Government for emergency management: Issues and challenges. *Journal of e-Governance*, 33:100–107.

Moon, M.J. (2002). The evolution of E-Government among municipalities: Rhetoric or Reality? *Public Administration Review*, 62(4):424–433.

Moon, J.W., and Kim, Y.G. (2001). Extending the TAM for a world-wide-web context. *Information and Management*, 38:217–230.

Muafi, R., Gusaptono, H., Effendi, M.I., and Charibaldi, N. (2012). The Information Technology (IT) Adoption Process and E- Readiness to Use within Yogyakarta Indonesian Small Medium Enterprises (SME). *International Journal of Information and Communication Technology Research*, 2(1), Accessed April 1, 2014. http://esjournals.org/journaloftechnology/archive/vol2no1/vol2no1_5.pdf

Muir, A., and Oppenheim, C. (2002). National Information Policy Developments Worldwide in Electronic Government. *Journal of Information Science*, 28(3):173–186.

Mulozi, D.L. (2008). Rural access: options and challenges for connectivity and energy in Zambia. International Institute for Communication and Development (IICD) thematic report, Accessed April 2, 2014. http://www.iicd.org/files/Zambia-Rural-Access-Report.pdf

Mtingwi, J., and Van Belle, J-P. (2012). The State of E-Government and M-Government Readiness in Malawi. *International Journal of Information Technology and Computer Science*, 6: 58–68.

Mutula, S.M. (2010). Deploying Development Informatics in Bridging the Digital Divide: Challenges and Opportunities. In: *11th DIS Annual Conference 2010, 2–3 September, Richardsbay, University of Zululand, South Africa,* Accessed April 3, 2014. http://www.lis.uzulu.ac.za/research/conferences/2010/DIS%20conferenceFP%20Mutula%20Sept%20%2025%20final.pdf

Mutula, S.M. (2013). E-Government Divide: Implications for sub-Saharan Africa. In: *Information Ethics for Africa: Cross-cutting Themes.* Pretoria: African Centre of Excellence for Information Ethics,59–69, Accessed April 15, 2014. http://www.africainfoethics.org/pdf/ie_africa/chapter_6.pdf

Mutula, S.M. and Van Brakel, P. (2006). An evaluation of e-readiness assessment tools with respect to information access: Towards an integrated information rich tool. *International Journal of Information Management*, 26(3):212–223.

Naidoo, G. (2004). Introduction of E-governance and its implications for developing countries. In: Gupta. M.P. (ed.) *Towards E-Governance Management Challenges*, 145–154. New Delhi. India. Tata McGraw Hill Publishing Company.

Naidoo, G., and Van Jaarsveldt. (2004). Electronic government: Strategies and Implementations: E-governance in South Africa: A perspective on initiatives, readiness and development issues. In: Gupta, M.P. (ed.). *Towards E-governance Management Challenges*, 138–144. New Delhi. India. Tata McGraw Hill Publishing Company.

Nanayakkara, C. (2007). A Model of User Acceptance of Learning Management Systems: a study within Tertiary Institutions in New Zealand, Accessed April 4, 2014. http://litteacher.com/StuffFromMac/Walden/Application/A%20Model%20of%20User%20Acceptance%20of%20Learning%20Management%20Systems.pdf

Napoli, J., Ewing, M.T., and Pitt, L.F. (2008). Factors Affecting the Adoption of the Internet in the Public Sector. *Journal of Nonprofit and Public Sector Marketing*, 7:77–88.

Navarra, D.D., and Cornford, T. (2007). The state, democracy and the limits of new public management: Exploring alternative models of e-Government. Presented at the *e-Government Workshop '06 (Egov06) September 11 2006, Brunel University, London, UB8 3PH*, 1–14, Accessed April 1, 2014. http://is2.lse.ac.uk/wp/pdf/wp155.pdf

Ndou, V.D. (2004). E-Government for developing countries: opportunities and challenges. *The Electronic Journal on Information Systems in Developing Countries*, 18(1):1–24.

NeGP Report. (2007). *Draft Report of the first phase of NeGP Impact Assessment Study.* Ahmedabad: Indian Institute of Management, Ahmedabad.

Ngulube, P. (2007). The Nature and Accessibility of E-Government in Sub Saharan Africa, *International Review of Information Ethics*, Vol. 7, Accessed April 3, 2014.

Ngulube, P. (2010). Mapping mixed methods research in library and information science journals in Sub-Saharan Africa: 2004–2008. *The International Information and Library Review*, 42:252–261.

Ngulube, P., Mokwatlo, K., and Ndwandwe, S. (2009). Utilisation and prevalence of mixed methods in library and information research in South Africa 2002–2008. *South African Journal of Library and Information Science*, 72(2):105–116.

Noh, Y.K. (2009). ICT development in Korea, Accessed March 30, 2014. http://www.tiaonline.org/gov_affairs/events/Young_Noh_Presentation.ppt.

Nordfors, L., Ericson, B., Lindell, H., and Lapidus, J. (2009). E-Government of Tomorrow: Future Scenarios for 2020. Gullers Group, Accessed March 30, 2014. http://www.vinnova.se/upload/epistorepdf/vr-09-28.pdf

Norris, P. (2001). *Digital Divide? Civic Engagement, Information Poverty and the Internet in Democratic Societies*. Cambridge: Cambridge University Press.

Nour, M., AbdelRahman, A., and FadlAllah, A. (2008). A Context-Based Integrative Framework for e-Government Initiatives. *Government Information Quarterly*, 25:448–461.

NOVOSEC. (2008). Authentication in E-Government, Authentication mechanisms and areas of application, Accessed April 11, 2011. https://www.bsi.bund.de/SharedDocs/Downloads/EN/BSI/ Egovernment/4_Authen_en_pdf.pdf?__blob=publicationFile

Nurdin, N., Stockdale, R., and Scheepers, H. (2011). Examining the Role of the Culture of Local Government on Adoption and Use of E-Government Services, Accessed March 6, 2014. http://link.springer.com/chapter/10.1007%2F978-3-642-15346-4_7#page-1.

Nyirenda, J., and Cropf, R. (2009). The Prospects for e-Government and eGovernance in Sub-Saharan Africa: A Case Study of Zambia. *Americas Conference on Information Systems (AMCIS)*, Conference Proceedings. Paper 261, Accessed April 1, 2014. http://aisel.aisnet.org/amcis2009/261.

Ochara-Muganda, N., and Van Belle, J.P. (2010). A Proposed Framework for E-Government Knowledge Infrastructures for Africa's Transition Economies, *Journal of e-Government Studies and Best Practices*, Accessed March 12, 2014. http://www.ibimapublishing.com/journals/JEGSBP/2010/303226/303226.pdf

OECD. (2004). E-Transformation Turkey Project: Turkish Case for e-Government. In: *OECD Meeting of Senior Officials from Centres of Government on Using New Tools for Decision-Making: Impacts on Information, Communication and Organisation, 7–8 October 2004, Istanbul, Turkey*, Accessed April 1, 2014. http://unpan1.un.org/intradoc/groups/public/documents/UNPAN/UNPAN025638.pdf

O'Cathain, A., Murphy, E., and Nicholl, J. (2007). Integration and publications as indicators of 'yield' from mixed methods studies. *Journal of Mixed Methods Research*, 1:147–163.

Ok, H-Y. (2011). New Media Practices in Korea. *International Journal of Communication*, 5:320–348, Accessed March 18, 2014. http://ijoc.org/ojs/index.php/ijoc/article/viewFile/701/527

Okot-Uma, R.W. (2000). *Electronic Governance: Re-Inventing Good Governance*. Commonwealth Secretariat, London.

Olson, J.R., and Boyer, K.K. (2003). Factors influencing the utilisation of Internet purchasing in small organisations. *Journal of Operations Management*, 21:225–245.

Ooh, K.L., Lean, O.K., Zailani, S., Ramayah, T., and Fernando, Y. (2009). Factors influencing intention to use e-Government services among citizens in Malaysia. *International Journal of Information Management*, 29(6):458–475.

Ojo, A., Janowski, T., and Estevez, E. (2007). *Determining progress towards e-Government: What are the core indicators?* UNU-IIST Report, No. 360. Macao, International Institute for Software Technology, United Nations University.

Osman, I.H., Anouze, A.L., Irani, Z., Lee, H., Balcı, A., Medeni, T.D., and Weerakkody, *V. (2011)*. A new COBRAS framework to evaluate e-government services: a citizen centric perspective. In:, *eGov Workshop'11 (1GOV11) March 17–18, 2011, Brunel University, West London, UB83PH 1*, Accessed April 15, 2014. http://www.iseing.org/tgovwebsite/tgovworkshop2011/CRCPDF/tGOV-3/Paper%203.pdf

Osterweil, L.J., Schweik, C.M., Sondheimer, N.K., and Thomas, C.W. (2004). Analyzing Processes for E-Government Application Development: The Emergence of Process Definition Languages. *Journal of E-Government*, 1(4): 63–87,

Othman, J.B., and Mokdad, L. (2010). Enhancing data security in ad hoc networks based on multipath routing. *Journal of Parallel and Distributed Computing*, 70(3):309–316.

Palvia, S.C.J., and Sharma, S.S. (2007). E-Government and E-Governance: Definitions/Domain Framework and Status around the World, Accessed March 17, 2014. http://www.iceg.net/2007/books/1/1_369.pdf

Pankowska, M. (2008). National frameworks' survey on standardization of e-government documents and processes for interoperability. *Journal of Theoretical and Applied Electronic Commerce Research*, 3(3), 64–82.

Panuwatwanich, K., Stewart, R.A., and Mohamed, S. (2009). Critical pathways to enhanced innovation diffusion and business performance in Australian design firms. *Automation in Construction*, 18(6):790–797.

Papadopoulou, P., Nikolaidou, M., and Martakos, D. (2010). What Is Trust in E-Government? A Proposed Typology. In: *Proceedings of the 43rd Hawaii International Conference on System Sciences (HICSS-43, 2010), Koloa, Kauai, Hawaii*. 1 – 10. Accessed April 20, 2014. http://cgi.di.uoa.gr/~peggy/papers/HICSS%202010.pdf

Paré, R. (2002). E-democracy and E-Government: how will these affect libraries? The Case of Canada. In: *68th IFLA Council and General Conference 18–24 August 2002,* Accessed March 25, 2014. http://archive.ifla.org/IV/ifla68/papers/107-090e.pdf

Park, H.M. (2008). *Hypothesis Testing and the Statistical Power of a Test*. Technical working paper. The University of Information Technology Services (UITS), Center for Statistical and Mathematical Computing, Indiana University.

Park, E.G., Lamontagne, M., Perez, A., Melikhova, I., and Bartlett, G. (2009). Running ahead toward interoperable e-Government: The government of Canada metadata framework. *International Journal of Information Management*, 29(2):145–150.

Park, S. Y. (2009). An Analysis of the Technology Acceptance Model in Understanding University Students' Behavioral Intention to Use e-Learning. *Educational Technology and Society*, *12* (3), 150–162.

Partnership on Measuring ICT for Development. (2009). Revisions and Additions to the Core List of ICT Indicators. Background paper for the *7th World Telecommunication/ICT Indicators Meeting, Cairo, Egypt, 3–5 March 2009. New York: United Nations Statistics Division,* Accessed March 10, 2014. http://unstats.un.org/unsd/statcom/doc09/BG-ICTIndicators.pdf

Pascual, P.J. (2003*). E-Government*. E-Asean Task Force, UNDP-APDIP.

Pathak, R. D., and Prasad, R. S. (2006). Role of E-governance in tackling corruption: The Indian Experience. In: Raza Ahmad (Ed.), *The role of public administration in building a harmonious society*. Philippines: Asian Development Bank, 434–463.

Pavlou, P. (2003). Consumer acceptance of electronic commerce: Integrating trust and risk with the technology acceptance model. *International Journal of Electronic Commerce,* 7(3):101–134.

Pedersen, P. (2005). Adoption of mobile internet services: An exploratory study of mobile commerce early adopters. *Journal of Organisational Computing and Electronic Commerce,* 15(3):203–222.

Pereira, J. (2009). *Zambia Aid effectiveness in the health sector*. Action for Global Health, Accessed March 30, 2014. http://www.actionforglobalhealth.eu/fileadmin/user_upload/doc_library/AE_Zambia_Case_Study_Final_version.pdf

Peters, R.M., Janssen, M., and Engers, T.M.V. (2004). Measuring e-Government impact: existing practices and shortcomings. In: *Conference Proceedings, 6th International Conference on Electronic Commerce (ICEC'2004). October 25–27, 2004, Delft, The Netherlands*. 480–489. Accessed April 20, 2014. http://dl.acm.org/citation.cfm?id=1052281

Petrauskas, R., Bilevičienė, T., and Kiškienė, A. (2008). E-Inclusion as the Part of E-Government Development in Lithuania. *Viešoji Politika IR Administravimas*, Nr. 23, Accessed April 3, 2014. http://www.ktu.lt/lt/mokslas/zurnalai/vpa/vpa23/VPA_Nr.23_R.Petrauskas_p.48-58.pdf

Pilling, D. and Boeltzig, H. (2007). Moving toward e-government: effective strategies for increasing access and use of the Internet among non-Internet users in the U.S. and U.K. In: *Proceedings of the 8th Annual International Digital Government Research Conference, 35–46. Bridging Disciplines and Domains, PA, USA, 20–23 May, 2007*. 35–46. Accessed April 20, 2014. http://dl.acm.org/citation.cfm?id=1248467

Polit, D.F., and Hunfgler, B.P. (1995). *Nursing research: Principles and methods*. 6th ed. Philadelphia: Lippincott.

Polit, D.F. and Beck, C.T. (2004). *Nursing research: Principles and methods*. 7th ed. Philadelphia: Lippincott, Williams and Wilkins.

Powell, M. (2006). *Rethinking education management information systems: Lessons from and options for less-developed countries*. Infodev Working Paper No. 6, Accessed March 20, 2014. http://www.infodev.org/en/Publication.504.html.

Potnis, D., and Pardo, T. (2008). The United Nations e-Government Readiness Index: a work in progress. In: *Proceedings of the 2008 international conference on Digital government research. Montreal, Canada, May 18–21, 2008*. 365–366. Accessed April 20, 2014. http://dl.acm.org/citation.cfm?id=1367895

Potnis, D., and Demissie, D. (2009). Barriers to Socio-economic Opportunities in Africa: An e-Government Perspective In: *iConference Proceedings* (2009), Accessed March 29, 2014. http://works.bepress.com/cgi/viewcontent.cgi?article=1018&context=devendra_potnis.

Prattipati, S. N. (2003). Adoption of e-governance: Differences between countries in the use of online government services. *Journal of American Academy of Business*, 3(1/2): 386–391.

Prybutok, V., Zhang, X., and Ryana, S. (2008). Evaluating leadership, IT quality, and net benefits in an e-Government environment. *Information and Management*, 45:143–152.

Public law. (2002). USA PUBLIC LAW 107–347—DEC. 17 2002, Accessed March 20, 2014. http://www.gpo.gov/fdsys/pkg/PLAW-107publ347/pdf/PLAW-107publ347.pdf

Pudaruth, S., Moloo, R.K., Mantaye, A., and Bibi, J.N. (2010). A Survey of E-Learning Platforms in Mauritius. *Proceedings of the World Congress on Engineering 2010 (WCE 2010), June 30 – July 2, 2010, London, U.K., Vol. I*, Accessed March 16, 2014. http://www.iaeng.org/publication/WCE2010/WCE2010_pp415-420.pdf

Pudjianto, B., and Hangjung, Z. (2009). Factors Affecting e-Government Assimilation in Developing Countries, Accessed April 1, 2014. http://www.cprsouth.org/wp-content/uploads/drupal/Boni%20Pudjianto.pdf

Ralyte, J., Jeusfeld, M.A., Backlund, P., Kuhn, H., and Arni-Bloch, N. (2008). A knowledge-based approach to manage information systems interoperability. *Information Systems Journal*, 33:754–784.

Rahman, M.M., and Rajon, A.A. (2012). An Effective Framework for Implementing Electronic Governance in Developing Countries: Bangladesh Perspective. *International Journal of Computer and Information Technology (IJCIT)*, 3(1), Accessed April 4, 2014. http://www.ijcit.org/ijcit_papers/vol3no1/IJCIT-120704.pdf

Raj, D. (1972). *The Design of Sample Surveys.* McGraw-Hill Book Company, New York.

Ramayah, T. (2005). Doing e-research with e-library: determinants of perceived ease of use of e-library. *International Journal of Technology, Knowledge and Society,* 1(4):71–82.

Raus, M., Liu, J-W., and Kipp, A. (2010). Evaluating IT innovations in a business-to-government context: A framework and its applications. *Government Information Quarterly*, 27:122–133.

Ravi, R. (2009). E-Government Unit Ministry of Communication and Information Technology E-Government Interoperability Framework (e-GIF) Government of the Islamic Republic of Afghanistan e-GIF Implementation, Management and Compliance, VERSION 1.0, May 2009. Ministry of Communication and Information Technology, Government of the Islamic Republic of Afghanistan, Kabul.

Remenyi, D., Williams, B., Money A., and Swartz, E. (1998). *Doing Research in Business and Management: An Introduction to Process and Method*, London: SAGE.

Rodger, J.A., Pendharkar, P.C., and Bhatt, G.D. (1996). Diffusion theory and the adoption of software innovation: Common errors and future issues. *The Journal of High Technology Management Research*, 7(1):1–13.

Rogers, E. (1962). *Diffusion of innovations*, New York, USA: The Free Press.

Rokhman, A. (2011). Potential Users and Critical Success Factors of e-Government Services: The Case of Indonesia. *International Conference on Public Organization: ICONPO 2011,* 231–244. Yogyakarta: University of Muhammadiyah Yogyakarta.

Rorissa, A., and Demissie, D. (2010). An analysis of African e-Government service websites. *Government Information Quarterly*, 27:161–169.

Rose, G., and Straub, D. (1998). Predicting General IT Use: Applying TAM to the Arabic World. *Journal of Global Information Management, 6*(3):39–46.

Roundtable Report (2002). Singapore, ICA 36th Conference, Singapore, October 2002, Accessed August 12, 2011, http://unpan1.un.org/intradoc/groups/public/documents/APCITY/UNPAN011283.pdf

Rowley, J. (2011). E-Government stakeholders—who are they and what do they want? *International Journal of Information Management,* 31:53–62.

Rowley, J. (2004). Researching people and organisations. *Library Management,* 25(4/5):208–214.

Roy, R. (2006). E-Service delivery and new governance capacities: 'Service Canada' as a case study. *International Journal of Services Technology and Management,* 7(3):253–271.

Saade, R.G., and Bahli, B. (2005). The impact of cognitive absorption on perceived usefulness and perceived ease of use in online learning: An extension of the technology acceptance model. *Information and Management*, 42:317–327.

Saadé, R.G., and Kira, D. (2007). Mediating the impact of technology usage on perceived ease of use by anxiety. *Computers and Education*, 49(4):1189–1204.

SADC. (2002). SADC e-Readiness Review and Strategy Recommendations of the SADC e-Readiness Task Force, Accessed March 7, 2014. http://unpan1.un.org/intradoc/groups/public/documents/cafrad/unpan006872.pdf .

SADC e-Readiness Task Force. (2002). SADC e-Readiness Review and Strategy – Recommendations of the SADC e-Readiness Task Force, Accessed March 29, 2014. http://schoolnetafrica.org/fileadmin/resources/SADC_report.pdf .

Sahin, I. (2006). Detailed review of Rogers' diffusion of innovations theory and educational technology-related studies based on Rogers' theory. *The Turkish Online Journal of Educational Technology*, 5(2), 14–23.

Sahraoui, S. (2007). E-inclusion as further stage of e-Government. *Transforming Government: People, Process and Policy*, 1(1):44–58.

Salant, P., and Dillman, D.A. (1994). *How to Conduct Your Own Survey*, New York: Wiley.

Salman, A. (2010). ICT, the New Media (Internet) and Development: Malaysian Experience. *The Innovation Journal: The Public Sector Innovation Journal*, 15(1).

Sampath, S. (2005). *Sampling theory and methods*. 2nd ed. Alpha Science International, UK.

Sander, J.I., Bell, P.J., and Rice, S.D. (2005). MIS Sustainability in Sub-Saharan Africa: Three Case Studies from The Gambia. *International Journal of Education and Development using Information and Communication Technology (IJEDICT)*, 1(3):135–159.

Sanson-Fisher R. (2004). Diffusion of innovation theory for clinical change. *Medical Journal of Australia*, 180(6):S55–S56.

Sarantis, D., Charalabidis, Y., and Askounis, D. (2011). A goal-driven management framework for electronic government transformation projects implementation. *Government Information Quarterly*, 28:117–128.

Sarker, P.P. (2001). Questioning the ICT Revolution: Structural Analysis of Information Society, Accessed April 2, 2014. http://unpan1.un.org/intradoc/groups/public/documents/apcity/unpan006303.pdf

Saunders, M., Lewis, P., and Thornhill, A. (2002). *Research methods for business students*, 3rd ed. Prentice Hall, Harlow.

Saxena, K.B.C. (2005). Towards excellence in e-Governance. *International Journal of Public Sector Management*, 18(6):498–513.

Seo, K-I. (2011). Innovating Public Procurement through Korea ON-line E-Procurement System. 33 PowerPoint slides, Accessed March 10, 2014. http://slideplayer.us/slide/728306/ .

Schooley, B.L., and Horan, T.A. (2007). Towards end-to-end government performance management: Case study of interorganizational information integration in emergency medical services (EMS). *Government Information Quarterly*, 24:755–784.

Schuppan, T. (2009). E-Government in developing countries: Experiences from sub-Saharan Africa. *Government Information Quarterly*, 26:118–127.

Sciadas, G. (2002). *Monitoring the digital divide*. UNESCO, Orbicom-CIDA Project Report. Montreal: Orbicom. Accessed May 4, 2006. http://www.orbicom.uqam.ca/projects/ddi2002/ddi2002.pdf

SCM. (2005). Delivering Reduction in Administrative Burden', SCM Network to Reduce Administrative Burdens, 2005, Accessed August 6, 2010, http://ec.europa.eu/information_society/newsroom/cf/ document.cfm?action=display&doc_id=391&ei=j_FQTuqFAse2hAfF6JDVBg&usg=AFQjCNHSTUZS89y5e1uCXWWUjl2wU6mjmw.

Scott, J., and Marshall, G., eds. (2005). *Oxford dictionary of sociology*, 3rd ed. New York: Oxford University Press.

Scott, W.R. (2004).Institutional Theory: Contributing to a Theoretical Research Program. In: Ken G. Smith and Michael A. Hitt (Eds), *Great Minds in Management: The Process of Theory Development*. Oxford UK: Oxford University Press.

Seifert, J. W., and Petersen, R.E. (2002). The Promise of All Things E? Expectations and Challenges of Emergent Electronic Government. *Perspectives on Global Development and Technology*, 1(2):193–212.

Sharma, S.K., and Gupta, J.N.D. (2003). Building Blocks of an E-Government – A Framework. *Journal of Electronic Commerce in Organizations*, 1(4): 34–48.

Sharma, S.K. (2006). An E-Government Services Framework.. In: Khosrow-Pour, M. (Ed.), *Encyclopedia of Commerce, E-Government and Mobile Commerce*, 373–378. Information Resources Management Association, Idea Group Reference, USA.

Shanbhag, S. (2006). Alternative Models of Knowledge Production: a Step Forward in Information Literacy as a Liberal Art. *Library Philosophy and Practice*, 8(2), Accessed March 10, 2014. http://www.webpages.uidaho.edu/~mbolin/shanbhag.pdf

Shareef, A.M., Kumar, V., Kumar, U., and Dwivedi, Y.K. (2011). E-Government Adoption Model (GAM): Differing service maturity levels. *Government Information Quarterly*, 28:17–35.

Sharifi, M., and Manian, A. (2010). The study of the success indicators for pre-implementation activities of Iran's E-Government development projects. *Government Information Quarterly*, 27(1):63–69.

Shareef, M.A., Kumar, V., Kumar, U., and Dwivedi, Y.K. (2011). E-Government Adoption Model (GAM): Differing service maturity levels. *Government Information Quarterly*, 28, 17–35.

Shareef, M., Ojo, A., and Janowski, T. (2008). A readiness assessment framework for egovernment planning: design and application. In: *2nd International Conference on Theory and Practice of Electronic Governance (ICEGOV2008)*. Cairo, Egypt: ACM.

Shen, C.C., and Chiou, J-S. (2010). The impact of perceived ease of use on Internet service adoption: The moderating effects of temporal distance and perceived risk. *Computers in Human Behavior*, 26(1):42–50.

Shehadi, R.T., Khoury, R., Kassatly, F., and Lamaa, A. (2013). Self-Sustainable E-Government: A Road Map toFinancial Independence and Value Creation. *American Journal of Modeling and Optimization*, 1(3), 43–46.

Sheridan, W., and Riley, T. (2006). Comparing e-Government vs. e-governance. Commonwealth Center for e-Governance, Accessed March 24, 2014. http://www.egovmonitor.com/node/6556.

Simenda, K. (2009). Electronic/Mobile Government in Africa: Progress Made and Challenges Ahead. Addis Ababa, Ethiopia, Accessed May 17, 2013, http://www.unpan.org/emgkr_africa.

Singh, S. (2007). Department of Information and Computer Science. UNISA. South Africa. (Interview on 26th August 2007).

Singletary, L., Akbulut, A., and Houston, A. (2002). Innovative software use after mandatory adoption. In: *Proceedings of the 8th Americas Conference on Information Systems, Dallas, TX, USA*, 1135–1138, Accessed April 15, 2014. http://sighci.org/amcis02/RIP/Singletary.pdf

Sipior, J.C., and Ward, B.T. (2005). Bridging the Digital Divide for e-Government Inclusion: A United States Case Study. *Electronic Journal of e-Government*, 3 (3):137–146.

Smith, M.L. (2011). Limitations to building institutional trustworthiness through e-Government: a comparative study of two e-services in Chile. *Journal of Information Technology*, 26:78–93.

Sorrentino, M., and Niehaves, B. (2010). Intermediaries in E-Inclusion: A literature review. In: *Proceedings of the 43rd Hawaii International Conference on System Sciences*. IEEE Computer Society, 1–10.

Srivastava, S.C., and Teo, T.S.H. (2007). E-Government payoffs: evidence from cross-country data. *Journal of Global Information Management*, 15(4):20–40.

Stafford, T.F., and Turan, A.H. (2011). Online tax payment systems as an emergent aspect of governmental transformation. *European Journal of Information Systems*, 1–15.

Stamoulis, D., Theotokis, D., Martakos, D., and Gyftodimos, G. (2003). A teleological Development of Design-Decisions-Independent' Information Systems. In: N Patel, Ed. *Adaptive Evolutionary Information Systems*. Idea Publishing Group, 81–104.

Stanimirovic, D., and Vintar, M. (2013). Conceptualization of an Integrated Indicator Model for the Evaluation of e-Government Policies. *Electronic Journal of e-Government,* 11(2), 293–307.

Stiftung, B. (2002). Balanced E-Government: E-Government – Connecting Efficient Administration and Responsive Democracy: A study by the Bertelsmann Foundation, Accessed April 2, 2014. http://www.eamericas.org/documentos/BertelsmanFoundationeGov02.pdf .

Stokes, D.E. (1997). *Pasteur's quadrant: Basic science and technological innovation.* Washington, DC: Brookings Institution Press.

Straub, D. (1994). The Effect of Culture on IT Diffusion: E-mail and Fax in Japan and the US. *Information Systems Research*, 5(1):23–47.

Straub, D., Keil, M., and Brenner, W. (1997). Testing the technology acceptance model across cultures: A three country study. *Information and Management*, 33:1–11.

Subbiah, A., and Ibrahim, O. (2011). Value Co-Creation Process: A Case of E-Services for G2C in Malaysia. *European Journal of Social Sciences,* 19(3):443–449.

Suinat, O. (2007). E-Government Leadership, Accessed April 1, 2014. http://cif.docrix.ru/docs/5/index-36226.html

Sundaravej, T. (2010). Empirical validation of unified theory of acceptance and use of technology model. *Journal of Global Information Technology Management,* 13 (1), 5–27.

Sutinen, E., and Tedre, M. (2010). ICT4D: A computer science perspective. Lecture Notes in Computer Science, 221–231, Accessed July 20, 2011, http://link.springer.com/chapter/10.1007%2F978-3-642-12476-1_16#page-2.

Syamsuddin, I., and Hwang, J–S. (2010). A New Fuzzy MCDM Framework to Evaluate E-Government Security Strategy, In: *Proceedings of the IEEE 4th International Conference on Application of Information and Communication Technologies AICT2010,* Accessed April 1, 2014. https://www.researchgate.net/publication/224185924_A_new_fuzzy_MCDM_framework_to_evaluate_e-government_security_strategy.

Takahashi, T. (2000). *Brazil, Ministry of Science and Technology 2001,* Information Society in Brazil: Green Book, Ministry of Science and Technology, Brasilia.

Talbot, C. (2008). Measuring public value – A competing values approach: A paper for The Work Foundation. Herbert Simon Institute, Manchester Business School, UK, Accessed April 2, 2014. http://www.theworkfoundation.com/Assets/Docs/measuring_PV_final2.pdf

Tan, B.C.C., Pan, S.L., and Cha, V. (2008). *The evolution of Singapore's government infocomm plans: Singapore's e-Government journey from 1980 to 2007.* Singapore: National University of Singapore.

Tassabehji, R. (2005). Inclusion in e-Government: A Security Perspective. In: *E-Government Workshop '05 (eGOV05), Brunel University,* Accessed April 16, 2014. http://www.iseing.org/egov/egov05/source%20files/papers/cameraready-41-p.pdf

Tassabehji, R. and Elliman, T. (2006). Generating Citizen Trust in e-Government using a Trust Verification Agent: A Research Note. In: *European and Mediterranean Conference on Information Systems (EMITS),* Accessed April 1, 2014. http://www.iseing.org/emcis/emcis2006/Proceedings/Contributions/EGISE/eGISE4.pdf .

Tashakkori, A., and Creswell, J.W. (2007). Editorial: the new era of mixed methods. *Journal of Mixed Methods Research,* 1:3–7.

Tavana, M., Zandi, F., and Katehakis, M.N. (2013). A hybrid fuzzy group ANP–TOPSIS framework for assessment of e-government readiness from a CiRM perspective. *Information and Management*, 50, 383–397.
Teddlie, C., and Tashakkori, A. (2009). *Foundations of mixed methods research: Integrating quantitative and qualitative approaches in social and behavioral research*. Thousand Oaks, CA: Sage.
Teofilovic, N. (2002). The Reality of Innovation in Government. *The Innovation Journal,* Accessed April 3, 2014. http://www.innovation.cc/scholarly-style/reality.pdf
The Guardian. (2009). Nice talking to you – mobile phone use passes milestone. Tuesday 3 March 2009, Accessed April 3, 2014. http://www.guardian.co.uk/technology/2009/mar/03/mobile-phones1.
Thorbjornsen, H., Supphellen, M., Nysveen, H., and Pedersen, P.E. (2002). Building brand relationship online: a comparison of two interactive Applications. *Journal of interactive marketing*, 16(3):17–34.
Thong-Tee, C.T. (2003). Singapore's Policy and Regulatory Update for APEC. Telecommunications and Information Working Group. Taipei, Accessed April 3, 2014. http://aimp.apec.org/Documents/2009/TEL/TEL39-PLEN/09_tel39_plen_011.pdf
Titah, R., and Barki, H. (2006). E-Government adoption and acceptance: A literature review. *International Journal of Electronic Government Research*, 2(3):23–57.
Trimi, S., and Sevrani, K. (2010). Development of M-government Projects in a Developing Country: The Case of Albania. *International Journal of Information Technology Project Management (IJITPM)*, 1(3), 46–58.
Trusler, J. (2003). South African E-Government Policy and Practices: A Framework to Close the Gap, In Traunmüller, Roland (Ed.). "Electronic Government". In: *Proceedings 2nd International Conference EGOV2003*, Prague, Sep.2003. Lecture Notes in Computer Science, Springer-Verlag: Berlin, 2003, 504–507.
Tushman, M., and O'Reilly III, C. (2007). Research and relevance: implications of Pasteur's quadrant for doctoral programs and faculty development. *Academy of Management Journal,* 50(4):769–774.
UN e-Government Report (2003). *UN Global E-government Survey 2003,* Accessed April 3, 2014. http://unpan1.un.org/intradoc/groups/public/documents/un/unpan016066.pdf
UN e-Government Report (2008). *UN E-Government Survey 2008: From E-Government to Connected Governance*. UN White paper, Accessed April 15, 2014. http://unpan1.un.org/intradoc/groups/public/documents/un/unpan028607.pdf
UN e-Government report (2012). *United Nations E-Government Survey 2012: E-Government for the People,* Accessed April 3, 2014. http://unpan1.un.org/intradoc/groups/public/documents/un/unpan048065.pdf
UN e-Government Survey (2010). Leveraging e-Government at a time of financial and economic crisis, Accessed April 3, 2014. http://unpan1.un.org/intradoc/groups/public/documents/un/unpan038851.pdf
United Nations Department of Economics and Social Affairs (UNDESA). (2004). *E-Government Readiness Assessment Methodology,* Accessed April 3, 2014. http://unpan1.un.org/intradoc/groups/public/documents/un/unpan014224.pdf
United Nations Department of Economics and Social Affairs (UNDESA). (2005). *Global e-Government Readiness Report 2005: From e-Government to e-Inclusion,* Accessed April 15, 2014. *http://unpan1.un.org/intradoc/groups/public/documents/un/unpan021888.pdf*.

Valdés, G., Solar, M., Astudillo, H., Iribarren, M., Concha, G., and Visconti, M. (2011). Conception, development and implementation of an e-Government maturity model in public agencies. *Government Information Quarterly*, 28 (1): 176–187

Vencatachellum, I., and Pudaruth, S. (2010). Investigating E-Government Services Uptake in Mauritius: A User's Perspective. *International Research Symposium in Service Management,* Accessed April 3, 2014. http://www.uom.ac.mu/sites/irssm/papers/Vencatachellum%20&%20Pudaruth%20~%2073.pdf

Venkatesh, V., and Davis, F.D. (1996). A model of the antecedents of perceived ease of use: Development and test. *Decision Sciences*, 27(3):451–481.

Venkatesh, V., and Davis, F.D. (2000). A theoretical extension of the technology acceptance model: Four longitudinal field studies. *Management Science*, 46(2):186–204.

Venkatesh, V., Morris, M.G., and Davis, G.B. (2003). User acceptance of information technology: Toward a unified view. *MIS Quarterly*, 27(3):425–478.

Verdolini, E., and Galeotti, M. (2011). At home and abroad: An empirical analysis of innovation and diffusion in energy technologies. *Journal of Environmental Economics and Management*, 61(2):119–134.

Vernadat, F.B. (2010). Technical, semantic and organizational issues of enterprise interoperability and networking. *Annual Reviews in Control*, 34:139–44.

Verdegem, P. (2011). Social Media for Digital and Social Inclusion: Challenges for Information Society 2.0 Research and Policies. Paper presented at the *3rd ICTs and Society Meeting (June 29 – July 2, 2010; Internet Interdisciplinary Institute – IN3; Castelldefels – Barcelona, Spain),* Accessed April 17, 2014. http://www.triple-c.at/index.php/tripleC/article/viewFile/225/214.

Visser, W., and Twinomurinzi H. (2008). E-Government and Public Service Delivery: Enabling ICT to put 'People First' – A Case Study from South Africa, *Journal of Systemics, Cybernetics and Informatics*, 6(6):36–41, Accessed April 3, 2014. http://www.iiisci.org/journal/CV$/sci/pdfs/QP476DK.pdf

Votis, K., Alexakos, C., Vassiliadis, B., and Likothanassis, S. (2008). An Ontologically-Principled Service-Oriented Architecture for Managing Distributed E-Government Nodes. *Journal of Network and Computer Applications*, 31(2):131–148.

Wang, L., Rosenberg, M., and Lo, M. (2008). Ethnicity and utilization of family physicians: A case study of Mainland Chinese immigrants in Toronto, Canada. *Social Science and Medicine*, 67(9):1410–1422.

Wang, Y-S., and Shih, Y-W. (2009). Why do people use information kiosks? A validation of the Unified Theory of Acceptance and Use of Technology. *Government Information Quarterly*, 26(1):158–165.

Wangpipatwong, S., Chutimaskul, W. and Papasratorn, B. (2008). Understanding Citizen's Continuance Intention to Use e-Government Website: a Composite View of Technology Acceptance Model and Computer Self-Efficacy. *The Electronic Journal of e-Government*, 6(1):55–64.

Warkentin, M., Gefen, D., Pavlou, P., and Rose, G. (2002). Encouraging citizen adoption of E-Government by building trust. *Electronic Markets*, 12(3):157–162.

Weerakkody, V., Dwivedi, Y. K., Brooks, L., Williams, M. D., and Mwange, A. (2007). E-Government implementation in Zambia: Contributing Factors. *Electronic Government, An International Journal*, 4(4):484–505.

Weerakkody, V., El-Haddadeh, R., Sabol, T., Ghoneim, A., and Dzupka, P. (2012). E-government implementation strategies in developed and transition economies: A comparative study. *International Journal of Information Management*, 32, 66– 74.
Wescott, C.G. (1999). Guiding principles on civil service reform in Africa: an empirical review. *International Journal of Public Sector Management*, 12(2): 145–170
Wescott, C.G. (2003). E-Government to combat corruption in the Asia Pacific Region. In: 11th *International Anti-Corruption Conference, Seoul, Republic of Korea, 25 to 28 May 2003,* Accessed April 3, 2014. http://ieeexplore.ieee.org/stamp/stamp.jsp?arnumber=04680403 .
Wescott, C.G. (2009). E-Government in the Asia-Pacific Region. *Systemises, Cybernetics and Informatic*, 3(6): 37–42, Accessed April 3, 2014. http://www.iiisci.org/journal/CV$/sci/pdfs/P749171.pdf
Wescott, C. G. (2010). Uneven Progress in Meeting E-Government Challenges in Asia-Pacific (March 13, 2010). Asia Pacific Governance Institute Working Paper No. 1, Accessed April 3, 2014. https://papers.ssrn.com/sol3/Data_Integrity_Notice.cfm?abid=1570134.
West, D. M. (2000). Assessing e-Government: The Internet, Democracy, and Service Delivery by State and Federal Government, Accessed March 13, 2014. http://www.insidepolitics.org/egovtreport00.html.
West, D.M. (2003). Global E-Government. Center for Public Policy, Brown University, Accessed April 3, 2014. http://www.insidepolitics.org/egovt03int.html.
West, D.M. (2004). E-Government and the transformation of service delivery and citizen attitudes. *Public Administration Review*, 64(1):15–27.
West, D.M. (2006). Global e-Government, Accessed April 2, 2014. http://www.InsidePolitics.org.
Widodo, A.P., Istiyanto, J.E., Wardoyo, R., and Santoso, P. (2013). E-Government Interoperability Framework based on a Real Time Architecture. *International Journal of Computer Science Issues (IJCSI)*, 10(1), 1694–0814.
Williams, M., Rana, N., Dwivedi, Y., and Lal, B. (2011). Is UTAUT really used or just cited for the sake of it? A systematic review of citations of UTAUT's originating article. In: *ECIS 2011 Proceedings,* Accessed April 3, 2014. http://aisel.aisnet.org/cgi/viewcontent.cgi?article=1230&context=ecis2011.
Wilson, M (1996). *Asking questions,* In: Sapsford, R and Jupp, V.J. (Eds.), *Data Collection and Analysis.* London: *Sage*. 94–120.
Wilson, G., and Stacey, E. (2003). Online interaction impacts on learning: Teaching the teachers to teach online. In: *Proceedings of the 20th Annual Conference of the Australasian Society for Computers in Learning in Tertiary Education. 7–10 December 2003, Adelaide, Australia.* Accessed: http://epubs.scu.edu.au/cgi/viewcontent.cgi?article=1166&context=tlc_pubs (Accessed 4 April 2014).
Wihlborg, E., and Palm, J. (2008). Who is governing what? Governing local technical systems-an Issue of accountability. *Local government studies*, 34(3):349–362.
Wimmer, M.A., Scholl, H.J., Grönlund, A., and Andersen, K. (2006). Wimmer (Eds.): Electronic Government. In: *EGOV 2006.* Lecture Notes in Computer Science, 4084. Springer-Verlag Berlin Heidelberg, 269–280.
Wixom, B., and Todd, P. (2005). A theoretical integration of user satisfaction and technology acceptance. *Information Systems Research,* 16(1):85–102.

Wolff, H., Chong, H., and Auffhammer, M. (2011). Classification. Detection and consequences of data error: Evidence from the Human Development Index. *The Economic Journal*, 121:843–870.

Wonglimpiyarat, J., and Yuberk, Y. (2005). In support of innovation management and Roger's Innovation Diffusion theory. *Government Information Quarterly*, 22(3):411–422.

Wong, W. and Welch, E. (2004). Does e-Government promote accountability? A comparative analysis of web site openness and government accountability. *Governance: An International Journal of Policy, Administration, and Institutions*, 17(2):275–297.

Wood, M., and Welch, C. (2010). Are 'Qualitative' and 'Quantitative' Useful Terms for Describing Research? *Methodological Innovations Online*, 5(1):56–71.

Workman, M. (2005). Expert decision support system use, disuse, and misuse: a study using the theory of planned behaviour. *Computers in Human Behavior*, 21(2):211–231.

World Bank. (2007). "Public Value of IT" Frameworks, Accessed April 3, 2014. http://siteresources.worldbank.org/EXTINFORMATIONANDCOMMUNICATIONANDTECHNOLOGIES/Resources/282822-1188575147431/PublicValueITFrameworks2007.pdf

World Bank. (2003). *World Development Indicators*. Accessed: http://www.worldbank.org/data/wdi2003/ (Accessed 10 January 2009).

World Information Technology and Services Alliance (WITSA). (2000). *International Survey of E-Commerce*, Accessed April 3, 2014. http://www.witsa.org/papers/EComSurv.pdf

Wright, W., Smith, R., Jesser, R., and Stupeck, M. (1999). Information Technology, Process Reengineering and Performance Measurement: A Balanced Scorecard Analysis of Compaq Computer Corporation. *Communications of the Association for Information Systems*, 8(1):1–47.

Wu, R. C-Y. (2007). Enterprise integration in e-Government. *Transforming Government: People, Process and Policy*, 1(1):89–99.

Wu, I.L. (2003). Understanding senior management's behavior in promoting the strategic role of IT in process reengineering: use of the theory of reasoned action. *Information and Management*, 41(1):1–11.

Wynne, M.E., Perry, K.A., and Cooper, L.F. (2007). Digital Inclusion: The Next Step in Addressing the Digital Divide. Microsoft White Paper – Innovating for Inclusion: A Digital Inclusion Guide for Those Leading the Way, Accessed April 5, 2014. http://download.microsoft.com/download/c/d/f/cdf8d9fa-c7b6-4524-b516-198e7812a85f/78403_071128_PublicSector_Manuscript_f1t0_mg.pdf

Yamane. T. (1967). *Elementary Sampling Theory*. Prentice-Hall, Inc., Englewood Cliffs, NJ.

Yildiz, M. (2007). E-Government research: reviewing the literature, limitations, and ways forward. *Government Information Quarterly*, 24:646–665.

Yin, R. (2003). *Applications of Case Study Research*. Sage Publications, London.

Yin, R.K. (1997). The abridged version of case study research, design and methods. In: L. Bickman and D.G. Rog (Eds), *Handbook of applied social research methods*. Thousand Oaks, CA: Sage, 229–259.

Yonazi, J., Sol, H., and Boonstra, A. (2010). Exploring Issues Underlying Citizen Adoption of e-Government Initiatives in Developing Countries: The Case of Tanzania. *Electronic Journal of e-Government*, 8(2):176–188.

Yu, J., Ha, I., Choi, M., and Rho, J. (2005). Extending the TAM for a t-commerce. *Information and Management*, 42:965–976.

Yuen, H.K.A. and Ma, W.W.K. (2008). Exploring Teacher Acceptance of e-Learning Technology. *Asia-Pacific Journal of Teacher Education*, 36(3):229–243.

Zarei, B., Ghapanchi, A., and Sattary, B. (2008). Toward National E-government Development Models for Developing Countries: A Nine-Stage Model. *The International Information and Library Review*, 40: 199–207.

Zefferer, T. (2011). *Mobile Government: E-Government for Mobile Societies. Stocktaking of Current Trends and Initiatives*. Vienna: Secure Information Technology Center.

Zhan-qi, D., Xue, Y-W., and Zhang, P-Z. (2009). An Analysis on the Negative Effects of E-Government Information Opening: Case Study of Coal Administrative Information Opening in Shanxi Province. In: *2009 Second International Conference on Information and Computing Science, 1: 289–292.May 21–May 22, Manchester, England, UK,* Accessed April 3, 2014. http://www.computer.org/csdl/proceedings/icic/2009/3634/01/3634a289-abs.html.

Zhang, L., Wen, H., Li, D., Fu, Z., and Cui, S. (2010). E-learning adoption intention and its key influence factors based on innovation adoption theory. *Mathematical and Computer Modelling*, 51(11–12):1428–1432.

Zhao, J.J., and Zhao, S.J. (2010). Opportunities and threats: A security assessment of state e-Government websites. *Government Information Quarterly,* 27:49–56.

Zhou, Z., and Hu, C. (2008). Study on the E-government Security Risk Management. *International Journal of Computer Science and Network Security*, 8(5):208–213.

Zhou, T., Lu, Y., and Wang, B. (2010). Integrating TTF and UTAUT to explain mobile banking user adoption. *Computers in Human Behavior*, 26: 760–767.

Zhu, K., Kraemer, K., and Xu S. (2006). The Process of Innovation Assimilation by Firms in Different Countries: A Technology Diffusion Perspective on E-Business. *Management Science,* 52(10):1557–1576.

Zhu, K., Xu, S., and Dedrick, J. (2003). Assessing drivers of e-business value: results of a cross-country study. In: *Twenty-Fourth International Conference on Information Systems, Seattle, Washington, U.S.A. 14–17 December 2013, 1–13,* Accessed April 3, 2014. http://web.merage.uci.edu/kzhu/PDFfiles/Papers_Abstract/ICIS03_EBvaluedrivers_ZhuXuDedrick.pdf

About the Authors

Kelvin J. Bwalya, PhD, is a Senior Lecturer in Computer Information Systems in the Department of Library and Information Studies, University of Botswana. He is also a Post Doctoral Research Fellow at the University of Kwa Zulu Natal, and a Senior IT reviewer for the Tertiary Education Council, Botswana. His PhD is in Information Systems (Information Management) from the University of Johannesburg, He also has a Master's Degree in Computer Science from the Korea Advanced Institute of Technology and a Bachelor's Degree in Electrical Engineering from the Moscow Power Engineering Technical University. His research interests include all aspects of computer information systems (e-Government, database design, process modelling, virtual reality, knowledge management systems, community informatics, etc.) and competitive intelligence.

Prof Stephen Mutula is currently the Acting Dean & Head of School, School of Social Sciences, University of Kwa Zulu Natal, South Africa. He holds a PhD in Information Science (University of Johannesburg, South Africa), Master's Degree in Information Science (University of Wales, UK), Postgraduate Diploma in Computer Science (University of Nairobi, Kenya) and Bachelors Degree in Education – Mathematics and Chemistry (Kenyatta University, Kenya). He has published extensively in international refereed journals and books. He is a first co-author of book entitled: Web Information Management: A Cross disciplinary textbook, published by Chandos Publishing, London, 2007. He is also the author of "Digital Economics: SMEs and e-Readiness", published in 2009 by IDEA Group Publishers, USA. He is an Honorary Research Fellow of the University of Zululand, South Africa. He has won several international excellence awards for his distinguished research work from various academic societies such as the Emerald Literati Club, UK.

Index

Accountability 3, 7, 14, 17, 20, 28, 38, 63, 123, 184, 280
Adaptive Learning 129, 149, 269
Adele (Agence pour le Développement de l'Administration Electronique) 106, 107
Adoption 10, 11, 127, 139, 157, 276
Adoption Models 127, 133
Adopt Public Private Partnership (PPP) 167, 170, 182, 238, 239, 270
Africa 9, 31, 34, 40, 58, 169, 271
Analytic Network Process (ANP) 123
Assessment Metrics 9, 95, 117
Association of South East Asian Nations (ASEAN) 85, 86, 306
Authentication 130, 218, 226, 237, 159
Balanced Score Card (BSC) 110, 111
Bertelsmann Foundation 116, 126, 306, 331
Botswana 7, 8, 35, 58, 175
Bartlett's Test 158, 264
Bhoomi project 48
Business processes 4, 5, 15, 18, 20, 23, 26, 27, 28, 31, 47, 63, 120
Back-offices 59, 79, 123
Biometrics 279, 280
Brazil 32, 126, 150, 161, 227
Brazil e-Government Standards for Interoperability (e-PING) 161, 229
Bureaucracy 39
Business 2, 3, 4, 5, 10, 14, 15, 18, 20, 21, 22, 23, 25, 29, 86, 87, 120
Business Processes Assessment 120
Business Process Management (BPM) 16
Business Process Re-engineering (BPR) 16, 154, 210, 238, 252, 234, 252, 267
Canada 33, 40, 81, 128, 159
Case Study 177, 179, 183, 185, 187, 189, 210, 218, 252, 234, 252, 265
Centre for Public Policy of the Brown University (CPP-BU) 110
Change Management 41, 55, 120, 151, 170, 173, 182, 216, 236, 238-239,
Citizen 5, 6, 7, 12, 14, 16, 19, 20, 21, 22, 26, 29
Civil service 41, 58, 165, 170, 172
Civil Society Organisation (CSOs) 133
CJIT Benefits Management framework 108, 109
Cost-Benefit Analysis (CBA) 101, 102
Community-based technologies 258
Community informatics 258, 259
Component-based e-readiness assessment framework 123
Conceptual Model 114, 260
Confidential 128, 159, 247, 248, 262
Context-aware 236-244, 267, 273, 285, 286
Correlation coefficient 263
Corruption 4, 5, 7, 17, 20, 26, 365, 45, 47, 48, 52, 184
Correlation Matrix 198, 264, 265
Cost-Benefit-Analysis (CBA) 101
Culture 11, 33, 50, 51, 60, 61, 82, 126
Cultural homogeneity 103
Customer Readiness 121
Customer Relationship Management (CRM) 110
Critical Success Factor 12, 28
Data interoperability 150, 154, 155
Decision-making 5, 7, 17, 19, 20, 45, 52, 67, 70, 96, 107, 118, 123, 138, 165, 224
Deloitte's Citizen Advantage model (CAM) 114
Demand 2, 22, 24, 30, 58, 69, 102, 112, 121, 124, 166, 174, 187, 192,
Democracy 160, 183, 184, 282
Design 1, 8, 10, 15, 24, 37, 42, 48, 50, 252, 254, 256, 260, 262, 269, 273, 284, 286, 287
Design of e-Government 8, 116, 124, 123, 146, 148, 148, 152, 230, 269, 156, 287
Developing Country 305, 332
Development informatics 131
Diffusion 86, 92, 96, 102, 134, 144, 158, 168, 273
Digital divide 2, 36, 51, 53, 54, 55, 89, 103
Digital Access Index (DAI) 90
Digital opportunities 104
E-Administration 21, 116, 126, 162, 283, 288, 290

E-economy 91, 92, 167
E-Commerce 45, 49, 54, 56, 57, 81, 83, 87, 88, 92, 138, 167, 168
E-Consultation 26, 27, 118, 219
Economic Intelligence Unit (EIU) 87
Economic Value Added (EVA) 13, 100
E-Decision-making 118
Electronic Data Interchange for Administration, Commerce, and Transport (EDIFACT) 149
E-Democracy 21, 31, 56, 80, 94, 99, 162, 282, 287
E-Document 218
Efficiency 4, 6, 12, 14, 16, 24, 28, 30, 32, 55, 64, 77, 94, 101
Effectiveness 102, 108, 134, 138, 162, 184, 220, 237
Effervescent e-Government 6, 8, 123, 132, 149, 267
E-Governance 24-28, 43, 56, 63-65, 77, 78, 228, 287
E-Government 1-335
E-Government applications 1, 2, 11-14, 24-45, 59-61, 73, 74, 78, 79, 93, 102, 114
E-Government assessment 114, 116, 117, 122-126
E-Government consumers 19, 62, 122, 123, 127, 214, 235, 268, 277, 285
E-Government designers 9, 122, 181
E-Government Economic (eGEP) Project Framework 111, 112
E-Government Framework 105, 116, 122, 143, 145, 184, 170
E-Government Interoperability frameworks (e-GIFs) 2, 221, 222, 226, 230, 234, 235
E-Government Assessment Framework (EAF Version 2.0) 106
E-government benefits 4, 5, 7, 9, 14, 15, 17, 26, 28, 40, 43, 44
E-government development 50, 51, 53, 57-59, 63, 64, 73, 79, 93, 104, 114
E-Government Development Models (EGDMs) 10
E-Government implementation 4, 16, 39, 103, 17, 120, 121, 235, 236-245, 264-274
E-Government Index 1, 57, 118
E-Government Maturity Models 16, 63, 76, 78
E-Government portal 31, 33, 34, 98, 101, 159
E-Government practitioners 12, 79, 131
E-Government Readiness 2, 23, 40, 52, 53-55, 58-92, 105, 114, 117, 119, 123
E-Government researchers 143, 153, 232, 241, 277
E-Government strategy 12, 15, 18, 38, 47, 55, 59, 69, 70, 105, 155, 170, 237
E-Government Interoperability Framework (e-GIF) 2, 3, 12, 86, 245, 221-238, 240, 267
E-Government Funding Frameworks 268, 273
E-Government Interoperability Frameworks 12, 18, 62, 147, 149, 153, 170, 221
E-Government Metadata Standard (e-GMS) 149, 150, 226,
E-Health 18, 56, 80, 81, 283
E-Learning 30, 54, 56, 57, 80, 81, 87, 128, 141, 169, 296
Emerging economies 17
Enterprise Architectures (EAs) 149, 227
E-Engagement 26
E-Passports 18
E-Participation 18, 23, 27, 29, 40, 45, 51-54, 61, 68, 77, 98, 118, 125
E-Procurement 4, 16, 17, 21, 25, 29, 45, 47, 64, 125, 149, 179, 184,
Equity 4, 98
E-Readiness 86, 90, 34, 52-57, 80-92, 99, 102, 117, 123, 126
E-Services 88, 108, 117, 128, 131, 165, 166, 220, 239
E-Service delivery 110, 111, 116, 126
E-Society 86, 91, 167
E-Tendering 4, 14, 68
European Union Interoperability Framework (EUIF) 149
E-Voting 18, 20, 25, 26, 27, 68, 71, 99, 138, 160, 296
Exploratory Factor Analysis (EFA) 192, 264, 265
eXtensible Markup Language (XML) 147-155
Factors 2, 6, 8, 11, 16, 18, 22, 51-54, 127, 196, 220-225, 230, 231, 212, 216

Failure 59, 63, 93, 99, 125, 157, 174-177, 179-182, 232, 245, 127
Future technologies 218, 279
Frameworks 93, 105, 114, 116, 143, 145, 220-223, 227, 231, 268, 269, 240, 267
Freedom of expression 4
French MAREVA framework 106, 107, 112
Front-end e-government applications 24, 74, 214, 267
Gambia 11, 42, 174, 175, 179, 181, 182
Gambia Personnel Management Organisation (PMO) 175-177
Gaussian normal data 195, 199, 205, 209, 211
Governance 3, 5, 7, 12, 14, 15, 16, 17, 19, 20
Government 3, 4, 24
Government to Business (G2B) 28, 29, 31, 32, 41, 47, 106, 171
Government to Citizens (G2C) 29, 28, 31, 32, 69, 106
Government-to-Employees (G2E) 30, 31
Government to Government (G2G) 28, 30, 31, 32, 65, , 69, 106, 111, 121, 160, 170
Greece 162-164
Gross Domestic Product (GDP) 90, 172
Harvard Centre for International Development (CID) 56, 84
Heterogeneity 14, 149, 152, 225, 242, 282
Hierarchical Multiple Regression analysis 264
Human Capital Index 9, 118, 119
ICT Infrastructure 6, 8, 23, 33, 35, 41, 52, 54, 56, 57, 73, 85, 86, 91, 97, 99, 101, 116
ICT Investment 99, 100, 101, 104, 114, 269
ICT Evaluation 93, 95, 97
ICT policy 40, 58, 84, 90, 132, 185, 216, 237
Impact 44, 45, 47, 48, 54, 55, 59, 61, 78, 85
Individual adoption 128, 262
Information and Communication Technologies (ICTs) 1-10, 14, 18-21, 46-52
Internal Rate of Return (IRR) 101, 108
Information Society 7, 42, 81, 88, 92, 97, 104, 159, 162, 163, 164, 167, 172, 230
Information Society Index (ISI) Report 88
Information Systems (IS) 6, 25, 35, 110, 137, 143, 152, 154, 170, 175, 186, 187, 222-225, 239
Information Technology (IT) 56, 87, 137, 163, 171, 182, 245
Innovation Diffusion Theory (IDT) 134
Integration Technologies 144, 146, 147, 149, 151
Internet Voting 18, 20, 27, 68
Interoperability 38, 41, 70, 146-156, 243, 277, 284
Institutional frameworks 7, 9, 12
Integration 143-175, 178, 185, 186, 191, 221-239
Interactive Voice Response (IVR) 270
International Data Corporation's (IDC) 88
Information Management 4, 16, 42, 45, 119, 175, 185, 243, 276, 281
Implementation 145-152, 219, 286, 270-273, 242, 256
Italian e-Government Architecture (SPCoop Enterprise Architecture) 149
Internet-based government 28
Knowledge 4, 6, 7, 10, 19, 20, 21, 49, 50, 54, 58, 60, 79, 86, 88, 92, 103
Knowledge Assessment Methodology (KAM) Report 86, 88
Knowledge-Based Economies (KBEs) 6, 49, 79
Knowledge economies 58
Knowledge sharing 7
Komolgorov-Smirnov and Shapiro-Wilk test 266
Leadership 9, 22, 23, 34, 37, 57, 58, 109, 121
Legal framework 99, 101, 122, 151, 156, 168, 171, 174, 218, 236
Legal interoperability 151, 224
Location-Based Services (LBS) 276
Local-context 117
Malawi 7, 186, 281
Mahalanobis distance 188, 194, 196, 196, 200, 202, 205, 207, 212
Mauritius Government Intranet System (GINS) 170
Methodology 85, 88, 53, 57, 104, 107, 110, 112, 241-254
Millennium Development Goals (MDGs) 81
Mixed Methods Research 253, 257, 265, 267
M-Government 28, 164, 274, 275, 278, 280

Models of e-Government maturity 16, 24, 35, 63
Motivation of e-Government 17
Mozambique 174, 230
Multi-dimensional 1, 2, 8, 9, 13, 18, 43, 44, 51-57, 95, 247
Multimedia Messaging Service (MMS) 28
Multivariate Normal Distribution 191, 263
Multi-disciplinary 275
Multicolinearity 263
Natural Language Processing Systems 278
Net Present Value (NPV) 100
Networked Readiness Index (NRI) 86, 89
Netizens 280
Nordic Trust Fund 271
Online Government 28, 31, 57, 111
Online Procedures Enhancement for Civil Applications (OPEN) 47, 48
Ontology 148, 152
Operational efficiency 101, 111, 184
Organisational factors 18, 43, 52, 128, 157, 260
Organization for the Advancement of Structured Information Standards (OASIS) 148, 153
Organizational Interoperability 224
Organisational Readiness Assessment 119
Participatory 4, 5, 7, 17, 19-21, 45, 60, 69-71
Pasteur's quadrant 246, 247
Payback Period (PP) 101
Perceived Ease of Use (PEOU) 18, 129, 154, 138, 140, 142, 191-195
Perceived Usefulness (PU) 18, 129, 136, 137, 143, 197, 208, 260, 262
Personal Digital Assistants (PDAs) 28, 216, 276
Personal factors 128
Policy, [*See ICT policy*]
Public Administration 3, 5, 9, 26, 57, 68, 105, 107, 118, 161-165, 182, 224, 274, 216, 219, 289
Public Key Infrastructure (PKI) 130, 171
Public Private Partnerships (PPP) 4, 123
Public service 1, 3, 5, 7, 12, 17, 18-24, 39, 44, 45, 65
Public Service Value (PSV) 100, 149
Public Return on Investment (PROI) 100
Public Value of IT (PVIT) 101
Principal Component Analysis (PCA) 192, 264, 265
Privacy 35, 37, 54, 56, 60, 71, 78, 82, 87, 110, 125, 159, 280, 283, 284
Process interoperability 150, 228, 230
Project Management 96, 106, 155, 228, 237, 273, 238
Qualitative research 248, 249-253, 257
Quantitative research 108, 112, 117, 118, 188, 248-253, 266, 257
Regulatory frameworks 7, 12, 23, 50, 54, 59, 85, 91, 97, 99, 113, 183, 248
Regression 191-213, 234, 263, 264
Reliability 83, 84, 56, 83, 84, 97, 190, 250, 253, 263-265
Research Model 258-261, 277
Return on Assets (ROA) 100
Return on Investment (ROI) 15, 99, 100
RFID 168, 278, 280
Ripple effect 7
Salford Process Re-engineering method Involving New Technologies' (SPRINT) 151
Scalable e-Government applications 94, 23, 94, 151, 155, 243, 274
Secure Socket Layer (SSL) 150
Semantic interoperability 149, 151, 154
Service Delivery 1, 3, 6, 12, 15, 17, 27, 30, 35, 41, 45, 49, 59, 63, 69
Service Level Agreement (SLA) 121, 238
Service Manager 121
Service transparency 3, 21, 26, 30, 38, 41, 46, 47, 52, 87, 99, 102, 114, 123, 131
Seychelles 8, 40, 58
Shapiro-Wilk Test 191, 264
Shareholder Value Analysis (SVA) 114
Short Message Service (SMS) 28
Singapore 40, 127, 128, 165, 166
Socio-economic 1-5, 9, 14, 15, 18-20, 34, 40, 43, 54, 55, 61, 80
Social inclusion 4, 5, 17, 21, 45, 59, 88, 102, 125, 132, 288
Social infrastructure 60
Social Return on Investment (SROI) 100
South Africa 58, 154, 172, 174, 231
South Korea 127, 164, 167-169, 281

Southern African Development Community (SADC) 8, 58, 81, 307
Statistical Indicators Benchmarking the Information Society (SIBIS) 86, 88
Standard Cost Model (SCM) 113
Strategy 12, 15, 18, 24, 34, 35, 37, 42, 47, 50, 55, 76, 98, 104, 236, 239, 267
Sub-Saharan Africa 10, 11, 34, 59
Success 132, 155, 157, 159, 165, 174, 180, 184, 226, 235, 232, 230
Supply 2, 22, 51, 97, 102, 105, 123, 158, 167, 235, 237, 254, 274
Sweden 46, 85
Technical interoperability 129, 150, 225
Technology Acceptance Model (TAM) 129, 136, 137, 140, 142, 145, 262, 258
Technique for Order Preference by Similarity to Ideal Solution (TOPSIS) 123
Telecommunication 7, 9, 34, 42, 83
Telecommunications Infrastructure Index 9, 117, 119
Theory of Planned Behaviour (TPB) 135, 136, 142
Theory of Reasoned Action (TRA) 134, 142
Thrust, Resistance and Navigation Strategy Form (TRANSFORM), 124
Tied Aid Financing 271
Total Quality Management (TQM) 16
Traditional public service 12, 274
Transparency [*See Service Transparency*]
Trust 16, 34, 46, 48, 59, 60, 83, 88, 96, 122
Universal Access (UA) 83, 84, 103, 104, 187, 238
UK Criminal Justice IT (CJIT) 108
United Nations (UN) 57, 68, 78, 106, 118
United Nations Department of Economic and Social Affairs (UNDESA) 7, 9, 106
United Nations Division for Public Economics and Public Administration (UNDPEPA) 57, 68
United Nations Public Administration Network (UNPAN) 118
Unified Theory of Acceptance and Use of Technology (UTAUT) 139, 140, 141, 143, 144
Uptake 33, 34, 54, 80, 82, 118, 130, 137, 146, 163, 165, 217, 235, 263
Usability 34, 38, 54, 61, 69, 75, 87, 99, 111, 116, 131, 217
Virtual Network 183, 268, 277
Web Measure Index 106, 117, 118, 119
Web Portals 111, 150
Wearable Computing Devices 278
Web Services Description Language (WSDL) 150, 151, 155, 225
World Information Technology and Services Alliance's (WITSA) 56, 57, 86, 87, 92
Zambia 7, 10, 58, 61, 235, 253
Zambia Integrated Financial Management Information System (IFMIS) 186, 188
Zinnar ontology 149
Zambia Public Service Capacity Building Project (PSCAP) 185, 187
Zambia Revenue Authority – ZRA 184, 185, 214, 296